WITHDRAWN

Formability and Workability of Metals

Plastic Instability and Flow Localization

ASM Series in Metal Processing

Series Editor

HAROLD L. GEGEL, FASM
Senior Scientist
Air Force Wright Aeronautical Laboratories

---

1. **Metal Forming: Fundamentals and Applications**
   Taylan Altan, Soo-Ik Oh, and Harold L. Gegel
2. **Formability and Workability of Metals: Plastic Instability and Flow Localization**
   S.L. Semiatin and J.J. Jonas
   Other volumes in preparation

Formability and Workability of Metals
Plastic Instability and Flow Localization

S.L. Semiatin
Battelle Columbus Laboratories
Columbus, Ohio

and

J.J. Jonas
McGill University
Montreal, Canada

American Society for Metals
Metals Park, Ohio 44073

Copyright © 1984
by the
AMERICAN SOCIETY FOR METALS
All rights reserved

No part of this book may be reproduced, stored in a retrieval system, or transmitted, in any form or by any means, electronic, mechanical, photocopying, recording, or otherwise, without the prior written permission of the publisher.

Nothing contained in this book is to be construed as a grant of any right of manufacture, sale, or use in connection with any method, process, apparatus, product or composition, whether or not covered by letters patent or registered trademark, nor as a defense against liability for the infringement of letters patent or registered trademark.

Library of Congress Cataloging in Publication Data

Semiatin, S.L.
  Formability and workability of metals.

  (ASM series in metal processing; 2)
  Includes bibliographical references and index.
  1. Metals—Formability. 2. Metal-work. 3. Metals—Plastic properties. I. Jonas, J.J. II. Title.
  III. Title: Flow localization. IV. Series.
  TA460.S45 1984   620.1'633   84-3037
  ISBN 0-87170-183-9
  SAN 204-7586
PRINTED IN THE UNITED STATES OF AMERICA

Cover photograph: Cross-sections of titanium alloy compressor blades showing the development of shear bands in an actual forging. These shear bands are a manifestation of flow localization which limits workability in the conventional forging of blades.

To
W.W. Sunderland
and
C.R. Thompson

FOREWORD

The American Society for Metals is responding to the technical needs of a growing fraternity of scientists, engineers, and production managers of the second- and third-tier industrial base who are being challenged by rapid advances in the technology of automation.

The introduction of computer-aided and robotic technologies into the manufacturing process has caused managers to rethink manufacturing operations in terms of providing the full market value of which they are capable. The up-to-date factory is striving to reach the "ideal" goal of stockless production, which can be achieved only through closer relationships between design and manufacturing and between the designer and the parts vendor. In general, a productivity gap has always existed between vendors and users, because vendors traditionally have not been partners with their customers. The parts and material suppliers must now improve the quality of their products and their productivity to bring their production capabilities in line with new trends in world manufacturing.

The quality of products produced by the factory of the future will depend on the parts vendor's ability to change from a job-shop mode of production to one of zero lead time with repetitive production of discrete units that are free of defects.

The ASM Process Modeling Activity members are formulating a series of monographs that will link the components of process modeling and focus on its use to facilitate modernization of the vendor industries served by the society.

Although the range of process modeling is very broad, these monographs will focus primarily on the metalworking community. They will be aimed at supporting the continuing education of graduate engineers, and each monograph will have sufficient technical depth to be useful as reference material for university courses at the graduate and upper-undergraduate student levels. The monographs will link equipment or machinery dynamics, material-behavior modeling, numerical methods for process simulation, interface phenomena, and process economics. One of the aims of this series is to underscore the fact that process modeling is intimately associated with process simulation, die (mold) design and manufacturing, and process control.

The theory and examples contained in these monographs provide the basis for understanding the value of computer-aided engineering and manufacturing (CAE/CAM) as a productivity and part-quality enhancement tool. CAE/CAM systems will serve as a direct link between the designer and the parts vendor, making the vendor a "partner" in the total manufacturing operation.

In preparing these monographs, the authors have drawn extensively from the existing literature and the published results of active research programs in processing science. In particular, the Air Force Office of Scientific Research (AFOSR) program on processing science has had significant influence. This research encompassed materials, mechanics, interface phenomena, and equipment characteristics in a unified approach to the modeling of deformation processes. The various components of the modeling system were integrated by means of an interactive computer program that facilitates the simulation of material flow in arbitrarily shaped dies. The analytical models make possible the design of dies based on metal-flow simulation and the development of a process-control algorithm for feedforward control of metalworking presses; furthermore, they provide the means for using process control as a method of guaranteeing quality assurance of net-shape products. Shop-floor validation of process modeling for the design of near-net-shape products having a controlled set of microstructures and properties has been a rewarding result of this research.

It is a pleasure to acknowledge the support provided by AFOSR and, in particular, Dr. T.E. Walsh, Electronic and Materials Science, for his continued support. The stimulation and guidance provided by Dr. Frank Kelley, Dr. H.M. Burte, Dr. N.M. Tallan, and colleagues of the Air Force Wright Aeronautical Laboratories/Materials Laboratory throughout the program is also gratefully acknowledged. Special thanks are also due to Dr. George Dieter, Dean of the College of Engineering at the University of Maryland, and Dr. Roger N. Wright, Professor at Rensselaer Polytechnic Institute, who provided consultative advice. Special recognition must be given to Dr. Shiro Kobayashi, Professor of Mechanical Engineering at the University of California—Berkeley, for his dedicated research, which has significantly advanced the analysis of metalworking processes. Finally, it is a pleasure to acknowledge Dr. Taylan Altan, of Battelle Columbus Laboratories, who was the principal investigator for the AFOSR processing science program.

Harold L. Gegel
Series Editor

PREFACE

The ability to form metals into useful shapes is often limited by the occurrence of flow localization or fracture. In this monograph, the interaction of forming conditions and intrinsic material properties is examined to define the conditions under which it is impossible to distribute deformation uniformly during metalworking. It deals not only with the concentration of plastic flow under tensile loading conditions, but also with the occurrence of flow localization under bulk forming conditions. In addition, related topics of flow localization, as it occurs in metalcutting, ballistics, and geology, are also discussed briefly. Another monograph in the ASM Series in Metal Processing deals with fracture-controlled formability.

Much of the work discussed in this book has been conducted under the auspices of the U.S. Air Force; the assistance and enthusiastic encouragement of Harold Gegel, Atwell Adair, and Alan Rosenstein of this organization are gratefully acknowledged. In addition, Dr. Jonas would like to express his appreciation to McGill University for granting a sabbatical leave (spent at the Centre de Mise en Forme des Matériaux, Ecole Nationale Supérieure des Mines de Paris), during which time the monograph was written, as well as to the Natural Sciences and Engineering Research Council of Canada and the Quebec Ministry of Education (FCAC program) for supporting several projects, the results of which are summarized in this monograph.

The authors would also like to thank their colleagues for their fruitful comments that helped clarify many points discussed in this book. In particular, the comments and insights of T. Altan, G. Canova, N. Christodoulou, P. Dadras, J. Duffy, A.K. Ghosh, E.W. Hart, S.S. Hecker, A.L. Hoffmanner, U.F. Kocks, H.A. Kuhn, G.D. Lahoti, F.A. Nichols, E. Rauch, and J.F. Thomas, Jr., are appreciated. Additionally, M. Azrin, N. Christodoulou, R. Komanduri, H.A. Kuhn, and F.A. Nichols graciously supplied some of the illustrations. The authors also thank M. Linton, C. Sullivan, B. Pierpoint, R. Underwood, and J. Rieser for their assistance in the preparation of the manuscript. The patience and efforts of the ASM staff, in particular T. Gall and B. Sanders, in the production of this book are also greatly appreciated.

Lastly, the authors express their sincere appreciation to their families—without whose understanding and moral support, the writing of this monograph would not have been possible.

Lee Semiatin
John J. Jonas
October, 1983

CONTENTS

1 Introduction 1

Flow Localization at Cold Working Temperatures 2
Flow Localization at Warm and Hot Working
Temperatures 7
References 10

2 Fundamental Definitions and Workability Tests Used in Flow Localization Studies 13

Fundamental Definitions 14
    Stress 14
    Strain 16
    Stress-Strain-Strain Rate Relationships 17
    Yield Function and Associated Flow Rule 18
Workability Tests 23
    Uniaxial Compression Test 23
    Torsion Test 26
    Sidepressing Test 29
    Uniaxial Tension Test 31
    Plane-Strain Compression/Tension Tests 34
    In-Plane and Punch-Stretching Tests 37
    References 40

3 Flow Localization in Bulk Forming: Isothermal Deformation 43

Flow Localization/Surface Fracture at Cold
Working Temperatures 44
    Description of Flow Localization Phenomenology
    at Cold Working Temperatures 44

Flow Localization Analysis 46
Flow Localization Due to Flow Softening:
Axisymmetric Deformation 51
  Flow Localization Parameter 52
  Correlation Between the Flow Localization
  Parameter and Observations 55
  Other Forms of the Flow Localization Parameter 61
  Kinetics of Flow Localization in Uniaxial
  Compression of Specimens with Geometric and
  Mechanical Defects 64
  Flow Localization in the Presence of Metallurgical
  (Strength) Defects 68
Flow Localization Due to Flow Softening:
Plane-Strain Deformation 69
  Flow Localization Parameter 69
  Workability Diagrams for Shear Bands 71
  Process Modeling of Shear Band Development
  in Ti-6242Si 76
  Process Modeling of Shear Band Development
  in Hypothetical Materials 79
Flow Localization Due to Flow Softening: Torsion 85
  Flow Localization Parameter 85
  Application of Flow Localization Parameter to
  Torsion of Ti-6242Si 87
Sources of Flow Softening in Metals 93
  Work Softening at Elevated Temperatures by
  Dynamic Recovery Processes 93
  Work Softening at Elevated Temperatures as a
  Result of Dynamic Recrystallization 96
  Flow Softening Due to the Reversal of
  Strengthening Mechanisms 97
  Flow Softening Due to Textural Effects 100
  Practical Examples of Texture Softening 103
  Flow Softening Arising from Adiabatic Heating—
  Strain-Hardening Materials 109
  Flow Softening Arising from Adiabatic Heating—
  Nonhardening Materials 113
References 116

4 Flow Localization in Bulk Forming: Nonisothermal Deformation 121

Analysis of Flow Localization in Nonisothermal
Upsetting 122
Flow Localization in Upsetting of Ti-6242Si:
Observations 124

Comparison of Model and Experimental Predictions
of Flow Localization in Nonisothermal Upsetting of
Ti-6242Si 128
Flow Localization During the Nonisothermal
Sidepressing of Ti-6242Si 131
   Flow Localization During the Sidepressing of
   α + β Microstructure Ti-6242Si—Mechanical Press
   Deformation Rate 132
   Flow Localization During the Sidepressing of
   α + β Microstructure Ti-6242Si—Hydraulic Press
   Deformation Rate 135
   Other Shear Band Observations—α + β
   Microstructure Blade Forging 139
Flow Localization in Torsion 140
   Analysis 140
   Application of Flow Localization Analysis for
   Torsion 142
Summary 147
References 148

5 Instability and Flow Localization in Uniaxial Tension 149

Tension Testing of Round Bars—Instability 149
   Considère's Analysis 150
   Hart's Analysis 151
Tension Testing of Round Bars—Flow Localization 154
   Localization in the Presence of Deformation
   Defects—Hart/Duncombe/Nichols Necking
   Strain 155
   Localization in the Presence of Geometric
   Defects—Ghosh and Ayres/Marciniak/
   Hutchinson and Neale Necking Strain 159
   Critical Assessment of the Simplified Necking
   Theories 162
   Differential Equation for Flow Localization in
   Engineering Materials 166
   Approximate Graphical Solution to the Instability
   Relations 172
   Flow Localization Under Superplastic Flow
   Conditions 174
   Instability Analysis Including Rate Sensitivity
   of the Work Hardening Rate 177
   Experimental Observations Relating to the
   Detailed Analyses of Flow Localization 183
Tension Testing of Sheet Metals 188
   Diffuse Instability and Diffuse Necking in Sheet
   Metals 188

Local Instability and Localized Necking in Sheet
Metals 191
Bifurcation Theory 194
Summary 196
References 197

6 Instability and Flow Localization During Sheet Forming 199

Swift's Diffuse Instability Criterion 200
Hill's Local Instability Criterion 204
Flow Localization for $\rho^* > 0$ 207
    Marciniak-Kuczynski Analysis 207
    Sowerby-Duncan Interpretation of the M-K
    Analysis 211
    Experimental Correlations with the M-K
    Theory 214
    Forming Limits for Out-of-Plane Stretching 217
    Other Analyses of Sheet Metal Forming Limits
    for $\rho^* > 0$ 219
Summary 221
References 222

7 Related Problems of Flow Localization 225

Flow Localization During Metalcutting 225
    Flow Localization Analysis for Orthogonal Cutting .. 226
    Formation of Shear-Localized Chips—
    Comparison of Measurements and Predictions 230
Flow Localization During Impact Loading of Metals ... 232
    Staker's Contained Cylinder Experiments 233
    Two-Slice Model for Adiabatic Flow Localization
    in Simple Shear 234
    Two-Slice Model Calculations for Staker's
    Fragmenting Shell Experiments 238
Geological Shear Zones 242
References 243

Appendix A. Kinetics of Flow Localization in Uniaxial Compression 245

Appendix B. Effect of Stress Triaxiality on the Propagation of Necks and Bulges 251

Appendix C. Development of Adiabatic
Shear Bands in Torsion 257

Appendix D. M-K Analysis for Flow Localization .. 267

Index 277

1

INTRODUCTION

The intrinsic ability of metals and alloys to be worked into various simple and complex shapes forms the basis for the manufacturing operations known as deformation processes. These processes account for a sizable proportion of the manufactured goods made in industrialized countries each year. Thus, a thorough understanding of the deformation process and the factors limiting the forming of sound parts is important, not only from a scientific or engineering viewpoint, but also from an economic viewpoint. Other volumes in this series treat various aspects of deformation modeling. These include physical metallurgy, flow stress data and constitutive relations, die-workpiece interface phenomena, forming equipment, and numerical techniques. The purpose of this volume is to review and summarize the modes by which defects may form during deformation processing.

In this volume, forming limited by instability and flow localization will be treated. The approach to be taken will be largely phenomenological; that is, the description of the flow localization processes will be based on macroscopic or gross phenomena amenable to mathematical description using the fundamental equations of plasticity mechanics[1-4]—the equilibrium equation, the yield function and associated flow rule, etc. Through this means, the propensity for flow localization may be estimated using easily measured material properties, such as the flow stress as a function of strain, strain rate, and temperature, and applied to a large number of alloy systems. At various points in this volume, however, the microscopic mechanisms underlying observed flow behavior will be discussed to emphasize the effect of metallurgical state on flow phenomenology.

It is not surprising that the flow localization or fracture modes that limit the capacity to carry out deformation processes are greatly affected by the forming temperature, deformation rate, and stress state. Perhaps the most important of these factors is the forming temperature, or the temperature of the workpiece, i.e., the metal being shaped. For a large number of metals, it has been found that the extent to which they may be worked before failure is a strong function of the workpiece homologous temperature T_H. This is the ratio of the workpiece temperature T to the melting point of the metal T_{MP}, or in the case of alloys, the solidus temperature (Figure 1.1).

At cold working temperatures ($T_H \leq 0.25$), the workability is generally modest. These temperatures are most often employed for moderate amounts of deformation under primary or bulk forming conditions involving compressive loading of the workpiece, or for secondary or sheet-forming applications involving tensile loading. Because such operations are often carried out at room temperature, cold working enables the forming of parts to close dimensional tolerances and avoids the problems of nonuniform thermal contraction upon cooling, which are often encountered in warm and hot working. At warm working temperatures ($0.25 \leq T_H \leq 0.6$), the workability is usually at a minimum. For this reason, warm working is generally reserved for bulk forming operations that require small deformations and for applications in which a decrease in workpiece temperature offers an energy savings (in terms of reduced heating costs) when compared to the same operation performed under hot working conditions.

At hot working temperatures ($T_H \geq 0.6$), the workability of metals usually reaches a peak. Thus, major shaping operations such as rolling, forging, and extrusion are typically performed under hot working conditions. Hot working also has the advantage of generally low working loads, because the flow stress of most metals tends to decrease with increasing temperature.[5] With this as background, the specific flow localization phenomena to be discussed in the following chapters are summarized below.

Flow Localization at Cold Working Temperatures

As discussed in the forthcoming chapters, flow instability and flow localization may be attributed to one or more of the following causes:
    (i) The destabilizing influence of area reduction during tensile deformation (tensile instability).
    (ii) The accentuation of strain gradients by frictional effects.

(iii) Flow softening, or an exhaustion of strain-hardening capacity due to the effect of deformation heating, for example.

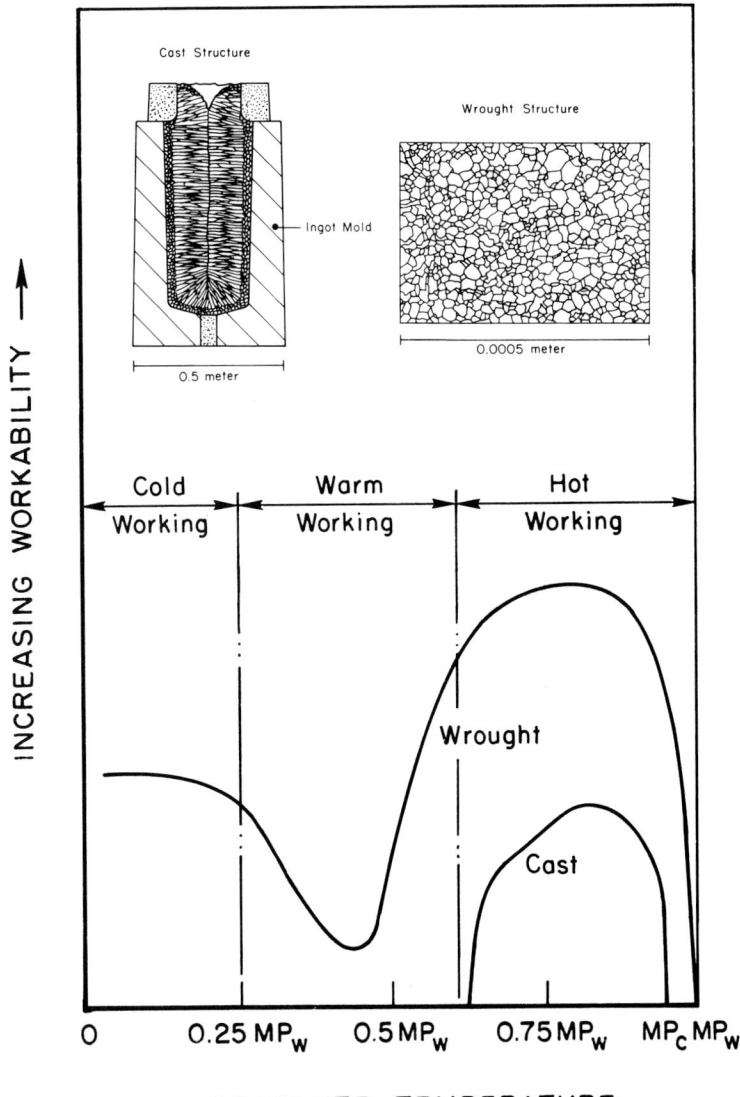

Figure 1.1. Relative workability of coarse-grained cast metals and wrought-and-recrystallized metals as a function of homologous temperature.

(iv) Heat transfer between the dies and the workpiece (i.e., chilling).

At cold working temperatures, the first three of these phenomena have been found to lead to flow localization, whereas the latter three have been observed to lead to flow localization at warm and hot working temperatures.

During bulk forming at cold working temperatures, friction may cause plastic deformation to localize within the workpiece, as well as cause free surface bulging, which can generate secondary tensile stresses and thus tensile instability and flow localization at the surface of the workpiece. In the former instance, friction causes zones of limited deformation, often called dead-metal zones, to be generated in the area of the workpiece in contact with the dies.[6] Separating these areas of limited deformation from the deforming bulk are thin regions of much higher than normal deformation crossing many grains, commonly known as shear bands (Figure 1.2). Often the variation of hardness from the dead-metal zones to the shear bands to the deformed bulk makes the finished part unacceptable for its intended use. When these variations are not great, the other friction-related category of flow localization, bulging, may lead to dimensional variations that render the part unacceptable. In this case, the tensile stresses associated with bulging frequently lead to flow localization in regions where the metal is slightly weaker than elsewhere, or where

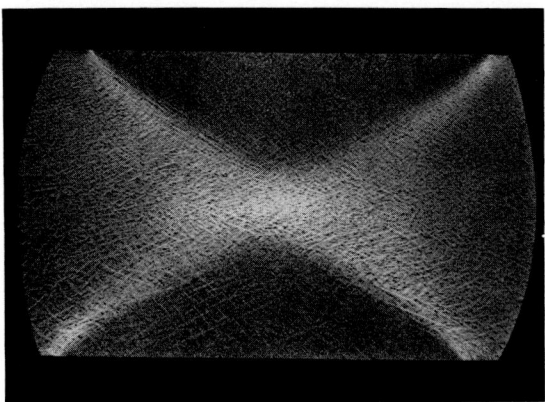

Figure 1.2. Transverse section of steel upset specimen deformed at room temperature under conditions of high friction. The dark dead-metal zones on the top and bottom of the specimen are separated from the deformed bulk by narrow regions of high deformation, or shear bands, which etch lighter in the above macrograph.

some metallurgical inhomogeneity (such as an inclusion) is present. Models similar to that of Marciniak-Kuczynski for flow localization in sheet forming may then be employed to estimate the amount of deformation that can be applied prior to marked localization and final fracture.[7-11] Fractures at the free surface of the workpiece usually cause rejection of a finished part.

A third source of flow localization in bulk forming at cold working temperatures is the flow softening that occurs following the exhaustion of strain-hardening capacity. This may occur because of effects such as the achievement of stable deformation textures, dissolution of precipitates, or thermal softening arising from deformation heating (Figure 1.3).[12-19] Following the flow stress maximum in these instances, flow typically localizes into shear bands. Examples

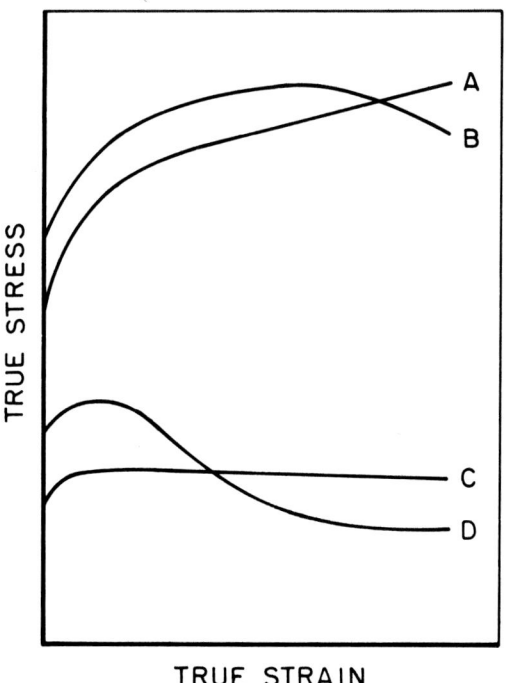

Figure 1.3. Typical flow curves for metals deformed at cold working temperatures (A—low strain rate, B—high strain rate) and at hot working temperatures (C, D). Strain hardening persists to large strains for curve A. The flow stress maximum and flow softening in curve B arise from deformation heating. The steady-state flow stress exhibited by curve C is typical of metals that dynamically recover. The flow stress maximum and flow softening in curve D may result from a number of metallurgical processes.

of these phenomena are most prevalent in plane strain operations such as flat sheet rolling and certain forging operations. When shear bands occur as a result of deformation heating, they are often referred to as adiabatic shear bands. As might be expected, these defects are found typically in parts formed at high strain rates at which the deformation heating does not have time to be conducted into the tooling. A number of simple criteria have been developed to predict the strain at which the flow stress passes through a maximum under these conditions and thus the onset of flow localization.[12, 20-24] The detailed process by which flow localizes following the flow stress maximum has only recently come under investigation.[25-28]

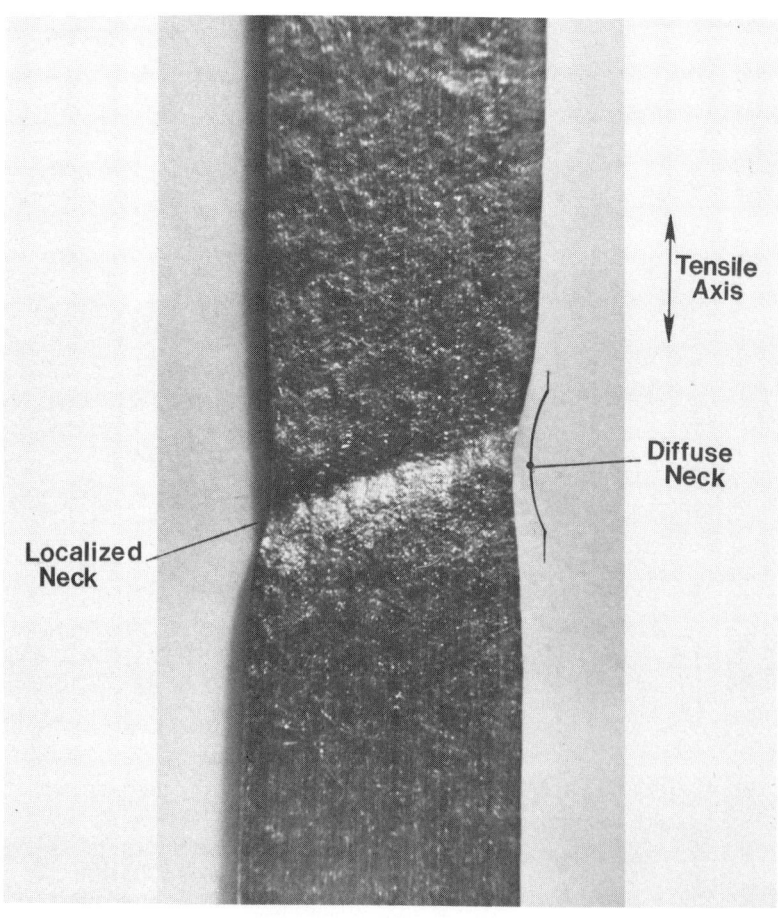

Figure 1.4. Diffuse and localized necks in an 1100 aluminum sheet tensile specimen.

Flow localization phenomena are also important in determining the amount of useful deformation that can be imposed on a workpiece in secondary forming operations performed on metal sheets. Under these conditions, the destabilizing process associated with geometric softening (i.e., the decrease with strain of the cross-sectional area which bears the forming load) leads to two stages of unstable flow. The first is known as "diffuse" necking (so called because its extent is much greater than the sheet thickness); the second is termed localized necking (through-thickness thinning), which is terminated by final separation, or fracture (Figure 1.4). The strain levels at which these phenomena occur in operations in which one of the in-plane strains in the sheet is negative are fairly easy to predict from the criteria developed by Swift[29] and Hill.[30] On the other hand, when both in-plane strains are positive, as in sheet metal stretching operations, the presence of some material inhomogeneity must be postulated to account for the shift in strain state to that of plane strain, as the latter is the one that describes the through-thickness thinning generally observed to precede fracture. The flow localization process in these cases is best described by models, such as that postulated by Marciniak and Kuczynski[7, 8] for in-plane stretching, that concentrate on the properties of the sheet metal itself. A more difficult problem to analyze in the field of sheet forming, and one of greater practical importance, is that of flow localization during punch stretching. Under these conditions, out-of-plane deformation and workpiece/tooling interactions tend to retard flow localization and enable larger deformations to be attained prior to failure.[31, 32]

Flow Localization at Warm and Hot Working Temperatures

Most of the metalworking processes performed at warm and hot working temperatures are carried out under compressive loading and thus fall into the category of bulk forming. At warm working temperatures, where ductility is usually low, workability is typically limited by grain-boundary or triple point cracking and not by a generalized flow localization process.[33] At the higher hot working temperatures, several modes of localization may limit workability.

Perhaps the most common occurs in conventional hot working operations in which the hot workpiece is deformed by tooling that is not preheated or tooling that is heated to a temperature much less than that of the workpiece. Because of this temperature difference, heat transfer between the workpiece and tooling occurs, causing chilling of the part of the workpiece in contact with the tooling. Furthermore, since the flow stress of most metals decreases rapidly with temperature in the hot working regime (Figure 1.5), the chilled zone of metal does not deform as rapidly as the bulk of the workpiece. Thus, the flow localizes between the chill zone and the deforming bulk in a manner analogous to that caused by friction and the occurrence of rigid zones at cold working temperatures (Figure 1.6). The extent of the chilling and, thus, the severity of the localization in hot working are determined, of course, by the amount of heat transfer between the tooling and the workpiece. This heat transfer is in turn affected by the contact time and the heat transfer characteristics of the lubricant interface. By using glass lubricants and by employing equipment with fast rams (e.g., mechanical presses and hammers in forging), the effects of chilling on flow localization at hot working temperatures can be minimized.[34, 35]

Another way of reducing the strain localization tendencies at hot working temperatures is through the use of tooling heated to the same, or nearly the same, temperature as the workpiece. These so-

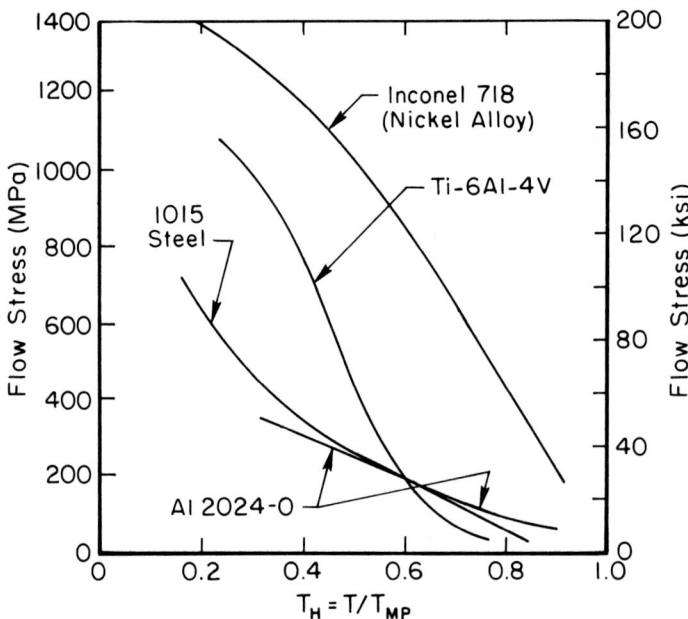

Figure 1.5. Flow stress of several common engineering alloys at a strain rate of 1 sec.$^{-1}$ as a function of homologous temperature.

called isothermal hot working operations are receiving increasing attention commercially. However, care must be exercised in applying this technology because of the flow softening or negative strain hardening that is an attribute of many alloys at hot working temperatures.[36] As mentioned above, flow softening promotes the occurrence of strain localization, the mode of which depends on the geometry of the metalworking operation. Axisymmetric modes of forming may lead to bulging types of deformation if flow softening metals are employed.[36] In contrast, plane-strain modes of deformation often produce flow localization in the form of shear bands.[37, 38] These and the other modes of localization are discussed in the chapters that follow.

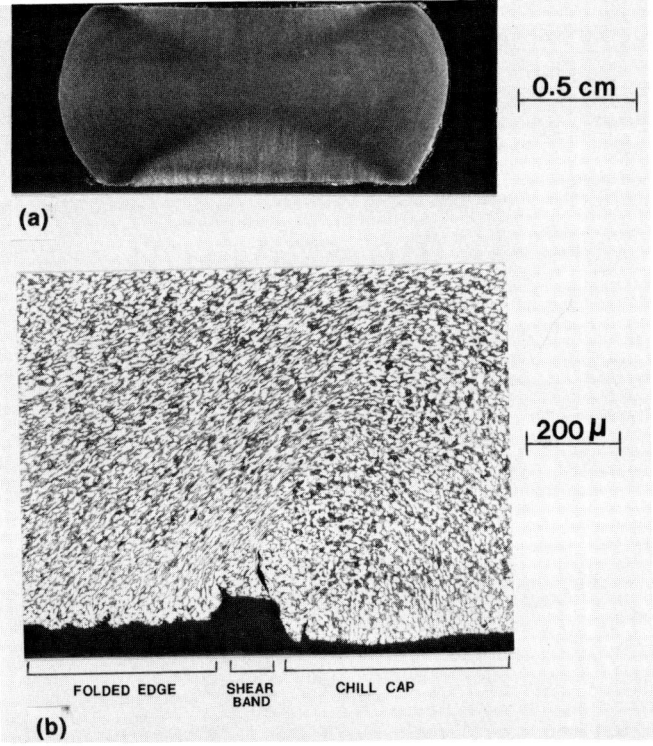

Figure 1.6. (a) Macrograph and (b) micrograph of a Ti-6Al-2Sn-4Zr-2Mo-0.1Si upset specimen with a starting microstructure of equiaxed alpha that was non-isothermally compressed in a mechanical press (strain rate ≈ 10 sec.$^{-1}$). Specimen preheat temperature: 913 °C (1675 °F), die temperature: 191 °C (375 °F).

References

[1] R. Hill: *The Mathematical Theory of Plasticity*, Oxford University Press, London, 1950.
[2] A. Mendelson: *Plasticity: Theory and Application*, Macmillan, New York, 1968.
[3] W. Johnson and P.B. Mellor: *Engineering Plasticity*, Van Nostrand Rheinhold, London, 1973.
[4] W.A. Backofen: *Deformation Processing*, Addison-Wesley, Reading, MA, 1972.
[5] H. Suzuki, S. Hashizume, Y. Yabuki, Y. Ichihara, S. Nakajima, and K. Kenmochi, *Rept. Inst. Indust. Sci., Univ. of Tokyo,* March, 1968, vol. 18, No. 3, p. 1.
[6] M. Cooke and C. Larke: *J. Inst. Metals,* 1945, vol. 71, p. 371.
[7] Z. Marciniak and K. Kuczynski: *Inter. J. Mech. Sci.,* 1967, vol. 9, p. 609.
[8] Z. Marciniak, K. Kuczynski, and T. Pokora: *Inter. J. Mech. Sci.,* 1973, vol. 15, p. 789.
[9] S. Kobayashi: *J. Eng. Ind., Trans. ASME,* 1970, vol. 92B, p. 391.
[10] H.A. Kuhn and P.W. Lee: *Met. Trans.,* 1971, vol. 2, p. 3197.
[11] P.W. Lee and H.A. Kuhn: *Met. Trans.,* 1973, vol. 4, p. 969.
[12] H.C. Rogers: *Ann. Rev. Mat. Sci.,* 1979, vol. 9, p. 283.
[13] K. Brown: *J. Inst. Metals,* 1972, vol. 100, p. 341.
[14] P.S. Mathur and W.A. Backofen: *Met. Trans.,* 1973, vol. 4, p. 643.
[15] I.L. Dillamore, J.G. Roberts, and A.C. Bush: *Metal Sci.,* 1979, vol. 13, p. 73.
[16] R.J. Asaro: *Formability—Analysis, Modeling, and Experimentation,* S.S. Hecker, A.K. Ghosh, and H.L. Gegel, eds., p. 61, The Metallurgical Society of AIME, New York, 1978.
[17] S. Kobayashi, C.H. Lee, Y. Saida, and S.C. Jain: Technical Report AFML-TR-70-90, University of California, Berkeley, CA, July, 1970.
[18] S.L. Semiatin, G.D. Lahoti, and S.I. Oh: *Material Behavior Under High Stress and Ultrahigh Loading Rates,* J. Mescall, ed., Plenum Press, New York, 1983, p. 119.
[19] S.S. Hecker, M.G. Stout, and D.T. Eash: *Proc. Conf. On Plasticity of Metals at Finite Strain: Theory, Experiment, and Computation,* Stanford University, Stanford, CA, June 29—July 1, 1981, E.H. Lee and R.L. Mallett, eds., p. 162, Rennselaer Polytechnic Institute, Troy, NY, 1982.
[20] R.F. Recht: *J. Appl. Mech., Trans. ASME,* 1964, vol. 31E, p. 189.
[21] R.S. Culver: *Metallurgical Effects at High Strain Rates,* R.W. Rohde et al., eds., p. 519, Plenum Press, New York, 1973.
[22] U.S. Lindholm, A. Nagy, G.R. Johnson, and J.M. Hoegfeldt: *J. Eng. Mat. Techn., Trans ASME,* 1980, vol. 102, p. 376.
[23] M.R. Staker: *Acta Met.,* 1981, vol. 29, p. 683.
[24] G.B. Olson, J.F. Mescall, and M. Azrin: *Shock Waves and High Strain Rate Phenomena,* M.A. Meyers and L.E. Murr, eds., p. 221, Plenum Press, New York, 1981.
[25] J.J. Jonas, R.A. Holt, and C.E. Coleman: *Acta Met.,* 1976, vol. 24, p. 911.
[26] J.J. Jonas and B. Baudelet: *Acta Met.,* 1977, vol. 25, p. 43.
[27] J.J. Jonas and N. Christodoulou: *Scripta Met.,* 1978, vol. 12, p. 393.

[28] J.J. Jonas, N. Christodoulou, and C. G'Sell: *Scripta Met.*, 1978, vol. 12, p. 565.
[29] H.W. Swift: *J. Mech. Phys. Solids*, 1952, vol. 1, p. 1.
[30] R. Hill: *J. Mech. Phys. Solids*, 1952, vol. 1, p. 19.
[31] A.K. Ghosh and S.S. Hecker: *Met. Trans.*, 1974, vol. 5, p. 2161.
[32] A.K. Ghosh and S.S. Hecker: *Met. Trans. A*, 1975, vol. 6A, p. 1065.
[33] R.C. Koeller and R. Raj: *Acta Met.*, 1978, vol. 26, p. 1551.
[34] S.L. Semiatin and G.D. Lahoti: *Sci. American*, August, 1981, vol. 245, No. 2, p. 98.
[35] S.L. Semiatin and G.D. Lahoti: *Met. Trans. A*, 1983, vol. 14A, p. 105.
[36] J.J. Jonas and M.J. Luton: *Advances in Deformation Processing*, J.J. Burke and V. Weiss, eds., p. 215, Plenum Press, New York, 1978.
[37] S.L. Semiatin and G.D. Lahoti: *Met. Trans. A*, 1981, vol. 12A, p. 1705.
[38] S.L. Semiatin and G.D. Lahoti: *Met. Trans. A*, 1982, vol. 13A, p. 275.

2
FUNDAMENTAL DEFINITIONS AND WORKABILITY TESTS USED IN FLOW LOCALIZATION STUDIES

During practical metalworking operations, flow localization generally occurs under complex conditions of loading and deformation. Because of this, the source of a flow localization problem is often difficult to pinpoint or quantify. As a result, means of avoiding such occurrences, be they of a metallurgical nature or should they require a change in processing conditions, are often selected on the basis of a trial-and-error procedure or on experience-based judgments. An alternative is to perform simulative experiments known as workability or formability tests in order to gage the tendency for flow localization.[1] For bulk forming performed under compressive loading conditions, these include experiments based on compression (either axisymmetric or plane strain), plane-strain sidepressing, and torsion. The Swift cup test, in-plane stretching, Hecker's punch-stretching technique, as well as the conventional tensile test, are valuable in diagnosing and understanding flow localization phenomena during secondary forming operations such as deep drawing and stretching. In this chapter, these techniques will be described briefly to prepare the groundwork for a detailed description of localization problems in subsequent chapters. Before reviewing these methods, however, the definitions of certain quantities to be used throughout this monograph will be given.

Fundamental Definitions

The description of any deformation process typically involves specification of the loads applied to bring about shape changes and the deformations themselves. Many general textbooks that treat this subject are available. These texts include those by Dieter, McClintock and Argon, Backofen, and Johnson and Mellor; the interested reader should consult them for detailed treatments of the topics that follow.[2-5]

STRESS

The description of the loadings used to carry out deformation processes fall into two general categories. The external (applied) loading is generally described in terms of *surface tractions,* or forces per unit area. A second category of tractions concerns those within the body, but their values vary with orientation. If we examine a plane whose orientation relative to the fixed spatial axes x, y, z is defined by the cosines n_x, n_y, n_z of the angles between the plane and these axes, the tractions $\underline{T}$ on this plane relative to the x, y, z axes are:

$$\begin{pmatrix} T_x \\ T_y \\ T_z \end{pmatrix} = \begin{pmatrix} \sigma_{xx} & \sigma_{xy} & \sigma_{xz} \\ \sigma_{yx} & \sigma_{yy} & \sigma_{yz} \\ \sigma_{zx} & \sigma_{zy} & \sigma_{zz} \end{pmatrix} \begin{pmatrix} n_x \\ n_y \\ n_z \end{pmatrix} ,$$

or simply

$$\underline{T} = \underline{\underline{\sigma}}\,\underline{n} . \qquad (2.1)$$

In this equation, $\underline{\underline{\sigma}}$ is known as the stress tensor. It may be noted that in general the traction vector lies at an arbitrary angle relative to the arbitrarily oriented plane. However, the vector may be resolved into components normal to the plane and lying in the plane. Such components are called normal stress components and shear stress components, respectively. Similarly, the terms σ_{xx}, σ_{yy}, and σ_{zz} are known as normal components of the stress tensor, or simply normal stresses. The remaining terms of the tensor are known as shear components of the stress tensor, or simply shear stresses. From equilibrium considerations, it may be shown that $\sigma_{xy} = \sigma_{yx}$, $\sigma_{xz} = \sigma_{zx}$, and $\sigma_{yz} = \sigma_{zy}$.

It is sometimes convenient to examine the state of stress relative to axes other than those originally used. Because stress is a tensor quantity, the transformation can be carried out by pre- and post-multiplication by the direction cosine matrix. Denoting the transformed stress tensor relative to the x', y', z' axes by $\underset{\sim}{\sigma}'$, we have:

$$\underset{\sim}{\sigma}' = \begin{pmatrix} a_{x'x} & a_{x'y} & a_{x'z} \\ a_{y'x} & a_{y'y} & a_{y'z} \\ a_{z'x} & a_{z'y} & a_{z'z} \end{pmatrix} \begin{pmatrix} \sigma_{xx} & \sigma_{xy} & \sigma_{xz} \\ \sigma_{yx} & \sigma_{yy} & \sigma_{yz} \\ \sigma_{zx} & \sigma_{zy} & \sigma_{zz} \end{pmatrix} (a)^T$$

$$= a \underset{\sim}{\sigma} a^T \quad . \tag{2.2}$$

In this expression, the terms a_{ij} are the direction cosines between the "new" i'th axes and the "old" j'th axes.

For simple two-dimensional problems of plane stress ($\sigma_{zz} = \sigma_{xz} = \sigma_{yz} = 0$), which are prevalent in situations such as sheet forming, a geometrical construction known as Mohr's circle is useful in performing the transformation of stresses. In these situations, the stress tensor is

$$\underset{\sim}{\sigma} = \begin{pmatrix} \sigma_{xx} & \sigma_{xy} & 0 \\ \sigma_{yx} & \sigma_{yy} & 0 \\ 0 & 0 & 0 \end{pmatrix} \quad ,$$

or

$$\underset{\sim}{\sigma} = \begin{pmatrix} \sigma_{xx} & \sigma_{xy} \\ \sigma_{yx} & \sigma_{yy} \end{pmatrix} \quad . \tag{2.3}$$

Here it is assumed that σ_{xx} is the algebraically largest normal stress component. Using the Mohr's circle construction, these stresses are plotted in a coordinate system in which normal stress is the abscissa, and shear stress is the ordinate. Such a diagram in which $\sigma_{xx} > 0$, $\sigma_{yy} < 0$, and $\sigma_{xy} > 0$ is shown in Figure 2.1. Note that a positive σ_{xy} is plotted *below* σ_{xx} and *above* σ_{yy}. For a counterclockwise rotation of the x, y axes by an angle θ, the transformed stress components are found by rotating the diameter connecting the points σ_{xx}, σ_{xy} and σ_{yy}, σ_{xy} by an amount 2θ in the same direction. It can also be observed that there is an orientation for which $\sigma_{xy} = 0$. This defines the *principal directions* of stress and the *principal stresses* σ_1 and σ_2. Even under arbitrary three-dimensional states of stress, a set of reference axes exists with respect to which off-diagonal terms of the stress tensor are equal to zero. It should also be noted that, at an angle of 45° (2θ = 90°) to the principal directions, the shear stresses are a maximum. For the special case of pure shear (all stress components except σ_{xy} equal to zero), the Mohr's circle is centered at the origin.

STRAIN

The deformations that a plastically deforming body undergoes may also be described using a tensor quantity. In the flow theory of plasticity, such a description is usually done in terms of infinitesimal or incremental strains. This is because of the difficulty of defining a large strain measure that obeys the tensor transformation law (for example, Equation 2.2) during an arbitrary deformation that may also include large rotations of material elements. Certain Lagrangian strain measures (i.e., strain measures referred to material axes rather than Eulerian, or spatial, axes) do meet these requirements, but their application can be difficult and hence will not be employed.

Attention shall focus on the strain increment tensor $d\underset{\sim}{\varepsilon}$,* relative to the Eulerian, or spatially fixed axes x, y, z:

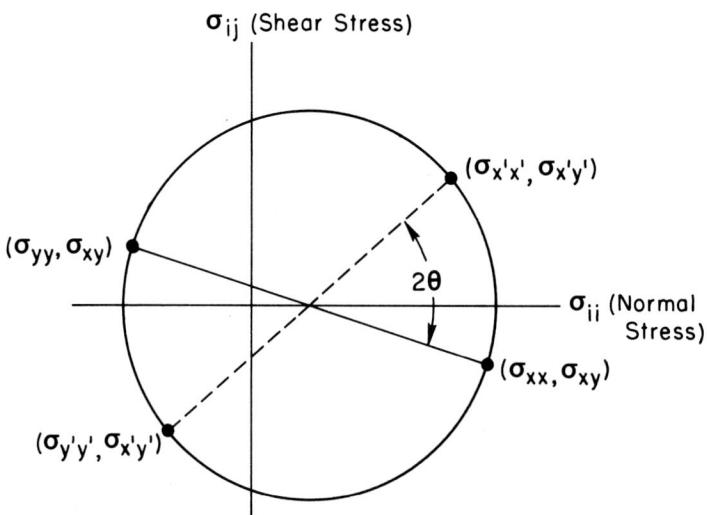

Figure 2.1. Mohr's circle for stress.

---

*In this monograph, all strains (and strain increments) will be assumed to be permanent, or plastic, strains that remain in the workpiece after the loads are removed. For most deformation processes, the elastic, or instantly recoverable, portion of the strain is small and can be neglected with respect to the plastic strains, as can the anelastic strains, which are recoverable with the passage of time.

$$d\underset{\sim}{\varepsilon} = \begin{pmatrix} d\varepsilon_{xx} & d\varepsilon_{xy} & d\varepsilon_{xz} \\ d\varepsilon_{yx} & d\varepsilon_{yy} & d\varepsilon_{yz} \\ d\varepsilon_{zx} & d\varepsilon_{zy} & d\varepsilon_{zz} \end{pmatrix} \quad . \tag{2.4}$$

For small total strains, the value of $d\underset{\sim}{\varepsilon}$ is unchanged with respect to a Lagrangian frame of reference. The diagonal terms $d\varepsilon_{xx}$, $d\varepsilon_{yy}$, and $d\varepsilon_{zz}$ are *normal* strain increments that describe contractions or elongations along the chosen directions. The remaining terms are *shear* strain increments that describe shearing deformation, or the change in angle between imaginary intersecting lines in the body. Because of the usual definition of strain increment in terms of displacement gradients, $d\varepsilon_{xy} = d\varepsilon_{yx}$, $d\varepsilon_{xz} = d\varepsilon_{zx}$, and $d\varepsilon_{yz} = d\varepsilon_{zy}$ in general. Also, because metals are incompressible (i.e., they suffer no volume change while undergoing plastic deformation), it can be shown that $d\varepsilon_{xx} + d\varepsilon_{yy} + d\varepsilon_{zz} = 0$. Hence, the description of the evolving deformation at any particular point requires specification of five strain increments only. It should be remembered that the values of these strain increments generally vary from point to point in a body undergoing an arbitrary deformation; they also vary in a body undergoing a nominally simple deformation, but within which flow localization is occurring.

Because the strain increment is a tensor, it obeys the same transformation laws as does the stress tensor, and a Mohr's circle representation may be used to analyze two-dimensional strain-transformation problems. Further, there exist directions of the coordinate axes for which the shear strain increment components of the tensor vanish. As with the stress tensor, these directions are called principal directions, and the normal strains in this orientation are the principal strains $d\varepsilon_1$, $d\varepsilon_2$, and $d\varepsilon_3$. For a plastically isotropic material and certain materials that show special classes of plastic anisotropy, the principal directions of stress coincide with the principal directions of strain increment.

STRESS-STRAIN-STRAIN RATE RELATIONSHIPS

Several relationships have been proposed to relate the stresses, the integrated strains, and strain rates in metals undergoing plastic flow. At cold working and warm working temperatures, metals deformed under a uniaxial stress state usually obey a stress-strain-strain rate relation of the form:

$$\sigma_1 = f(\varepsilon_1) \cdot g(\dot{\varepsilon}_1) \quad . \tag{2.5}$$

The strain dependence $f(\varepsilon_1)$ often follows one of several simple forms, such as those proposed by Hollomon[6] or Voce:[7]

Hollomon: $\sigma_1 = K\varepsilon_1^n$ (2.6)

Voce: $\sigma_1 = \sigma_o + \sigma_s [1 - \exp(-\varepsilon_1/\varepsilon_o)]$. (2.7)

In these equations, K, n, σ_o, σ_s, and ε_o are constants that vary from one material to another. The strain hardening exponent in the Hollomon equation, n (equal to $(\partial \ln\sigma_1/\partial \ln\varepsilon_1)|_{\dot\varepsilon,T}$), is an important parameter in gaging the formability of sheet metals. The strain-rate dependence of the stress, $g(\dot\varepsilon_1)$, often follows a power-law dependence, viz.:

$$g(\dot\varepsilon_1) \sim \dot\varepsilon^m \quad . \quad (2.8)$$

With this form for $g(\dot\varepsilon_1)$, the strain-rate hardening exponent or parameter, m, is equal to $(\partial \ln\sigma_1/\partial \ln\dot\varepsilon_1)|_{\varepsilon,T}$ and is readily determined experimentally by tension or compression testing. The m value defined in engineering flow laws such as Equation (2.8) is obtained by comparing the flow stress from two continuous flow curves for two different strain rates. On the other hand, the constant-state or state variable rate-sensitivity parameter, M_{sv}, is obtained from tension or compression tests, during which the strain rate is suddenly changed by a given amount. For most applications, the former rate sensitivity (m) is applicable.

At hot working temperatures, $\sigma_1 - \varepsilon_1$ plots often exhibit a steady-state or plateau flow stress ($\sigma_{ss} = \sigma_o + \sigma_s$ in the Voce relation, Equation 2.7), which depends only on the deformation temperature and the imposed strain rate. For many metals, it has been found that a relation of the following form adequately models this dependence:[8, 9]

$$\dot\varepsilon_1 \exp(Q/R_g T) = A_s (\sinh \alpha^+ \sigma_1)^{m'} \quad . \quad (2.9)$$

Here, A_s, α^+, and m' are material constants, and Q is the activation energy for the micromechanical process that characterizes the hot working flow behavior. The quantity R_g has its usual definition as the gas constant.

YIELD FUNCTION AND ASSOCIATED FLOW RULE

Because metalworking operations are rarely performed under uniaxial states of stress, some method must be devised to extrapolate the material behavior determined under such conditions to that expected during loading along other more general stress and strain paths. The concepts used for this purpose are known as effective stress and effective strain.[4]

The effective stress is defined using the analytical description of the yield locus. The yield locus is the locus of all possible combinations of stress states that will give rise to yielding or plastic flow in a material characterized by a given mechanical or hardness state. The yield loci most often employed are the von Mises yield locus for metals that are isotropic or Hill's anisotropic generalization for metals with orthotropic physical symmetry:

von Mises: $(\sigma_{xx} - \sigma_{yy})^2 + (\sigma_{yy} - \sigma_{zz})^2 + (\sigma_{zz} - \sigma_{xx})^2 + 6\sigma_{xy}^2$
$$+ 6\sigma_{yz}^2 + 6\sigma_{zx}^2 = 2\sigma_o^2 \quad . \quad (2.10)$$

Hill: $H(\sigma_{xx} - \sigma_{yy})^2 + F(\sigma_{yy} - \sigma_{zz})^2 + G(\sigma_{zz} - \sigma_{xx})^2 + 2N\,\sigma_{xy}^2$
$$+ 2L\,\sigma_{yz}^2 + 2M\,\sigma_{zx}^2 = 1 \quad . \quad (2.11)$$

In the von Mises locus, σ_o is the yield stress in uniaxial tension or compression. The Hill locus above is applicable only when the stress tensor axes x, y, z coincide with the principal directions of anisotropy. For a rolled sheet material, these axes are the rolling direction (R.D.), the transverse direction (T.D.), and the sheet normal (S.N.). In the special case of a sheet loaded in plane only by the principal stresses σ_1 and σ_2, the Hill locus takes the form:

$$H(\sigma_1 - \sigma_2)^2 + F\,\sigma_2^2 + G\,\sigma_1^2 = 1 \quad . \quad (2.12)$$

With the further simplification of plastic anisotropy that is rotationally symmetric around the sheet normal (i.e., planar isotropy), this yield locus becomes (Figure 2.2):[4]

$$\sigma_1^2 + \sigma_2^2 - [2R/(1 + R)]\,\sigma_1\sigma_2 = \sigma_o^2 \quad . \quad (2.13)$$

The normal plastic anisotropy parameter, R, is the ratio of the incremental width strain, $d\varepsilon_2$, to the incremental thickness strain, $d\varepsilon_3$, in a sheet tensile test. As before, σ_o is the yield stress in uniaxial tension. Note that for an isotropic material (R = 1), Equation (2.13) reduces to the von Mises criterion for conditions of plane stress.

With the above definition of the yield loci, the effective stress $\bar{\sigma}$ can now be defined. For an isotropic material loaded arbitrarily, it is given by:

$$\bar{\sigma} = \sqrt{\tfrac{1}{2}\{(\sigma_{xx} - \sigma_{yy})^2 + (\sigma_{yy} - \sigma_{zz})^2 + (\sigma_{zz} - \sigma_{xx})^2\} + 3\sigma_{xy}^2 + 3\sigma_{yz}^2 + 3\sigma_{zx}^2}$$ (2.14a)

For a uniaxial stress state such as simple tension or compression, $\bar{\sigma} = \sigma_{xx}$, the axial stress. Thus, if yielding occurs in the arbitrarily loaded material when the stress components have the values given in Equation (2.14a), then $\bar{\sigma}$ is the uniaxial stress that would produce yielding in the material at the same state of strain hardening. For a state of pure shear, $\bar{\sigma} = \sqrt{3}\,\sigma_{xy}$. The effective stress $\bar{\sigma}$ for an anisotropic sheet loaded biaxially by principal stresses, σ_1 and σ_2, is:[5]

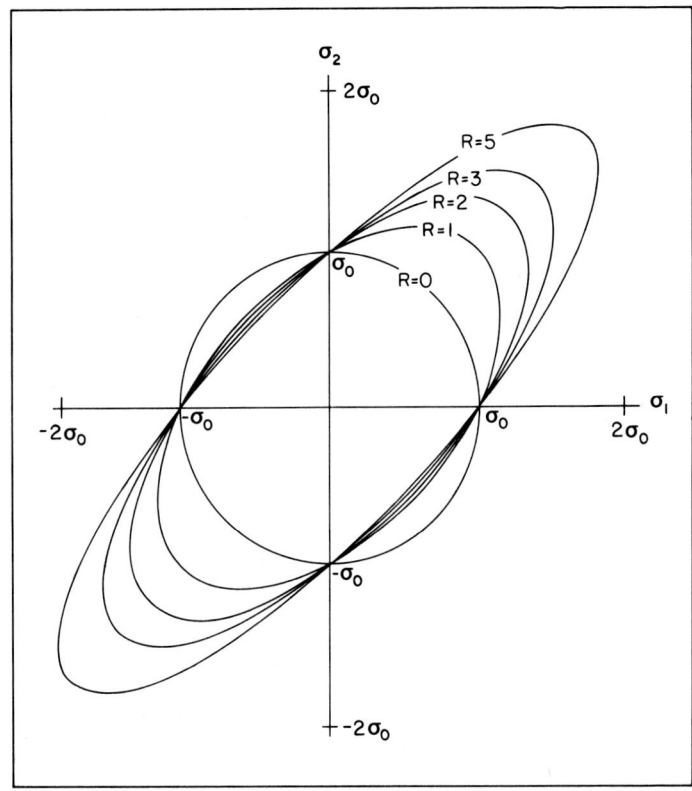

Figure 2.2. Plane-stress yield loci for sheet metals exhibiting various degrees of plastic anisotropy, or R values.[4]

$$\bar{\sigma} = \sqrt{3\,(1 + R)/2\,(2 + R)}\,\{\sigma_1^2 + \sigma_2^2$$
$$- (2R/(1 + R))\,\sigma_1\sigma_2\}^{1/2} \quad . \tag{2.14b}$$

Again, it has been assumed that the anisotropy is rotationally symmetric and characterized by the R parameter.

The definition of the effective strain follows from a set of equations known as the associated flow rule, or Levy-Mises relations. This is a set of equations that relates the components of the stress tensor and those of the strain increment tensor. For an isotropic material, these relations are

$$\left.\begin{array}{l} d\varepsilon_{xx} = \{\sigma_{xx} - \tfrac{1}{2}\,(\sigma_{yy} + \sigma_{zz})\}\,d\lambda \\ d\varepsilon_{yy} = \{\sigma_{yy} - \tfrac{1}{2}\,(\sigma_{zz} + \sigma_{xx})\}\,d\lambda \\ d\varepsilon_{zz} = \{\sigma_{zz} - \tfrac{1}{2}\,(\sigma_{xx} + \sigma_{yy})\}\,d\lambda \\ d\varepsilon_{xy} = 3\,\sigma_{xy}\,d\lambda \\ d\varepsilon_{yz} = 3\,\sigma_{yz}\,d\lambda \\ d\varepsilon_{zx} = 3\,\sigma_{zx}\,d\lambda \quad . \end{array}\right\} \tag{2.15a}$$

Similarly, the strain increments for a sheet with rotationally symmetric plastic anisotropy (characterized by R), which is loaded by the principal stresses σ_1 and σ_2, are given by:

$$\left.\begin{array}{l} d\varepsilon_1 = [(R + 1)\,\sigma_1 - R\sigma_2]\,d\lambda \\ d\varepsilon_2 = [(R + 1)\,\sigma_2 - R\sigma_1]\,d\lambda \\ d\varepsilon_3 = (-\sigma_1 - \sigma_2)\,d\lambda \quad . \end{array}\right\} \tag{2.15b}$$

The term $d\lambda$ in both sets of Equations (2.15) is a constant whose value depends on the hardness state of the material. Equations (2.15) are in incremental form for two reasons. First, it allows the relationship between the stresses and strains to be quasilinearized. A second, more important, argument comes from thermodynamics and the idea of maximum work.[10] This argument states that any arbitrary increment of plastic deformation applied to a body requires the least *internal* energy input when the work performed by the *externally* applied stresses through the *external* strain increment is a *maximum*. The external work is a maximum when $d\varepsilon_{ij} = (\partial\bar{\sigma}/\partial\sigma_{ij})\,d\lambda$, or $\underset{\sim}{d\varepsilon} \propto \nabla \cdot \bar{\sigma}$.

In other words, maximum external work is obtained when the strain increments are proportional to the gradient of the yield locus, as it is defined in stress space. For this reason, the effective stress or yield locus is often called the plastic potential, or the potential function whose gradient is proportional to the plastic strain increments. One of the most important properties of gradient functions leads to the fact that the strain increments are perpendicular to the yield locus. This property is employed often in the analysis of metal forming problems. For example, the measurement of R values, mentioned previously, allows an indirect method of determining the yield locus of textured sheet metals (Fig. 2.3).

With the definitions of the plastic strain increments, Equations (2.15), the effective strain is defined as that combination of increments required to make the product of effective stress and effective strain increment equal to the work increment dW performed under conditions of uniaxial tensile or compressive stress (dW = $\sigma_{xx} d\varepsilon_{xx}$) or pure shear (dW = $2\sigma_{xy} d\varepsilon_{xy}$). For an isotropic material, the effective strain increment is thus:

$$d\bar{\varepsilon} = \sqrt{{}^2/_9 \{(d\varepsilon_{xx} - d\varepsilon_{yy})^2 + (d\varepsilon_{yy} - d\varepsilon_{zz})^2 + (d\varepsilon_{zz} - d\varepsilon_{xx})^2\} + {}^4/_3 d\varepsilon_{xy}^2 + {}^4/_3 d\varepsilon_{yz}^2 + {}^4/_3 d\varepsilon_{zx}^2}$$

Similarly, the effective strain-rate increment for an isotropic metal is defined by:

$$d\bar{\dot{\varepsilon}} = \sqrt{{}^2/_9 \{(d\dot{\varepsilon}_{xx} - d\dot{\varepsilon}_{yy})^2 + (d\dot{\varepsilon}_{yy} - d\dot{\varepsilon}_{zz})^2 + (d\dot{\varepsilon}_{zz} - d\dot{\varepsilon}_{xx})^2\} + {}^4/_3 d\dot{\varepsilon}_{xy}^2 + {}^4/_3 d\dot{\varepsilon}_{yz}^2 + {}^4/_3 d\dot{\varepsilon}_{zx}^2} \quad (2.17)$$

For a sheet with rotationally symmetric plastic anisotropy loaded in plane stress, the effective strain increment is:

$$d\bar{\varepsilon} = \sqrt{2(2+R)/3(1+2R)^2} \{(d\varepsilon_1 - Rd\varepsilon_3)^2 + (d\varepsilon_2 - Rd\varepsilon_3)^2 + R(d\varepsilon_1 - d\varepsilon_2)^2\}^{1/2} \quad (2.16b)$$

Now that effective stress and strain have been defined, the method by which they can be related through stress, strain, strain-rate relationships can be described. This is most easily done for conditions of proportional straining, in which the ratio of the strain (and strain-rate) increments remains fixed. For this type of deformation, the differential signs may be eliminated from Equations (2.16) and (2.17). These equations and Equation (2.14), or similar equations for anisotropic metals, may then be inserted into equations such as (2.6), (2.7), (2.8), and (2.9) by replacing σ_1 with $\bar{\sigma}$, ε_1 with $\bar{\varepsilon}$, and $\dot{\varepsilon}$ with $\bar{\dot{\varepsilon}}$. For nonproportional straining, the stress, strain, strain-rate relationships can be obtained only by using the differential forms of Equations (2.6), (2.7), (2.8), and (2.9) in conjunction with Equations (2.14), (2.16), and (2.17) and integrating over the strain path employed.

Workability Tests

UNIAXIAL COMPRESSION TEST

One of the most common and the simplest of all workability tests is the uniaxial compression or upset test. It is used to obtain flow stress data and workability estimates for a number of bulk forming processes. In the test, a right cylindrical specimen is compressed between flat, parallel dies. When the test is used to determine the

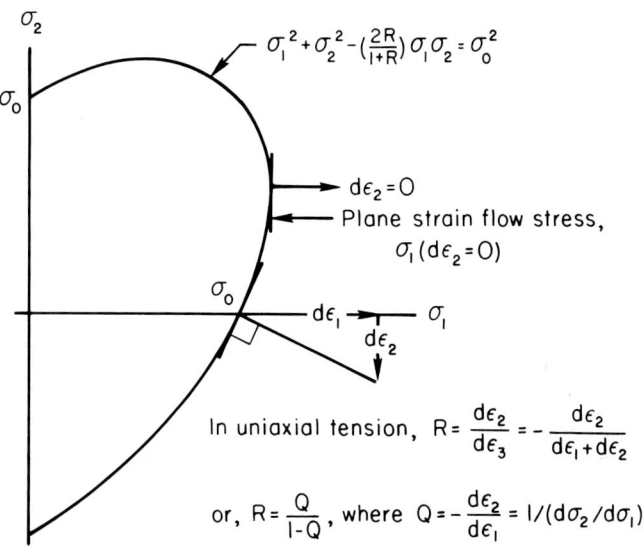

Figure 2.3. Relationship between R value and yield locus shape under conditions of uniaxial tension.

deformation resistance, or flow stress, as a function of strain, strain rate, and temperature, dies heated to the same temperature as the specimen and appropriate lubricants are used to ensure that the deformed shape of the specimen remains as close to cylindrical as possible, i.e., without chilling or appreciable bulging. Die materials include hot work die steels and tungsten carbide (for $T \leq 500$ °C, or 932 °F) and nickel-base superalloys, TZM molybdenum, and silicon nitride (for $T > 500$ °C, or 932 °F). A variety of die heating methods are available, including furnace heating and induction heating. Furthermore, a variety of lubricants may be employed. At ambient and slightly higher temperatures, common lubricants include PTFE (Teflon®) film, graphite, and molybdenum disulfide. At temperatures between 100 °C (212 °F) and 550 °C (1022 °F), graphite, applied by spraying a water-based solution, is the lubricant most frequently used. A variety of glasses that melt and retain a certain degree of viscosity at high temperatures are the usual lubricant choices above 550 °C (1022 °F).

Details regarding test procedures and data analysis of the compression test, when used for flow stress determination, are contained in another volume of the monograph series. Briefly, however, the important relationships used to reduce measured load-stroke data, if the deformation is uniform, are the following:*

Axial true strain, ε_1: $\bar{\varepsilon} = -\varepsilon_1 = -\ln(h/h_o)$ (2.18)

$h \equiv$ instantaneous height of the specimen
$h_o \equiv$ original height of the specimen

Axial true strain rate, $\dot{\varepsilon}_1$: $\dot{\bar{\varepsilon}} = -\dot{\varepsilon}_1 = -(v/h)$ (2.19)

$v \equiv$ crosshead speed

Axial true stress, σ_1: $\bar{\sigma} = -\sigma_1$ (2.20)

$\qquad = -(P/A) = -(Ph/A_o h_o)$

$P \equiv$ instantaneous load
$A \equiv$ instantaneous cross-sectional area
$A_o \equiv$ original cross-sectional area

Often the compression test is used to obtain workability data for use in bulk forming process design. For example, insight into the

---

*Note that compressive strains, strain rates, and stresses are negative. Similarly, the crosshead speed (v) and compressive load (P) associated with the test are also negative.

modes of flow localization and free surface fracture is often obtained by running compression tests on specimens of various h_o/d_o ratios (d_o = original specimen diameter) under different conditions of lubrication. The free surfaces of the specimens are gridded by photographic or electrochemical means, and grid measurements following deformation are used to obtain failure loci (Figure 2.4).[11]

The upset test is also commonly used to establish the modes of strain localization during nonisothermal metalworking operations (tooling and workpiece at different initial temperatures). In these cases, specimens heated to a particular temperature are compressed various amounts between flat dies that are heated to somewhat lower temperatures. The localization phenomena produced in this way are studied through a variety of means. These include (1) metallographic techniques in which chill zones and free-surface bulging can be measured directly and (2) analysis of the load-stroke curves through comparison with load-stroke curves from isothermal compression tests. The application of powerful finite-element techniques, which use material property data and processing conditions as inputs, is also proving useful in establishing the sequence of localization events during nonisothermal compression and other nonisothermal metalworking operations.

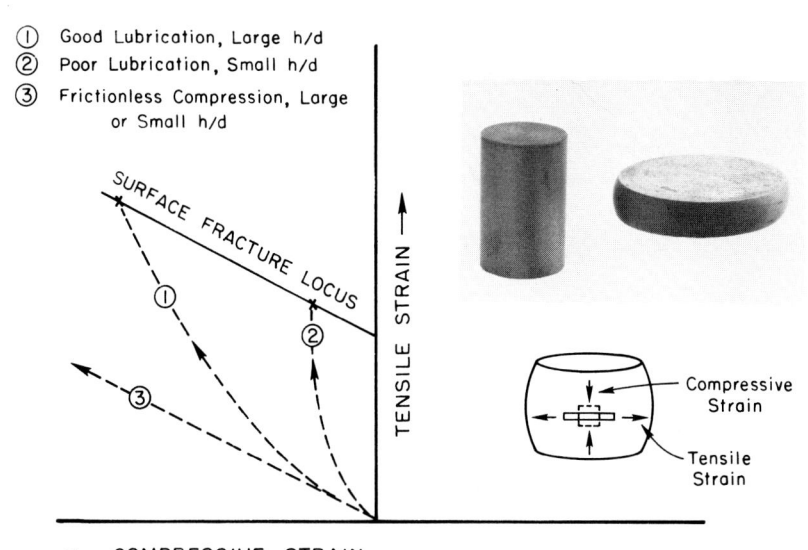

Figure 2.4. Typical failure locus of metals that develop surface cracks during bulk forming, an example of which is shown in the photograph. Locus is in terms of the free-surface compressive and tensile principal strains at failure.[11]

tions. With the aid of these techniques, the effects of working speed, die-workpiece temperature difference, the heat transfer characteristics of the lubricant interface, etc., on chilling and flow localization can be determined.

TORSION TEST

The torsion test may also be used to obtain flow stress data and workability estimates for bulk forming processes. Often it is chosen over the uniaxial compression test because very large strains can be achieved without the problems of lubricant breakdown and bulging.

Flow Stress Data. When the torsion test is used for the measurement of flow stress data, solid or tubular round bars are generally deformed at constant twisting rate, $\dot{\theta}$. Denoting the radial coordinate by r and the gage length by ℓ (Figure 2.5), the strain field during uniform deformation does not vary with axial position and is simply

$$\Gamma(r) = r\theta/\ell \quad , \tag{2.21}$$

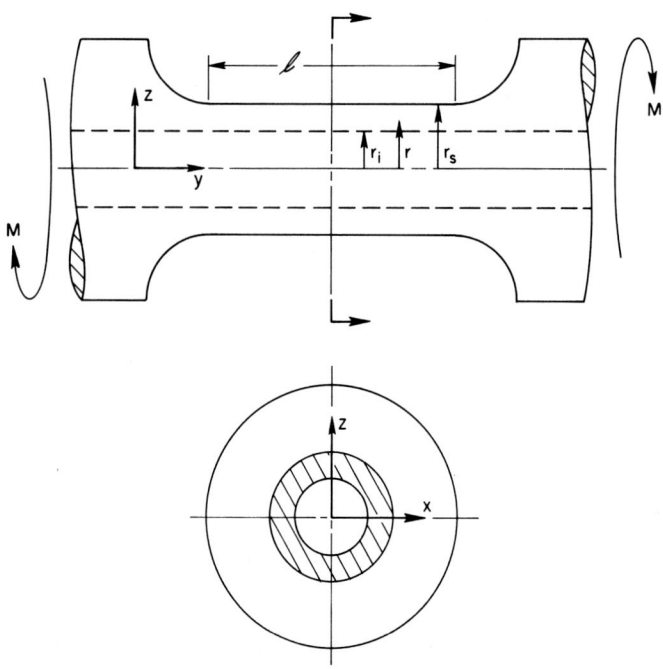

Figure 2.5. Nomenclature for a torsion test on a tubular specimen.

where θ is the amount of twist, and $\Gamma = 2\varepsilon_{xy} = \sqrt{3}\,\bar{\varepsilon}$, for an isotropic von Mises material. It has been shown that the relation between Γ and $\bar{\varepsilon}$ holds even at large strains.[12] For most practical purposes, the strain $\Gamma(r_s) = \theta\,r_s/\ell$ at the outer radius r_s is generally employed to characterize the material with the associated values of surface strain rate and shear stress.

The stress field in the torsion test is also fairly simple:

$$\sigma_{xy} = \tau(r) = \tau(\Gamma,\dot{\Gamma},T) = \tau(\theta,\dot{\theta},r,T) \quad . \tag{2.22}$$

In this expression, the shear strain rate $\dot{\Gamma}$ is simply related to $\dot{\theta}$ during uniform deformation in much the same manner that Γ is related to θ:

$$\dot{\Gamma}(r) = r\dot{\theta}/\ell \quad . \tag{2.23}$$

To obtain $\tau(\Gamma,\dot{\Gamma},T)$ from the measured data in the torsion test, that is to say, from the torque, M, versus twist, θ, data, several analyses may be applied.[13-15] These analyses are used primarily for converting solid bar torque data into shear stress-shear strain form. Analysis of the thin-walled tube torsion test is very simple, because the shear stress and shear strain are assumed not to vary across the wall thickness. Another analysis for the thick-walled tube case, which reduces to the published results in the various limits, can be given as follows. As in the other analyses, the effects of deformation heating on τ will be assumed to be negligible. This is a good approximation for slow deformation rates at which the heat generated has time to dissipate into the grips or surroundings. Furthermore, it will be assumed that the flow law for the material is of the form:

$$\tau = G\,\Gamma^n\dot{\Gamma}^m \quad , \tag{2.24}$$

in which G, n, and m are material constants.

The analysis is performed by noting that the torque M is equal to the moment produced by the shear stresses τ acting over the entire cross section of the torsion specimen. If the inner radius and outer radius of the specimen are r_i and r_s, respectively, the torque is therefore:

$$M = 2\pi \int_{r_i}^{r_s} \tau\,r^2\,dr \quad . \tag{2.25}$$

On substituting Equations (2.21), (2.23), and (2.24), Equation (2.25) becomes:

$$M = \frac{2\pi G\theta^n \dot\theta^m}{\ell^{(n+m)}} \int_{r_i}^{r_s} r^{2+n+m} dr \qquad (2.26)$$

or

$$M = \frac{2\pi G\theta^n \dot\theta^m}{\ell^{(n+m)}} \left(\frac{r^{3+n+m}}{3+n+m}\right)\bigg|_{r_i}^{r_s} . \qquad (2.27)$$

On further algebraic manipulation, we obtain:

$$M = \frac{2\pi G\theta^n \dot\theta^m}{(3+n+m)\,\ell^{n+m}} (r_s^{3+n+m})\{1 - (r_i/r_s)^{3+n+m}\}$$

or

$$M = \frac{2\pi \tau}{(3+n+m)} r_s^3\{1 - (r_i/r_s)^{3+n+m}\} . \qquad (2.28)$$

In the above equation, τ is the shear stress associated with the outer radius shear strain Γ_s and strain rate $\dot\Gamma_s$, respectively, so that

$$\tau(\Gamma_s,\dot\Gamma_s) = \frac{(3+n+m)\,M}{2\pi\, r_s^3\{1 - (r_i/r_s)^{3+n+m}\}} . \qquad (2.29)$$

For constant n and m, it is easily shown that $n = (\partial \ln\tau/\partial \ln\Gamma)_{\dot\Gamma,T}$ is equal to $(\partial \ln M/\partial \ln\theta)_{\dot\theta,T}$ and that $m = (\partial \ln\tau/\partial \ln\dot\Gamma)_{\Gamma,T}$ is equal to $(\partial \ln M/\partial \ln\dot\theta)_{\theta,T}$. Thus, Equation (2.29) reduces to the familiar Fields and Backofen[14] relation when r_i is set to zero, i.e., for the case of a solid bar. Moreover, in the limit of $r_i \to r_s$, i.e., for the case of the thin-walled tube, the term $(r_i/r_s)^{3+n+m}$ in Equation (2.29) may be expanded using the binomial expansion after noting that

$$r_i/r_s = [1 - (\Delta/r_s)] \quad , \qquad (2.30)$$

in which $\Delta = r_s - r_i$. Neglecting infinitesimals of the second or greater order, the thin-walled tube equation relating M and τ is then obtained:

$$\tau = M/2\pi\, r_s^2\, \Delta \quad . \qquad (2.31)$$

The flow stress data obtained from the torsion test can be readily compared to data from compression tests through the use of the definitions of effective stress and effective strain. Assuming a von Mises material, for compression, $\bar{\sigma} = -\sigma_1$ and $\bar{\varepsilon} = -\varepsilon_1$. For torsion, $\bar{\varepsilon} = \Gamma/\sqrt{3}$ and $\bar{\sigma} = \sqrt{3}\tau$. For a variety of metals, several investigators have shown that the $\bar{\sigma}$-$\bar{\varepsilon}$ relationships derived from the two test methods agree at least approximately.[16] However, there are numerous metals for which a comparison based on these definitions does not bring the two types of data into full agreement. In these cases, the torsion equivalent stresses are almost invariably *lower* than the compression ones. Examples are Type 304 stainless steel, aluminum, and ETP copper deformed at cold working temperatures (Figure 2.6a).[15, 17, 18] For these alloys, even a comparison at equal amounts of plastic work does not bring the data into coincidence. These discrepancies have been attributed to differences in the rates of dislocation accumulation and in texture development in torsion and other modes of deformation.[12] At hot working temperatures, where such differences are minimal, flow curves obtained by various test methods, however, frequently show fairly good agreement (Figure 2.6b).

Workability Analysis. The torsion test is also useful in the analysis of flow localization and shear band formation. In these instances, a fine axial scribe line is often placed on the entire length of the gage section. Following twisting, variations in the angle ϕ between this line and the axial direction may be used to follow the development of nonuniformities in the strain distribution. When the flow has localized at some point along the gage length, ϕ will be greater there than it is elsewhere. If we assume that the angle is roughly constant and equal to ϕ_u outside the region of localized deformation, the surface shear strain in the homogeneous part of the specimen at the onset of localization, Γ_s^u, is

$$\Gamma_s^u = \tan \phi_u \quad . \tag{2.32}$$

Similarly, the amount of surface shear strain within the region of localization, Γ_s^b, where the angle is equal to say ϕ_b, is

$$\Gamma_s^b = \tan \phi_b \quad . \tag{2.33}$$

SIDEPRESSING TEST

The plane-strain sidepressing test has been shown to be of great use in the simulation of forging operations in which the flow localizes in the form of shear bands.[19, 20] Because it involves the lateral compression of long bars of round or square cross section between flat parallel dies, the sidepressing test is simulative of forging operations such as those used to make steam and gas turbine engine blades.

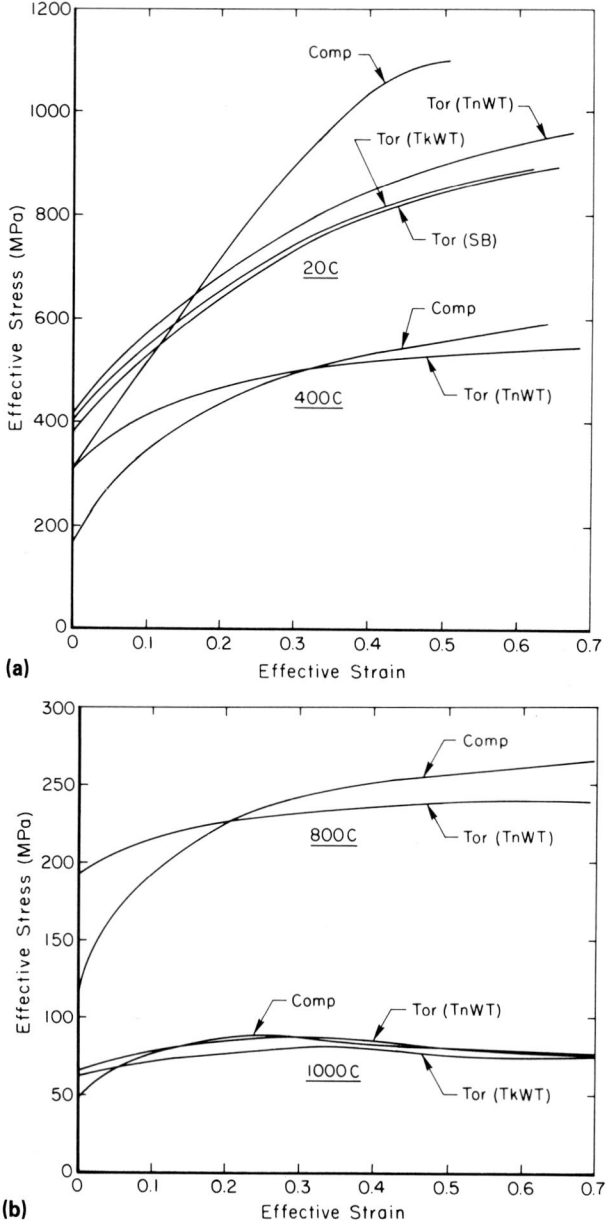

Figure 2.6. Von Mises effective stress-strain curves for Type 304L stainless steel at (a) cold working and (b) hot working temperatures, determined for an effective strain rate of 0.01 sec.$^{-1}$. Curves are from compression tests (Comp) and torsion tests (Tor) of thin-walled tubes (TnWT), thick-walled tubes (TkWT), and solid bars (SB).[17]

This test has been performed on metals at cold working temperatures, as well as hot working temperatures.[19, 20] At hot working temperatures, it has been useful for studying flow localization phenomena under isothermal, as well as nonisothermal, conditions.

Even when there is no flow localization as such, deformation during the sidepressing of round bars is very nonuniform. Nevertheless, an average effective strain may still be calculated based on the reduction of the initial diameter of the round bar d_o to some subsequent height h. Since $\varepsilon_{zz} = \varepsilon_{yz} = \varepsilon_{zx} = 0$ because of plane strain, and assuming $\varepsilon_{xy} = 0$, from volume constancy, we obtain $\varepsilon_{yy} = -\varepsilon_{xx}$ (where ε_{xx} is the compressive strain) for a von Mises material. Hence, $-\bar{\varepsilon}$ is equal to $(2/\sqrt{3}) \varepsilon_{xx} = 1.155 \varepsilon_{xx} \approx 1.155 \ln(h/d_o)$.

A simple technique has also been developed to determine the reduction at which shear bands are initiated in sidepressing. It makes use of metallographic observations and the fact that, in plane strain, shear bands initiate along the zero-extension directions or slip lines of plasticity theory. The method assumes that true initiation takes place before it is visible metallographically. Thus, the height h* associated with true initiation, which corresponds to the moment when the slip lines are perpendicular, can be found by back extrapolation from the earliest moment at which they are visible metallographically. The extrapolation technique employs a construction based on the assumption that, once shear bands are initiated, deformation proceeds more or less by block shear. For the purposes of argument, assume that shear bands are initiated as shown in Figure 2.7a. Deformation proceeds by shearing along the shear bands AOD and COB and by deformation of the blocks AOB, BOD, DOC, and COA, which leads to the rotation and bending of the shear bands evident in Figure 2.7a. At higher levels of deformation, the geometry assumes the form shown in Figure 2.7b. The "block" AOB has deformed into the shape shown. For the geometry studied, the deformation of block AOB may be approximated by the deformation of the area A'OB' (Figure 2.7a) into the area A"OB" (Figure 2.7b). Thus, by measuring the angle θ_h and height $h(\theta_h)$ (Figure 2.7b) at which shear bands are first observed in metallographic sections, the height at initiation h* (which corresponds to $\theta_h = 90°$) may be estimated:

$$h^* = h(\theta_h) \sqrt{\tan(\theta_h/2)} \qquad (2.34)$$

UNIAXIAL TENSION TEST

Probably the most common of all workability tests, the uniaxial tensile test is used to determine flow stress data for the analysis of flow localization in secondary forming operations such as those used to fabricate sheet metal products. These tests are usually performed on round bars or thin sheet specimens.

For round bars, the axial true strain ε_1 during uniform deformation is given by*

$$\varepsilon_1 = \ln \frac{\ell}{\ell_o} , \qquad (2.35)$$

where ℓ is the instantaneous gage length and ℓ_o is the original gage length. The axial true stress σ_1 is*

$$\sigma_1 = \frac{P}{A} = \frac{P\ell}{A_o \ell_o} , \qquad (2.36)$$

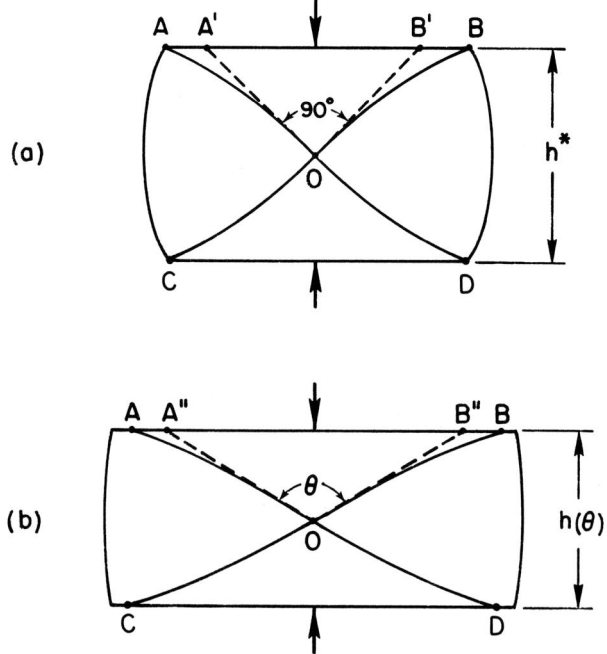

Figure 2.7. Construction used to determine reduction at which shear bands initiate in sidepressing. (a) Geometry corresponding to reduction at which shear bands initiate and (b) geometry corresponding to reduction at which shear bands are first observed in metallographic sections.

---

*In tension, the axial stress, axial strain, and load are all positive.

where P = applied load and A and A_o are the instantaneous and original cross-sectional areas of the specimen. Prior to necking at $\bar{\varepsilon}_1 = \varepsilon_u$, Equations (2.35) and (2.36) also define the effective strain $\bar{\varepsilon}$ and effective stress $\bar{\sigma}$, respectively. Flow properties (i.e., $\bar{\sigma}$ versus $\bar{\varepsilon}$) following necking may be obtained by measuring the diameter of the necked section and the profile radius of the neck during neck development. The strain field, in terms of the principal strains, is (assuming isotropy) given approximately by:

$$\left.\begin{array}{l}\varepsilon_1 = \ln(A_o/A) \\ \\ \varepsilon_2 = \varepsilon_3 = 1/2 \ln(A/A_o)\end{array}\right\} \quad (2.37)$$

The effective strain at any section of the neck continues to be $\bar{\varepsilon} = \varepsilon_1$, as it was for $\varepsilon_1 < \varepsilon_u$. Calculation of the corresponding effective stress is not as easy, because the stress state is triaxial. In this case, the Bridgman analysis[21] has been found to be useful for estimating the transverse principal stresses, which, with the axial stress ($\sigma_1 = P/A$), can be inserted into Equation (2.14) to obtain the effective stress. The flow localization process of necking in round bars is terminated by fracture. This event is often characterized by the final percent reduction in area, RA, or true axial fracture strain ε_{1_f}:

$$RA = [(A_o - A_f)/A_o] \times 100 \quad (2.38)$$

$$\varepsilon_{1_f} = \ln(A_o/A_f) \quad (2.39)$$

In these equations, A_f is the cross-sectional area at the fracture.

The flow curve for sheet metals may be determined in tension tests similar to those on round bars. These tests are usually performed at room temperature because most sheet forming is done in this manner. For uniform deformation, Equations (2.35) and (2.36), based on the overall gage length ℓ, may be used to obtain the flow curve. Once straining becomes nonuniform, the overall gage length can no longer be used; nevertheless, the local strains can be measured from the changes in the local gage lengths, defined for example in terms of grid lines or circles applied by electrochemical or photographic means. These can be used in turn to define the true stress. Unlike the round bar tension test, however, flow stress measurements are rarely attempted beyond the onset of necking during sheet tensile testing. Although the local strains are not measured with great frequency, one further type of measurement, in addition to the axial one, is often made during uniform deformation. This usually consists of the principal width strain, ε_2, which is determined as a function of the axial strain ε_1. From volume constancy, the thickness strain ε_3 may also be estimated, and plots of ε_2 versus ε_3 may be prepared. From these, the R value, or *normal* plastic anisotropy parameter, may be obtained:

$$R = d\varepsilon_2/d\varepsilon_3 \quad , \tag{2.40}$$

and the shape of the yield locus inferred through Equation (2.13). The R value is important in estimating the deep drawability of sheet metals.[4, 22, 23] Sheet metals with R's ≥ 1 have fair to good deep drawability, whereas metals with R < 1 are difficult to deep draw.

Unfortunately, the R value is generally a function of the orientation of the tensile specimen with respect to the rolling direction in the original sheet. This is the situation for metals such as drawing-quality, aluminum-killed (DQAK) low-carbon steel, and many sheet titanium alloys. When this is the case, an average R value, $\bar{R}$, is used in Equations (2.13), (2.14b), (2.15b), and (2.16b):

$$\bar{R} = \frac{R_{0°} + 2R_{45°} + R_{90°}}{4} \quad , \tag{2.41}$$

where the subscripts refer to the angle between the tensile axis and the rolling direction. Additionally, an estimate of the planar plastic anisotropy can be obtained from

$$\Delta R = \frac{R_{0°} - 2R_{45°} + R_{90°}}{2} \quad . \tag{2.42}$$

The value of ΔR may be used to assess the tendency to form ears during deep drawing.

PLANE-STRAIN COMPRESSION/TENSION TESTS

Because large strain flow stress data are often needed to solve sheet forming problems and because it is difficult to obtain these data from uniaxial tension experiments, the latter are frequently supplemented by plane-strain compression tests (Figure 2.8). In this test, a well-lubricated thin sheet is indented on both sides by narrow flat parallel punches whose breadth, b, exceeds the sheet breadth. When the width of the punches, w, is much greater than the instantaneous thickness of the sheet, h, the deformation zone is largely confined to the region directly between the punches.[24-26] Under these circumstances, the nondeforming metal outside the deformation zone prevents transverse flow, and thus the strain state is one of plane deformation. Because the thickness and longitudinal strains are both principal strains to a good approximation, this translates into $d\varepsilon_3 = -d\varepsilon_1$.

For the purposes of the analysis that follows, let the principal stresses in the plane strain compression test be denoted by σ_3^* and σ_2^* (see Figure 2.9). Note that σ_3^* and σ_2^* are both negative, and that $\sigma_3^* < \sigma_2^*$. The stress state associated with the test can be usefully compared with that for plane-strain tension. This is because the plastic deformation of metals is generally considered to be unaffected by the hydrostatic component of the stress state. Thus, the stress deviators in the plane-strain tensile test of Figure 2.9, in which $\sigma_1 = -\sigma_3^*$ and $\sigma_2 = \sigma_2^* - \sigma_3^*$, are identical to those of the plane-strain compression test. Note, however, that σ_1 and σ_2 are both positive in the case of the tensile test. Because $d\varepsilon_2$ is equal to zero, from Equations (2.15b), we have

$$\sigma_2/\sigma_1 = R/(1 + R) \quad . \tag{2.43}$$

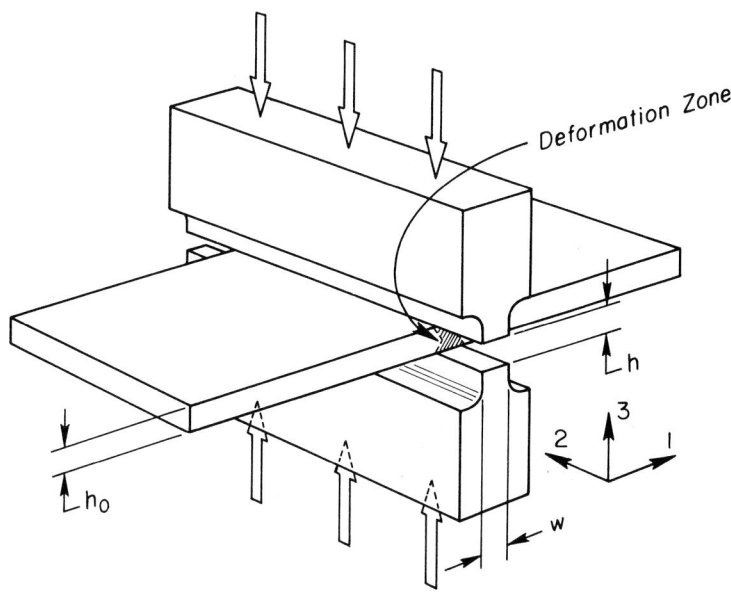

Figure 2.8. Schematic of the plane-strain compression test for sheet metals.[24]

On substituting this into the definition for the effective stress, Equation (2.14b), the following relation is obtained:

$$\bar{\sigma}_1 = \sqrt{\frac{3(1 + 2R)}{2(1 + R)(2 + R)}} \,\bar{\sigma}_1 \qquad (2.44)$$

When $R = 1$, $\bar{\sigma} = \sigma_1/1.15 = -\sigma_3^*/1.15$. From Equation (2.16b), we can derive the effective strain increment $d\bar{\epsilon}$ in plane-strain compression or tension:

$$d\bar{\epsilon} = \sqrt{\frac{2(2 + R)(1 + 3R + 2R^2)}{3(1 + 2R)^2}} \, d\epsilon_1 \qquad (2.45)$$

When $R = 1$, $d\bar{\epsilon} = 1.15\, d\epsilon_1$.

The comparison of data from plane-strain compression and sheet tensile tests offers a convenient method of judging the reliability of Hill's formulation of plastic anisotropy. For a tensile test on an anisotropic sheet, the stress and strain fields are:

$$\sigma_1 > 0,\ \sigma_2 = \sigma_3 = 0 \qquad (2.46)$$

$$\left.\begin{array}{l} d\epsilon_2/d\epsilon_1 = -R/(1 + R) \\ d\epsilon_3/d\epsilon_1 = -1/(1 + R) \end{array}\right\} \qquad (2.47)$$

The latter follow from Equations (2.15b). Using Equations (2.14b) and (2.16b), $\bar{\sigma}$ and $\bar{\epsilon}$ are given by:

$$\bar{\sigma} = \sqrt{\frac{3(1 + R)}{2(2 + R)}} \,\sigma_1 \qquad (2.48)$$

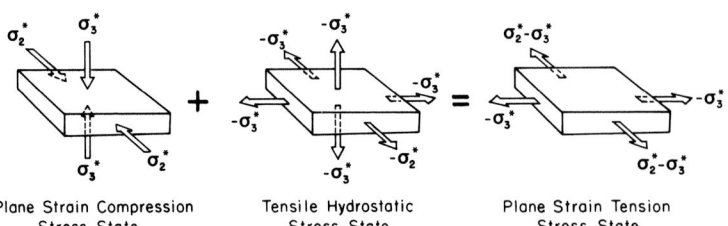

Plane Strain Compression Stress State   Tensile Hydrostatic Stress State   Plane Strain Tension Stress State

Figure 2.9. Schematic illustrating the equivalence of plane-strain compression and plane-strain tension loading of sheet metal.[4]

$$d\bar{\varepsilon} = \sqrt{\frac{2(2 + R)}{3(1 + R)}}\, d\varepsilon_1 \qquad (2.49)$$

At equal effective strains and stresses, the ratio of the two maximum principal stresses is thus:*

$$\sigma_{1_{\text{plane strain}}}/\sigma_{1_{\text{uniaxial}}} = (1 + R)/\sqrt{1 + 2R} \qquad (2.50)$$

When comparing actual measured plane-strain compression and uniaxial tension flow stress data, the minimum and maximum, respectively, principal stresses should be evaluated at equivalent levels of plastic work to prevent biasing the results through the definitions selected for $\bar{\sigma}$ and $\bar{\varepsilon}$. Such comparisons between measurements and Equation (2.50) show good agreement in some cases and fair to poor agreement in other cases (Figure 2.10). This may arise from the observation that the $\bar{\sigma}$ versus $\bar{\varepsilon}$ curves determined in plane-strain experiments are often *lower* than those established in axisymmetric testing.[29] As in the case of torsion testing, this may be due to the lower rates of dislocation accumulation and of texture development under these conditions.

IN-PLANE AND PUNCH-STRETCHING TESTS

The in-plane and punch-stretching tests are employed to study the process of flow localization in sheet metal forming. In the in-plane stretching test, originally developed by Marciniak and co-workers,[30] sheets that are clamped at their edges are stretched by flat-bottomed punches of various circular and elliptical cross sections. Another sheet of material is placed between the punch and the test specimen, which contains a hole similar in shape to the punch cross section, but smaller in size. The purpose of this second sheet is to minimize the effects of friction and to enhance strain uniformity in the test specimen. The use of differently shaped punches produces different strain paths in which ε_1 and ε_2 are both positive.

For the punch-stretching test, as developed by Hecker,[31] square and rectangular sheets clamped at their edges by a circular draw bead are stretched by a hemispherical punch. In this test, the strains in a square sheet vary over the stretched dome from a strain state near plane strain ($\varepsilon_1 > 0$, $\varepsilon_2 = 0$) near the flange of the sheet to one ap-

---

*Here, as above, the *minimum* principal stress in the plane-strain compression test $\sigma_3{*}$ is taken as equal to the negative of the *maximum* principal stress σ_1 in the "equivalent" plane-strain tensile test.

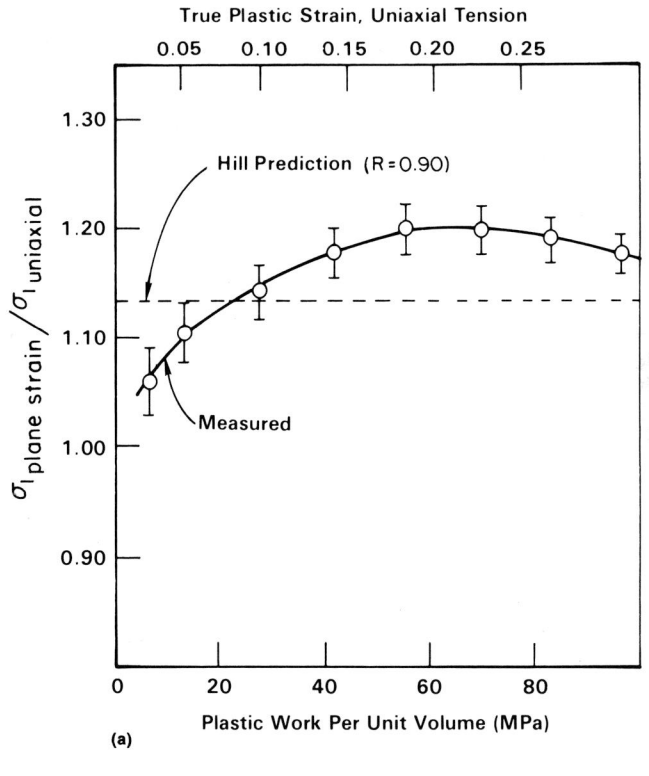

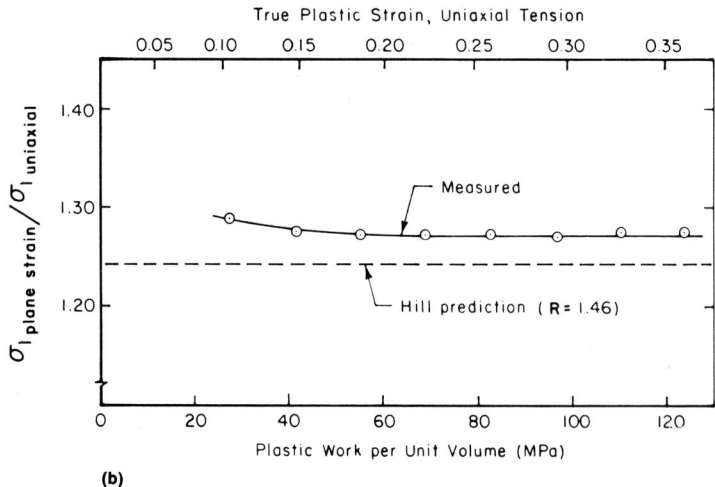

Figure 2.10. Ratio of the plane-strain flow stress and uniaxial tension flow stress, compared at equal levels of plastic work for (a) a hot rolled aluminum-killed, low-carbon steel[27] and (b) a cold rolled and annealed aluminum-killed, drawing-quality low-carbon steel.[28]

proximating balanced biaxial tension at the pole ($\varepsilon_1 = \varepsilon_2$). When square sheets are used, flow localization and failure usually occur near the flange (poor lubrication) or at the pole (good lubrication). When rectangular sheets are employed, in which case only the two narrow ends of the sheet are clamped, lateral drawing in of the sheet is possible, and depending on the exact ratio of the length and width of the sheet, flow localization and failure may occur under a variety of strain states within the range $\varepsilon_1 > 0$ and $\varepsilon_2 \leq 0$.

The strain paths and failure strains in the stretched sheets in both the in-plane and punch-stretching tests are measured through the prior application of grids (consisting of either a cartesian grid line network or, more commonly, a repetitive pattern of small circles) onto the test specimens. These patterns are applied through a variety of electroetching and photographic techniques. After stretching the sheet specimens, measurement of the grid spacing near the failure site al-

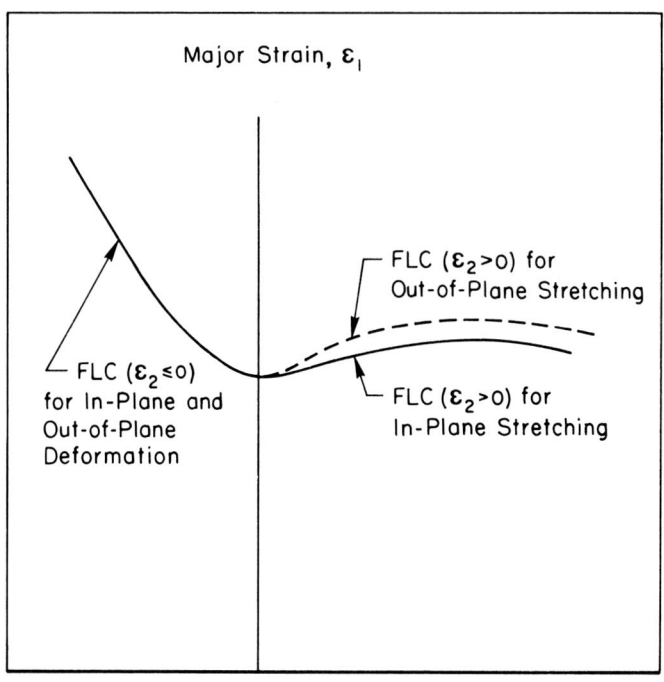

Figure 2.11. Typical forming limit diagrams, or loci of principal surface strains at failure, for sheet metals deformed in-plane and out-of-plane (as in punch forming).[32-35]

lows the determination of the strains at the onset of flow localization (if fracture occurs following through-thickness thinning) or the strains at fracture (if fracture occurs without noticeable through-thickness thinning). The principal strains at failure are most easily obtained with circular grids because the principal axes of strain lie along the major and minor axes of the ellipses into which the circles deform under proportional loading conditions ($d\varepsilon_2/d\varepsilon_1$ = constant). Both types of tests promote this kind of straining.

The failure data from both the in-plane and punch-stretching tests are most conveniently presented in terms of ε_1 (denoted the *major* strain) versus ε_2 (denoted the *minor* strain) diagrams (Figure 2.11). Since Keeler,[32] who studied strain states for which $\varepsilon_2 \geq 0$, and Goodwin,[33] who studied strain states for which $\varepsilon_2 < 0$, were among the first to present data in this way, these are often called Keeler-Goodwin diagrams, especially when the data are for low-carbon steels. Other names, such as forming limit curves (FLC's) and forming limit diagrams (FLD's) are also widely used when referring to these plots. Although this will be discussed in more detail in a later chapter, it has been found that the FLD's are usually higher for out-of-plane or punch stretching, as compared to in-plane stretching (Figure 2.11).[34, 35] This arises because friction and strain gradients, inherent in punch stretching, delay the localization of plastic flow. Hence, the deformation method must be specified when describing failure processes in terms of FLD's.

References

[1]   H.J. McQueen and J.J. Jonas: *Metal Forming—Interrelation Between Theory and Practice*, A.L. Hoffmanner, ed., p. 393, Plenum Press, New York, 1971.
[2]   G. Dieter: *Mechanical Metallurgy*, McGraw-Hill, New York, 1976.
[3]   F.A. McClintock and A.S. Argon: *Mechanical Behavior of Materials*, Addison-Wesley, Reading, MA, 1966.
[4]   W.A. Backofen: *Deformation Processing*, Addison-Wesley, Reading, MA, 1972.
[5]   W. Johnson and P.B. Mellor: *Engineering Plasticity*, Van Nostrand Rheinhold, London, 1973.
[6]   J.H. Hollomon: *Trans. AIME*, 1945, vol. 162, p. 268.
[7]   E. Voce: *J. Inst. Metals*, 1948, vol. 74, p. 537.
[8]   W.J. McG. Tegart: *Ductility*, p. 133, ASM, Metals Park, OH, 1968.
[9]   H.J. McQueen and J.J. Jonas: *Treatise on Materials Science and Technology, Vol. 6: Plastic Deformation of Metals*, R.J. Arsenault, ed., p. 393, Academic Press, New York, 1975.
[10] R. Hill: *The Mathematical Theory of Plasticity*, Oxford University Press, London, 1950.

[11] H.A. Kuhn and P.W. Lee: *Met. Trans.,* 1971, vol. 2, p. 3197.
[12] S.C. Shrivastava, J.J. Jonas, and G. Canova: *J. Mech. Phys. Solids,* 1982, vol. 30, p. 75.
[13] A. Nadai: *Theory of Flow and Fracture of Solids, Vol. 1,* McGraw-Hill, New York, 1950.
[14] D.S. Fields and W.A. Backofen: *Proc. ASTM,* 1957, vol. 57, p. 1259.
[15] G. Canova, S. Shrivastava, J.J. Jonas, and C. G'Sell: *Formability of Metallic Materials—2000 A.D., ASTM STP 753,* J.R. Newby and B.A. Niemeier, eds., p. 189, ASTM, Philadelphia, 1981.
[16] F.A. Hodierne: *J. Inst. Metals,* 1962-1963, vol. 91, p. 267.
[17] S.L. Semiatin and J.H. Holbrook: *Met. Trans. A.,* 1983, vol. 14A, p. 1681.
[18] D.J. Lloyd: *Met. Sci.,* 1980, vol. 14, p. 193.
[19] S. Kobayashi, C.H. Lee, Y. Saida, and S.C. Jain: Technical Report AFML-TR-70-90, University of California, Berkeley, CA, July, 1970.
[20] S.L. Semiatin and G.D. Lahoti: *Met. Trans. A,* 1981, vol. 12A, p. 1705.
[21] P.W. Bridgman: *Large Plastic Flow and Fracture,* McGraw-Hill, New York, 1952.
[22] W.T. Lankford, S.C. Snyder, and J.A. Bauscher: *Trans. ASM,* 1950, vol. 42, p. 1197.
[23] R.L. Whiteley: *Trans. ASM,* 1960, vol. 52, p. 154.
[24] A.B. Watts and H. Ford: *Proc. Inst. Mech. Engrs.,* 1952-1953, vol. 1B, p. 448.
[25] J.F.W. Bishop: *J. Mech. Phys. Solids,* 1958, vol. 6, p. 132.
[26] H. Ford: *Proc. Inst. Mech. Engrs.,* 1948, vol. 159, p. 115.
[27] S.L. Semiatin: Ph.D. Thesis, Department of Metallurgy and Materials Science, Carnegie-Mellon University, Pittsburgh, PA, 1977.
[28] A.K. Ghosh and W.A. Backofen: *Met. Trans.,* 1973, vol. 4, p. 1113.
[29] H. Ford: *J. Inst. Metals,* 1968, vol. 96, p. 65.
[30] Z. Marciniak and K. Kuczynski: *Inter. J. Mech. Sci.,* 1967, vol. 9, p. 609.
[31] S.S. Hecker: *Metals Eng. Quart.,* 1974, vol. 14, No. 4, p. 30.
[32] S.P. Keeler: "Circular Grid System—A Valuable Aid for Evaluating Sheet Metal Formability," Paper 680092, SAE Automotive Engineering Congress, Detroit, January, 1968.
[33] G.M. Goodwin: "Application of Strain Analysis to Sheet Metal Forming Problems in the Press Shop," Paper 680093, SAE Automotive Engineering Congress, Detroit, January, 1968.
[34] A.K. Ghosh and S.S. Hecker: *Met. Trans.,* 1974, vol. 5, p. 2161.
[35] A.K. Ghosh and S.S. Hecker: *Met. Trans. A,* 1975, vol. 6A, p. 1065.

FLOW LOCALIZATION IN BULK FORMING: ISOTHERMAL DEFORMATION

By far the largest number of observations of flow localization phenomena in bulk forming processes are related to processes carried out under nominally isothermal conditions, or conditions in which the workpiece and tooling have the same initial temperature. At low strain rates, any deformation heat that is developed is dissipated into the tooling, and thus temperature changes in the workpiece are negligible. At high strain rates, deformation, or adiabatic, heating raises the workpiece temperature, but only limited heat transfer between the workpiece and the tooling occurs because of the short deformation times. For purposes of discussion, therefore, flow localization under nominally isothermal conditions focuses, for the most part, on the workpiece material and its flow properties. Tooling-workpiece interactions are restricted to the effects of friction on the imposed strain state.

In this chapter, attention will be focused on flow localization in bulk metalworking processes at both cold and hot working temperatures. As mentioned in Chapter 1, the approach will be largely phenomenological. Where appropriate, however, the metallurgical processes leading to particular categories of material behavior will be discussed.

Flow Localization/Surface Fracture at Cold Working Temperatures

The first strain localization problem to be discussed is that of flow localization leading to fracture on the free surface of the workpiece in operations such as forging and rolling. These phenomena are most common at cold working temperatures.[1-6] In these cases, flow localization is initiated at surface inhomogeneities or imperfections when barreling is produced by factors such as friction. As a result, secondary tensile stresses are developed that cause the imperfections to grow until fracture occurs.

DESCRIPTION OF FLOW LOCALIZATION PHENOMENOLOGY AT COLD WORKING TEMPERATURES

Although the exact sequence by which barreling occurs can be dependent on a variety of geometric and material parameters, gross trends can nevertheless be discerned from simple upsetting tests. In these experiments, the occurrence of localization and surface fracture is studied by compressing cylindrical specimens of various initial height-to-diameter ratios (h_o/d_o) between flat dies under various conditions of lubrication. From tests of this sort, it is found that the amount of barreling for a given height reduction, and thus the driving force for flow localization, increases with decreasing specimen aspect ratio (smaller h_o/d_o) and decreased lubrication (more friction). Viewed differently, the maximum reduction obtainable without fracture decreases with decreasing aspect ratio and decreased lubrication. This trend may have been expected intuitively. However, Lee, Kuhn, and Erturk[2,3] and others have laid a firm experimental and theoretical foundation for this expectation.

In an extended series of experiments, Lee and Kuhn upset cylinders of different h_o/d_o's between flat, parallel dies under various conditions of lubrication (good lubrication, no lubrication, no lubrication with roughened die surfaces, etc.). Prior to deformation, the free surfaces of the specimens were gridded at the "equator" to enable tracking of the deformation path that was followed. Specifically, the surface axial strain ε_{zz} and hoop strain $\varepsilon_{\theta\theta}$, both of which are principal strains, were measured. The dependence of these strains on the overall height reduction of the cylinder is depicted schematically in Figure 3.1. At small reductions or height strains, the ratio of $-\varepsilon_{zz}$ to $\varepsilon_{\theta\theta}$ is fairly constant. Because of barreling, this ratio is less than the value of 2, which would be expected for a homogeneous, isotropic material. As the reduction is increased, the $-\varepsilon_{zz}$ dependence exhibits a perturbation that leads to a decrease in the slope of the $-\varepsilon_{zz}$ versus height strain relationship until it is less than that of the $\varepsilon_{\theta\theta}$ versus height strain relation or even zero. In the latter event, a condition of plane strain is introduced, during which $d\varepsilon_{\theta\theta} = -d\varepsilon_{rr}$. This type of flow readily leads to strain localization and to final fracture.

The flow localization and fracture process in a series of experiments similar to the one just described can also be interpreted through plots of $\varepsilon_{\theta\theta}$ versus ε_{zz} (Figure 3.2). Good lubrication during upsetting and large values of h_o/d_o, both of which minimize barreling, promote large amounts of strain prior to the onset of localization and fracture. As indicated above, the latter are associated with the con-

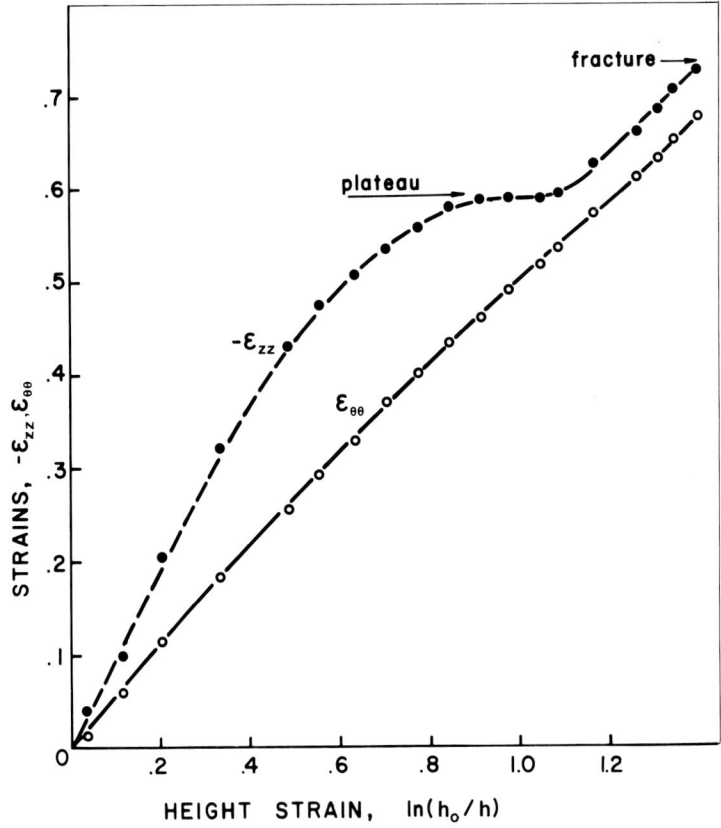

Figure 3.1. Axial strain ε_{zz} and circumferential strain $\varepsilon_{\theta\theta}$ measured at the equator versus overall height strain imposed during room-temperature upset test ($h_o/d_o = 1.50$) on cold drawn 1045 steel. Note the strain perturbation at a height strain of approximately 0.8.[1,2]

Flow Localization in Bulk Forming: Isothermal Deformation   45

dition $d\varepsilon_{zz} = 0$. Poor lubrication and small values of h_o/d_o, on the other hand, lead to early localization and fracture. Perhaps the most interesting feature of these plots is that the loci of the failure strains for most metals lie along a straight line whose slope is $-1/2$. In other words, the failure loci are parallel to the strain path, characterizing a state of frictionless, homogeneous compression. Only the intercept on the circumferential strain axis varies from one metal to another. Because of this, only one upset test need be conducted for a given metal to determine its entire surface failure locus. The graphical summary of data of this type is often called a workability diagram.

FLOW LOCALIZATION ANALYSIS

The importance of surface imperfections, which are assumed to give rise to the flow localization phenomenon just described, can be deduced by employing a model similar to the one originally proposed by Marciniak and Kuczynski[7] to characterize the process by which through-thickness necks develop during the stretching of sheet

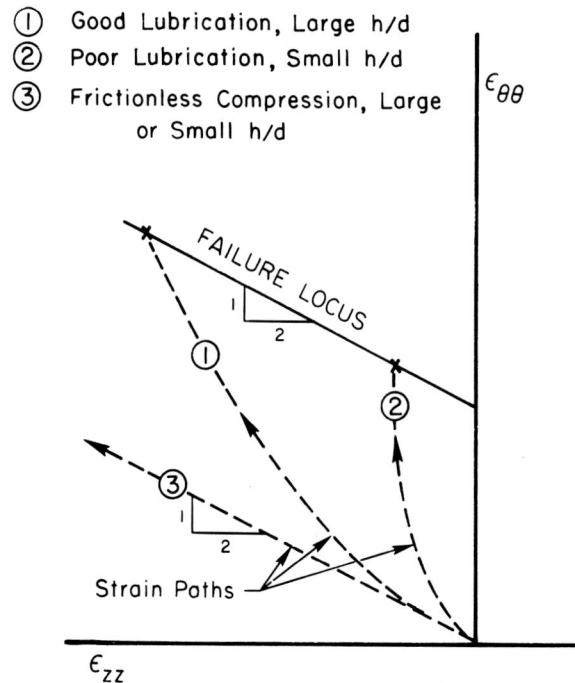

Figure 3.2. Strain paths and typical failure locus, depicting the influence of initial aspect ratio (h_o/d_o) and lubrication during upset testing.

metal. The analysis below follows that of Lee and Kuhn[2] for an isotropic material, which was in turn based on the work of Marciniak and Kuczynski.

Although the surface imperfection on which attention will be focused can take several forms (strength imperfection, work-hardening defect, etc.), the one that will be dealt with in this chapter and is most easily visualized is the geometric defect consisting of a local irregularity in radius or height. The growth of these defects can be described in terms of the R and Z models, using the Lee-Kuhn terminology as depicted in Figure 3.3. Note that in the R and Z models,

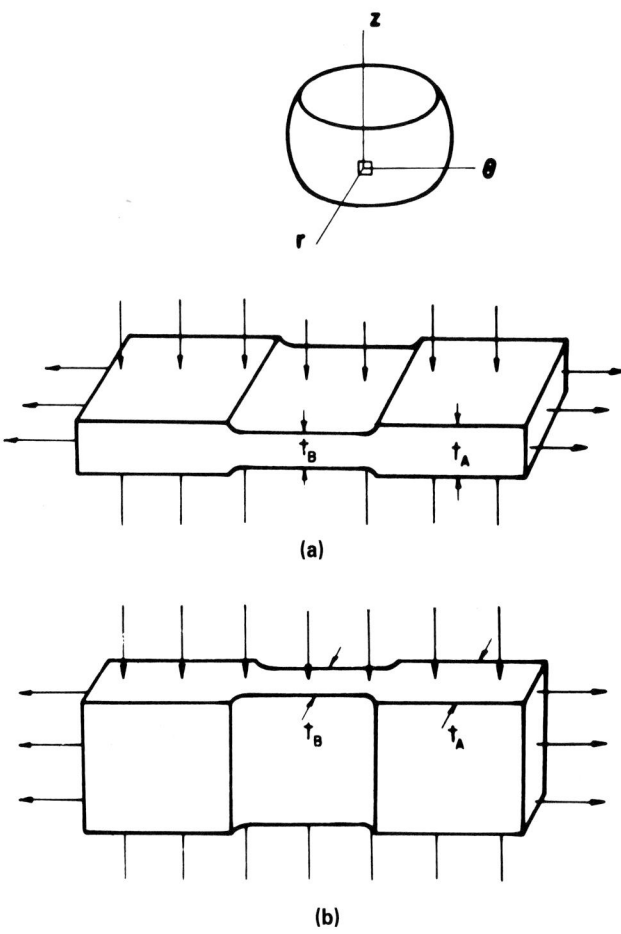

Figure 3.3. Material elements used as models for plasticity analysis of localized thinning and fracture of metals. (a) R model and (b) Z model.[2]

the incipient "trough" lies along the radial or axial directions, respectively.

The localization analysis is used to estimate the strain history in the region of the imperfection (B) from a knowledge of the imposed, or gross, strain field (in region A) and equilibrium considerations. It begins by noting that the principal axes of stress and strain at the "equatorial" free surface lie parallel to the r, θ, and z axes. With the definition of the strain ratio, K*, in region A (assumed to remain constant during the flow localization process),

$$K^* = -d\varepsilon_{zz_A}/d\varepsilon_{\theta\theta_A} \quad , \tag{3.1}$$

the effective strain increment $d\bar{\varepsilon}_A$ in region A (i.e., the region outside the irregularity) is found from Equation (2.16a) to be

$$d\bar{\varepsilon}_A = (2/\sqrt{3}) \, d\varepsilon_{\theta\theta_A} (1 - K^* + K^{*2})^{1/2} \quad , \tag{3.2}$$

and, since $\sigma_{RR} = 0$ at the surface, the stress ratio r* and effective stress $\bar{\sigma}_A$ in region A can be deduced from Equations (2.15a) and (2.14a), respectively:

$$r^* = \sigma_{zz_A}/\sigma_{\theta\theta_A} = (2K^* - 1)/(K^* - 2) \quad , \tag{3.3}$$

and

$$\bar{\sigma}_A = \sigma_{\theta\theta_A} (1 - r^* + r^{*2})^{1/2} \quad . \tag{3.4}$$

The stresses and thus the effective stress in the imperfection (region B) can be found by employing force equilibrium considerations. Characterizing the imperfection by $f = t_B/t_A$ (Figure 3.3), equilibrium requires that:

$$\sigma_{\theta\theta_B} = \sigma_{\theta\theta_A}/(t_B/t_A) = \sigma_{\theta\theta_A}/f \tag{3.5}$$

for both types of defect. If we assume that σ_{zz} is the same in both regions,* we have

$$\sigma_{zz_B}/\sigma_{\theta\theta_B} = (\sigma_{zz_A}/\sigma_{\theta\theta_A}) \, f = r^* \, f \quad . \tag{3.6}$$

---

*Such an assumption is probably valid for the R model, but not for the Z model. Although Lee and Kuhn do not discuss this, the Z model formulation should probably include $d\varepsilon_{zz}$ continuity. The formulation of Equations (3.6) through (3.10) would then be somewhat different.

The effective stress in region B is then, from Equation (2.14a):

$$\bar{\sigma}_B = \sigma_{\theta\theta_B}(1 - r^* f + r^{*2} f^2)^{1/2} \qquad (3.7)$$

A relationship between $\bar{\sigma}_B$ and $\bar{\sigma}_A$ can be obtained by combining Equations (3.4), (3.5), and (3.7):

$$\bar{\sigma}_B = (\bar{\sigma}_A/f)\{(1 - r^* f + r^{*2} f^2)/(1 - r^* + r^{*2})\}^{1/2} \qquad (3.8)$$

The effective stress relationship of Equation (3.8) can be transformed into the analogous one for effective strain by assuming a form for the constitutive equation. If we assume that $\bar{\sigma} \propto \bar{\varepsilon}^n$ (i.e., no rate sensitivity) and neglect the rotation of the principal strain axis associated with the gradual change in strain path,

$$\bar{\varepsilon}_B = \bar{\varepsilon}_A\{(1 - r^* f + r^{*2} f^2)/(1 - r^* + r^{*2}) f^2\}^{1/2n} \qquad , \qquad (3.9)$$

which can be evaluated for each increment of $d\bar{\varepsilon}_A$ (Equation 3.2).

With the aid of the above expression for $\bar{\varepsilon}_B$ and the stress ratio $\sigma_{zz_B}/\sigma_{\theta\theta_B}$ (Equation 3.6), the flow rule (Equation 2.15a) and definition of effective strain (Equation 2.16a) can be used to calculate the strain increments in the region of the imperfection:

$$\left.\begin{array}{l} d\varepsilon_{\theta\theta_B} = d\bar{\varepsilon}_B(1 - r^* f/2)/(1 - r^* f + r^{*2} f^2)^{1/2} \quad , \\[6pt] d\varepsilon_{zz_B} = d\bar{\varepsilon}_B(r^* f - 1/2)/(1 - r^* f + r^{*2} f^2)^{1/2} \quad , \end{array}\right\} \qquad (3.10)$$

and

$$d\varepsilon_{rr_B} = d\bar{\varepsilon}_B(-r^* f/2 - 1/2)/(1 - r^* f + r^{*2} f^2)^{1/2} \quad .$$

The easiest way to estimate the growth of the inhomogeneity is by numerical evaluation of Equations (3.10), after assuming that K*, and hence r*, remain constant. This is done by selecting suitable values for K* and r* and assuming some initial imperfection ratio, say f_o. Using appropriately small increments of $d\varepsilon_{\theta\theta_A}$, the increments in $\bar{\varepsilon}_A$ (Equation 3.2) and $\bar{\varepsilon}_B$ (Equation 3.9) can be found, from which $d\varepsilon_{\theta\theta_B}$, $d\varepsilon_{zz_B}$, and $d\varepsilon_{rr_B}$ are determined. Finally, with the aid of these increments, the change in the inhomogeneity factor, df, is calculated. For the R model, it is given by

$$df = f_o(d\varepsilon_{zz_B} - d\varepsilon_{zz_A}) \qquad , \qquad (3.11)$$

and for the Z model, by

$$df = f_o (d\varepsilon_{rr_B} - d\varepsilon_{rr_A}) \quad . \tag{3.12}$$

By employing Equations (3.2) and (3.9) to (3.12), as described above, and repeatedly incrementing $d\varepsilon_{\theta\theta_A}$, the values of f can be continuously updated. Finally, when $f = 0$, or when the ratio $d\varepsilon_{rr_B}/d\varepsilon_{\theta\theta_B}$ (R model) or $d\varepsilon_{zz_B}/d\varepsilon_{\theta\theta_B}$ (Z model) is suitably small, a strain state near plane strain is reached and the ensuing localization is considered to be terminated by fracture* (Figure 3.4).

The variation in the localization strain, or limit strain as it is often called, predicted by these models follows a trend very similar to the measured failure loci of metals (compare Figures 3.4 and 3.5). The major drawback of the analysis lies in the need to set an initial value for f_o. A similar deficiency occurs in the analysis of necking in sheet stretching. However, the analyses do offer considerable insight into the effects of material properties such as n (and m in modified models similar to that just presented)[8] and stress ratio on the limit strains.

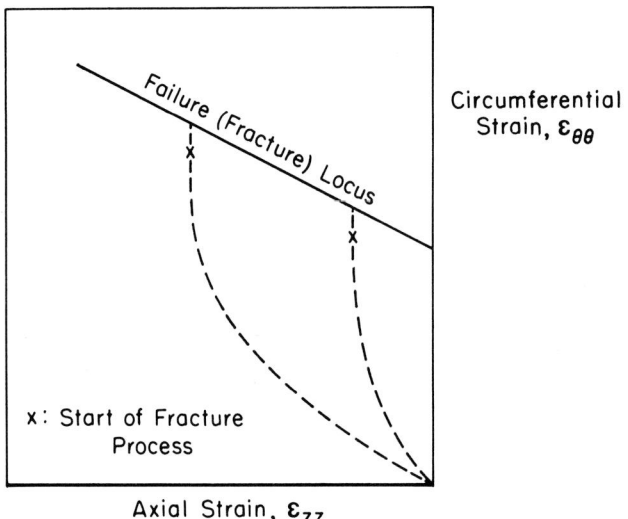

Figure 3.4. Relation between end of flow localization and start of the fracture process during upsetting of specimens that fail by surface fracture.

---

*In fact, the strains at which fracture occurs have been shown to correlate well with the Cockcroft and Latham fracture criterion.[3]

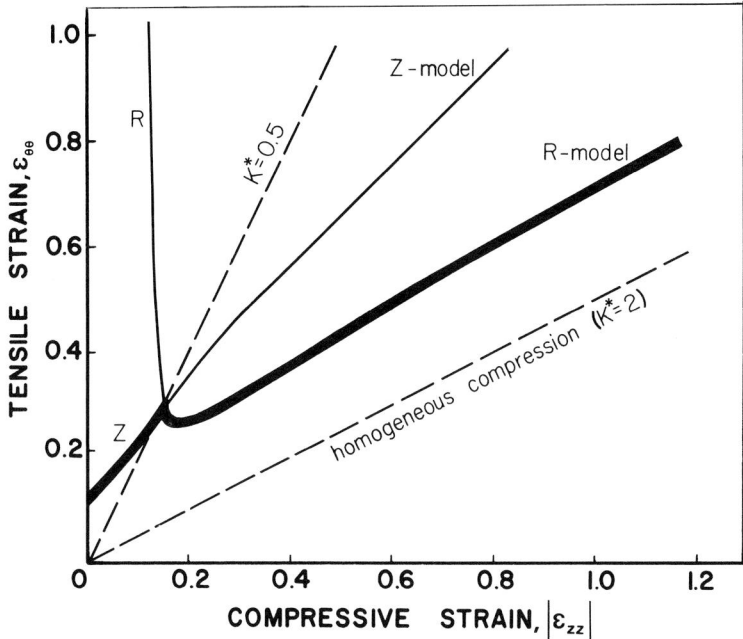

Figure 3.5. Locus of limit strains for the R and Z models. The lower parts of each model are used to construct the actual failure locus (heavy line). Calculations were based on $f_o = 0.99$, $n = 0.25$, and a prestrain of 0.10, resulting in a flow curve of the form $\bar{\sigma} = K(\bar{\varepsilon} + 0.10)^{0.25}$ [2]

Flow Localization Due to Flow Softening: Axisymmetric Deformation

The second class of problem involving flow localization under nominally isothermal conditions concerns that which occurs as a result of flow softening, or as it is sometimes called, negative work hardening.[9] This type of flow localization is most often seen under hot working conditions, in which flow softening may result from a variety of sources, both metallurgical and physical. However, it may also occur at cold working temperatures, at which the most common source of flow softening is deformation heating. In this and the following sections, the phenomenological basis for the localization of strain in materials that exhibit flow softening will be discussed. Finally, this chapter will be concluded with a summary of the common flow softening mechanisms in metals and alloys.

FLOW LOCALIZATION PARAMETER

It has been observed that the mode of flow localization due to flow softening varies depending on the deformation state or strain path followed. Under conditions of axisymmetric deformation, such as uniaxial compression, flow concentration takes the form of localized bulges, which are analogous to necks in the tension testing of round bars.[9, 10] By contrast, when a plane-strain loading path is followed, the localization is free to become more concentrated, leading to the formation of macroscopic shear bands. The latter topic will be discussed later after the characteristics of unstable flow during axisymmetric compression have received due consideration.

The effect of material properties on the rate of flow localization may be established using a method originated by Hart for the study of tensile necking.[11, 12] As in the tensile case, during axisymmetric upsetting, a necessary, but not sufficient, condition for *significant* flow localization is that the applied load pass through a maximum. The degree of flow localization following the load maximum is then determined by examining the rate of growth of imperfections in the workpiece[13] in a manner analogous to that described above for flow localization and surface fracture at cold working temperatures. Before discussing the results of this approach, the flow localization parameter α, whose magnitude is quite useful in ranking materials according to their tendency for strain concentration, will first be derived.

The flow localization parameter α is based on the variations in strain, strain rate, and temperature within the workpiece required to maintain force equilibrium. In the absence of inertial effects, the axial force F transmitted through a cylindrical workpiece remains constant. Denoting an axial coordinate by x, defined with respect to specimen or material coordinates (and not spatial, or Eulerian, coordinates), this condition is $dF/dx = 0$, or in normalized terms, $d\ln F/dx = 0$. Under uniaxial stress conditions, the axial force is simply $F = \sigma A$, in which $A \equiv$ the cross-sectional area of the workpiece and $\sigma \equiv \sigma_1$, the axial principal stress. Thus, at any time t, force equilibrium requires

$$\left(\frac{\partial \ln F}{\partial x}\right)\bigg|_t = 0 = \left(\frac{\partial \ln A}{\partial x}\right)\bigg|_t + \left(\frac{\partial \ln \sigma}{\partial x}\right)\bigg|_t . \quad (3.13)$$

In the most general case, the normalized gradient in cross section (with respect to x) at any instant of time (the first term on the right-hand side of Equation 3.13) can be expressed in terms of the variation in initial cross section A_o and the total strain ε at any point,[14]

$$\left(\frac{\partial \ln A}{\partial x}\right)\bigg|_t = \frac{d \ln A_o}{dx} - \left(\frac{\partial \varepsilon}{\partial x}\right)\bigg|_t , \qquad (3.14)$$

because of the constant volume assumption. Note that when $A_o(x)$ = constant, i.e., no geometric or machining imperfections or defects, Equation (3.14) reduces to the familiar expression $dA/A = -d\varepsilon$, derivable from the constant-volume assumption.

The outcome of the analysis embodied by Equation (3.13) now hinges on the particular constitutive model selected to describe the material behavior (and hence the second term of the right-hand side of Equation 3.13). For simplicity, a dependence $\sigma = \sigma(\varepsilon, \dot{\varepsilon}, T)$ will be assumed, in which the influence of each of ε, $\dot{\varepsilon}$, and T can be described independently of the other two. Such a description is known to be inaccurate,[15] but will nevertheless be employed here because of the relative simplicity of the results to which it leads. Accordingly, any variation in the flow stress of the material, $d\sigma$, is considered to involve the following three components:

$$d\sigma = \left(\frac{\partial \sigma}{\partial \varepsilon}\right)\bigg|_{\dot{\varepsilon},T} d\varepsilon + \left(\frac{\partial \sigma}{\partial \dot{\varepsilon}}\right)\bigg|_{\varepsilon,T} d\dot{\varepsilon} + \left(\frac{\partial \sigma}{\partial T}\right)\bigg|_{\varepsilon,\dot{\varepsilon}} dT . \qquad (3.15)$$

Here, ε, $\dot{\varepsilon}$, and T denote the axial (principal) strain, (principal) strain rate, and temperature, respectively, all of which are field quantities whose values depend on x and t.* The effect of various material properties on flow localization may be identified now. The first parenthetical term in Equation (3.15) is typically a flow stabilizing influence at cold working temperatures and neutral or destabilizing at hot working temperatures when flow softening is occurring. The second one, the strain-rate hardening term, is usually stabilizing, and the third term, the temperature-dependent one, is typically destabilizing because of thermal softening. Often the strain hardening term and the thermal softening term are lumped together, and a normalized, constant strain-rate strain hardening rate γ' is defined as:

$$\gamma' = \left(\frac{1}{\sigma}\frac{d\sigma}{d\varepsilon}\right)\bigg|_{\dot{\varepsilon}}$$

$$= \left\{\left(\frac{\partial \sigma}{\partial \varepsilon}\right)\bigg|_{\dot{\varepsilon},T} d\varepsilon + \left(\frac{\partial \sigma}{\partial T}\right)\bigg|_{\varepsilon,\dot{\varepsilon}} dT\right\}\bigg/\sigma d\varepsilon . \qquad (3.16)$$

---

*Note that in the present instance, as the stress field is that of uniaxial compression, strains, strain rates, and stresses are all negative. For use in generalized problems, Equation (3.15) can also be stated in terms of the effective stress, strain, and strain rate.

With this definition and that of the rate sensitivity parameter, $m = (\partial \ln\sigma/\partial \ln\dot\varepsilon)|_{\varepsilon,T}$, the second term on the right-hand side of Equation (3.13) is easily found to be:

$$\left(\frac{\partial \ln\sigma}{\partial x}\right)\bigg|_t = \gamma'\left(\frac{\partial \varepsilon}{\partial x}\right)\bigg|_t + m\left(\frac{\partial \ln\dot\varepsilon}{\partial x}\right)\bigg|_t \quad . \tag{3.17}$$

Combining Equations (3.13), (3.14), and (3.17), the following is obtained, after rearrangement, for the load equilibrium equation:

$$m\left(\frac{\partial \ln\dot\varepsilon}{\partial x}\right)\bigg|_t = \left(\frac{\partial \varepsilon}{\partial x}\right)\bigg|_t (1 - \gamma') - \frac{d\ln A_o}{dx} \quad . \tag{3.18a}$$

This final expression relates the axial strain-rate and strain *gradients* to the material properties and A_o (x). Alternatively, a formulation that relates the *variation* of ε, $\dot\varepsilon$, and A_o between a given material point and its neighbor may be written:

$$m\, \delta\ln\dot\varepsilon = (1 - \gamma')\,\delta\varepsilon - \delta\ln A_o \quad . \tag{3.18b}$$

The α parameter is defined as $-\delta\ln\dot\varepsilon/\delta\varepsilon$. In the case of no initial variation of cross section ($\delta\ln A_o = 0$), an initial variation in hardness state (due to mechanical damage, or so-called "hammer blows," for example) may give rise to strain and strain rate gradients whose growth may be gaged by the α parameter obtained from Equation (3.18b):

$$\alpha = -\frac{\delta\ln\dot\varepsilon}{\delta\varepsilon} = \frac{\gamma' - 1}{m} \quad . \tag{3.19}$$

When there are initial geometric (or machining) defects, Equation (3.19) may still be used to study flow localization, because the term $\delta\ln A_o$ is typically small relative to $(1 - \gamma')\,\delta\varepsilon$.

The flow localization parameter α defined above can be used to estimate the tendency of a material to form marked or catastrophic strain concentrations. It also gives the rate of localization at imperfections during upsetting after a load maximum or minimum. It should be emphasized that it is a function solely of the material properties, γ' and m, either or both of which may be functions of ε, $\dot\varepsilon$, and T. Thus, to determine the propensity to form strain concentrations, flow curves from constant strain rate compression tests and estimates of m (based on continuous flow curves for two different strain rates) are required, and α should be examined as a function of strain and the nominal strain rate and temperature. In general, however, materials that strain harden or show minimal flow softening resist flow localization. Furthermore, materials that flow soften appreciably resist strain concentration (i.e., have low rates of flow localization) as long as the rate sensitivity is sufficiently large (about 0.2 or higher). The application of Equations (3.18b) and (3.19) to obtain the detailed kinetics of flow localization is discussed more fully in Appendix A.

CORRELATION BETWEEN THE FLOW LOCALIZATION PARAMETER AND OBSERVATIONS

By definition, flow localization in upsetting corresponds to $\alpha > 0$. This corresponds to materials that exhibit $\gamma' > 1$, that is to say, a fairly large flow softening rate (as σ and ε are both negative in compressive deformation).* In actuality, Jonas, Holt, and Coleman[13] have suggested and Semiatin and Lahoti[16, 17] have verified that materials will show significant flow localization when $\alpha \geq 5$, approximately. It was mentioned above that flow localization in axisymmetric deformation states such as upsetting is manifested by localized bulges of the workpiece. Several cases of such flow localization will now be described.

Perhaps the first reported instance of flow instability under compressive loading is that of Jonas and Luton.[9] While establishing the general sources of flow softening at elevated temperatures, they found unusual, localized bulges in specimens of oxidized uranium isothermally upset at 850 °C (1562 °F) and $\dot{\varepsilon} \approx -1.5 \times 10^{-3}$ sec.$^{-1}$. For this material, the stress-strain curves (Figure 3.6) showed large amounts of flow softening whose magnitude depended on the holding time prior to testing, during which oxide layers of increasing thickness developed on the specimen surface. Although the detailed mechanisms of flow softening will be discussed later, it appears that, in this case, it was due to the progressive breakup of the oxide layer. For specimens that had been held in the presence of 10 ppm oxygen for 4 hours or longer prior to compression, localized bulges were formed on the specimens as a result of the flow softening behavior (Figure 3.7). The flow curves for these holding times show maximum values of γ' of approximately 5 at strains of 0.05 (Figure 3.6). Since m for this material is about 0.18,[18] the maximum value of α (Equation 3.19) during the deformation is approximately $(5 - 1)/0.18 \approx 22$, a number

---

*When $\gamma' = 1$, the rate of flow softening just compensates for the rate of geometric hardening or area increase. Thus $\gamma' > 1$ is needed to permit the development of nonuniform flow.

much greater than 5, which is the minimum value of α for significant flow localization.

Other correlations between the α parameter and observations of unstable bulging in isothermal hot upsetting are summarized in Table 3.1. For the α/β titanium alloy Ti-6Al-2Sn-4Zr-2Mo-0.1Si (Ti-6242Si), flow softening is observed at a variety of hot working temperatures and strain rates.[16, 19] The extent of flow softening is small when the alloy has been α/β processed and has an equiaxed alpha, or α + β, preform or starting microstructure (Figure 3.8). Larger degrees of flow softening are noted, on the other hand, in the constant strain rate flow curves of the Ti-6242Si alloy that has been beta worked or beta annealed to give a Widmanstätten alpha, or β, preform or starting microstructure (Figure 3.8). Calculations of the α parameter

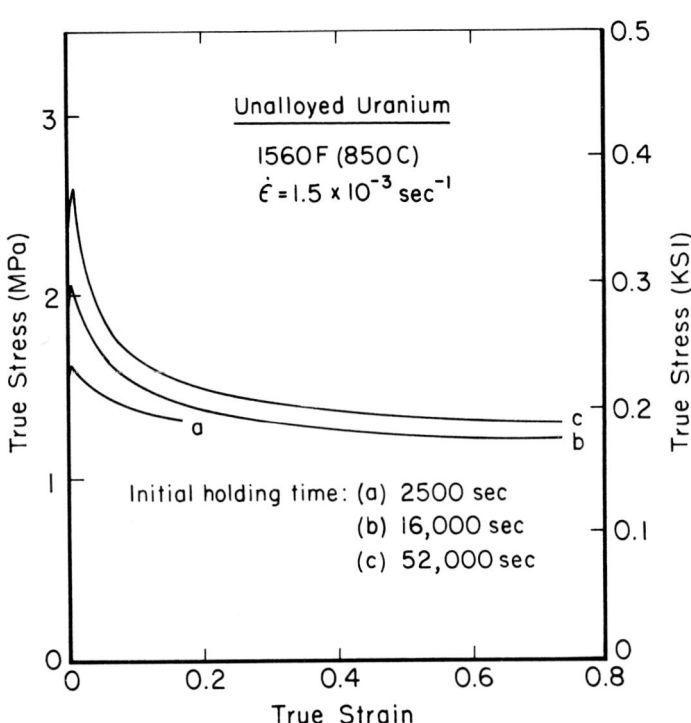

Figure 3.6. Compression flow curves for unalloyed depleted uranium tested in the gamma phase field that exhibit high levels of flow softening. Test specimens were held at 850 °C (1560 °F) in an atmosphere containing 10 ppm oxygen for the times indicated prior to testing. The external oxide layer formed on holding led to high initial flow stresses, but it broke up rapidly with strain beyond a few percent deformation.[9]

Table 3.1.
α_{max} Values for Upsetting of Ti-6242Si, Ti-10-2-3, and U-700

Material/Condition	Test Parameters, T(°C), $\|\dot{\varepsilon}\|(sec.^{-1})$	γ'_{max}	m	$\alpha_{max} = \dfrac{\gamma'_{max} - 1}{m}$	Bulging?
Ti-6242Si/ α/β Worked + Annealed	913, 10	0.63	0.206	<0	No
Ti-6242Si/ β Worked + Annealed	913, 10	1.67	0.134	5.0	Yes
Ti-10-2-3/ β Annealed	704, 10^{-3}	1.58	0.22	2.6	Yes
	704, 10^{-1}	1.65	0.13	5.0	Yes
	704, 10	1.40	0.08	5.0	Yes
	816, 10^{-3}	0.42	0.29	<0	No
	816, 10^{-1}	0.48	0.18	<0	No
	816, 10	0.34	0.16	<0	No
U-700/Hot Rolled	1038, 25	1.63	0.12	5.3	Yes

γ'_{max} = maximum value of γ' for ε between 0 and 0.7.

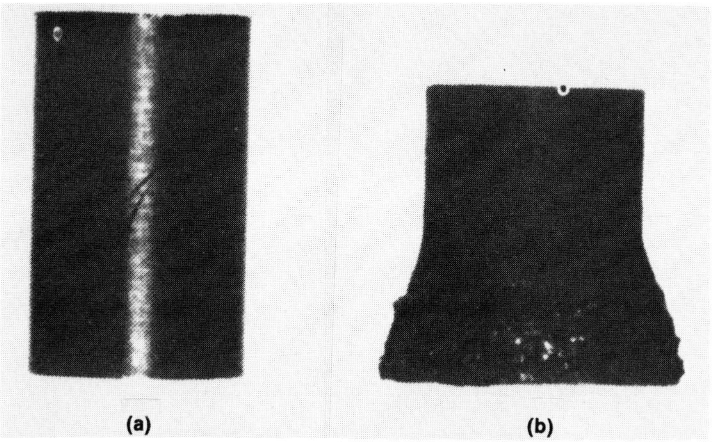

Figure 3.7. (a) Undeformed and (b) deformed compression specimens of oxidized, unalloyed depleted uranium. The deformed specimen, which exhibits large amounts of flow softening (Figure 3.6) and flow localization at one end, was upset 20 percent at 850 °C (1560 °F).[9]

from the flow stress data correlate well with localized bulging observations for this alloy as well (see Table 3.1 and Figure 3.9).[10] It should be noted that a shear type of deformation occurred during the upsetting, at 913 °C (1675 °F) and 10 sec.$^{-1}$, of a sample containing a β microstructure (Figure 3.9). This effect may be rationalized as being caused by poor alignment of the compression tooling, lack of sufficient or uniform lubrication at the die-workpiece interface, as well as other material influences (e.g., texture) that might cause the deformation state to change from axisymmetric localized bulging to a largely plane-strain mode involving localized shear.

This transition from somewhat localized bulging to highly localized shearing has also been documented for the hot isothermal upsetting of Ti-10V-2Fe-3Al (Ti-10-2-3) and nickel alloy U-700. For Ti-10-2-3, no localized bulging is observed at 816 °C (1500 °F) at any strain rate between 10^{-3} and 10 sec.$^{-1}$ (Figure 3.10). This is as expected, since $\alpha_{max} < 5$ under these conditions (Table 3.1). For deformation at 704 °C (1300 °F), α values greater than or equal to 5 are attained at a variety of strain rates (Table 3.1). However, the mode of instability varies from extremely mild bulging ($\dot{\varepsilon} = 10^{-3}$ sec.$^{-1}$, $\alpha_{max} \approx 2$) to pronounced bulging ($\dot{\varepsilon} = 10^{-1}$ sec.$^{-1}$, $\alpha_{max} \approx 5$) to bulging plus

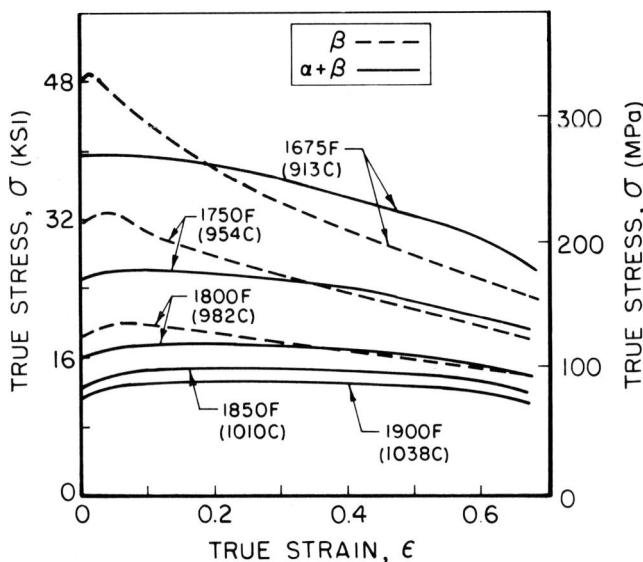

Figure 3.8. Compression flow curves for Ti-6242Si with either an equiaxed alpha (α + β) or Widmanstätten alpha (β) starting microstructure, determined as a function of temperature for a strain rate of 10 sec.$^{-1}$.[10]

Figure 3.9. Isothermal hot compression specimens of Ti-6242Si reduced in height by 50 percent at 913 °C (1675 °F), $\dot{\varepsilon} \approx 10$ sec.$^{-1}$. Starting microstructures were (a) $\alpha + \beta$ and (b) β. In the former case, $\alpha_{max} < 0$, whereas in the latter, $\alpha_{max} = 5$.[10]

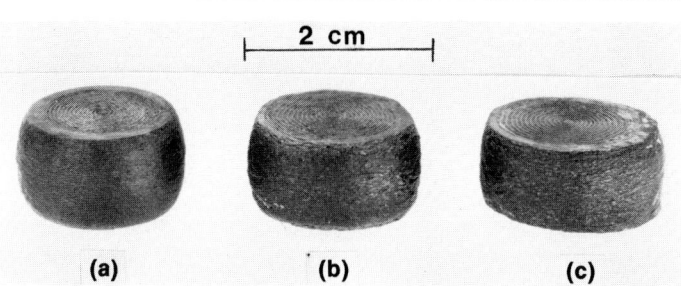

Figure 3.10. Isothermal hot compression specimens of Ti-10V-2Fe-3Al reduced in height by 50 percent at 816 °C (1500 °F) and strain rates of (a) 10^{-3}, (b) 10^{-1}, and (c) 10 sec.$^{-1}$. Note the absence of flow localization in all instances.

shearing deformation ($\dot{\varepsilon} = 10$ sec.$^{-1}$, $\alpha_{max} \approx 5$) (Figure 3.11). From these observations, it appears that deformation heating, whose magnitude increases with strain rate, in conjunction with the above variables (tooling misalignment, etc.) is of great importance in the flow localization process. More will be said later about the effects of deformation heating on flow localization in the analytical treatments presented below.

As a last example, in a different alloy class, the unstable flow of U-700 is described next. For this nickel alloy, flow softening giving rise to large values of α is evident at a variety of hot working temperatures. It is highly marked at 1038 °C (1900 °F) (Table 3.1). When cylindrical specimens are isothermally upset at 25 sec.$^{-1}$ and the tooling is well aligned, localized bulging occurs at moderately high reductions of 50 percent (Figure 3.12a). Surprisingly, however, a small misalignment of the tooling, such that the dies are inclined at an angle of only 2°, leads to bulging plus shearing at a reduction of 50 percent (Figure 3.12c). Similarly, if a larger reduction is imposed at the same temperature and strain rate, both bulging and shearing are

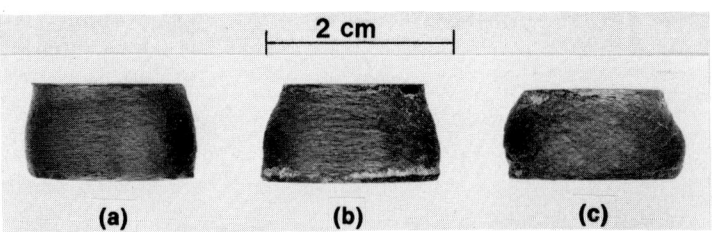

Figure 3.11. Isothermal hot compression specimens of Ti-10V-2Fe-3Al reduced in height by 50 percent at 704 °C (1300 °F) and strain rates of (a) 10^{-3}, (b) 10^{-1}, and (c) 10 sec.$^{-1}$. Note the increasing degree of flow localization as the strain rate is increased.

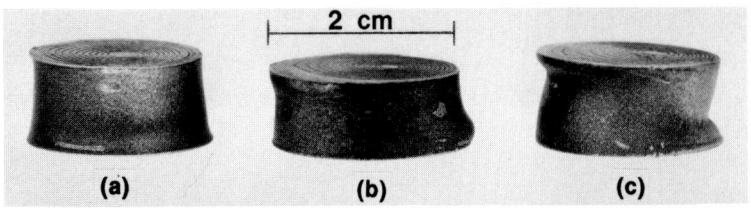

Figure 3.12. Isothermal hot compression specimens of U-700 tested at 1038 °C (1900 °F), $\dot{\varepsilon} = 25$ sec.$^{-1}$. Reductions were (a) 50, (b) 60, and (c) 50 percent. For (c), the compression dies were misaligned by 2°.

noted (Figure 3.12b). In this instance, lubricant breakdown and nonuniform frictional conditions may be surmised to have caused the observed behavior.

In summary, the occurrence of flow softening when accompanied by rate sensitivities resulting in values of $\alpha = (\gamma' - 1)/m \geq 5$ leads to flow localization during upsetting. Although the mode of localization often involves localized bulging, second-order influences such as tooling misalignment and insufficient lubrication can introduce a component of highly localized shear. In addition, it appears from the observations that deformation heating has a marked effect on the degree of flow localization.

OTHER FORMS OF THE FLOW LOCALIZATION PARAMETER

The previous analysis for the α parameter, which was expressed in terms of strain and strain-rate gradients (Equation 3.19), can also be given in the form of grid-length gradients (and the rate of change of grid-length gradients) and gradients in cross-sectional area (as well as gradients in the rate of change of cross section). For this purpose, it must first be recalled that

$$\dot{\varepsilon} = -\dot{A}/A = \dot{\ell}/\ell \qquad (3.20)$$

so that*

$$\delta \ln \dot{\varepsilon} = \delta \ln \dot{A} - \delta \ln A \qquad (3.21)$$

and

$$\delta \ln \dot{\varepsilon} = \delta \ln \dot{\ell} - \delta \ln \ell \qquad (3.22)$$

Here ℓ is the spacing of a uniform grid applied at the beginning of an experiment and before the imposition of any mechanical damage or hammer blows. Thus, $\delta \ln \ell_o = 0$ and, because of volume constancy,

$$\delta \varepsilon = \delta \ln \ell = \delta \ln A_o - \delta \ln A \qquad (3.23)$$

With the help of relations (3.21), (3.22), and (3.23) above, Equation (3.18a) can now be rewritten in the following four alternative forms:

---

*When $\dot{A}$ and $\dot{\ell}$ are negative (tension and compression, respectively), in the expressions that follow, $\delta \ln \dot{A}$ and $\delta \ln \dot{\ell}$ must be replaced by $\delta \dot{A}/\dot{A}$ and $\delta \dot{\ell}/\dot{\ell}$, respectively. Similar remarks apply to $\delta \ln A$ and to $\delta \ln \ell$.

$$m \left.\frac{\partial \ln \dot{A}}{\partial x}\right|_t = (\gamma' - 1 + m) \left.\frac{\partial \ln A}{\partial x}\right|_t - \gamma' \frac{d \ln A_o}{dx} \quad , \tag{3.24}$$

and

$$m \left.\frac{\partial \ln \dot{\ell}}{\partial x}\right|_t = (1 - \gamma' + m) \left.\frac{\partial \ln \ell}{\partial x}\right|_t - \frac{d \ln A_o}{dx} \quad , \tag{3.25}$$

in terms of gradients, and

$$m \,\delta \ln \dot{A} = (\gamma' - 1 + m)\, \delta \ln A - \gamma' \delta \ln A_o \quad , \tag{3.26}$$

and

$$m \,\delta \ln \dot{\ell} = (1 - \gamma' + m)\, \delta \ln \ell - \delta \ln A_o \tag{3.27}$$

in terms of variations or differences. The latter two expressions can in turn be converted into the following more useful formulations:

$$m \,\delta \ln \dot{A} = (1 - \gamma' - m)\, \delta \varepsilon - (1 - m)\, \delta \ln A_o \quad , \tag{3.28}$$

and

$$m \,\delta \ln \dot{\ell} = (1 - \gamma' + m)\, \delta \varepsilon - \delta \ln A_o \quad . \tag{3.29}$$

When the rate of flow localization becomes appreciable, the $\delta \ln A_o$ term can be neglected in comparison with the $\delta \varepsilon$ term, as above, so that the rate of flow localization can be expressed as:

$$\alpha_A = -\frac{\delta \ln \dot{A}}{\delta \varepsilon} \simeq \frac{\gamma' - 1 + m}{m} \quad , \tag{3.30}$$

and

$$\alpha_\ell = -\frac{\delta \ln \dot{\ell}}{\delta \varepsilon} \simeq \frac{\gamma' - 1 - m}{m} \quad . \tag{3.31}$$

These two alternative definitions of the α parameter, one assessing the rapidity of localization in terms of *area* rate differences and the other in terms of *length* rate differences, provide further means of predicting (and measuring) the rate of development of nonuniformities during deformation.

Note that the critical conditions for the *onset* of detectable flow localization associated with the three α parameters are slightly different, being given by:

$$\gamma' = 1, \gamma' = 1 - m, \text{ and } \gamma' = 1 + m$$

in the $\delta\ln\dot{\varepsilon}$, $\delta\ln\dot{A}$, and $\delta\ln\dot{\ell}$ forms, respectively. However, once the rate of strain concentration becomes appreciable, the important point is that it is inversely proportional to the rate sensitivity m for all the formulations. Also, during the interval when the rate of flow softening, as given by γ', is significant (i.e., when $\gamma' > 1$) the rate of localization is approximately proportional to $(\gamma' - 1)$, the relevant functions of γ' being $(\gamma' - 1)$, $(\gamma' - 1 + m)$, and $(\gamma' - 1 - m)$, respectively, for the three forms.

The qualitative similarities and quantitative differences between the three alternative methods of describing the development of strain concentrations can be seen in Figure 3.13, which was calculated for a simulated *tension* test of a strain-hardening material.[20] Here, Y'/Y_i' represents the area-rate gradient $\delta\ln\dot{A}$ normalized by its initial value:

$$\delta\ln\dot{A}_i = -\delta\ln A_o \left[(1 - m)/m\right] \quad . \tag{3.32}$$

In a similar way, Z'/Z_i' and λ'/λ_i' represent the length-rate gradient $\delta\ln\dot{\ell}$ and strain-rate gradient $\delta\ln\dot{\varepsilon}$ normalized by their initial values:

$$\delta\ln\dot{\ell}_i = -\delta\ln A_o/m \quad , \tag{3.33}$$

and

$$\delta\ln\dot{\varepsilon}_i = \delta\ln\dot{\ell}_i = -\delta\ln A_o/m \quad . \tag{3.34}$$

The flow localization results in Figure 3.13 demonstrate the kinetics of the process in terms of the three possible measures of area-rate, length-rate, and strain-rate gradients or variations. These kinetics have been established by applying Equations such as (3.18b), (3.26), (3.27), (3.28), and (3.29) in a numerical procedure which assumes (a) for a boundary condition, a fixed overall, or average, axial strain rate during the deformation; (b) a given initial geometric defect size; and (c) a given material flow law. Details of the solution procedure are contained in References 20, 21, and Appendix A.

From Figure 3.13, it is evident that the length-rate gradient increases most rapidly, because from Equation (3.22),

$$\delta\ln\dot{\ell} = \delta\ln\dot{\varepsilon} + \delta\ln\ell \quad , \tag{3.35}$$

and all these terms are *positive* so that $\delta \ln \dot{\ell} > \delta \ln \dot{\varepsilon}$. Conversely, the area-rate gradient increases the least quickly, because from Equation (3.21),

$$\delta \ln \dot{A} = \delta \ln \dot{\varepsilon} + \delta \ln A \quad , \tag{3.36}$$

and, in this case, $\delta \ln \dot{A} > 0$ (for tension), whereas $\delta \ln A < 0$, so that $\delta \ln \dot{A} < \delta \ln \dot{\varepsilon}$. Despite these differences in the apparent kinetics of flow localization, it should be noted that the three formulations all describe the same experiment and the same process of strain concentration.

KINETICS OF FLOW LOCALIZATION IN UNIAXIAL COMPRESSION OF SPECIMENS WITH GEOMETRIC AND MECHANICAL DEFECTS

The detailed influence of flow softening on the concentration of strain during uniaxial compression has been determined by Jonas,

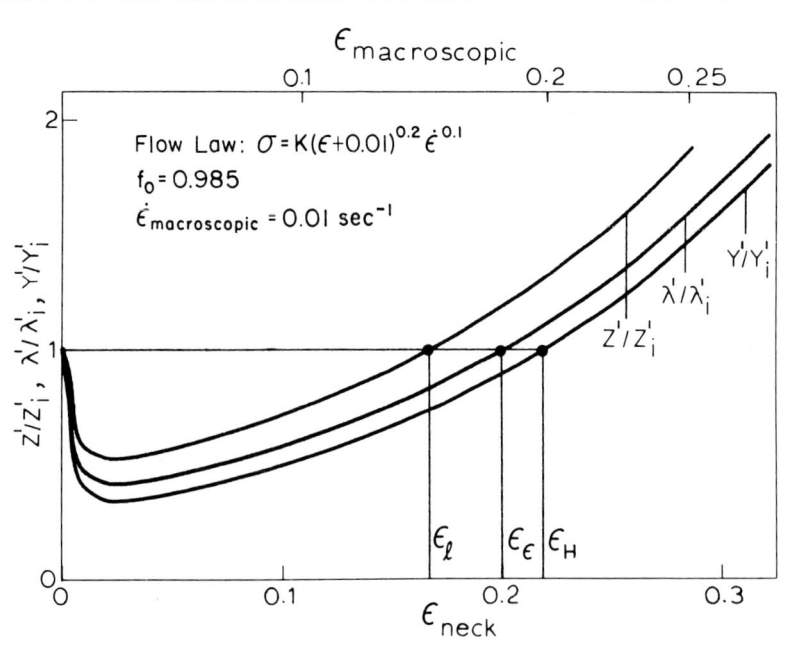

Figure 3.13. Dependence of the normalized length-rate gradient Z'/Z'_i, strain-rate gradient λ'/λ'_i, and area-rate gradient Y'/Y'_i on strain during a simulated tensile test.[20]

64 Flow Localization in Bulk Forming: Isothermal Deformation

Holt, and Coleman by employing equations such as those above,* and is illustrated in Figure 3.14.[13] In this case, the material was considered to obey the following flow softening relation (Figure 3.15):

$$\sigma = -79.24\,(-\dot{\varepsilon})^{0.1}\,[1 - \exp(25\,\varepsilon_t)](-\varepsilon_t)^{-0.375} \qquad (3.37)$$

Here, $\varepsilon_t = -0.01 + \varepsilon$ (i.e., the sample was assumed to have undergone a uniform prestrain of -0.01 prior to testing), the strain rate $\dot{\varepsilon} = -0.01\text{ s}^{-1}$, and the rate sensitivity $m = 0.1$. Note that $(-\dot{\varepsilon}) > 0$ and $(-\varepsilon_t) > 0$ because of the sign conventions associated with compression. In Figure 3.14a, A represents the behavior of the *uniform* part of the specimen, A_b that of an incipient bulge caused by mechanical damage ("hammer blow"), and A_g that of a geometric or machining defect. For illustrative purposes, an unreasonably large 7 percent geometric defect was assumed, leading to an initial value for A_g of 93. In the case of the hammer blow defect, the bulge (A_b) and uniform (A) areas were both 100 (in arbitrary units) prior to the damage incident, after which A_b was an unreasonably large, but illustratively useful, 125 units.

By comparing Figures 3.14a and 3.15, it can be seen that bulge development coincides with the period of rapid flow softening. It is also apparent that geometric or machining defects** are much more likely to produce flow localization than deformation defects, inasmuch as 25 percent of the latter is required to produce a response approximately equivalent to that of 7 percent of the former. In Figure 3.14b, the dependence on overall strain of the strain rate within the geometric and deformation defects is illustrated and compared with that of the uniform part of the specimen. Similarly, in Figure 3.14c, the growth and decay of the strain gradients $\lambda_g = (\partial\varepsilon/\partial x)|t$ (geometric) = $\delta\varepsilon$ (geometric) and $\lambda_b = (\partial\varepsilon/\partial x)|_t$ (deformation) = $\delta\varepsilon$ (deformation) are depicted as functions of the overall strain. It is evident from Figure 3.14b that, in the early stages of straining, $-\delta\ln\dot{\varepsilon}$ decreases from its

---

*See Appendix A for a detailed discussion of the application of the flow localization equations for "two-slice" models such as that employed by Jonas, Holt, and Coleman.[13] In real situations involving significant bulging (in compression) or necking (in tension), modifications to the localization equations to account for stress triaxiality are required. These are discussed in Appendix B.

**The influence of *metallurgical* or *strength* defects has not yet been considered in detail. However, it will be demonstrated below that metallurgical and geometric defects are formally equivalent and lead to the same types of behavior. From a practical point of view, they are both more important than deformation defects,[13, 20] which have rather different characteristics (Figure 3.14).

initial value $-\delta\ln\dot{\varepsilon}_i = \delta\ln A_o/m$, then increases, but does not reach it again until the *first* Considère strain ε_c is attained, i.e., until the strain is reached at which $\gamma' - 1 = 0$ for the first time. At strains beyond ε_c, $-\delta\ln\dot{\varepsilon}$ increases rapidly, attains a maximum, and then decreases until it is again equal to $-\delta\ln\dot{\varepsilon}_i = \delta\ln A_o/m$ at the *second* Con-

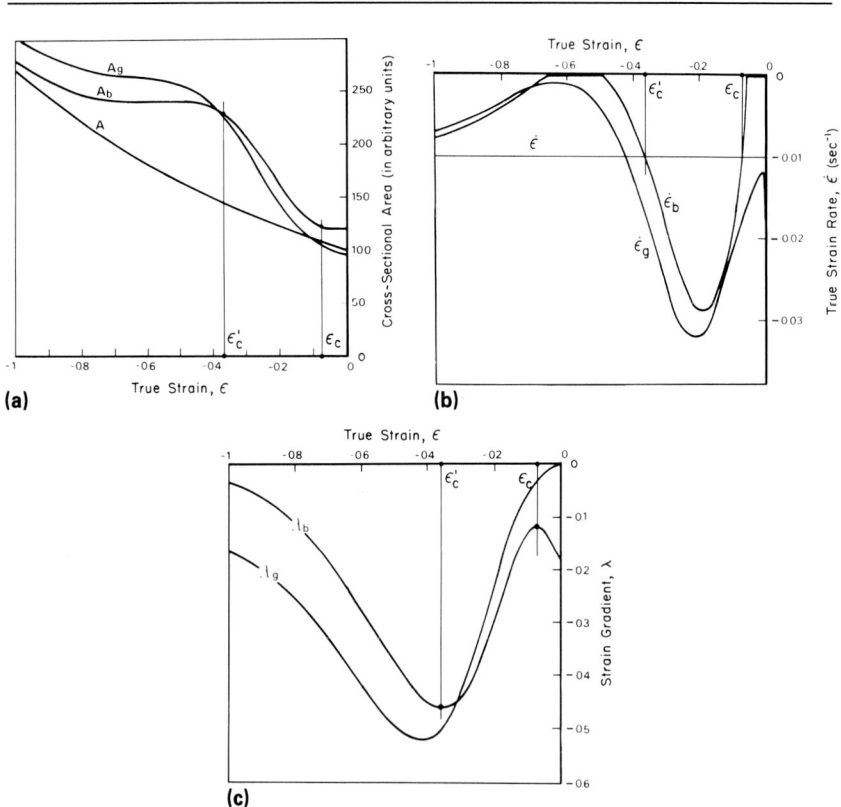

Figure 3.14. (a) Change in cross-section with strain during compression testing of a flow softening material. Curve A represents the uniform region of the specimen, A_b that of an incipient bulge caused by mechanical damage, and curve A_g a geometric or machining defect. Prior to upsetting A = 100, A_g = 93, and A_b = 125, in arbitrary units. (b) Comparison of the strain rates in the uniform part of the compression specimen ($\dot{\varepsilon}$) with those in the regions of mechanical ($\dot{\varepsilon}_b$) and geometric ($\dot{\varepsilon}_g$) damage. Note that $\dot{\varepsilon}_b = \dot{\varepsilon}$ at the Considère strains, ε_c and ε'_c, and that $\dot{\varepsilon}_g < \dot{\varepsilon}$ from the beginning of the test. (c) Comparison of the strain gradients in the vicinity of the mechanical defect (λ_b) and of the geometric defect (λ_g). The severity of the mechanical defect strain gradient decreases with strain until ε_c is reached, increases until ε'_c is attained, and then decreases again. λ_g is initially zero, and the values of the slope $\partial\lambda_g/\partial\varepsilon$ are equal at $\varepsilon = 0$, $\varepsilon = \varepsilon_c$, and $\varepsilon = \varepsilon'_c$.[13]

sidère strain ε'_c. Thus, the period of significant bulge formation, and therefore of strain concentration, corresponds to the interval between the first and second Considère strains; that is, it covers the time interval during which $(\gamma' - 1) > 0$ (see also Figures 3.14c and 3.15).

At strains greater than the second Considère strain ε'_c, $-\delta\ln\dot\varepsilon$ decreases to less than $\delta\ln A_o/m$ and then becomes negative (i.e., $\delta\ln\dot\varepsilon$ becomes positive). Under these conditions, the absolute magnitude of λ_g decreases gradually until the strain gradient it describes

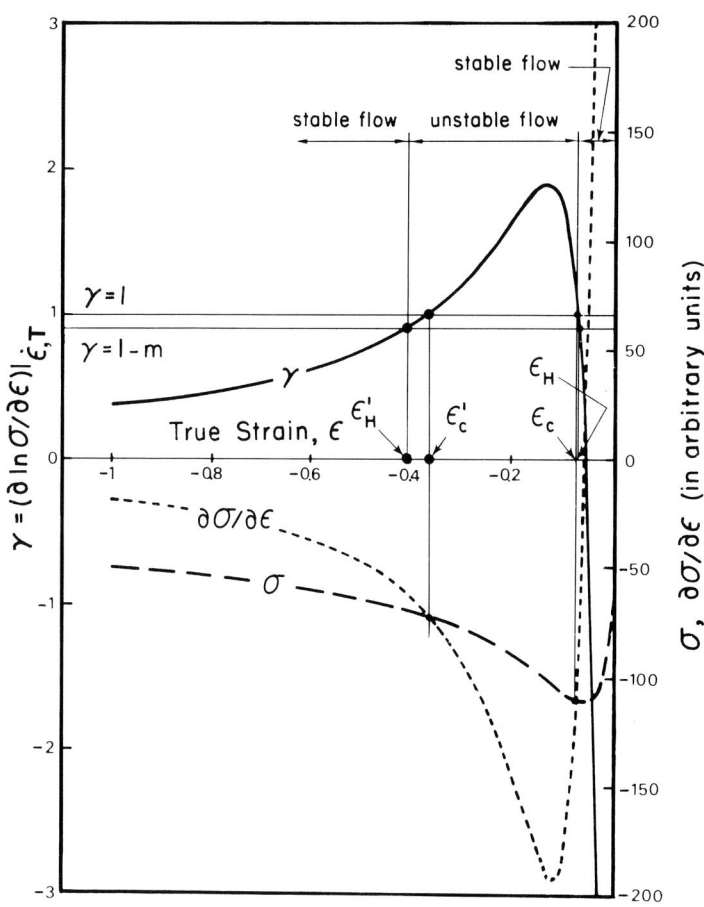

Figure 3.15. The dependence of σ, $\partial\sigma/\partial\varepsilon$, and γ on true strain ε during the compression testing of a flow softening material whose flow localization characteristics in the presence of deformation and geometric defects are described in Figure 3.14.[13]

Flow Localization in Bulk Forming: Isothermal Deformation   67 is barely perceptible visually. This corresponds to the period of bulge propagation.

The *extent* of the flow localization produced during the interval between the first and second Considère strains depends on a certain integral of $(\gamma' - 1)/m$.[21] Because the integral contains the product of $(\gamma' - 1)/m$ times the strain* in an *exponential*, it is very sensitive to the values of both m and $(\gamma' - 1)$. A detailed analysis of the flow localization process will not be given in this book; for a more complete treatment, the reader is referred to References 15 and 21. Of importance here, however, is the central role such treatments give to the expression $(\gamma' - 1)/m$. Because this term appears in an exponential and because of the values of the other experimental coefficients, the analyses support the experimental observation that appreciable strain concentrations in uniaxial compression are associated with values of $(\gamma' - 1)/m$ above about 5. Such approaches[13, 15, 21] also underline the importance of the *product* of $(\gamma' - 1)$ and $1/m$; that is, neither flow softening alone (in the presence of high m) nor low rate sensitivity alone (in the absence of significant flow softening) is sufficient to produce strain concentrations of industrial interest.

FLOW LOCALIZATION IN THE PRESENCE OF METALLURGICAL (STRENGTH) DEFECTS

When the strain begins to concentrate during metal forming, the site of the localization is generally taken to be the position of greatest weakness within the specimen. In the analysis described above, the weakness was considered, for convenience, to be usually a lack of cross section $\delta \ln A_o$. However, local weaknesses can also be identified with *metallurgical* causes and can indeed be present at positions of uniform section, where $\delta \ln A_o = 0$ for example. The most common causes of metallurgical weakness are local variations in grain orientation (texture), grain size, solute content, precipitate fineness, and effectiveness of heat treatment. The latter heading includes such diverse phenomena as differences (due to temperature or cooling rate gradients) in the completeness of annealing, quenching, tempering, etc. It can also involve local differences in thermal-mechanical history. These differences can lead to local variations in the rate sensitivity or in the strain-hardening coefficient of interest, γ, γ', or n. These will not be considered here. Instead, it is simpler to deal for the moment only with variations in strength. Thus, in the case of a simple

---

*The exponential concerned is $\exp[(1 - \gamma')\varepsilon/m]$, where it should be noted that $\varepsilon < 0$ in compression.[21]

parabolic law material, for instance, for which the flow stress is given by:

$$\sigma = K \dot{\varepsilon}^m \varepsilon^n \tag{3.38}$$

where K is the strength coefficient, the local differences in flow stress can be readily described by the term $\delta \ln K$ or $d \ln K/dx$.[20] This term can then be added to relations such as (3.18b) or to Equations (3.24) to (3.29) to give expressions such as:

$$m \, \delta \ln \dot{\varepsilon} = (1 - \gamma') \, \delta \varepsilon - \delta \ln A_o - \delta \ln K \quad . \tag{3.39}$$

In this case, the flow will localize at the larger of the two defects, $\delta \ln A_o$ or $\delta \ln K$, or at the largest *combination* of defects.

At elevated temperatures, the constitutive relations are rarely parabolic in form, adopting instead an approximately exponential dependence on strain, leading to a saturation stress σ_s (in the absence of flow softening and of changes in temperature). Under such conditions, the flow stress can be specified by a relation of the type:

$$\sigma = B(T) \dot{\varepsilon}^m [1 - \exp(-\varepsilon/\varepsilon_o)] \tag{3.40}$$

where ε_o is a characteristic strain, and the saturation stress is $\sigma_s = B(T) \dot{\varepsilon}^m$. Although the characteristic strain ε_o generally depends on strain rate, this dependence can be neglected for the present purpose. The metallurgical defect can then be described once again by a term similar to the one introduced above for the parabolic law, namely $\delta \ln B$. Analogous expressions can also be found for other constitutive laws.[15] The important point is that the term $\delta \ln K$ or $\delta \ln B$ plays the same role in Equation (3.39) as $\delta \ln A_o$ did in Equation (3.18b); thus, a one or two percent strength defect has an influence equivalent to that of a one or two percent geometric defect.

Flow Localization Due to Flow Softening: Plane-Strain Deformation

FLOW LOCALIZATION PARAMETER

During bulk forming under plane-strain conditions of deformation, a more common mode of flow localization than localized bulging is possible. This is the formation of shear bands, or narrow regions of internally localized plastic flow crossing many grains. Because they are planar or two-dimensional defects, shear bands usually are not observed under axisymmetric conditions of flow such as during upsetting, unless friction, tool misalignment, or other effects produce a shift in the strain state, as mentioned previously.

During plane-strain deformation, flow localization in the form of shear bands is favored over flow localization in the form of bulges. This may be shown by comparing the flow localization parameters associated with shear banding on the one hand and with localized bulging on the other. The former is evaluated by focusing on the shear stresses and shear strains along the slip-line directions, because (1) it has been observed experimentally that shear bands are initiated along them,[22] and (2) geometric hardening effects (which are flow stabilizing) vanish along these directions. First, the shear stress on these planes is denoted by τ, the displacement coordinate perpendicular to them by x' (which lies parallel to the conjugate set of slip-line directions), and the shear strain and shear strain rate attributable to τ by Γ and $\dot{\Gamma}$, respectively. Next, for simplicity, consideration is restricted to regions where the slip lines have no curvature, i.e., where they are neither converging nor diverging.* Under these conditions, the cross-sectional area A_τ subject to the maximum shear stress does not vary with x' ($dA_\tau/dx' = 0$), nor does τ itself ($d\tau/dx' = 0$). It is further assumed that similar strain hardening and rate sensitivity coefficients defined above for tensile and compressive deformation apply to deformation by shear. For the present purpose, they are given by

$$\gamma'_\tau \equiv (\partial \ln\tau/\partial \Gamma)|_{\dot{\Gamma}} \text{ and } m \equiv (\partial \ln\tau/\partial \ln\dot{\Gamma})|_{\Gamma,T} \quad . \tag{3.41}$$

Then, recalling Equation (3.17) for uniaxial deformation, it is seen that

$$\left(\frac{\partial \ln\tau}{\partial x'}\right)\bigg|_t = \gamma'_\tau \left(\frac{\partial \Gamma}{\partial x'}\right)\bigg|_t + m \left(\frac{\partial \ln\dot{\Gamma}}{\partial x'}\right)\bigg|_t \quad , \tag{3.42a}$$

which, for $d\tau/dx' = 0$, leads to the equation in variational terms

$$0 = \gamma'_\tau \delta\Gamma + m \delta\ln\dot{\Gamma} \quad . \tag{3.42b}$$

With this expression, a flow localization parameter α_τ may be defined:

---

*This could be a region of symmetry, such as that situated at the center of a round bar that has been sidepressed, for example.

$$\alpha_\tau \equiv \frac{\delta \ln \dot{\Gamma}}{\delta \Gamma} = -\frac{\gamma'_\tau}{m} \qquad (3.43)$$

Assuming that the material is isotropic and that the von Mises criterion holds so that $\tau = \bar{\sigma}/\sqrt{3}$, $\Gamma = \sqrt{3}\,\bar{\varepsilon}$, and $\dot{\Gamma} = \sqrt{3}\,\dot{\bar{\varepsilon}}$, Equation (3.43) reduces to an expression for the flow localization parameter α:

$$\alpha \equiv \frac{\delta \ln \dot{\bar{\varepsilon}}}{\delta \bar{\varepsilon}} = -\frac{\left(\frac{\partial \ln \bar{\sigma}}{\partial \bar{\varepsilon}}\right)\bigg|_{\dot{\bar{\varepsilon}}}}{m} = \frac{\gamma'}{m} \qquad (3.44)$$

In Equation (3.44), γ' is the normalized flow softening rate in compression, for which $\varepsilon = -\bar{\varepsilon}$, and is identical to the γ' in Equations (3.16) through (3.19). Note also that $\delta \ln \dot{\bar{\varepsilon}}/\delta \bar{\varepsilon} = -\delta \ln \dot{\varepsilon}/\delta \varepsilon$, because $\varepsilon = -\bar{\varepsilon}$ for deformation in compression.

Equations (3.43) and (3.44) specify that the rate at which shear strain-rate concentrations develop in plane strain is proportional to the ratio of the normalized flow softening rate to the strain-rate sensitivity parameter. When relation (3.44) is compared to (3.19), it is evident that in plane-strain deformation, the tendency for shear band formation is greater than that for localized bulging. This is simply because of the absence of the term representing the change in cross-sectional area in the former case; that is, at a given strain, $(\gamma'/m) > (\gamma' - 1)/m$, where (-1) is the "area" term. It is not surprising, therefore, that shear bands commonly develop under plane-strain conditions of mechanical working. It is preferable for this reason to determine the effect of material properties on the occurrence of shear bands from deformation studies carried out under plane-strain conditions of testing.

WORKABILITY DIAGRAMS FOR SHEAR BANDS

A considerable amount of research has been conducted to establish a correlation between the occurrence of shear bands in plane-strain isothermal metalworking operations and the α parameter defined by Equation (3.44). Probably the most extensive investigation of this type was performed by Semiatin and Lahoti.[16, 23, 24] In the greater part of this work, the plane-strain isothermal sidepressing test was employed, and alloys including Ti-6242Si, Ti-10-2-3, and JBK-75 (an alloy similar to A286) were studied.

When shear bands were observed in metallographic sections of these alloys, their morphology followed identical patterns, which were a function of the reduction (Figure 3.16). At reductions close to that at which they were initiated, two complementary shear bands (forming an X in all specimens) intersected at approximately 90° at the center of the sidepressing. At this reduction, the general form of the shear bands was reminiscent of the slipline field solutions for sidepressing. With increasing reduction, however, the legs of the X rotated away from the primary compression axis, indicating that the shear bands are primarily associated with material, not spatial, elements; that is, they only form on the planes of maximum shear stress when the material coefficients adopt certain critical values in Equation (3.44). With still further deformation, the intersection of the shear bands led to the formation of a flat region of intense deformation at the center of the specimens, which eventually bowed towards one or the other of the die surfaces with increasing deformation.

As mentioned previously, the Ti-6242Si alloy exhibits a range of flow behaviors, depending upon the starting microstructure, nominal deformation temperature, and strain rate. Flow curves from constant strain rate isothermal hot compression tests for $\dot{\varepsilon} = 10$ sec.$^{-1}$

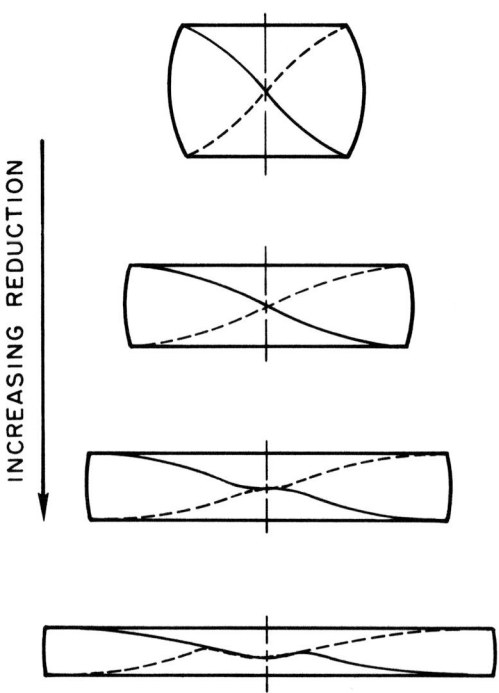

Figure 3.16. Schematic representation of the mechanism of shear band formation in isothermal sidepressing.[23]

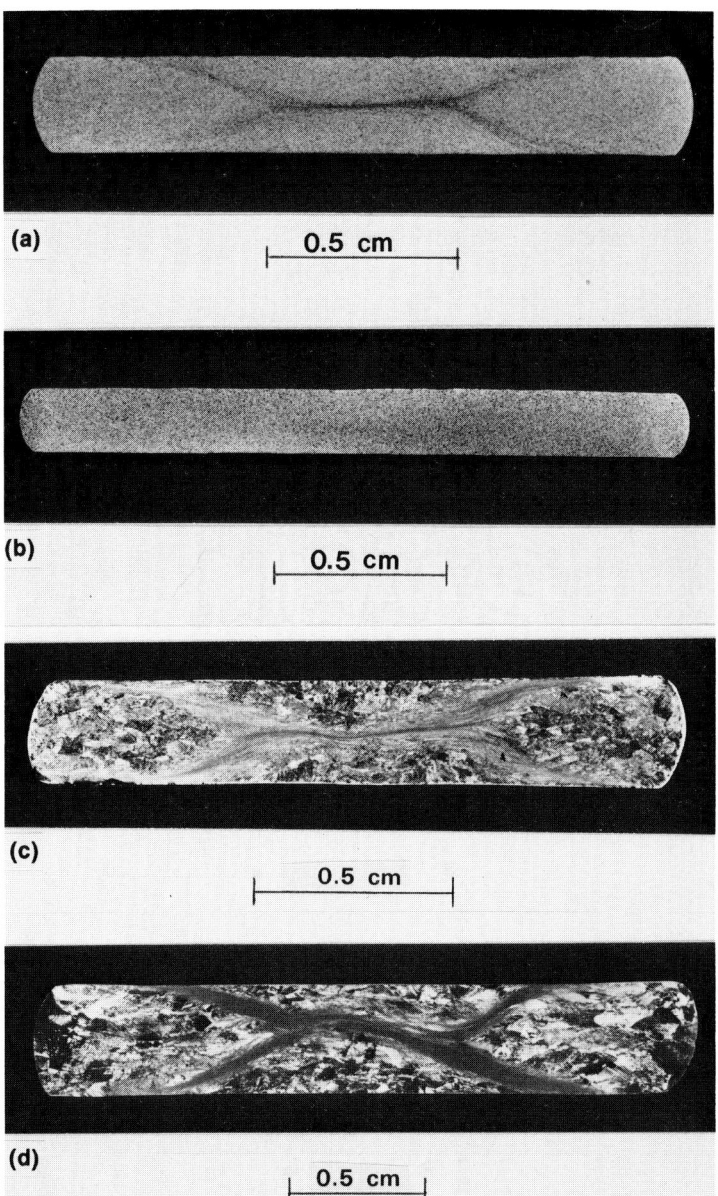

Figure 3.17. Transverse metallographic sections of isothermally sidepressed cylinders of Ti-6242Si with (a,b) an $\alpha + \beta$ microstructure and (c,d) a β microstructure. In all cases, $\dot{\varepsilon} \approx 10$ sec.$^{-1}$. Test temperatures and flow localization parameters were (a) 843 °C (1550 °F), $\alpha_{max} \approx 7.0$, (b) 913 °C (1675 °F), $\alpha_{max} \approx 3.0$, (c) 843 °C (1550 °F), $\alpha_{max} \approx 11$, and (d) 913 °C (1675 °F), $\alpha_{max} \approx 10$.[16, 23]

were presented above (Figure 3.8) for both the α + β and β microstructures. Similar flow curves have been obtained for deformation at other strain rates. From data of this sort, γ' and m can be calculated over the entire range and used to evaluate α parameters from Equation (3.44). The strain rates and temperatures at which $\alpha \geq 5$ at some strain in the range of 0 to 0.7 have been determined for the two microstructures. In addition, the strain rates and temperatures at which shear bands are generated in the isothermal hot sidepressing of round bars have been established from metallographic sections of a large number of experimental forgings (Figure 3.17).

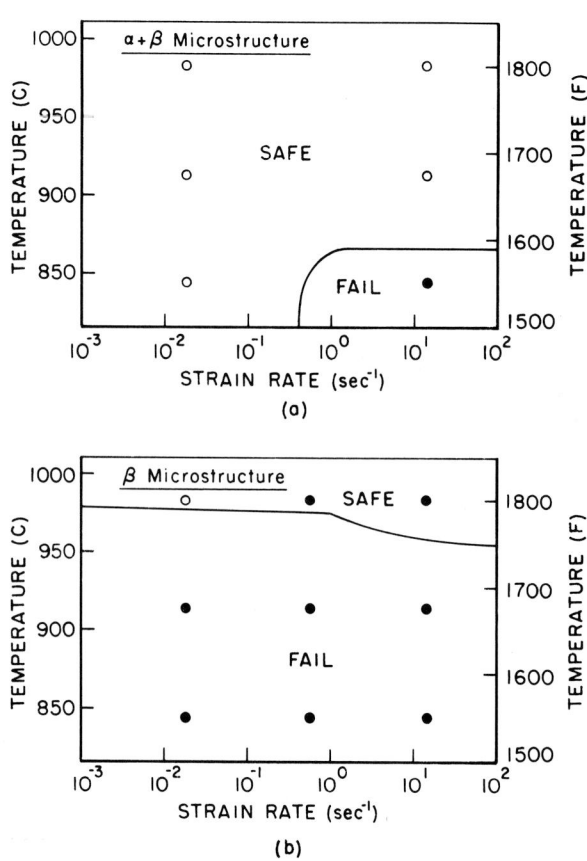

Figure 3.18. Workability maps for occurrence of shear bands in isothermal sidepressing of Ti-6242Si with (a) an α + β microstructure and (b) a β microstructure. Workability predictions (—) and forging conditions in which shear bands were (●) and were not (○) observed are noted.[23]

The comparison of α parameter predictions and experimental observations is best done on temperature-strain rate maps. Such maps or workability diagrams are shown in Figure 3.18 for Ti-6242Si having the two different preform microstructures. It can be seen that, with the exception of two points, the loci corresponding to $\alpha_{max} \geq 5$ separate regimes in which shear bands are and are not observed for this alloy. The small disagreement between the predicted locus and the β microstructure data may be due to the choice of an α value of 5 rather than 4 for the occurrence of noticeable flow localization. Also, experimental errors in the flow stress data affect the value of γ' and can change the position of the $\alpha = 5$ loci in this way. Thus, the α parameter provides an insight into the tendency to form shear bands as well as the likely degree of localization or severity of shear banding. Although the $\alpha = 5$ criterion is principally a rule of thumb, process modeling using finite element methods has confirmed the usefulness of this parameter. These results will be discussed in the next section.

The usefulness of the $\alpha = 5$ criterion has been further underscored by shear band formation observations in Ti-10-2-3 and JBK-75.[24] Isothermal hot sidepressings of Ti-10-2-3 in the beta annealed condition exhibited shear bands when deformation was carried out at 704 °C (1300 °F) and 10 sec.$^{-1}$ (Figure 3.19), but not when it was performed at 816 °C (1500 °F) and 10 sec.$^{-1}$. From constant strain rate flow curves, which showed varying degrees of flow softening, it was found that α_{max} (Equation 3.44) was approximately 16 in the former case, whereas it was only 1.8 in the latter. Hence, these observations agree well with the $\alpha = 5$ criterion. Similar agreement was found in a study of the solution-treated JBK-75 alloy. When sidepressings were made at 816 °C (1500 °F) and $\dot{\varepsilon} = 2.5$ sec.$^{-1}$, shear bands were gen-

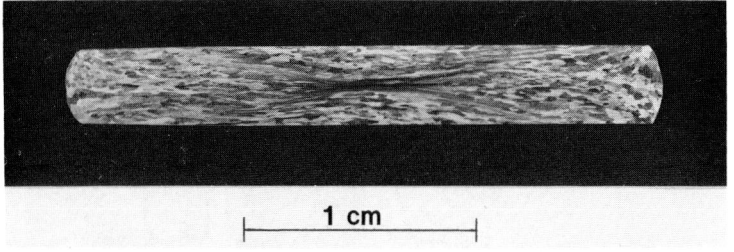

Figure 3.19. Transverse metallographic section of isothermally sidepressed cylinder of Ti-10V-2Fe-3Al deformed at 704 °C (1300 °F), $\dot{\varepsilon} \approx 10$ sec.$^{-1}$, for which $\alpha_{max} \approx 16$. Specimen sidepressed at 816 °C (1500 °F), $\dot{\varepsilon} \approx 10$ sec.$^{-1}$, for which $\alpha_{max} \approx 2.0$, exhibited no shear bands.[24]

erated; the corresponding flow curves led to α values as high as 17.5 (Figure 3.20). By contrast, at 982 °C (1800 °F) and 2.5 sec.$^{-1}$, the flow behavior is such that $\alpha_{max} \approx 2.5$, and no shear bands were observed in sidepressed specimens, as expected.

PROCESS MODELING OF SHEAR BAND DEVELOPMENT IN Ti-6242Si

Further insight into the mode of flow localization can be obtained through application of the sophisticated FEM techniques, which have been developed recently by Rebelo and Kobayashi[25] and Oh.[26] The large strain ALPID program developed by Oh was employed to simulate the isothermal hot sidepressing of round bars of Ti-6242Si of both the $\alpha + \beta$ and β microstructures. For this purpose, flow stress data measured in isothermal hot compression tests were used.[23] By combining features of the upper-bound and finite element methods of plasticity analysis,[27, 28] ALPID requires significantly less computation time for metalworking simulations than conventional methods. This is achieved partly by employing advanced types of elements with linear, quadratic, or cubic displacement distributions. By this means,

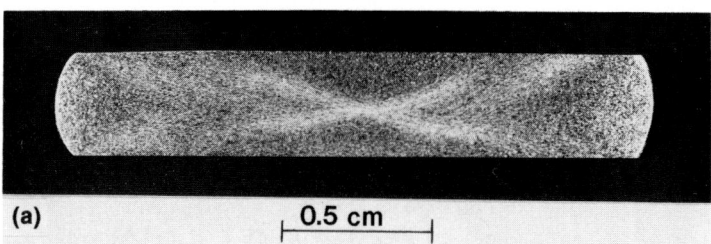

(a) 0.5 cm

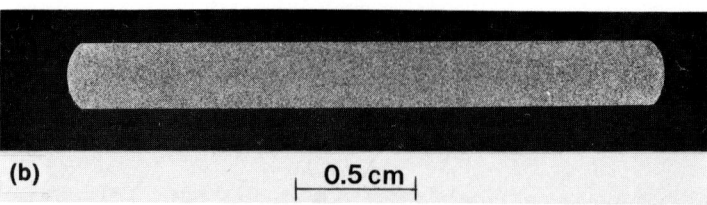

(b) 0.5 cm

Figure 3.20. Transverse metallographic sections of isothermally sidepressed cylinders of solution treated JBK-75 Alloy. (a) Sidepressed at 816 °C (1500 °F), $\alpha_{max} \approx 17.5$, and (b) sidepressed at 982 °C (1800 °F), $\alpha_{max} \approx 2.5$, $\dot{\varepsilon} \approx 2.5$ sec.$^{-1}$ in both cases.[24]

significantly fewer elements are required for simulation. Furthermore, the program can be applied to a wide range of workpiece and tool geometries; it can also treat materials with both rigid plastic, $\bar{\sigma} = \bar{\sigma}(\bar{\varepsilon})$, and rigid viscoplastic, $\bar{\sigma} = \bar{\sigma}(\bar{\varepsilon}, \dot{\bar{\varepsilon}})$, properties. Further details regarding ALPID can be obtained from another volume in this monograph series.

In the present application, the plane-strain version of ALPID was utilized for the viscoplastic deformation of Ti-6242Si. Because ALPID does not have the capability for calculating temperature changes during forging, flow stresses from constant strain rate compression tests that were not corrected for deformation heating[10] were used in the form $\bar{\sigma} = \bar{\sigma}(\bar{\varepsilon}, \dot{\bar{\varepsilon}})$. In this way, the effect of temperature increase on the flow stress is included implicitly in the independent variable of strain, because $\bar{\sigma} = \bar{\sigma}(\bar{\varepsilon}, \dot{\bar{\varepsilon}}, T) = \bar{\sigma}(\bar{\varepsilon}, \dot{\bar{\varepsilon}}, T(\bar{\varepsilon}))$ to a first approximation. Only when material elements undergo large changes in strain rate during sidepressing does this assumption come into question.

Because of symmetry considerations, the deformation in only one quadrant of the cross section of the cylindrical sidepressing needed to be examined. The discretization of this problem required 11 elements, each with nine nodal points. Runs with this quadrant divided into fewer or more elements showed this mesh to be optimal. For the boundary conditions, the die was assumed to move at a constant crosshead speed, and die-workpiece interface friction was characterized by a friction factor of 0.2 (interface shear stress = $0.2\,\bar{\sigma}/\sqrt{3}$), a value based on lubricant evaluations using the ring test.

Simulations for Ti-6242Si bars sidepressed at 913 °C (1675 °F) and an $\dot{\bar{\varepsilon}} \approx 10$ sec.$^{-1}$ demonstrated the power of the ALPID program. Predicted load-stroke curves agreed well with measured ones. In addition, the program readily predicted the nonuniform flow fields that developed in this case. This was ascertained by the comparison of predicted effective strain-rate fields with observed deformation patterns. The strain rate was chosen as the primary field quantity to inspect, as opposed to strain, because it is the best measure of the instantaneous tendency towards shear band formation. It does this by displaying deformation rate gradients, high values of which characterize shear bands. Strain, on the other hand, which is a cumulative variable, can mask current behavior if the flow localization develops at large strains; under these conditions, the relative differences in strain from one region to another are small and therefore difficult to detect.

Effective strain-rate contours for the two Ti-6242Si microstructures deformed at a crosshead speed of 9.14 mm/sec. (0.36 in./sec.) at 913 °C (1675 °F) show striking differences (Figure 3.21). The simulation results are consistent with experimental observations of uniform flow in the α + β material and of shear band formation in the β material (Figure 3.17). For the α + β microstructure, strain rate contours from the simulation do not exhibit large gradients across the cross section. Somewhat larger values of strain rate are apparent along the lines of velocity discontinuity in the classical slip-line field[22] at height reductions of 20 to 30 percent, but these disappear with increasing reduction.

By contrast, the β microstructure simulation shows large strain-rate gradients across the cross section (Figure 3.21). The regions of

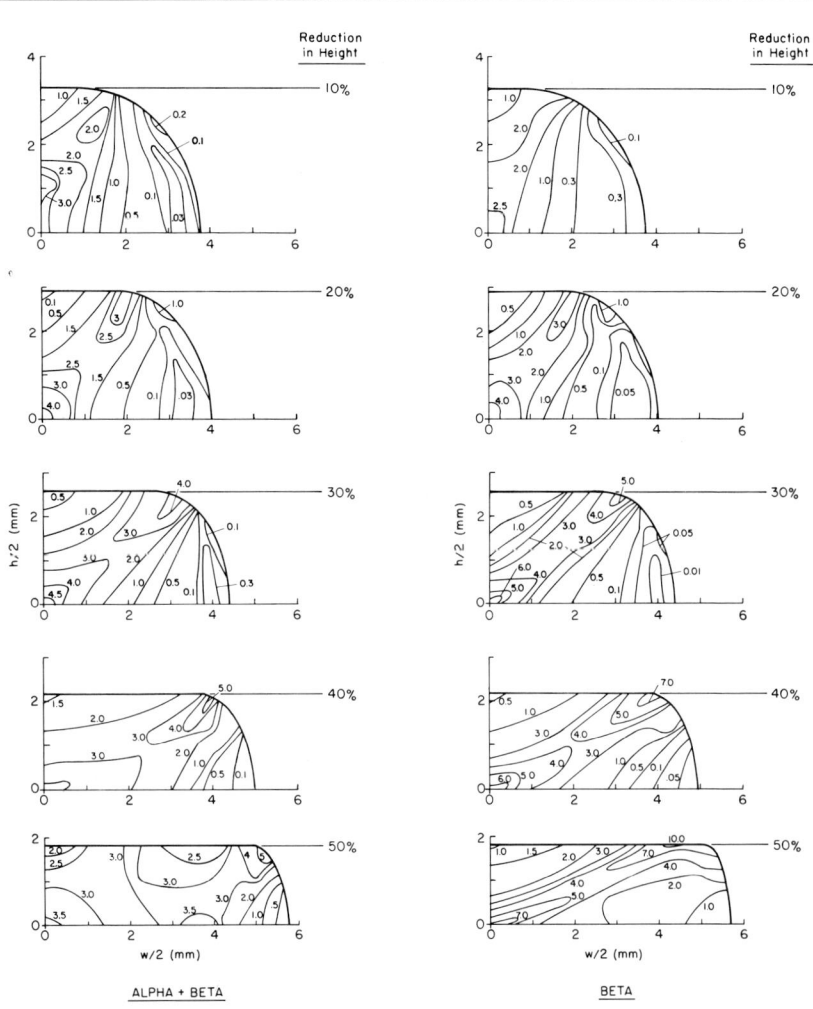

Figure 3.21. Strain-rate contour plots predicted by ALPID for isothermally side-pressed Ti-6242Si with α + β and β microstructures. Specimen temperature: 913 °C (1675 °F), Crosshead speed: 9.14 mm/sec. (0.36 in./sec.).[23]

Flow Localization in Bulk Forming: Isothermal Deformation

highest strain rate originate along the velocity discontinuities of the slip line field, but in this case, they persist to higher reductions and are observed to be related to individual material elements and not to particular spatial directions determined by the geometry. The high strain-rate region begins to rotate away from the ordinate at a reduction between 20 and 30 percent (in good agreement with the reduction at which shear bands are observed to initiate experimentally).[23] This is believed to indicate shear band initiation in the process simulation. It should be emphasized that such flow localization in the process simulation occurs as a natural consequence of the material properties and workpiece geometry. No instability criterion was inserted or needed to be inserted into the program to generate this deformation pattern. After 50 percent reduction in height, the flow field for the β microstructure simulation became so nonuniform that further computer simulation was not possible without remeshing. On the other hand, the simulation for the α + β case was run to 70 percent reduction without encountering any problems of this kind.

PROCESS MODELING OF SHEAR BAND DEVELOPMENT IN HYPOTHETICAL MATERIALS

An examination of ALPID simulation results for isothermal sidepressing employing hypothetical material properties further illustrates the power of such newly developed process modeling tools and offers a detailed insight into the flow localization phenomena resulting from flow softening. The hypothetical materials to be discussed are assumed to have flow stresses σ that depend on strain ε and strain rate $\dot{\varepsilon}$ as $\sigma = f(\varepsilon)g(\dot{\varepsilon})$; that is, the effects of these two experimental variables are taken to be clearly separable. At a constant strain rate, the flow stress dependence on strain, $f(\varepsilon)$, of most metals at hot working temperatures lies between two extremes (Figure 3.22). (Note in Figure 3.22 that the normalization factor σ^* includes a constant term, as well as the strain rate dependence $g(\dot{\varepsilon})$ of the flow stress.) One of the extremes of $f(\varepsilon)$ is a flow curve that shows an initial work-hardening interval followed by a flow-stress plateau (curve A in Figure 3.22). This curve is typical of much of the α + β microstructure data. The other extreme is a curve showing little or no initial work hardening, followed by a large amount of flow softening (curve B in Figure 3.22); the latter is typical of much of the β microstructure flow stress data. The large strain behavior of these two flow curves is characterized by approximately constant values of γ' (Equation 3.18: 0.0 for curve A and 1.25 for curve B. The rate sensitivity of the flow stress of the hypothetical materials, $g(\dot{\varepsilon})$, was assumed to follow a power-law relation, namely, $g(\dot{\varepsilon}) \sim \dot{\varepsilon}^m$, and the rate sensitivity exponent m was assumed to have values of either 0.0, 0.125, or 0.30. These values span those typically measured in compression tests. With these assumptions, the flow stress is completely described by σ = (const.) $\dot{\varepsilon}^m f(\varepsilon)$. As before, the temperature dependence of the flow stress is implicitly included in $f(\varepsilon)$. With these properties, α's (Equation 3.44) between 0 and ∞ were obtained, suggesting a wide range of tendencies to form shear bands.

Sidepressing simulations were run using ALPID and the same element grid that was used for the Ti-6242Si simulations. In all cases, an arbitrary crosshead speed of 9.14 mm/sec. (0.36 in./sec.) was selected. The crosshead speed was not important, because (1) the flow curves had preselected values of rate sensitivity m independent of strain rate; and (2) the effects of speed and heat transfer on the flow properties (e.g., flow softening due to deformation heating) were implicitly included in the flow curves postulated for the nominally isothermal constant strain-rate compression tests. The latter point follows from the previous argument that to a first approximation $\bar{\sigma}(\bar{\varepsilon}, \dot{\bar{\varepsilon}}, T)$ = $\bar{\sigma}(\bar{\varepsilon}, \dot{\bar{\varepsilon}}, T(\bar{\varepsilon})) = \bar{\sigma}(\bar{\varepsilon}, \dot{\bar{\varepsilon}})$.

As shown in Figure 3.23, the grid distortions predicted for the five selected cases display a strong influence of the material properties. For instance, the two cases for which α is less than 5 (case I, α = 0 and case II, α = 4.2) exhibit relatively uniform deformation at

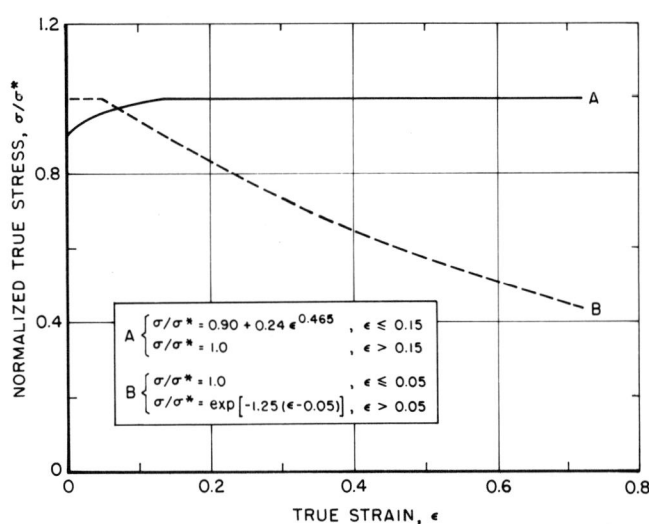

Figure 3.22. Hypothetical flow curves for metals deformed in the hot working regime. Curves show extremes of no flow softening (curve A) and a large amount of flow softening (curve B).[23]

reductions of 25, 37.5, and 47.5 percent. The simulation for these two cases was taken to 75 percent reduction, with only minor nonuniformities appearing in the second case at reductions greater than 40 percent. For case III (α undefined), case IV ($\alpha = 10$), and case V ($\alpha = \infty$), the grid distortions become increasingly nonuniform with increasing α at a given reduction, on the one hand, and with increasing reduction at a given α on the other. For cases IV and V, the deformation became so nonuniform after approximately 50 percent reduction that continuation of the simulation was impossible. The grid distortions in Figure 3.23 also pinpoint the regions of higher than average strain. These can be distinguished from the changes in the angles between intersecting grid lines; these indicate that the deformation is indeed

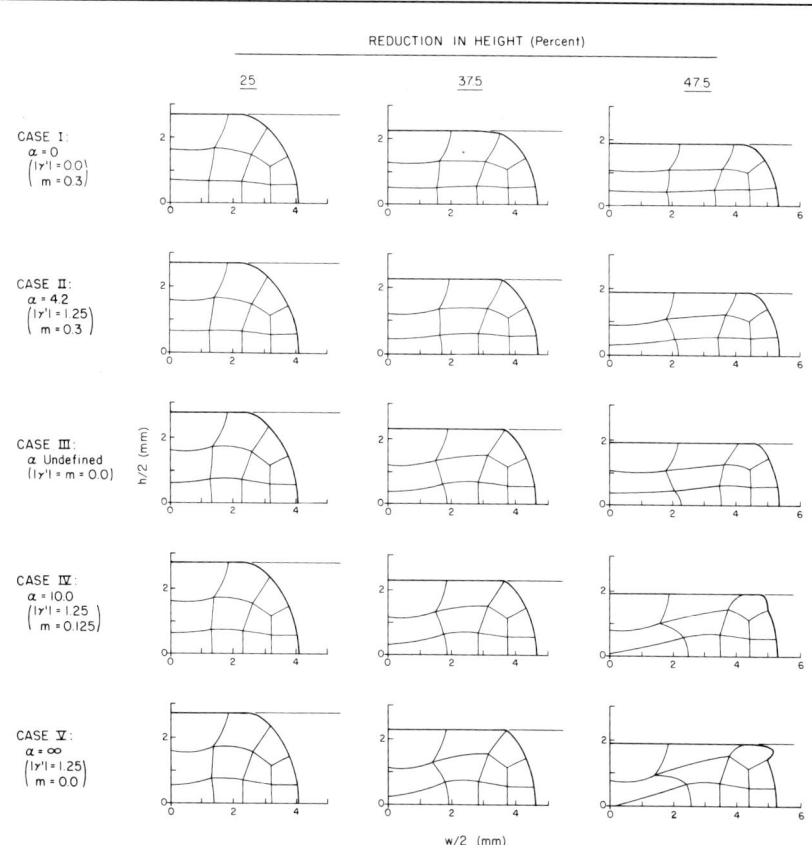

Figure 3.23. Predicted grid distortions for hypothetical metals (Figure 3.22) with varying degrees of flow softening rate, γ', and strain rate sensitivity parameter, m.[23]

Flow Localization in Bulk Forming: Isothermal Deformation

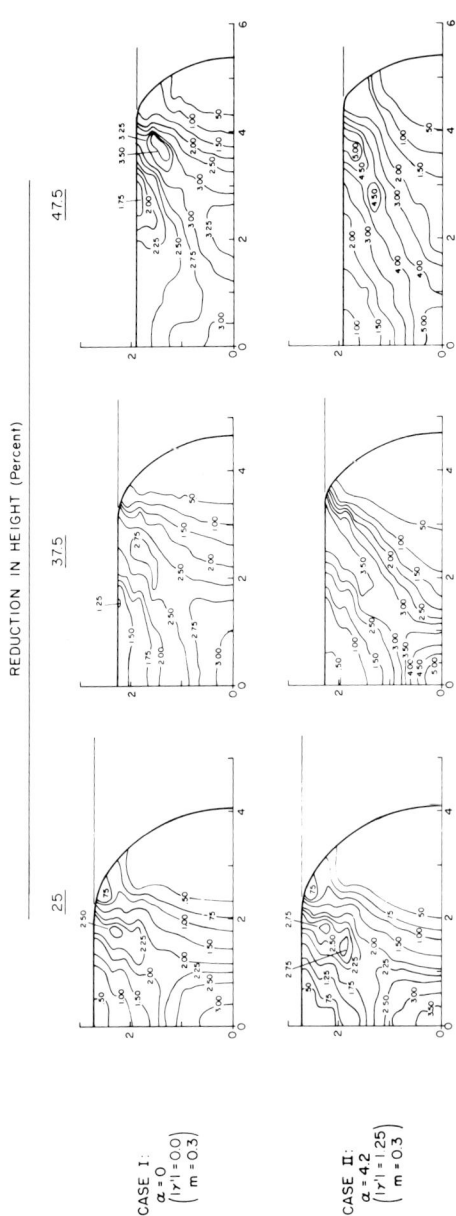

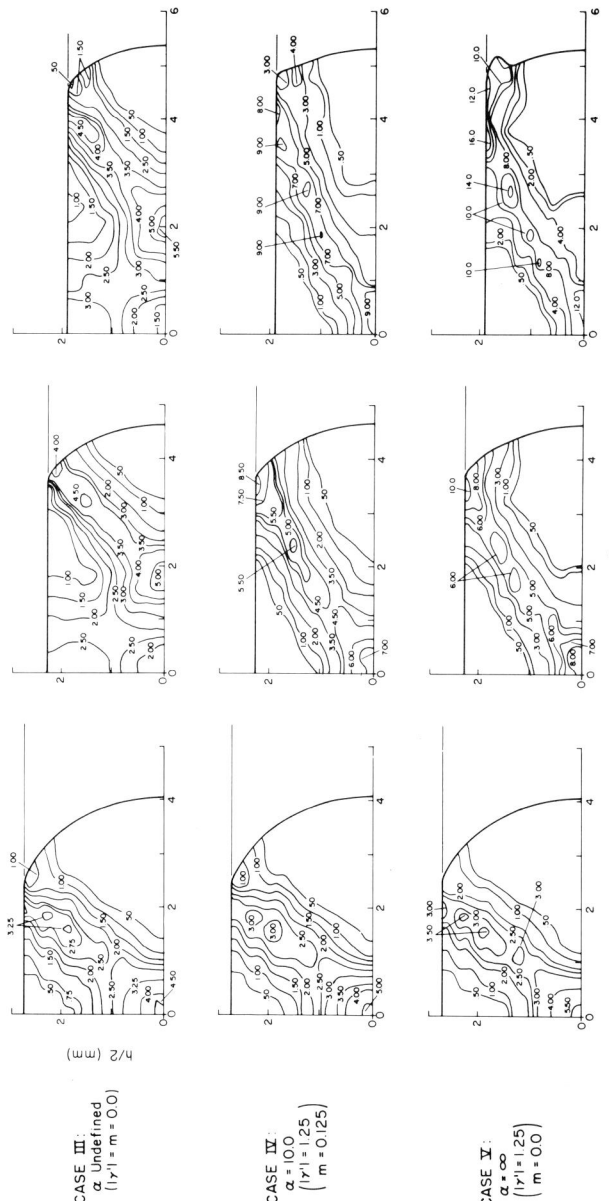

Figure 3.24. Predicted strain-rate contours for hypothetical metals with varying degrees of flow softening rate, γ', and strain rate sensitivity parameter, m.[23]

Flow Localization in Bulk Forming: Isothermal Deformation

predicted to localize along the directions observed in the metallographic sections.

The predicted effective-strain-rate contours (Figure 3.24) exhibit a trend similar to that for the grid distortions. The strain-rate gradients increase with increasing α. Modest ones are seen in cases II and III, and strong ones are shown in cases IV and V. In addition, the localizations observed in cases IV and V occur along lines that rotate toward the abscissa with increasing reduction. For all the cases, at a reduction of 25 percent, the regions of highest strain rate lie at 45° to the ordinate; at higher reductions, these regions begin to rotate. Hence, the initiation event (marked by the reduction at which the angle between the intersecting flow localizations deviates from 90°) is predicted to occur at reductions greater than 25 percent. Another interesting observation is the tendency for the regions containing the strain concentrations to form "flats" near the center of the specimen similar to those actually observed. This can be seen by comparing the 47.5 percent reduction patterns for cases IV and V to the observations in Figures 3.17 and 3.19. A related phenomenon is seen in case III, in which the strain-rate localization moves away from the center. These and other phenomena are highly suggestive of the block shearing required for shear band occurrence. The predicted velocity maps for these cases further confirm and illustrate the importance of the physical factors involved in the formation and retention of shear bands.

Comparison of α Parameter and Simulation Predictions. The simulation results for the wide range of material properties discussed above allow a more complete evaluation of the accuracy of the α-parameter method of predicting the occurrence of shear bands. As shown by the simulations, intense shear bands are definitely expected when α is 10 or greater. Furthermore, modest localizations can be expected when α is between 4 and 10. Thus, the use of α = 5 as a critical value for the appearance of shear bands is a useful engineering tool to obtain a first-order idea of when intense shear bands may be expected.

Another feature illustrated by the process simulation results is the fact that flow localization is a process and not an event. Strain and strain-rate concentrations do not occur instantaneously. For this reason, flow localization cannot be expected to appear fully developed when α first reaches some critical value (such as 5) at some point in the flow field. The application of this premise for cases IV and V, for example, would require flow localization to be detectable at the reduction at which some material element has undergone an effective strain of $\bar{\varepsilon} = 0.05$. Because of inhomogeneous deformation, this should occur at a reduction even less than that corresponding to an effective thickness strain of 0.05. By contrast, simulation shows that localizations are first developed at reductions between 25 and 37.5 percent, which correspond approximately to effective thickness strains between 0.33 and 0.54. For the cases studied experimentally, in a remarkably similar way, the initiation strain is considerably greater than the strain at which the α parameter first attains a value of 5.

Flow Localization Due to Flow Softening: Torsion

The simple torsion test offers another good method of studying the localization of plastic flow arising from flow softening. Extensive flow localization research in this area has been performed by Spretnak and his students, Lindholm, Jonas, Semiatin, and their co-workers.[17, 29-34] These workers have used a variety of solid and tubular round bars. The early work of Spretnak and Lindholm was limited to predicting the onset of flow instability, i.e., it concerned the amount of twist at which the torque passes through a maximum. These simple analyses are incapable of specifying whether the torque instability will or will not lead to appreciable flow localization, however. To do this, one must perform analyses similar to those presented above for localized bulging in upsetting and for shear band formation in plane-strain modes of deformation such as sidepressing. Although the torsion test is also a plane-strain mode of deformation, the radial variations of strain, strain rate, and, at high deformation rates, temperature along the cross section of the specimens make the analysis more complex than those applicable to some of the other deformation modes. These complications will be discussed in the next chapter; presently, a method by which a flow localization parameter can be derived for the torsion test will be discussed.

FLOW LOCALIZATION PARAMETER

A flow localization parameter for torsional deformation can be derived by noting that the applied torque M is a function of the shear flow stress (Equation 2.25), which itself depends on the effective strain $\bar{\varepsilon}$, effective strain rate $\dot{\bar{\varepsilon}}$, and temperature T. Because the strain and strain rate are functions of the amount of twist θ and twist rate $\dot{\theta}$, the torque can be said to be a function of θ, $\dot{\theta}$, and T, so that the following equilibrium condition is obtained:

$$\frac{d\ln M}{dz} = \left(\frac{\partial \ln M}{\partial \theta}\right)\bigg|_{\dot{\theta},T} \frac{d\theta}{dz} + \left(\frac{\partial \ln M}{\partial \ln \dot{\theta}}\right)\bigg|_{\theta,T} \frac{d\ln\dot{\theta}}{dz}$$

$$+ \left(\frac{\partial \ln M}{\partial T}\right)\bigg|_{\theta,\dot{\theta}} \frac{dT}{dz} = 0 \quad . \quad (3.45)$$

Here z is the axial coordinate along the torsion bar. At fixed $\dot{\theta}$, the normalized torque hardening (or softening) rate G is given by:

$$G \equiv \left(\frac{d\ln M}{d\theta}\right)\bigg|_{\dot{\theta}}$$

$$= \left\{\left(\frac{\partial \ln M}{\partial \theta}\right)\bigg|_{\dot{\theta},T} d\theta + \left(\frac{\partial \ln M}{\partial T}\right)\bigg|_{\theta,\dot{\theta}} dT\right\}\bigg/ d\theta \quad . \tag{3.46}$$

With this relation, Equation (3.45) can be rewritten

$$\frac{d\ln M}{dz} = G\frac{d\theta}{dz} + \left(\frac{\partial \ln M}{\partial \ln \dot{\theta}}\right)\bigg|_{\theta,T}\frac{d\ln\dot{\theta}}{dz} = 0 \quad . \tag{3.47}$$

If the rate sensitivity of the material does not vary greatly with deformation rate, then

$$\left(\frac{\partial \ln M}{\partial \ln \dot{\theta}}\right)\bigg|_{\theta,T} \approx \frac{\partial \ln \bar{\sigma}}{\partial \ln \dot{\bar{\varepsilon}}} = m \quad . \tag{3.48}$$

as shown in Reference 17. With this result, Equation (3.47) leads to a flow localization parameter in variational terms

$$A = \frac{\delta \ln \dot{\theta}}{\delta \theta} = -\frac{G}{m} \quad . \tag{3.49}$$

This result is analogous to Equation (3.44) for the α parameter and specifies that, for two neighboring slices of the specimen, the ratio of the difference in the logarithms of the twist rate over the difference in the angle of twist is proportional to the torque softening rate (note that −G is a positive quantity for a material that exhibits torque softening) and inversely proportional to the rate sensitivity. For the slice that has undergone the incrementally greater amount of twist, the ratio (when positive) specifies the amount by which the twist rate is higher in the "weaker" slice and is thus a measure of the current rate of flow localization. Thus, materials that require increasing torque with increasing twist during torsion and that have large positive rate sensitivities resist flow localization during torsion. Conversely, a material that exhibits a large degree of torque softening and possesses a low rate sensitivity can be expected to undergo flow localization rapidly at imperfections in the torsion specimen. Further, because the torque on the torsion specimen is a strong function of the shear stress of the material, flow localization occurs readily in materials that have stress-strain curves displaying large degrees of flow softening.

APPLICATION OF FLOW LOCALIZATION PARAMETER TO TORSION OF Ti-6242Si[17]

The application of the flow localization parameter will be discussed below for the isothermal hot torsion of Ti-6242Si. Torque-twist curves for tubular specimens of Ti-6242Si are shown in Figure 3.25 for the α + β microstructure and in Figure 3.26 for the β microstructure. Both sets of curves display torque maxima early in the deformation, and subsequently, the torque decreases with increasing twist. However, it should be noted that the β microstructure M-θ data show somewhat more negative slopes than the α + β microstructure M-θ data. These results are similar to those obtained from isothermal hot compression tests on the same alloy (see, for example, Figure 3.8), from which it can be seen that the degree of flow softening is again greater in the β microstructure than in the α + β microstructure material.

In the experiments described above, axial scribe lines were placed on the specimens prior to twisting. Examination after testing indicated that certain specimens, particularly those of the β microstructure, had undergone significant flow localization. For most of the α + β specimens, on the other hand, the angle between the specimen axis and the scribe line was fairly constant along the length of the scribe, indicating that the deformation was fairly uniform (e.g., Figure 3.27). In addition, surface shear strain measurements using the scribe line angles and Equation (2.32) were in agreement with calculations based on the amount of twist and the specimen geometry (Equation 2.21).

In contrast to the observations regarding the α + β specimens, the β specimen scribe lines showed definite evidence of flow localization (Figure 3.28). For each of these specimens, a large portion of the scribe line formed a small angle with the specimen axis, and a small portion formed a large angle with the specimen axis, indicative of a region of intense strain. Moreover, the microstructure in the regions with large scribe line angles was much more highly deformed than that of the rest of the gage section. Support for the occurrence of flow localization in the β microstructure hot torsion specimens was also obtained from the predictions of a simple deformation/heat transfer computer program that employs measured flow stress data and a two-dimensional (radial) heat transfer code to predict M-θ curves.[35]

For the α + β microstructure results (Figure 3.25), the levels of the measured torques corresponded well with predictions. Agreement of measurement and prediction was excellent at 913 °C (1675 °F) with a surface effective strain rate $\dot{\varepsilon}_s \simeq 0.9$ sec.$^{-1}$ over the entire range of twisting and was good at 816 °C (1500 °F) at $\dot{\varepsilon}_s \simeq 3.3$ sec.$^{-1}$, except at small values of twist. Comparison of measured and pre-

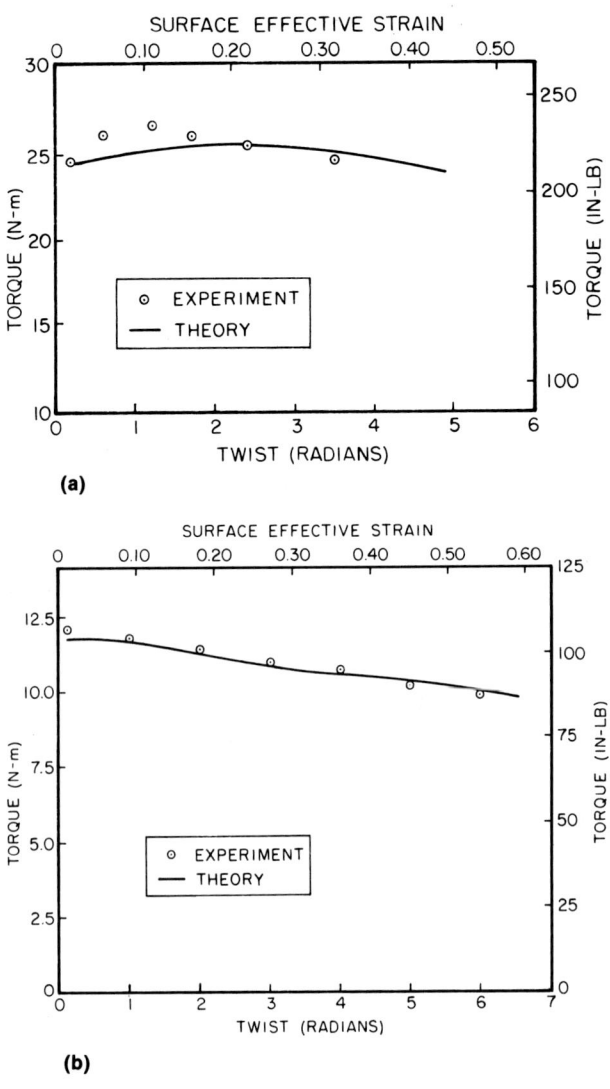

Figure 3.25. Comparison of experimental and theoretical torque-twist curves for α + β microstructure Ti-6242Si hot torsion specimens tested at (a) surface $\dot{\varepsilon} \approx 3.3$ sec.$^{-1}$, T = 816 °C (1500 °F) and (b) surface $\dot{\varepsilon} \approx 0.9$ sec.$^{-1}$, T = 913 °C (1675 °F).[17]

dicted torque-twist curves for the β microstructure material (Figure 3.26) does not show as good agreement. In all four cases analyzed, the measured torque-twist curve lay below the predicted one, and in three of these, the difference between measurement and prediction increased with the amount of twist. This difference was greatest at the lower temperatures and higher strain rates. This discrepancy can be attributed to the occurrence of flow localization that permitted the deformation to continue at torques less than those required for uniform deformation.

Parametric studies have also been carried out to compare the tendency of the α + β and β microstructures to undergo localized flow in torsion. Using the deformation/heat transfer model discussed above, constant twist rate torsion was simulated on the computer, and torque-

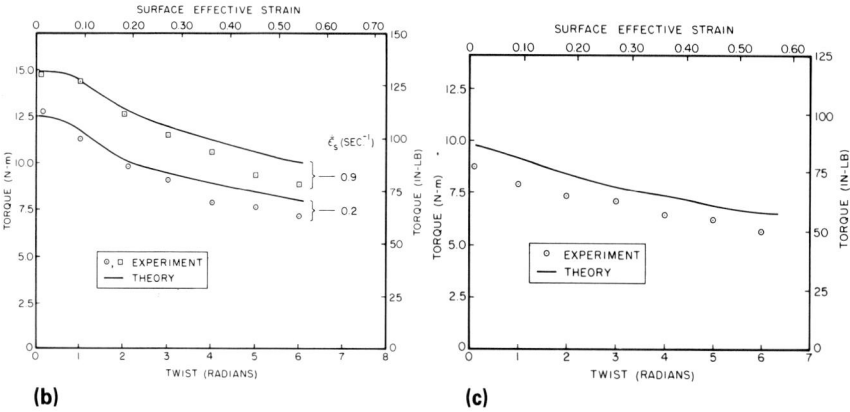

Figure 3.26. Comparison of experimental and theoretical torque-twist curves for β microstructure Ti-6242Si tested at (a) surface $\dot{\varepsilon} \approx 0.9$ sec.$^{-1}$, T = 816 °C (1500 °F), (b) surface $\dot{\varepsilon} \approx 0.2$ and 0.9 sec.$^{-1}$, T = 913 °C (1675 °F), and (c) surface $\dot{\varepsilon} \approx 0.9$ sec.$^{-1}$, T = 954 °C (1750 °F).[17]

twist curves for uniform, stable deformation were generated from hot compression data for the specimen design employed in the experiments. Examples of the results for torsion at 913 °C (1675 °F) are presented in Figure 3.29. It is evident from such plots that the β microstructure displays much more torque softening than the α + β microstructure. This is reasonable in view of the flow softening trend described above for the hot compression results (Figure 3.8).

A's were calculated (Equation 3.49) for the two microstructures from the torque-twist simulations (to obtain G's) and measured m's (Tables 3.2 and 3.3). The difference in the A factors for the two microstructures was quantified at two strain levels for the temperatures and strain rates used in the testing program. Relatively large A's were associated with the β microstructure, the maximum values for a given strain rate and temperature being generally greater than 0.55 (Table 3.2).* On the other hand, the maximum values of A for the α + β microstructure (Table 3.3) were in the range of 0.1 to 0.35,* i.e., considerably below those for the β microstructure. This difference explains why the β microstructure is susceptible to flow localization in torsion at the strain rates and temperatures studied, whereas the α + β structure is not. The analysis also showed that the localization tendency of the β microstructure is greatest at low strains, a conclusion supported by the experimental observations.

The marked flow localization observed in hot torsion tests is a manifestation of shear banding and is evidently related to shear

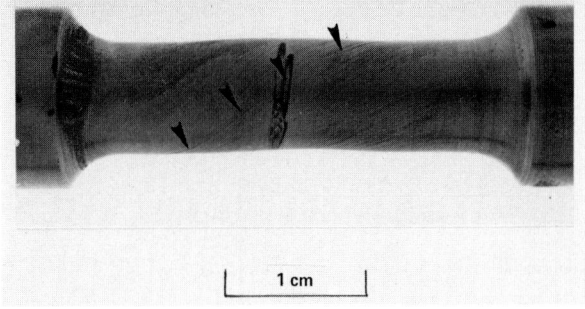

Figure 3.27. Hot torsion specimen of α + β microstructure Ti-6242Si that was tested at 913 °C (1675 °F), surface $\dot{\varepsilon} \approx 0.9$ sec.$^{-1}$. Small arrows indicate position of fine scribe line used to determine strain uniformity.[17]

---

*The numerical values of A and α associated with flow localization are not in the same range for reasons associated with the geometry of torsion testing, which will be discussed below.

band observations in Ti-6242Si deformed by other modes, such as isothermal plane-strain sidepressing. However, the torsion flow localization parameter $A = \delta \ln \dot\theta/\delta\theta$ is not directly comparable with $\alpha = \delta \ln \dot{\bar\varepsilon}/\delta\bar\varepsilon$, but must be recast into a more general form. This can be done with the aid of Equations (2.21), (2.23), and (3.49), which provide the necessary correspondence between the geometry of torsion testing on the one hand and that of tension and compression on the other:

$$A = \frac{\delta \ln \dot\theta}{\delta \theta} = \frac{\delta \ln \dot{\bar\varepsilon}}{\delta \bar\varepsilon}\left(\frac{r}{\sqrt{3}\ell}\right) = -\frac{G}{m}.$$

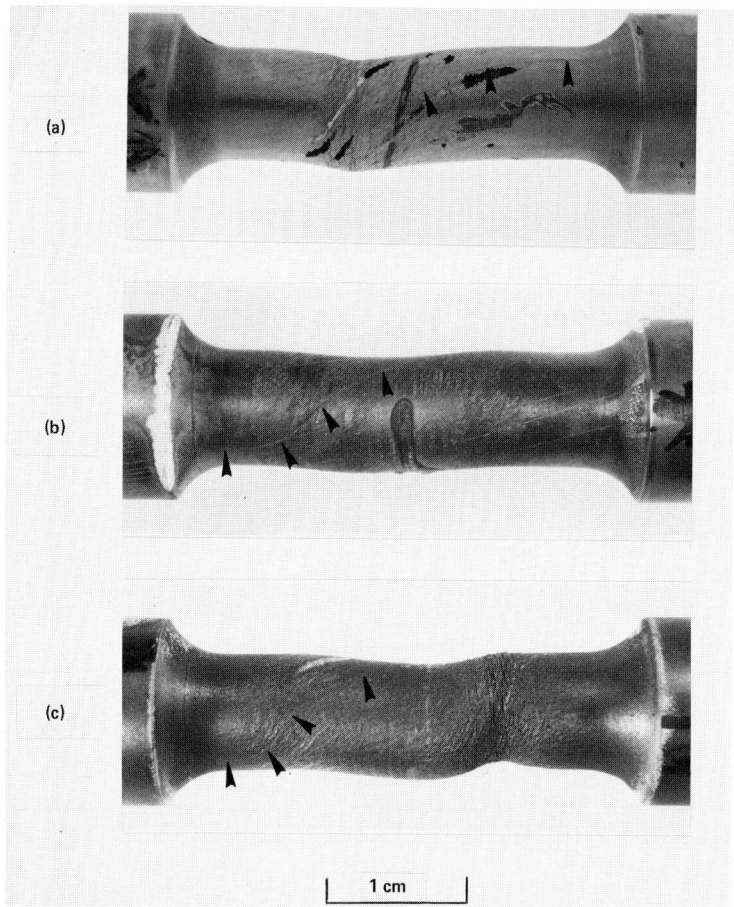

Figure 3.28. Hot torsion specimens of β microstructure Ti-6242Si twisted at surface $\dot\varepsilon \approx 0.9$ sec.$^{-1}$ and test temperatures of (a) 816 °C (1500 °F), (b) 913 °C (1675 °F), and (c) 954 °C (1750 °F). Small arrows indicate position of fine scribe lines used to determine strain uniformity.[17]

For the tubular torsion specimens employed, the average radius [$^1\!/_2$ ($r_i + r_s$)] can be used for r in the above expression, leading to:

$$\alpha \equiv \frac{\delta \ln \dot{\varepsilon}}{\delta \bar{\varepsilon}} = -\frac{13.9 \, G}{m}.$$

The values of α calculated in this way are given in Tables 3.2 and 3.3. The β specimens, which exhibited flow localization, had maximum values of α (at the selected strain rates and temperatures) greater than about 5 to 6. In contrast, the values for the $\alpha + \beta$ specimens were generally below 4. In isothermal sidepressing, it will be recalled, shear bands were observed when the combination of material properties led to α values greater than 5, but not when these were below 5. Hence, the competing softening and strain-rate hardening mechanisms can be concluded to play similar roles in the development of

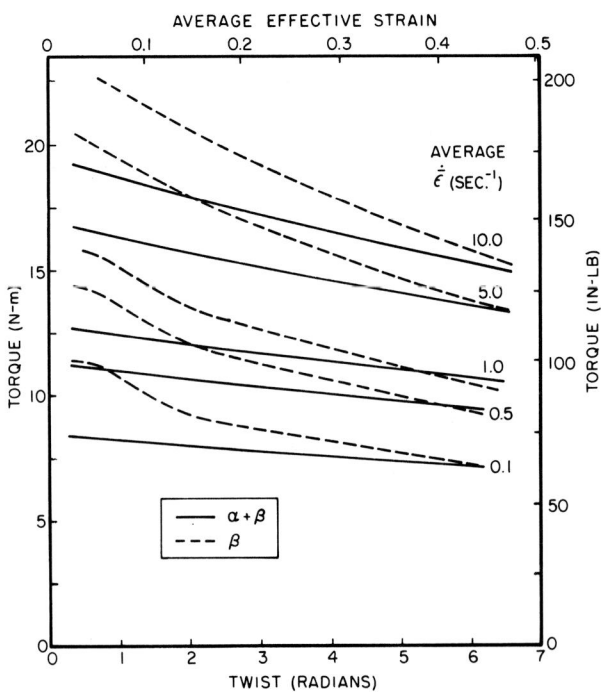

Figure 3.29. Torque-twist curves for Ti-6242Si from numerical model and measured compression flow stress data. Data for tests at 913 °C (1675 °F) and various average effective strain rates. (Average effective strain rate = 0.6 × surface effective strain rate for tubular specimen design employed.).[17]

Table 3.2.
Flow Localization Parameters for Ti-6242 of β Microstructure

Test Temperature °C (°F)	Average Effective Strain Rate* (sec.⁻¹)	Average Effective Strain**	m	$A \equiv -\dfrac{G}{m}$	α
816 (1500)	0.1	0.08	0.16	0.84	11.6
816 (1500)	0.1	0.32	0.16	0.43	6.0
816 (1500)	1.0	0.08	0.09	1.03	14.3
816 (1500)	1.0	0.32	0.09	0.85	11.8
913 (1675)	0.1	0.08	0.20	0.79	10.9
913 (1675)	0.1	0.32	0.20	0.31	4.3
913 (1675)	1.0	0.08	0.17	0.66	9.1
913 (1675)	1.0	0.32	0.17	0.39	5.4
954 (1750)	0.1	0.08	0.23	0.57	7.9
954 (1750)	0.1	0.32	0.23	0.31	4.3
954 (1750)	1.0	0.08	0.20	0.55	7.6
954 (1750)	1.0	0.32	0.20	0.32	4.4

*Avg. $\dot{\varepsilon} = 0.6\, \dot{\varepsilon}_s$ for specimen design employed.
**Avg. $\bar{\varepsilon} = 0.6\, \bar{\varepsilon}_s$ for specimen design employed.

regions of flow localization, i.e., of shear bands, in these and other deformation modes.

Sources of Flow Softening in Metals

The mechanical effect of flow softening on initiating plastic instability and on promoting the localization of strain has been described extensively above. In this section, the *physical* causes of flow softening under the categories of greatest concern to commercial metal processing and to high-temperature service are considered.

WORK SOFTENING AT ELEVATED TEMPERATURES BY DYNAMIC RECOVERY PROCESSES[9]

It is important to distinguish first between *flow* softening processes in general—those processes that lead to a decrease in flow stress

Table 3.3.
Flow Localization Parameters for Ti-6242 of α + β Microstructure

Test Temperature °C (°F)	Average Effective Strain Rate* (sec.$^{-1}$)	Average Effective Strain**	m	$A \equiv -\dfrac{G}{m}$	α
816 (1500)	0.1	0.08	0.17	0.27	3.8
816 (1500)	0.1	0.32	0.17	0.26	3.6
816 (1500)	1.0	0.08	0.09	<0	<0
816 (1500)	1.0	0.32	0.09	0.35	4.9
913 (1675)	0.1	0.08	0.23	0.14	1.9
913 (1675)	0.1	0.32	0.23	0.13	1.8
913 (1675)	1.0	0.08	0.17	0.22	3.0
913 (1675)	1.0	0.32	0.17	0.18	2.5
954 (1750)	0.1	0.08	0.26	0.08	1.1
954 (1750)	0.1	0.32	0.26	0.08	1.1
954 (1750)	1.0	0.08	0.21	0.12	1.7
954 (1750)	1.0	0.32	0.21	0.13	1.8

*Avg. $\bar{\dot{\varepsilon}} = 0.6\, \bar{\dot{\varepsilon}}_s$ for specimen design employed.
**Avg. $\bar{\varepsilon} = 0.6\, \bar{\varepsilon}_s$ for specimen design employed.

as a result of increasing strain—and *work* softening proper. The latter refers to a process of negative work hardening, i.e., to situations where the dislocation density decreases with strain, and includes dynamic recovery and dynamic recrystallization at elevated temperatures. Work softening generally occurs when a dislocation substructure formed in a previous operation is subjected to further straining at a higher temperature, a lower strain rate, or both. Under these conditions, the dislocation and sub-boundary densities, which had previously attained equilibrium or saturation levels or were tending to a stable configuration, become unstable with respect to continued deformation. During each unit of further strain, more dislocations are destroyed by recovery processes than are created by the additional strain. Thus, the dislocation density in the subgrain interiors is reduced, and the mean subgrain size is concurrently increased. Flow stress reductions of 20 to 40 percent can be produced in this way, with the FCC metals approaching the latter limit, while the former limit applies approximately to the BCC and HCP metals.

The relative amount of flow softening that can be attributed to work softening of this type depends on the ratio of the yield to the steady-state stress and, more precisely, on the ratio of the amount of work hardening previously achieved to the current yield stress. The BCC and HCP metals generally display relatively high yield stresses in the annealed condition at a given temperature and strain rate, a characteristic that reduces the *proportion* of work hardening that can be induced during straining. By contrast, the FCC metals have low yield stresses at similar temperature-corrected strain rates. Thus, for a fixed *absolute* amount of work hardening, the degree of work softening displayed by the latter materials is of course greater. A further factor of importance is the strain interval $\Delta\varepsilon$, during which the flow stress decrease takes place, as the value of

$$\gamma = \left(\frac{\partial \ln \sigma}{\partial \varepsilon}\right)\bigg|_{\dot\varepsilon,T} \text{ or of } \gamma' = \left(\frac{d \ln \sigma}{d\varepsilon}\right)\bigg|_{\dot\varepsilon}$$

depends on $\Delta\varepsilon$ as well as on $\Delta\ln\sigma$. When work softening can be attributed to dynamic recovery processes, $\Delta\varepsilon$ has been reported to be about 0.30 to 0.40,[36] with the largest fraction of the decrease occurring during the first 0.1 strain. Under these conditions, values of γ or γ' well above the critical level of 1.0 (e.g., 2 to 4) can be observed, at least over limited intervals of strain.

Note that appreciable work softening is required to produce flow localization under conditions of *axisymmetric* compression, e.g., upset forging, because of the stabilizing influence of the increasing cross-sectional area. Under these conditions, the rate of localization is proportional to the exponential of $(\gamma' - 1)/m$.[21] The rate of work softening required to initiate *shear* instabilities, which are more common during plane-strain conditions of deformation, is considerably less, on the other hand, because of the absence of the area-increase term, $1/m$. In this case, the rate of localization is proportional to the exponential of γ'/m, which exceeds the former quantity by a factor of $\exp(1/m)$.[21] In either case, under isothermal conditions, the harmful influence of work softening is considerably moderated by the high rate sensitivities characteristic of high-temperature flow, so that, only when $\gamma > 2$ does the concentration of strain become pronounced. By contrast, when adiabatic heating effects are involved as well, or when yield drops resulting from a variety of dislocating unpinning processes become important (see below), then lower rates of flow softening can lead to significant localization.

Work Softening as a Result of Strain Path Changes. When the strain path is changed, it is well known that Bauschinger effects can occur. In the present context, these are generally restricted to strain intervals of about 3 percent and can thus be termed "transient" effects. The behavior that *follows* the Bauschinger transient is of concern here. This type of phenomenon is observed when an approximately axisymmetric strain path* is followed by a period of plane-strain deformation. Because the work hardening rate at a given equivalent strain (or stress) is higher during axisymmetric tension or compression than under plane-strain conditions,[33, 37-39] a change in strain path from the former to the latter generally leads to a period of work softening, or to the temporary absence of work hardening. A similar work hardening transient is expected when the strain path is changed from rolling (plane-strain compression or pure shear) to *simple* shear, such as occurs during the formation of shear bands. The isothermal γ values associated with this type of behavior are not particularly large ($\gamma < 2$ in compression), so that the phenomenon does not lead to significant macroscopic instabilities. However, when combined with adiabatic heating considerations, which can become important on a microscale, or with texture change effects (see below), the decrease in work hardening rate that accompanies strain path changes can play a central role in the initiation and propagation of microscopic shear bands.

WORK SOFTENING AT ELEVATED TEMPERATURES AS A RESULT OF DYNAMIC RECRYSTALLIZATION[9]

Work softening occurs most frequently by the removal of *pairs* of dislocations by the usual mechanisms of dynamic recovery. However, dislocation removal during straining can also be accomplished by the motion of high angle grain boundaries, i.e., by dynamic recrystallization processes, that lead to the annihilation of dislocations on a more massive scale. Dynamic recrystallization is largely limited to the FCC metals[40] that have relatively low yield stresses. This mechanism can, in principle, produce flow stress decreases on the order of 50 percent or more, particularly when it is of the periodic or grain coarsening type.[41] The sharpest drops are associated with the purest materials, in which the extent of grain-boundary drag by solutes and precipitates is the least,[42] so that the resulting grain-boundary mobilities are very high. In commercial materials, on the other hand, the relative flow softening attributable to dynamic recrystallization is limited to about 20 percent, partly because of the inhomogeneous nature of the flow generally induced under normal testing

---

*Note that balanced biaxial tension is equivalent to uniaxial compression.

conditions, but also because of the grain-boundary drag produced by the typical levels of both solutes and fine particles. Nevertheless, *locally* high degrees of softening can be introduced in this way, which lead to the dangers described above when work softening is combined with adiabatic heating. In the absence of such a combination, the harmful effects of dynamic recrystallization are usually mitigated by the high rate sensitivities (0.1 to 0.2) that are associated with this mechanism.

FLOW SOFTENING DUE TO THE REVERSAL OF STRENGTHENING MECHANISMS

There are numerous strengthening mechanisms employed in improving the mechanical properties of metals. Most of these are unstable with respect to large deformations, especially when these are applied at elevated temperatures. Two exceptions to this rule are the cases of solute hardening and of dispersion strengthening, especially the former, which retains its influence during concurrent straining.* The remainder are all susceptible to reversal as the material attempts to attain its equilibrium configuration. These will now be examined briefly, although they have been reviewed in more detail elsewhere.[9]

Precipitation Strengthening. Generally speaking, precipitates must be very fine (<<50 Å, or 5 nm in diameter) and highly dispersed to provide a significant strengthening effect. At elevated temperatures, they only coarsen slowly, the rate-limiting step for this process being the diffusion rate of the component of the precipitate that is in *substitutional* solid solution in the matrix (or the slowest component, if there is more than one). Another consideration affecting the coarsening rate is the current *concentration* of this element in solution in the matrix; this can be very low in systems in which the solubility product at the temperature in question is minute.

Because of the above factors, the rate of static coarsening of common precipitates is generally low. Nevertheless, during concurrent deformation, the dynamic rates generally observed are several orders of magnitude higher.[43-45] This arises for a number of reasons, examples of which follow:

(i) The vacancies generated during straining raise their concentration to well above the equilibrium level, increasing the effective rate of diffusion.

---

*Although the flow stress of solute-hardened materials decreases as the temperature is increased, the strength *ratio* (with respect to the pure metal at the same temperature and strain rate) remains approximately constant.

(ii) The dislocations and sub-boundaries introduced by straining provide short-circuit paths for the frequently more rapid pipe diffusion process.

(iii) During static or dynamic recrystallization, the motion of grain boundaries accelerates diffusion in their immediate vicinity, in part because of the higher vacancy concentrations associated with them.[46]

(iv) Particles can be sheared by moving dislocations, a process which can reduce them to subcritical size, so that they undergo re-solution.

Somewhat similar phenomena can be involved in ordered systems, such as the gamma-prime-strengthened superalloys. In such cases, a further re-solution mechanism becomes available, attributable to the heating of the material above the gamma-prime solvus, either accidentally or because of adiabatic effects associated with straining.[47]

Spheroidization of Lamellar Structures. The rapid spheroidization of pearlite during high-temperature deformation is a well-known example of microstructural softening.[48, 49] The driving force for spheroidization comes from the difference between the relatively high surface energy of the very fine plates of cementite and the appreciably lower value associated with the fairly coarse spheroidized particles. The spheroidization is able to take place rapidly during metal processing because of the acceleration of the relevant diffusion mechanisms resulting from the factors described above pertaining to the effect of concurrent straining on the rate of *precipitate* coarsening. The softening, in turn, can be traced to the increase of the mean free path of the dislocations during this process, the initial value of which is very small and on the order of the plate spacing.

Somewhat similar considerations apply to the break-up of Widmanstätten and martensitic microstructures such as may be observed during subtransus hot working of various two-phase titanium alloys with a microstructure of acicular alpha (Figure 3.30).[50-52] However, these processes also involve the destruction of microtwins and of the dense arrangements of dislocations produced by quenching, processes that may be considered types of work (i.e., dislocation) softening.

Dislocation Channeling in Irradiated Materials. The mechanical stability of irradiated materials is of considerable interest to the nuclear power industry. These materials can be strengthened appreciably by the irradiation damage process, during which the vacancies generated condense into sessile dislocation loops and other defects. The loops introduce a component of dislocation strengthening that is, in this instance, unstable with respect to plastic deformation. Once dislocations begin to move on a particular slip plane, they can sweep the plane clear of the loops, reducing the local critical shear stress for flow considerably, and thereby enhancing the occurrence of the usual kinds of plastic instability and flow localization.[53]

Yield Drops. The occurrence of yield drops at ambient and moderately elevated temperatures is well known and has been studied by numerous workers. The formation of solute atmospheres around dislocations, which is frequently instrumental in producing pinning and subsequent unpinning, has also been studied. Because of the enor-

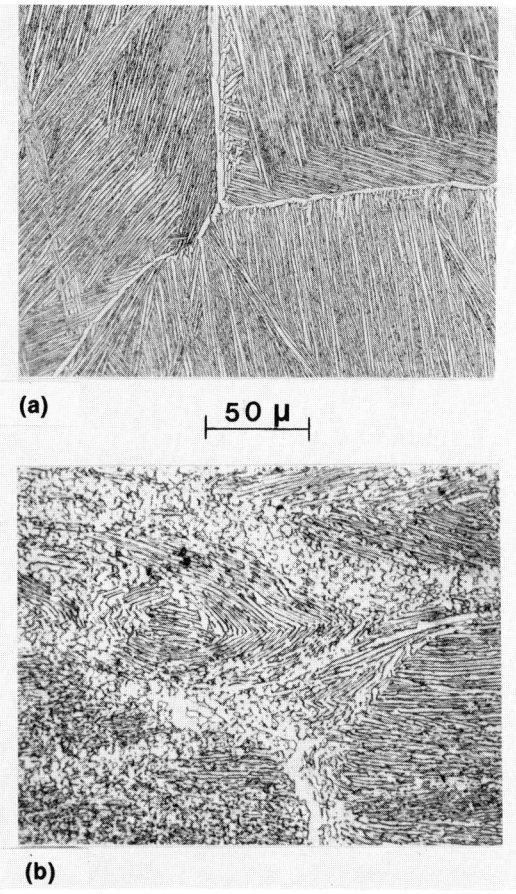

Figure 3.30. β microstructure in Ti-6242Si. (a) As received (i.e., as-beta annealed) material and (b) following subtransus compression at 900 °C (1650 °F) to a true axial strain of 1.0 at a strain rate of 2×10^{-3} sec.$^{-1}$.[52]

mous acceleration in diffusion rate that accompanies an increase in temperature into the hot working range, yield drops are not normally expected under these conditions. In effect, the times and temperatures involved should lead either to appreciable overaging or to the rapid motion of solutes behind gliding dislocations and therefore to an absence of observable effects. Nevertheless, distinct yield drops of considerable (relative*) amplitude have been detected at temperatures as high as 1200 °C. These have been observed, not only in BCC metals,[54-57] but in FCC[58] and HCP[59, 60] materials as well.

It is evident that the species involved in producing high-temperature yield drops are larger and more complex than those associated with the lower temperature phenomena. Thus, while H, C, N, and O are frequently cited as responsible at ambient and neighboring temperatures, as the latter is increased, the *substitutional* elements begin to become involved. At still higher temperatures, namely, in the hot working regime, the migrating species are likely to be composed of various complexes and atom groupings, such as clusters and ordered regions. Although the longer times of formation and slower rates of migration of these entities are consistent with the conditions under which their effects are observed, the details of these high-temperature aging processes remain largely unknown.

FLOW SOFTENING DUE TO TEXTURAL EFFECTS

Another type of flow softening, which does not necessarily involve work softening, however, is that due to texture changes. As such, its effects may be pronounced at both cold working and hot working temperatures. Texture softening occurs most dramatically in single crystals deforming by single slip. At the beginning of straining, there is little or no work hardening (the critical resolved shear stress τ_c is approximately constant), and the tensile (or compressive) flow stress σ depends principally on the Schmid factor, $\cos\theta_g \cos\phi_g$, as given by:

$$\sigma = \frac{\tau_c}{\cos\theta_g \cos\phi_g} \quad (3.50a)$$

where θ_g is the angle between the slip plane normal and the stress axis and ϕ_g that between the slip direction and the stress axis. If the angle between the tensile axis and the glide plane normal is initially small (e.g., 10 to 20°), then during extension, the normal is gradually tilted away from the tensile axis. Under these conditions, the Schmid

---

*With respect to the value of the lower yield stress.

factor increases towards its maximum value of 0.5 at 45°, and the axial stress *decreases* in direct proportion, as given by Equation (3.50a). Such geometrical softening can attain relative values as high as 70 percent.[61, 62]

In polycrystalline hexagonal materials, because of the dispersion of crystallite orientations, the proportions of flow softening that can be produced by texture modification are of course much smaller. These are reduced even further in the FCC and BCC metals, because there is less difference between the minimum and maximum values of the Schmid factors. Nevertheless, texture softening is not a negligible effect, particularly when it occurs in combination with other mechanisms, such as strain-path work softening or the break-up of Widmanstätten or martensitic microstructures (both of which have been discussed above). The magnitude of the effect in polycrystalline metals can be estimated from the relation:

$$\sigma = M_T \tau_c (\Gamma_{ss}) \qquad (3.50b)$$

Here σ is the applied stress component pertaining to a particular grain when it is deforming according to a selected strain path; Γ_{ss} is the accumulated slip on all the slip systems acting within the grain; τ_c is the critical shear stress for flow, which depends only on the total shear Γ_{ss} up to that point (i.e., it is assumed to be independent of strain path); and the Taylor factor M_T is equivalent to the value of $(\cos\theta_g \cos\phi_g)^{-1}$ for the *set* of active slip systems associated with the selected strain path and stress state.*

The rate of the flow stress increase in the grain can now be expressed in the form suggested by Gil Sevillano, van Houtte, and Aernoudt:[63]

$$\frac{d\sigma}{d\varepsilon} = \frac{dM_T}{d\varepsilon} \cdot \tau_c (\Gamma_{ss}) + M_T(\varepsilon) \cdot \frac{d\tau_c(\Gamma_{ss})}{d\varepsilon} \qquad , \qquad (3.51)$$

or

$$\frac{d\sigma}{d\varepsilon} = \frac{dM_T}{d\varepsilon} \cdot \tau_c + M_T \cdot \frac{d\tau_c}{d\Gamma_{ss}} \cdot \frac{d\Gamma_{ss}}{d\varepsilon} \qquad . \qquad (3.52)$$

$$\Rightarrow \frac{d\sigma}{d\varepsilon} = \tau_c \frac{dM_T}{d\varepsilon} + M_T^2 \frac{d\tau_c}{d\Gamma_{ss}} \qquad (3.53)$$

---

*Note that the increment of plastic work dW is given by $dW = \sigma d\varepsilon = \tau_c d\Gamma_{ss} = \tau_c M_T d\varepsilon$, so that the applied strain increment $d\varepsilon = d\Gamma_{ss}/M_T$.

The above expression shows clearly the individual contributions of texture change ($\tau_c \cdot d\bar{M}_T/d\varepsilon$) and of work hardening ($\bar{M}_T^2 \cdot d\tau_c/d\Gamma_{ss}$). However, for completeness, Equation (3.53) should be evaluated and then averaged for *all* the grains in the polycrystal, inasmuch as*

$$\bar{\sigma} = \overline{M_T \cdot \tau_c (\Gamma_{ss})} \tag{3.54}$$

The mean value of the product $M_T \cdot \tau_c$ can be decomposed[64] by introducing $\bar{\tau}_c$ defined by:

$$\bar{\tau}_c = \bar{\sigma}/\bar{M}_T = \overline{M_T \cdot \tau_c}/\bar{M}_T \tag{3.55}$$

This leads to

$$\bar{\sigma} = \bar{M}_T \cdot \bar{\tau}_c (\Gamma_{ss}) \tag{3.56}$$

so that

$$\frac{d\bar{\sigma}}{d\varepsilon} = \bar{\tau}_c \cdot \frac{d\bar{M}_T}{d\varepsilon} + \bar{M}_T^2 \cdot \frac{d\bar{\tau}_c}{d\bar{\Gamma}_{ss}} \tag{3.57}$$

This arises because the differences in the orientations of the individual grains produce different values of M_T pertaining to each grain, which in turn lead to different values of $\Gamma_{ss} = \int_0^\varepsilon d\Gamma_{ss} = \int_0^\varepsilon M_T(\varepsilon)d\varepsilon$ and therefore of $\tau_c (\Gamma_{ss})$, as well as of $d\tau_c/d\Gamma_{ss}$, $dM_T/d\varepsilon$, and $d\sigma/d\varepsilon$. Grains that are poorly oriented for slip in a given stress state have high values of M_T and therefore higher than average values of Γ_{ss} and τ_c at a given macroscopic strain ε. Here, $\bar{\tau}_c$ represents the flow stress of the "average" grain.

The slope represented by Equation (3.57) can be evaluated as long as the evolution law $M_T(\varepsilon)$ is known for each grain in a particular sample, so that $\bar{M}_T(\varepsilon)$ is also known. In this relation, $d\bar{\tau}_c/d\bar{\Gamma}_{ss}$ can be positive, zero, or negative. When it is positive and appreciable, as in the early stages of normal polycrystalline straining, texture softening cannot produce macroscopic instability effects. By contrast, when $d\bar{\tau}_c/d\bar{\Gamma}_{ss}$ is negative or zero, texture softening (i.e., $d\bar{M}_T/d\varepsilon < 0$) can lead to either localized or generalized (i.e., diffuse) strain concentration, depending on the detailed conditions.

---

*$\bar{\sigma}$ in Equations (3.54) through (3.59) refers to an average value of the σ defined in Equation (3.50b) and not the effective stress discussed previously and in subsequent sections of this monograph.

Equation (3.57) can also be expressed in the logarithmic formalism employed for the instability analyses presented earlier:*

$$\gamma = \left(\frac{\partial \ln \bar{\sigma}}{\partial \varepsilon}\right)\bigg|_{\dot{\varepsilon},T} \simeq \left(\frac{\partial \ln \bar{M}_T}{\partial \varepsilon}\right)\bigg|_{\dot{\varepsilon},T} + \bar{M}_T \cdot \left(\frac{\partial \ln \bar{\tau}_c}{\partial \Gamma_{ss}}\right)\bigg|_{\dot{\varepsilon},T} \quad . \quad (3.58)$$

PRACTICAL EXAMPLES OF TEXTURE SOFTENING

There are basically three types of conditions under which texture softening can take place. The first is when the mean Taylor factor decreases during deformation along a *fixed* strain path. The second, more important, case concerns the effect of *changes* in strain path on the evolution of the Taylor factor. These two cases involve the effect of deformation on materials that have an initially random texture, or at most a slight preferred orientation due to their processing history, which is largely fortuitous. The third case concerns marked textures that are specifically designed and produced by means of appropriate *heat treatments*, but that are unstable with respect to subsequent deformation. These three cases will be examined in turn, but first, the two principal methods used for determining the mean Taylor factor for metal deformation at cold working temperatures will be reviewed briefly.

Method of Full Constraints (Isostrain Method). When an increment of strain $d\varepsilon$ is applied to a material, the additional deformation is described, in the most general case, in terms of six components: the three diagonal or normal strain components (defined with respect to the *specimen* axes) and the three (symmetrical) off-diagonal or shear components. The six are not independent, however, because the constancy of volume during plastic deformation links the three diagonal components, so that only five are truly independent.[65] Thus, when a particular grain is deformed incrementally, five degrees of freedom (e.g., five independent slip systems in an FCC metal) are usually needed to permit the five strain increments to be imposed arbitrarily. This approach was introduced by Taylor in 1938,[65] and then by Bishop and Hill in 1951[66, 67] in a related form. It is known as the method of full constraints, because all five (six including volume constancy) components of the strain tensor are fully defined or imposed. Each

---

*Note that when Equation (3.58) is applied to compression, $+\bar{M}_T$ (i.e., in the second term of the right-hand side of the equation) must be replaced by $-\bar{M}_T$ because $d\bar{\Gamma}_{ss}/d\varepsilon = -\bar{M}_T$ in this case. Bearing in mind that $\bar{\sigma}$ and ε are also negative, $\gamma < 0$ and > 0 under flow hardening and flow softening conditions, respectively, in opposition to the tension case.

individual grain follows *exactly* the strain path imposed on the sample as a whole, and the method applies primarily to undeformed grains, which are initially equiaxed, and continues to apply at least approximately until the grain distortion attains a critical level that depends on the strain path being followed.[64] By means of this technique, the increment of total slip associated with a given imposed strain increment $d\varepsilon$ can be readily calculated for each grain, leading to the value of $M_T = d\Gamma_{ss}/d\varepsilon$ for that grain. The average Taylor factor $\bar{M}_T$ can then be determined, from which the evolution law $\bar{M}_T(\varepsilon)$ can be deduced, as well as the values of $\partial \bar{M}_T/\partial \varepsilon|_{\dot\varepsilon,T}$ needed for the application of Equations (3.57) and (3.58). The detailed dependence of $\bar{M}_T$ on ε depends, of course, on strain path.

Method of Relaxed Constraints. When the grain becomes sufficiently elongated, as in tensile deformation, one of the constraints on the strain can be removed or relaxed, and the central portion of the grain no longer suffers *exactly* the same shape change as the sample as a whole.[68] In the case of the elongated grains produced in wire drawing or tension, this means that there is a small incompatibility between the inner parts of each grain and the grain ends, which is assumed to be accommodated within the ends of the grains. In this case, only *four* independent slip systems are needed to produce the required *approximate* shape change in the central portion of the grain.

If, instead of being stretched, the grain is heavily compressed and assumes a pancake-like shape, the central portion is considered to be free to shear along *two* perpendicular directions, both of which are contained in the plane of the flattened grain. These two "free" shear components, which are no longer prescribed, permit the shape change to be accomplished by means of only *three* independent degrees of freedom (such as the three independent slip systems in FCC metals that deform by restricted glide). As before, the difference between the macroscopic strain imposed on the sample as a whole (five prescribed strain components plus one from volume constancy) and the strain accomplished by the central portion of the grain (three prescribed components plus one from volume constancy) is assumed to be absorbed or accommodated by the rims of the grains. Similar considerations apply to other strain paths, all of which involve only three or four independent slip systems at large strains, instead of the five employed at the initiation of macroscopic flow according to the full constraints analysis.[69, 70]

The relaxed constraints method is particularly suited to the calculation of grain rotations and therefore to the simulation of texture development at large strains, e.g., axial strains above about 0.7 in tension and compression, shear strains greater than 3 in torsion, and normal strains greater than about 1.25 in rolling.[64, 71] Like the full constraints technique, it permits the distribution of M_T values pertaining to a particular population of grains to be readily determined, so that the evolution law $\bar{M}_T(\varepsilon)$ can be established, together with the values of $(\partial \bar{M}_T/\partial \varepsilon)|_{\dot{\varepsilon},T}$ required for the application of Equations (3.57) and (3.58). It should be added that, as the grain shape evolves from the originally equiaxed to the finally distorted configuration, the method of $\bar{M}_T$ determination can be gradually converted from that of full to that of relaxed constraints.

Dependence of $\bar{M}_T$ on Strain and Strain Path for Radial Loading Paths. Several workers have investigated the effect of strain on $\bar{M}_T$ when the strain path is fixed, i.e., under conditions of proportional or radial loading.[63, 64, 72-74] These calculations have been largely restricted to BCC and FCC metals deformed at cold working temperatures and take only limited account of additional phenomena such as twinning and deformation and shear band formation.[75-77] Much less is known about texture evolution in HCP metals,[78] so that the remarks that follow apply primarily to the cubic metals. For these, the mean Taylor factor appears to change little during cold rolling or plane-strain compression, i.e., less than 4 percent if twinning is neglected, even though a distinct texture is being developed.[64, 71, 79] Thus, the $\partial \ln \bar{M}_T/\partial \varepsilon|_{\dot{\varepsilon},T}$ term in Equation (3.58) can be expected to take values of 0.04 or less, depending on the strain interval over which $\bar{M}_T$ is changing. Such small values are not likely to lead to texture-based instabilities at cold working temperatures.

Similar remarks apply to the case of torsion, where the mean Taylor factor first decreases[63] and then increases[64] with strain. Here, the increases and decreases are about 6 percent in the FCC metals and about 12 percent in the BCC metals.[64] As these take place over a macroscopic shear strain interval Γ of about 10, the coefficient $\partial \ln \bar{M}_T/\partial \Gamma|_{\dot{\varepsilon},T}$ is again small and therefore unlikely to provoke macroscopic flow localization.

The cases of FCC tension and BCC compression (assuming restricted glide in both cases) can be taken together, as in the absence of twinning, they are roughly equivalent. The mean Taylor factor *increases* by about 6 percent during the initial strain interval of about 1 and does not subsequently decrease.[63, 71] Thus, there is no crystallographic impetus for flow localization under these two conditions of straining. This is in contrast to the cases of FCC compression and BCC tension, which are again qualitatively similar. For these strain paths, $\bar{M}_T$ increases at first, up to a strain of about 0.6, after which it *decreases* by about 15 percent, leading to *negative* values (in tension) of $\partial \ln \bar{M}_T/\partial \varepsilon|_{\dot{\varepsilon},T}$ of approximately -0.30 to -0.40 in the vicinity of $\varepsilon = 1$. Thus, for tension, the occurrence of texture softening leads to the fulfillment of the isothermal instability condition $\gamma = 1$ (Equation 3.19) *earlier* than would be expected from purely work hardening considerations (i.e., from the values of $\partial \ln \tau_c / \partial \Gamma_{ss}|_{\dot{\varepsilon},T}$ alone).

For the case of FCC compression, because of the associated sign changes (see footnote regarding Equation 3.58), the texture softening component $\partial \ln \bar{M}_T / \partial \varepsilon|_{\dot{\varepsilon},T}$ is equal to 0.3 to 0.4 (i.e., it is *positive*). Thus, when τ_c = constant and only texture softening is occurring, $\gamma - 1$ remains negative and therefore still in the range of stable values. Because of the area increase term, for instability in compression, $\gamma > 1$ is required, which cannot be attained unless accompanied by sufficient dislocation softening (i.e., by $\partial \ln \tau_c / \partial \varepsilon|_{\dot{\varepsilon},T} > 0.6$).* Larger effects of the type described above are likely to be found in HCP materials; however, more data are required on the dependence of $\bar{M}_T$ on strain and strain path before a quantitative assessment of the phenomenon can be made.

In summary then, texture softening during deformation along a *fixed* strain path can occur under certain experimental conditions, notably during the compressive and tensile deformation of FCC and BCC materials, respectively. Such softening is not expected to be of industrial importance. However, texture softening can play a larger role either when there is a change in strain path or when the starting material is strongly textured. These two cases will now be examined using the formalism introduced above.

Effect of Strain Path Change on $\bar{M}_T(\varepsilon)$. There are basically two types of path changes of interest here. The first involves a change from one bulk path to another; the second concerns a change from the bulk path to a new localized path along a loading direction different from that of the bulk. The latter occurs when a shear band is formed, for example. The bulk-to-bulk processes include operations such as forging (compression) following rod rolling or extrusion (tensile elongation), and sheet metal forming (variety of strain paths) after rolling (plane-strain extension along the rolling direction). Although it is difficult to generalize about these operations, the following principles are likely to apply to many of the examples.

Under uniaxial conditions of straining (tension or compression), once a texture begins to form, the mean Taylor factor $\bar{M}_T$ *increases* above the random value,** as described earlier.[63, 71] If the strain

---

*Note that $d\varepsilon < 0$ in compression, so that $\partial \ln \tau_c / \partial \varepsilon|_{\dot{\varepsilon},T} > 0$ for work softening.

**By contrast, there is less change in $\bar{M}_T$ when plane-strain deformation is taking place.[64]

path is changed abruptly at a particular point in this operation, the $\bar{M}_T$ for deformation along the second path also changes instantaneously. This discontinuity in $\bar{M}_T$ is due *solely* to the alteration in the stress state (and to the associated modification in the set of slip or twinning systems being activated), as the texture cannot respond instantaneously to the path change. Because the first $\bar{M}_T$ value is *higher* than the random one, the second $\bar{M}_T$ pertaining to the new path is frequently *less* than the (now different) random texture value associated with the second path. However, this abrupt change in $\bar{M}_T$ is not relevant to the present discussion. Instead, the question of interest is the dependence of the second $\bar{M}_T$ on further straining, $\bar{M}_T(\varepsilon)$, i.e., whether $\partial \ln \bar{M}_T / \partial \varepsilon |_{\dot{\varepsilon},T} < 0$ or > 0.

Unfortunately, little is known at present about the effect of a path change on $\partial \ln \bar{M}_T / \partial \varepsilon |_{\dot{\varepsilon},T}$. Nevertheless, some insight into the problem can be gained from the work of Gil Sevillano, Van Houtte, and Aernoudt,[63, 80] which deals with bulk-to-localized path changes. Such path deviations arise, for example, when shear bands form during (1) flat rolling, (2) extrusion or wire drawing, and (3) upsetting of round bars in forging operations. In these instances, a simple shear strain path is suddenly adopted following prior deformation by (1) plane strain compression, (2) axisymmetric extension, and (3) axisymmetric compression, respectively.

Gil Sevillano and co-workers considered two types of FCC metals: copper, as an example of a material with a relatively high stacking fault energy (SFE), and 70/30 brass, with a relatively low SFE. They simulated the development of the rolling texture in the two materials using a Taylor type (full constraints) analysis. At selected rolling strains ($\varepsilon_{R.D.}$ = 0.2, 0.4, and 0.6 for the brass, and $\varepsilon_{R.D.}$ = 0.5, 1.0, 2.0, and 4.0 for the copper, where R.D. refers to the rolling direction), they changed the deformation mode (at the sites of the future shear bands within the homogeneous material) to *simple shear** and determined the value of $\bar{M}_T$ pertaining to the new strain path, as well as that of $\partial \bar{M}_T / \partial \varepsilon |_{\dot{\varepsilon},T}$. In the brass, after rolling strains of 0.2 to 0.4 (and for an angle of 40° between the rolling plane and the plane of the shear band), $(\partial \bar{M}_T / \partial \varepsilon)|_{\dot{\varepsilon},T}$ was about -0.1. In the copper, after rolling strains of 2.0 to 4.0 (and for an inclination of 35°), $(\partial \bar{M}_T / \partial \varepsilon)|_{\dot{\varepsilon},T}$ was about -0.08. These correspond to values of about -0.035 and -0.02 for $(\partial \ln \bar{M}_T / \partial \varepsilon)|_{\dot{\varepsilon},T}$ for the brass and copper, respectively.

---

*They used fixed end torsion for this purpose, which is equivalent to simple shear. Note that the displacement field associated with shear banding is that of *simple* shear and not *pure* shear. The latter leads to different textures and work hardening rates.[64]

Although negative, these rates of texture softening are rather low. Nevertheless, Gil Sevillano and co-workers considered that they differed sufficiently from zero (particularly for the 70/30 brass) to be responsible for the formation of shear bands in these materials at the strains indicated. This is because the rates of work hardening in simple shear (torsion), expressed for the present purpose as $\partial \ln \bar{\tau}_c/\partial \varepsilon|_{\dot{\varepsilon},T}$ (Equation 3.58), had dropped to about $+0.03$ in the two materials. However, it should be noted that the above authors made no allowance for the effect of *strain path change* on $\partial \ln \bar{\tau}_c/\partial \varepsilon|_{\dot{\varepsilon},T}$, which probably acts to reduce the *transition* work hardening rate to zero, or even to render it negative (see above). Furthermore, as they were concerned with isothermal conditions, they did not include a flow softening contribution from adiabatic heating. It can therefore be concluded that texture softening can accompany strain path changes and that such softening can help to promote the formation of shear bands and other forms of flow localization, particularly when account is taken of the true work softening ($\partial \ln \bar{\tau}_c/\partial \varepsilon|_{\dot{\varepsilon},T} < 0$) that follows the path change and the deformation heating and thermal softening produced in the localization.*

Effect of Heat Treatment on $\bar{M}_T(\varepsilon)$. Heat treatments are used to strengthen metals in numerous ways. Those that lead to the formation of martensitic, Widmanstätten, etc., microstructures must be considered carefully when reversal of their strengthening effects by deformation can lead to flow softening, as discussed previously. Here, consideration is restricted to those treatments that produce nonrandom textures of industrial interest. The best examples are the annealing treatments designed to raise the R value for subsequent sheet metal forming operations, although texture modification by suitable heat treatment is also widely employed in the manufacture of tubes and other parts made of hexagonal materials and to improve the physical properties of magnetic materials. Of particular interest is the relation between R value and texture and therefore between R value and $\bar{M}_T$. For present purposes, it is assumed that no other strengthening mechanisms are important and that the mean flow stress $\bar{\sigma}$ along a particular loading direction depends only on the mean values of M_T and τ_c in each grain, as given by:

$$\bar{\sigma} = \overline{M_T \cdot \tau_c} \quad , \tag{3.54}$$

or

$$\bar{\sigma} = \bar{M}_T \cdot \bar{\tau}_c \quad . \tag{3.56}$$

---

*Note that rates of texture softening well above the average rates calculated by Gil Sevillano et al.[80] can occur in particular grains such as the ones that first display microscopic shear bands.[71-79]

where $\bar{\tau}_c = \overline{M_T \cdot \tau_c}/\bar{M}_T$. Suppose now that a particular material is processed so that a high value of $\bar{M}_T$ applies to a certain stress state or loading path, i.e., that $\bar{M}_{T_{ht}} > \bar{M}_{T_{random}}$. Thus, for a fixed value of dislocation density and therefore of $\bar{\tau}_c$,

$$\bar{\sigma}_{ht} = \bar{M}_{T_{ht}} \cdot \bar{\tau}_c > \bar{\sigma}_{random} = \bar{M}_{T_{random}} \cdot \bar{\tau}_c \quad . \tag{3.59}$$

However, once such a material is deformed, the average Taylor factor may decrease and tend toward the stable value associated with the strain path selected. This process can be characterized in terms of the current value of $\partial \ln \bar{M}_T / \partial \varepsilon |_{\dot{\varepsilon},T}$, which is negative under these conditions. The effect of such a "path change," i.e., from the heat treated state to the new path, can be considerably greater than the ones produced by true path changes, such as those described earlier. The former generally fall in the range:

$$0 > \partial \ln \bar{M}_T / \partial \varepsilon |_{\dot{\varepsilon},T} > -1.0 \tag{3.60}$$

(i.e., with $d\varepsilon > 0$, as in tension). Although the lack of experimental data makes it difficult to be more precise, it is possible that the above limit is exceeded in hexagonal materials, in which strong heat treatment textures have been produced.[81]

FLOW SOFTENING ARISING FROM ADIABATIC HEATING—STRAIN-HARDENING MATERIALS

Deformation heating can lead to sizable amounts of flow softening and hence flow localization in alloys in which the flow stress is very temperature sensitive. The effect of deformation heating is usually most marked at high temperatures, because the temperature sensitivity of the flow stress is generally higher in this temperature range. However, there are many examples of deformation heating leading to strain localization at cold working temperatures where the softening is promoted by the high flow stress levels.

Previous analyses[31, 82-85] of the flow localization caused by deformation heating at cold working temperatures have concentrated solely on predicting the strain at which the flow curve passes through a maximum under adiabatic conditions. For example, the strain for instability along the maximum shear stress directions in plane strain can be calculated from[31, 82-85]

$$d\bar{\sigma} = 0 = \left(\frac{\partial \bar{\sigma}}{\partial \bar{\varepsilon}}\right)\bigg|_{\dot{\varepsilon},T} d\bar{\varepsilon} + \left(\frac{\partial \bar{\sigma}}{\partial \dot{\bar{\varepsilon}}}\right)\bigg|_{\bar{\varepsilon},T} d\dot{\bar{\varepsilon}} \\ + \left(\frac{\partial \bar{\sigma}}{\partial T}\right)\bigg|_{\bar{\varepsilon},\dot{\bar{\varepsilon}}} dT \quad . \tag{3.61}$$

This is done by neglecting the rate sensitivity; then the strain $\bar{\varepsilon}_c$ at which this condition is satisfied for a material whose isothermal flow curve is of the form $\bar{\sigma} = K\bar{\varepsilon}^n$ is given by

$$\bar{\varepsilon}_c = -\frac{\rho c n}{0.95 \left(\dfrac{\partial \bar{\sigma}}{\partial T}\right)\bigg|_{\bar{\varepsilon},\dot{\bar{\varepsilon}}}} \qquad (3.62)$$

In Equation (3.62), ρ is the density of the metal, and c is its specific heat. It has also been assumed that 95 percent of the deformation work is transformed into heat that is retained in the workpiece. Table 3.4 shows that for ductile (large n) metals whose flow stress is not too sensitive to temperature (e.g., normalized 1006 steel, annealed 304 stainless steel, and 6061-0 aluminum), large amounts of strain can be imposed before the onset of instability. In contrast, quenched and tempered steels such as 4340 can be deformed only small amounts before flow localization initiates. This is particularly striking in materials with the highest hardnesses and the lowest initial strain-hardening rates.

It is also instructive to determine the amount of quasistable post-uniform deformation beyond $\bar{\varepsilon}_c$ that can be expected. This can be done by determining the strain at which the α parameter reaches a critical value such as 5 or 10.* For the present class of materials, γ' is defined by**

$$\gamma' = -\left(\frac{d\ln\bar{\sigma}}{d\bar{\varepsilon}}\right)\bigg|_{\dot{\bar{\varepsilon}}} = -\left(\frac{\partial\ln\bar{\sigma}}{\partial\bar{\varepsilon}}\right)\bigg|_{\dot{\bar{\varepsilon}},T} - \left(\frac{\partial\ln\bar{\sigma}}{\partial T}\right)\bigg|_{\bar{\varepsilon},\dot{\bar{\varepsilon}}} \frac{dT}{d\bar{\varepsilon}} \qquad (3.63)$$

Under adiabatic conditions, dT is given, as before, by

$$dT = \frac{0.95\bar{\sigma}d\bar{\varepsilon}}{\rho c}, \qquad (3.64)$$

so that, for power-law hardening materials, Equation (3.63) becomes

---

*A more detailed discussion of the effect of adiabatic heating on flow localization is contained in Chapter 7 (shell fragmentation) and Appendix C (high speed torsion).

**Since γ' was defined before in terms of the uniaxial compression flow curve $\sigma(\varepsilon)$ (Equation 3.18), and since for this test $\bar{\sigma} = -\sigma$ and $\bar{\varepsilon} = -\varepsilon$, $\gamma' = (1/\sigma)(d\sigma/d\varepsilon)|_{\dot{\varepsilon}} = -(1/\bar{\sigma})(d\bar{\sigma}/d\bar{\varepsilon})|_{\dot{\bar{\varepsilon}}}$.

$$\gamma' = -\frac{n}{\bar{\varepsilon}} - \frac{0.95}{\rho c}\left(\frac{\partial \bar{\sigma}}{\partial T}\right)\bigg|_{\bar{\varepsilon},\dot{\bar{\varepsilon}}} \quad . \tag{3.65}$$

With the aid of Equation (3.62), this may be rewritten as

$$\gamma' = \frac{n}{\bar{\varepsilon}_c} - \frac{n}{\bar{\varepsilon}} \quad . \tag{3.66}$$

Returning to the question of shear band formation, the α parameter is given by Equation (3.44):

$$\alpha = \frac{\gamma'}{m} = \left(\frac{n}{\bar{\varepsilon}_c} - \frac{n}{\bar{\varepsilon}}\right)\bigg/m \quad . \tag{3.67}$$

Solving Equation (3.67) for $\bar{\varepsilon}(\alpha)$ and dividing by $\bar{\varepsilon}_c$, the normalized strain $\bar{\varepsilon}/\bar{\varepsilon}_c$ at which flow localization may be expected to become evident can be found from

$$\frac{\bar{\varepsilon}}{\bar{\varepsilon}_c} = \left(1 - \frac{\alpha m \bar{\varepsilon}_c}{n}\right)^{-1} \tag{3.68a}$$

or

$$\frac{\bar{\varepsilon}}{\bar{\varepsilon}_c} = \left(1 - \frac{\alpha m \rho c}{0.95(|\partial \bar{\sigma}/\partial T|)\big|_{\bar{\varepsilon},\dot{\bar{\varepsilon}}}}\right)^{-1} \quad , \tag{3.68b}$$

with α set to 5, for example. Note that the latter of Equations (3.68) has been derived by making use of Equation (3.62). It thus appears that large m and large ρc tend to increase the amount of quasistable deformation, and large $(|\partial \bar{\sigma}/\partial T|)|_{\bar{\varepsilon},\dot{\bar{\varepsilon}}}$ tends to decrease it. This result is plausible for m, in that it is qualitatively similar to the result obtained in the absence of adiabatic heating considerations.[86]

Estimates of $\bar{\varepsilon}/\bar{\varepsilon}_c$ for various materials evaluated on the basis of Equation (3.68) are given in Table 3.4. These estimates illustrate that 1006 steel, for example, with small $\partial \bar{\sigma}/\partial T$, can be expected to undergo large quasistable deformations prior to noticeable shear banding (at $\alpha \approx 5$), whereas the quenched and tempered 4340 steel (large $\partial \bar{\sigma}/\partial T$) can be expected to form shear bands almost immediately after $\bar{\varepsilon}_c$.

Table 3.4.
Flow Localization Tendencies of Various Alloys under Adiabatic Shear Band Conditions

Alloy (Condition)	$\rho\left(\dfrac{g.}{cm^3}\right)$	$c\left(\dfrac{cal.}{g.°C}\right)$	$n^\dagger$	$-\dfrac{\partial\bar{\sigma}^\dagger}{\partial T}$ (kPa/°C)	$m^\dagger$	$\bar{\varepsilon}_c$	$\dfrac{\bar{\varepsilon}(\alpha=5)}{\bar{\varepsilon}_c}$	$\dfrac{\bar{\varepsilon}(\alpha=10)}{\bar{\varepsilon}_c}$
1006 Steel (normalized)	7.86	0.11	0.24	625	0.01	1.45	1.43	2.53
1043 Steel (normalized)	7.83	0.11	0.12	750	0.01	0.61	1.34	2.03
4340 Steel (Q & T, $R_c = 26$)	7.83	0.11	0.092*	1075*	0.01	0.33	1.22	1.56
4340 Steel (Q & T, $R_c = 39$)	7.83	0.11	0.055*	1925*	0.01	0.11	1.11	1.25
4340 Steel (Q & T, $R_c = 52$)	7.83	0.11	0.043*	3100*	0.01	0.053	1.07	1.14
304 Stainless Steel (annealed)	8.03	0.09	0.50	1975	0.02	0.80	1.19	1.47
316 Stainless Steel (annealed)	8.03	0.11	0.35	2975	0.03	0.46	1.25	1.65
6061-0 Aluminum	2.71	0.23	0.24	500	0.002	1.33	1.06	1.12
Pure Titanium (mill annealed)	4.51	0.125	0.30	1250	0.025	0.60	1.33	2.00
Ti-6Al-4V (α/β Processed)	4.46	0.13	0.02	2300	0.015	0.022	1.09	1.32

†Data for room-temperature deformation at $\dot{\varepsilon} = 10\ \text{sec.}^{-1}$.
*Mechanical property data from quasistatic tests.

FLOW SOFTENING ARISING FROM ADIABATIC HEATING — NONHARDENING MATERIALS

An inspection of Equation (3.65) shows that, for materials that exhibit a steady-state flow stress (n = 0) at low strain rates, the flow softening rate due to adiabatic heating at high strain rates can be quite high, depending on the value of $(\partial \bar{\sigma}/\partial T)|_{\varepsilon,\dot{\varepsilon}}$. The occurrence of a steady state of flow is common at hot working temperatures, and so the occurrence of flow localization due to adiabatic heating can be of considerable practical importance in this regime.

The effect of adiabatic heating on shear band formation when n = 0 can be assessed using the α parameter, which from Equations (3.44) and (3.65) is found to be:

$$\alpha = \frac{\gamma'}{m} = -\frac{0.95\,(\partial \bar{\sigma}/\partial T)|_{\bar{\varepsilon},\dot{\bar{\varepsilon}}}}{\rho c m} \quad . \tag{3.69}$$

To determine the hot working temperatures and strain rates at which shear bands can be expected to form, one could assume an α = 5 criterion, as before, and measure $\bar{\sigma}$ versus T, as well as m as a function of strain rate and temperature. A somewhat simpler method, however, relies on the observation that high-temperature deformation processes are thermally activated and that the rate sensitivity of the flow stress is therefore related to its temperature dependence. Because of this relationship, it can be shown[16] that:

$$m = -\frac{R_g T^2}{Q\bar{\sigma}}\left[\left(\frac{\partial \bar{\sigma}}{\partial T}\right)\bigg|_{\bar{\varepsilon},\dot{\bar{\varepsilon}}}\right] \quad , \tag{3.70}$$

where Q is the experimental activation energy, R_g is the gas constant; and T is the absolute temperature. By inserting this relation into Equation (3.69), an expression that eliminates the necessity of measuring the slope of the $\bar{\sigma}$-T plot is obtained:

$$\alpha = \frac{0.95 Q \bar{\sigma}}{\rho c R_g T^2} \quad . \tag{3.71}$$

The application of Equation (3.71) to predict the flow localization caused by adiabatic heating will now be illustrated. For this purpose, the problem of the initiation of shear bands during the hot plane-strain sidepressing of Ti-6242 will be considered. The $\bar{\sigma}$-T plots pertaining to the α + β microstructure (presented in Figure 3.31) were obtained from hot compression testing. However, instead of plotting

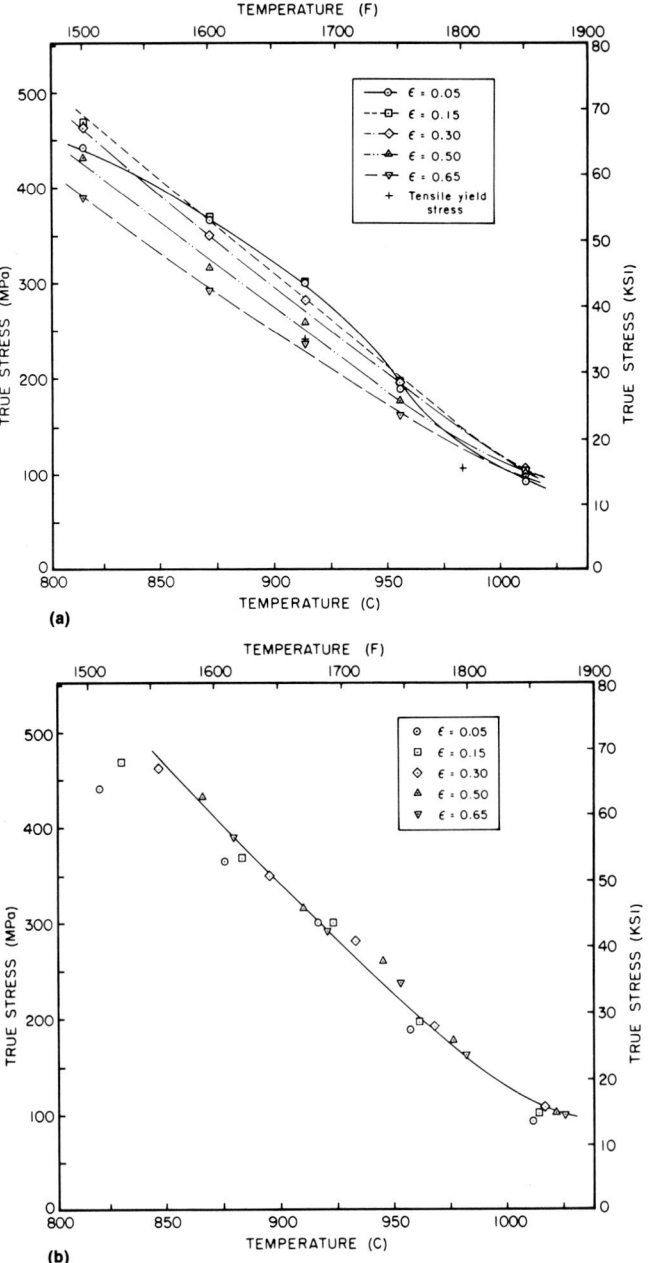

Figure 3.31. Flow stress versus temperature data at various strain levels for α + β microstructure Ti-6242Si compression specimens tested at $\dot{\varepsilon} = 10$ sec.$^{-1}$. (a) Measured data and (b) data in which deformation heating has been taken into account.[10]

the stresses in terms of the *nominal* test temperatures (Figure 3.31a), it is more useful for the present purpose to display them in terms of the *instantaneous* test temperatures (Figure 3.31b). The latter are defined as the initial test temperatures plus the increases due to deformation heating.[10] At strain rates of 1 sec.$^{-1}$ and higher, such heating is essentially adiabatic, and the temperature rise is therefore given by Equation (3.64). When the compression flow stresses are correlated with the *instantaneous* temperatures in this way, a single trend line is found to fit all the data (except that at low strains, $\varepsilon \lesssim 0.20$, where strain hardening is occurring). Thus, to a good approximation, the truly isothermal flow curves for the $\alpha + \beta$ microstructure exhibit a steady-state flow stress.

To obtain the activation energy Q needed in Equation (3.71), plots of log σ versus (1/T) pertaining to a variety of $\dot\varepsilon$'s must be prepared. As before, since $\sigma = \sigma\,(\dot\varepsilon \exp(Q/R_g T)) = \sigma\,(Z)$:

$$Q = -\frac{R_g \cdot \Delta \ln \dot\varepsilon}{\Delta(1/T)} \qquad (3.72)$$

For Ti-6242Si with the $\alpha + \beta$ microstructure, a value of $Q \simeq 150{,}000$ cal./mole was arrived at in this way. By setting α equal to 5, the temperature at which Equation (3.71) is satisfied can now be estab-

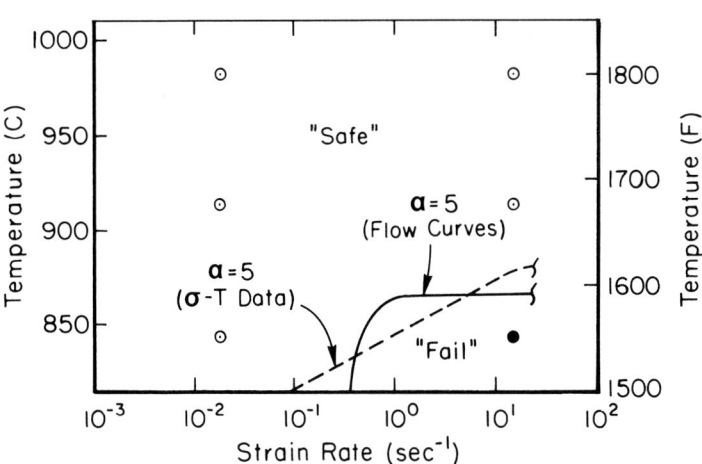

Figure 3.32. Comparison of shear band observations for $\alpha + \beta$ microstructure Ti-6242Si and the $\alpha = 5$ criterion based on measured flow stress data (solid line) and σ-T data in conjunction with equation (3.71) (broken line). Open and closed data points indicate conditions under which shear bands were not and were observed, respectively.

lished by examining the σ-T plots for each strain rate. The locus of temperatures and strain rates so determined is shown in Figure 3.32. It can be seen to compare favorably with the α = 5 locus established directly from measured flow curves and m values. Differences between the two predictions can be attributed to the neglect of low strain work-hardening effects when Equations (3.69) and (3.71) were derived.

References

[1] H.A. Kuhn and P.W. Lee: *Met. Trans.*, 1971, vol. 2, p. 3197.
[2] P.W. Lee and H.A. Kuhn: *Met. Trans.*, 1973, vol. 4, p. 969.
[3] H.A. Kuhn, P.W. Lee, and T. Erturk: *J. Eng. Mat. Technol., Trans. ASME*, 1973, vol. 95H, p. 213.
[4] S.K. Suh and H.A. Kuhn: *Modern Developments in Powder Metallurgy, Vol. 9*, p. 407, Metal Power Industries Federation, Princcton, NJ, 1977.
[5] S. Kobayashi: *J. Eng. Ind., Trans. ASME*, 1970, vol. 92B, p. 391.
[6] G. Cusminsky and F. Ellis: *J. Inst. Metals*, 1967, vol. 95, p. 33.
[7] Z. Marciniak and K. Kuczynski: *Inter. J. Mech. Sci.*, 1967, vol. 9, p. 609.
[8] R.L. Hewitt: *Quart. Bulletin*, National Research Council, Division of Mechanical Engineering and National Aeronautical Establishment, Ottawa, Canada, 1978, No. 1, p. 1.
[9] J.J. Jonas and M.J. Luton: *Advances in Deformation Processing*, J.J. Burke and V. Weiss, eds., p. 215, Plenum Press, New York, 1978.
[10] S.L. Semiatin, G.D. Lahoti, and T. Altan: *Process Modeling: Fundamentals and Applications to Metals*, T. Altan, H. Burte, H. Gegel, and A. Male, eds., p. 387, ASM, Metals Park, OH, 1980.
[11] E. Hart: *Acta Met.*, 1967, vol. 15, p. 351.
[12] F.A. Nichols: *Acta Met.*, 1980, vol. 28, p. 663.
[13] J.J. Jonas, R.A. Holt, and C.E. Coleman: *Acta Met.*, 1976, vol. 24, p. 911.
[14] J.J. Jonas and B. Baudelet: *Acta Met.*, 1977, vol. 25, p. 43.
[15] U.F. Kocks, J.J. Jonas, and H. Mecking: *Acta Met.*, 1979, vol. 27, p. 419.
[16] S.L. Semiatin and G.D. Lahoti: *Met. Trans. A*, 1981, vol. 12A, p. 1705.
[17] S.L. Semiatin and G.D. Lahoti: *Met. Trans. A*, 1981, vol. 12A, p. 1719.
[18] S.L. Robinson, O.D. Sherby, and P.E. Armstrong: *J. Nucl. Mater.*, 1973, vol. 46, p. 293.
[19] P. Dadras and J.F. Thomas, Jr.: *Met. Trans. A*, 1981, vol. 12A, p. 1867.
[20] J.J. Jonas, N. Christodoulou, and C. G'Sell: *Scripta Met.*, 1978, vol. 12, p. 565.
[21] N. Christodoulou and J.J. Jonas: *Res Mechanica*, 1982, vol. 5, p. 49.
[22] S. Kobayashi, C.H. Lee, Y. Saida, and S.C. Jain: Technical Report AFML-TR-90, University of California, Berkeley, CA, July, 1970.
[23] S.L. Semiatin and G.D. Lahoti: *Met. Trans. A*, 1982, vol. 13A, p. 275.

[24] S.L. Semiatin, G.D. Lahoti, and S.I. Oh: *Material Behavior under High Stress and Ultrahigh Loading Rates*, Plenum Press, New York, 1983, p. 119.
[25] N. Rebelo and S. Kobayashi: *Inter. J. Mech. Sci.*, 1980, vol. 22, p. 699.
[26] S.I. Oh: *Inter. J. Mech. Sci.*, 1982, vol. 24, p. 479.
[27] B. Avitzur: *Metal Forming: Processes and Analysis*, McGraw-Hill, New York, 1968.
[28] S. Kobayashi: *Metal Forming—Interrelation Between Theory and Practice*, A.L. Hoffmanner, ed., p. 325, Plenum Press, New York, 1971.
[29] R.H. Ernst and J.W. Spretnak: *Trans. Iron Steel Inst. Japan*, 1969, vol. 9, p. 361.
[30] D. Hauser: Ph.D. Thesis, Ohio State University, Department of Metallurgical Engineering, Columbus, OH, 1973.
[31] U.S. Lindholm, A. Nagy, G.R. Johnson, and J.M. Hoegfeldt: *J. Eng. Mat. Techn., Trans. ASME*, 1980, vol. 102, p. 376.
[32] G.R. Johnson: *J. Eng. Mat. Techn., Trans. ASME*, 1981, vol. 103, p. 201.
[33] G.R. Canova, S. Shrivastava, J.J. Jonas, and C. G'Sell: *Formability of Metallic Materials—2000 A.D.*, J.R. Newby and B.A. Niemeier, eds., p. 189, American Society for Testing and Materials, Philadelphia, 1982.
[34] E. Rauch, G.R. Canova, and J.J. Jonas: Unpublished Research, McGill University, Montreal, Quebec, 1982.
[35] G.D. Lahoti and T. Altan: *J. Eng. Mat. Techn., Trans. ASME*, 1975, vol. 97, p. 113.
[36] J.P. Immarigeon and J.J. Jonas: *Acta Met.*, 1971, vol. 19, p. 1053.
[37] J.J. Jonas, G.R. Canova, S.C. Shrivastava, and N. Christodoulou: *Plasticity of Metals at Finite Strain: Theory, Experiment, and Computation*, E.H. Lee and R.L. Mallett, eds., p. 206, Rennselaer Polytechnic Institute, Troy, NY, 1982.
[38] S.C. Shrivastava, J.J. Jonas, and G. Canova: *J. Mech. Phys. Solids*, 1982, vol. 30, p. 75.
[39] S.S. Hecker and M.G. Stout: *Deformation, Processing, and Structure*, G. Krauss, ed., p. 1, ASM, Metals Park, OH, 1984.
[40] H.J. McQueen and J.J. Jonas: *Treatise on Materials Science and Technology, vol. 6: Plastic Deformation of Metals*, R. J. Arsenault, ed., p. 393, Academic Press, New York, 1975.
[41] J.J. Jonas and T. Sakai: *Deformation, Processing, and Structure*, G. Krauss, ed., p. 185, ASM, Metals Park, OH, 1984.
[42] H.P. Stüwe: *Recrystallization of Metallic Materials*, F. Haessner, ed., p. 11, D. Riederer Verlag, Stuttgart, 1978.
[43] I. Weiss and J.J. Jonas: *Met. Trans. A*, 1980, vol. 11A, p. 403.
[44] T. Chandra, I. Weiss, and J.J. Jonas: *Metal Science*, 1982, vol. 16, p. 97.
[45] T. Chandra, I. Weiss, and J.J. Jonas: *Can. Met. Quart.*, 1981, vol. 20, p. 421.
[46] Y. Estrin and K. Lücke: *Acta Met.*, 1982, vol. 30, p. 983.
[47] M.C. Mataya and G. Krauss: *J. Applied Metalworking*, 1981, vol. 2, p. 28.
[48] E.A. Chojnowski and W.J. McG. Tegart: *Metal Sci.*, 1968, vol. 2, p. 14.

[49] J.L. Robbins, O.C. Shepard, and O.D. Sherby: *Trans. ASM*, 1967, vol. 60, p. 205.
[50] S. Nadiv and H.L. Gegel: Air Force Wright Aeronautical Laboratories, Dayton, OH, unpublished research, 1979.
[51] P. Dandras and J.F. Thomas, Jr.: *Res. Mechanica Letters*, 1981, vol. 1, p. 97.
[52] S.L. Semiatin, J.F. Thomas, Jr., and P. Dadras: *Met. Trans. A*, Nov. 1983, vol. 14A, p. 2363.
[53] C.E. Coleman, D. Mills, and J. van der Kuur: *Can. Met. Quart.*, 1972, vol. 11, p. 91.
[54] J.J. Jonas, B. Heritier, and M.J. Luton: *Met. Trans. A*, 1979, vol. 10A, p. 611.
[55] A.S. Rizkalla, R.A. Holt, and J.J. Jonas: *Zirconium in the Nuclear Industry (Fourth Conference), ASTM STP 681*, p. 497, American Society for Testing and Materials, Philadelphia, 1979.
[56] R. Choubey and J.J. Jonas: *Metal Science*, 1981, vol. 15, p. 30.
[57] R. Choubey, J.J. Jonas, R.A. Holt, and C.E. Ells: *Zirconium in the Nuclear Industry (Fifth Conference), ASTM STP 754*, D. G. Franklin, ed., p. 350, American Society for Testing and Materials, Philadelphia, 1982.
[58] A.A. Guimaraes and J.J. Jonas: *Met. Trans. A*, 1981, vol. 12A, p. 1655.
[59] A.S. Rizkalla, R. Choubey, and J.J. Jonas: *Zirconium in the Nuclear Industry (Sixth Conference)*, ASTM STP 824, p. 176, American Society for Testing and Materials, Philadelphia, 1984.
[60] P. Dadras and J.F. Thomas, Jr.: *Met. Trans. A*, 1983, vol. 14A, p. 1512.
[61] E. Schmid: *Metallwirtschaft*, 1928, vol. 7, p. 1011 (in German).
[62] W. Boas and E. Schmid: *Z. Phys.*, 1929, vol. 54, p. 16 (in German).
[63] J. Gil Sevillano, P. van Houtte, and E. Aernoudt: *Progress in Materials Science*, 1981, vol. 25, p. 69.
[64] G.R. Canova, U.F. Kocks, and J.J. Jonas: *Acta Met.*, 1984, vol. 32, p. 211.
[65] G.I. Taylor: *J. Inst. Met.*, 1938, vol. 62, p. 307.
[66] J.F.W. Bishop and R. Hill: *Phil. Mag.*, 1951, vol. 42, p. 414.
[67] J.F.W. Bishop and R. Hill: *Phil. Mag.*, 1951, vol. 42, p. 1298.
[68] H. Honneff and H. Mecking: *Proc. Fifth Inter. Conf. on the Textures of Materials (ICOTOM5), Vol. I*, G. Gottstein and K. Lücke, eds., p. 265, Springer Verlag, Berlin, 1978.
[69] U.F. Kocks and H. Chandra: *Acta Met.*, 1982, vol. 30, p. 695.
[70] U.F. Kocks and G.R. Canova: Proc. Second Risø Int. Conf., "Deformation of Polycrystals: Mechanisms and Microstructures," N. Hansen *et al.*, eds., p. 355, Risø National Laboratory, Roskilde, Denmark, 1981.
[71] C. Tomé, G.R. Canova, U.F. Kocks, N. Christodoulou, and J.J. Jonas: *Acta Met.*, 1984, vol. 32, in press.
[72] G.Y. Chin, W.L. Mammel, and M.T. Dolan: *Trans. TMS-AIME*, 1969, vol. 245, p. 383.
[73] J.M. Rosenberg and H. R. Piehler: *Met. Trans.*, 1971, vol. 2, p. 257.
[74] S.L. Semiatin, P.R. Morris, and H.R. Piehler: *Texture of Crystalline Solids*, 1979, vol. 3, p. 191.
[75] G.Y. Chin and B.C. Wonsiewicz: *Trans. TMS-AIME*, 1969, vol. 245, p. 871.

[76] B.C. Wonsiewicz and G.Y. Chin: *Met. Trans.*, 1970, vol. 1, p. 57.
[77] P. Van Houtte: *Proc. Fifth Inter. Conf. on the Textures of Materials (ICOTOM5), Vol. I*, G. Gottstein and K. Lücke, eds., p. 347, Springer Verlag, Berlin, 1978.
[78] D.R. Thornburg and H.R. Piehler: *Met. Trans. A*, 1975, vol. 6A, p. 1511.
[79] I.L. Dillamore and H. Katoh: *Met. Sci.*, 1974, vol. 8, p. 21.
[80] J. Gil Sevillano, P. Van Houtte, and E. Aernoudt: *Mémoires et Etudes Scientifiques Revue de Metallurgie*, 1980, vol. 77, p. 1043.
[81] W.F. Hosford and W.A. Backofen: *Fundamentals of Deformation Processing*, W.A. Backofen, J.J. Burke, L.F. Coffin, Jr., N.L. Reed, and V. Weiss, eds., p. 259, Syracuse University Press, Syracuse, NY, 1964.
[82] M.R. Staker: *Acta Met.*, 1981, vol. 29, p. 683.
[83] R.S. Culver: *Metallurgical Effects at High Strain Rates*, R.W. Rohde et al., eds., p. 519, Plenum Press, New York, 1973.
[84] R.F. Recht: *J. Appl. Mech., Trans. ASME*, 1964, vol. 31E, p. 189.
[85] G.B. Olson, J.F. Mescall, and M. Azrin: *Shock Waves and High-Strain-Rate Phenomena in Metals*, M.A. Meyers and L.E. Murr, eds., p. 221, Plenum Press, New York, 1981.
[86] A.K. Ghosh and R.A. Ayres: *Met. Trans. A*, 1976, vol. 7A, p. 1589.

FLOW LOCALIZATION IN BULK FORMING: NONISOTHERMAL DEFORMATION

Another common form of flow localization occurring during bulk forming is seen in the conventional hot working of metals. In such operations, contact between a hot workpiece and typically much cooler tooling leads to chilling of the workpiece, and the resulting nonuniform flow patterns may necessitate total redesign of processes such as forging, extrusion, and rolling. Because the development of flow localization in these circumstances involves a strong interaction between the workpiece and tooling, the total process design must, therefore, include consideration of material properties as well as processing parameters. The most important material property is probably the dependence of flow stress on temperature. For materials that show a strong dependence at hot working temperatures, temperature gradients set up due to chilling lead to strain and strain-rate gradients. In extreme cases, shear bands may develop. Processing parameters enter the picture through their effect on heat transfer. The amount of heat transfer is determined by the tooling-workpiece contact time (and thus equipment speed), the tooling-workpiece temperature difference, and the thermal characteristics of the tooling, workpiece, and lubricant interface.

In this chapter, the modes of flow localization in nonisothermal hot working will be discussed and applied to observations of the conventional forging behavior of Ti-6242Si. The discussion will center on flow localization in upsetting and lateral sidepressing of this alloy.

The importance of understanding both the influence of the material, as well as processing parameter effects, in establishing flow localization will be emphasized.

Analysis of Flow Localization in Nonisothermal Upsetting[1, 2]

Insight into the mode of flow localization during nonisothermal metalworking is most easily obtained through the analysis of the upset forging of a cylindrical workpiece. Denoting the forging direction by x, equilibrium requires that the gradient in net load F supported by the workpiece through its thickness must be equal to zero. If we again assume that the stress field is uniaxial (so that the axial stress σ is equal to the flow stress) and that $\sigma = \sigma\,(\varepsilon, \dot{\varepsilon}, T)$, an expression similar to Equation (3.13) is obtained. To emphasize the importance of temperature gradients in this situation, this equation (at a fixed time t), may be rewritten as:

$$0 = \frac{d\ln A}{dx} + \left\{ \left(\frac{\partial \ln \sigma}{\partial \varepsilon}\right)\bigg|_{\dot{\varepsilon},T} \frac{d\varepsilon}{dx} + \left(\frac{\partial \ln \sigma}{\partial \dot{\varepsilon}}\right)\bigg|_{\varepsilon,T} \frac{d\dot{\varepsilon}}{dx} + \left(\frac{\partial \ln \sigma}{\partial T}\right)\bigg|_{\varepsilon,\dot{\varepsilon}} \frac{dT}{dx} \right\} . \qquad (4.1)$$

With the assumption of uniaxial conditions, $dA/A = -d\varepsilon$ and the equation becomes:

$$0 = \left[\left(\frac{\partial \ln \sigma}{\partial \varepsilon}\right)\bigg|_{\dot{\varepsilon},T} - 1 \right] \frac{d\varepsilon}{dx} + \left(\frac{\partial \ln \sigma}{\partial \dot{\varepsilon}}\right)\bigg|_{\varepsilon,T} \frac{d\dot{\varepsilon}}{dx} + \left(\frac{\partial \ln \sigma}{\partial T}\right)\bigg|_{\varepsilon,\dot{\varepsilon}} \frac{dT}{dx} . \qquad (4.2)$$

It is seen that strain and strain-rate gradients are controlled by material properties (strain hardening or flow softening, strain rate hardening, and flow stress dependence on temperature) and temperature gradients that are established by a variety of material properties and process variables. Strain hardening and strain rate hardening tend to minimize flow localization under conditions involving temperature gradients. On the other hand, flow softening and negative dependence of flow stress on temperature tend to act in concert with temperature gradients to produce flow localization.

To separate the effects of thermal gradients and flow softening on flow localization, let us assume that the flow stress is not a function of strain at fixed strain rate and temperature. Many metals behave this way at large strains during hot working. Further, attention will be focused solely on the early stages of deformation, during which $d\ln A/dx = -d\varepsilon/dx$ is ~ 0. Even when chilling and flow localization have become severe, calculations show that the strain rate term in Equation (4.2) has much more influence on maintaining equilibrium than the term involving $d\varepsilon/dx$. With these assumptions, Equation (4.2) becomes:

$$\frac{d\ln\dot\varepsilon}{dx} = -\frac{(\partial\ln\sigma/\partial T)|_{\varepsilon,\dot\varepsilon}}{m}\frac{dT}{dx} \equiv \eta\frac{dT}{dx} \qquad (4.3)$$

The marked similarity between Equations (3.19) and (3.44) and Equation (4.3) should be noted. In the former, the destabilizing influence is flow softening, whereas for the latter, it is a thermal gradient in conjunction with a negative dependence of flow stress on temperature. In addition, in both instances, a large strain-rate sensitivity tends to act as a stabilizing influence.

For an idea of the temperature gradients that can be expected in the upsetting of cylinders, the classical solution for one-dimensional heat conduction between two semi-infinite bodies may be employed. If we assume perfect heat transfer between the two bodies, one at an initial temperature T_D and one at an initial temperature T_S, the temperature of the body whose initial temperature is T_S as a function of x and T ($T(x,t)$) is the following:[3]

$$\frac{T(x,t) - T_S}{T_D - T_S} = \frac{\sqrt{\rho_D c_D k_D}}{\sqrt{\rho_D c_D k_D} + \sqrt{\rho_S c_S k_S}} \cdot \text{erfc}\,(x/2\sqrt{k_S t/\rho_S c_S}) \qquad (4.4)$$

In this expression, ρ, c, and k denote density, specific heat, and thermal conductivity, respectively, and the subscripts D and S refer to the two bodies. Taking the partial derivative with respect to x of Equation (4.4), we obtain:

$$\frac{\partial T}{\partial x} = \frac{(T_S - T_D)\sqrt{\rho_D c_D k_D}}{(\sqrt{\rho_D c_D k_D} + \sqrt{\rho_S c_S k_S})(\sqrt{\pi k_S t/\rho_S c_S})} \cdot \exp\,(-\rho_S c_S x^2/4\,k_S t) \qquad (4.5)$$

Identifying S with the workpiece or specimen in the upsetting operation and D with the dies or tooling, Equation (4.5) may be employed in conjunction with Equation (4.3) to estimate the strain-rate gradients attributable to chilling if the heat generation due to deformation is neglected. Also, it should be kept in mind that Equation (4.5) is only valid for times that are short enough so that the chilling at one end of the workpiece is not influenced by the chilling at the other end. In general, however, Equation (4.5) gives useful insight into the effects of the die-workpiece temperature difference, thermal properties of the dies and workpiece, and working speed (i.e., time of deformation) on chilling and the development of thermal gradients.

Flow Localization in Upsetting of Ti-6242Si: Observations[2]

The application of Equations (4.3) and (4.5) will be illustrated below by examining the nonisothermal compression deformation of Ti-6242Si. Prior to this demonstration, however, some experimental observations will first be reviewed. These observations concern the nonisothermal upsetting of lubricated Ti-6242Si cylinders 1.02 cm (0.40 in.) in diameter × 1.52 cm (0.60 in.) high that have been preheated to either 913 or 954 °C (1675 or 1750 °F) and then deformed between H11 tool steel dies heated to 191 °C (375 °F). The deformations in all cases consisted of a 50 percent reduction in height ($\varepsilon \approx 0.7$) in a mechanical press at a nominal strain rate of 10 sec.$^{-1}$. In such a press, the strain rate drops off during the last third of the upset test,[4] so that the time required for such a deformation is approximately 0.09 sec., rather than 0.07 sec.

Metallographic examination of the nonisothermally upset specimens revealed that the deformation was strongly influenced by the formation of chill zones or chill caps (Figures 4.1 and 4.2).* This is particularly obvious for the $\alpha + \beta$ microstructure specimens, in which the chill caps etch somewhat lighter than the bulk of the specimen (Figures 4.1a, 4.1b, and 4.2). Support for the interpretation that this phenomenon is indeed due to chilling can be obtained from the load-stroke data. An example of data of this type is given in Figure 4.3

---

*In these and subsequent figures containing macrographs, the compression or forging axis is vertical, with the lower part of the specimen having been in contact with the bottom die and the upper part with the top die.

for the nonisothermal compression of an α + β specimen preheated to 954 °C (1750 °F). The measurement is compared to two predictions based on flow stress data measured in nominally isothermal compression tests (in which slight deviations from isothermal conditions occur because of deformation heating) and the specimen geometry employed in the nonisothermal compression tests. During the early stages of deformation, the measured load is nearly equal to that predicted for

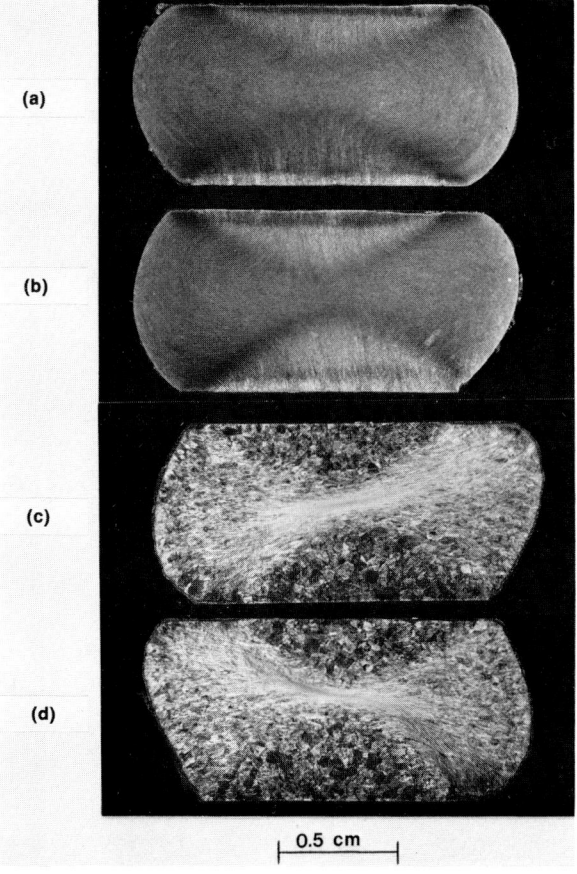

Figure 4.1. Axial cross sections of Ti-6242Si compression specimens nonisothermally deformed to 50 percent reduction in height in a mechanical press ($\dot{\varepsilon} \approx 10$ sec.$^{-1}$).$^{(2)}$ Preform microstructures, sample preheat temperatures, T_S, die temperatures, T_D, and dwell times, t_D, were the following: (a) α + β, T_S = 954 °C (1750 °F), T_D = 191 °C (375 °F), t_D = 0 sec. (b) α + β, T_S = 954 °C (1750 °F), T_D = 191 °C (375 °F), t_D = 5 sec. (c) β, T_S = 954 °C (1750 °F), T_D = 191 °C (375 °F), t_D = 0 sec. (d) β, T_S = 954 °C (1750 °F), T_D = 191 °C (375 °F), t_D = 5 sec.

isothermal deformation at 954 °C (1750 °F) (curve B). The difference may be attributed to the specimen preheat temperature being slightly higher than 954 °C (1750 °F). However, with increasing stroke, the measured load increases rapidly beyond the predictions based on isothermal deformation at either 954 °C (1750 °F) or 913 °C (1675 °F) (curve A). It can therefore be concluded that these higher working loads are due to chilling and the strong dependence of flow stress on temperature (Figure 3.31).

With the formation of chill caps, bands of localized shear passing through the corners of the specimen develop between (1) the regions of lower temperature and higher flow stress in the chill caps

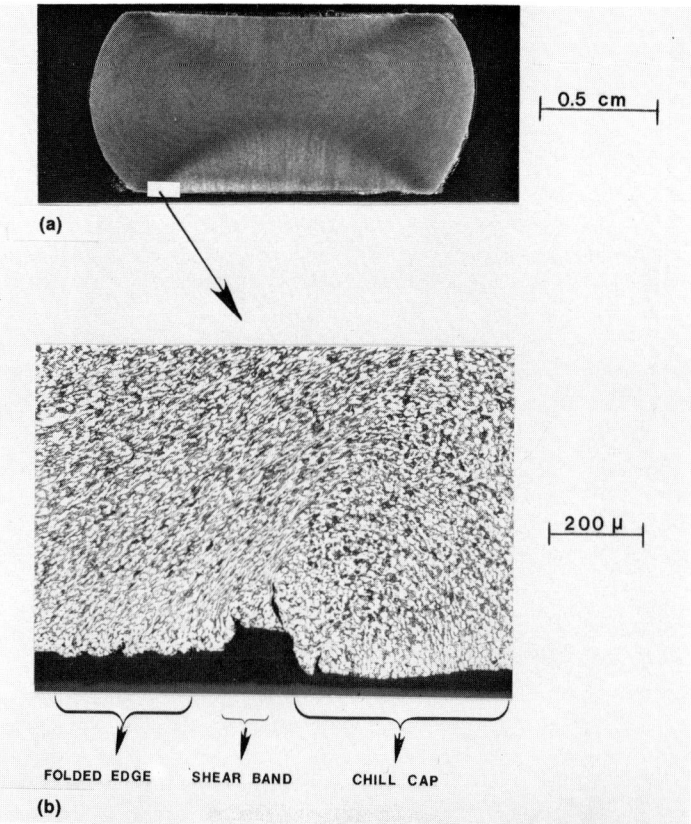

Figure 4.2. (a) Macrograph and (b) micrograph of α + β microstructure Ti-6242Si compression specimen nonisothermally deformed 50 percent in a mechanical press ($\dot{\varepsilon} \approx 10$ sec.$^{-1}$).[2] Preheat temperature: 913 °C (1675 °F), die temperature: 191 °C (375 °F), dwell time: 5 sec.

and (2) the deforming metal in the rest of the specimen (Figure 4.2). Metal then begins to flow along the shear bands. In particular, the specimen edges fold by shearing along the regions of localized deformation leading to bulge formation, a phenomenon that is very common in cold compression tests with poor lubrication.[5]

Careful examination of the chill zones and bands of localized deformation in specimens of the α + β and β microstructures reveals an interesting difference, however. For the α + β specimens (Figures 4.1a, 4.1b, and 4.2), the chill zones are caps that are relatively undeformed. For test temperatures of 913 and 954 °C (1675 and 1750 °F) and at 50 percent reduction in height, the caps comprise no more than about two thirds of the specimen (when the measurement is made along the central axis of the specimen). It is also interesting to note that the effect of increasing the dwell time on the dies prior to deformation is small, leading to only a slightly larger chill cap on the

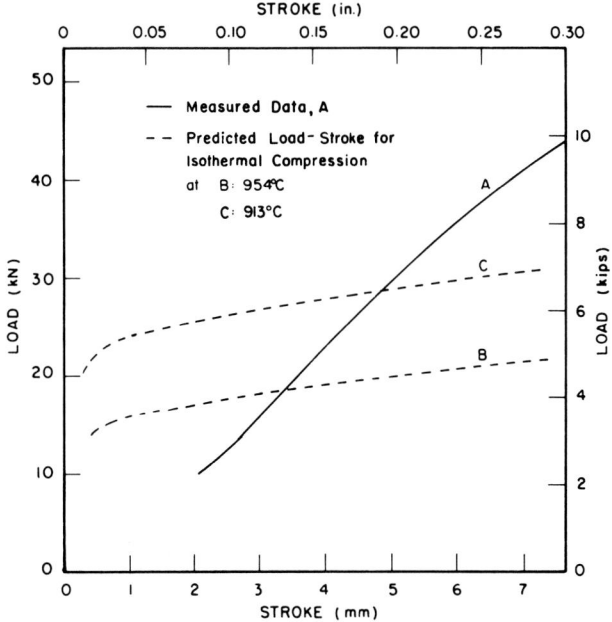

Figure 4.3. Measured load-stroke data for nonisothermal hot compression of 1.02 cm (0.4 in.) diameter, 1.52 cm (0.6 in.) high α + β microstructure Ti-6242Si specimen preheated to 954 °C (1750 °F) and deformed in a mechanical press ($\dot{\varepsilon} \approx 10$ sec.$^{-1}$) between dies heated to 191 °C (375 °F). Data are compared to load-stroke curves predicted for isothermal compression at 954 °C (1750 °F) and 913 °C (1675 °F).[2]

bottom as opposed to the top of a specimen after a dwell time of 5 sec. (Figure 4.1b). Further microscopic examination of the shear bands bordering on chill caps reveals that they do not extend over the entire height of the specimen. For this reason, the nonisothermal hot compression of the material containing the α + β microstructure may be thought of as analogous to axisymmetric deformation between conical rather than flat dies. Hence, the bulge profiles for the α + β samples are relatively symmetric about the specimen axes.

In contrast to the α + β microstructure specimens, the β microstructure specimens exhibit shear bands that pass *totally* through the cross sections (Figures 4.1c and d), and the chill caps essentially penetrate into the entire specimen. This phenomenon is similar to the occurrence of shear bands during the *isothermal* hot compression of β specimens.[6] Under isothermal conditions, it has been shown that such shear bands result from the flow softening taking place in material containing the β microstructure. The flow localization during the nonisothermal compression of a β microstructure specimen is more severe, however, because the effect of die chilling on the development of strain gradients reinforces the basic tendency of the β specimens to deform nonuniformly. It should be noted that the morphology of flow localization and shear banding in the β material is associated with highly asymmetric specimen cross sections (Figures 4.1c and d), which are unlike the relatively symmetric bulges found in the α + β specimens. This observation is strongly suggestive of the block-shearing type of deformation indicative of a change of deformation state from axisymmetric to plane strain.

Comparison of Model and Experimental Predictions of Flow Localization in Nonisothermal Upsetting of Ti-6242Si

The experimental observations described above will now be compared with model predictions based on Equations (4.3) and (4.5). Strictly speaking, Equation (4.3) is only applicable to the α + β experiments, because the β microstructure exhibits large degrees of flow softening $[(\partial\sigma/\partial\varepsilon)|_{\dot{\varepsilon},T} < 0]$. To obtain an estimate of the instantaneous temperature and through this the strain rate gradients for the α + β tests, it is assumed that nonisothermal upsetting occurs with sequential steps of deformation followed by intervals of heat transfer. That is to say, in applying the heat transfer analysis, it is assumed that an increment of deformation is imposed during some time Δt, and this

Table 4.1
Physical Properties of Ti-6242Si and H11 Tool Steel[1]

	Density, ρ (g./cc)	Specific Heat, c (cal./g. °C)	Thermal Conductivity, k (cal./sec. cm °C)
Ti-6242Si*	4.4	0.23	0.040
H11**	7.8	0.11	0.080

*Properties for T ~ 900 °C (1650 °F).
**Properties for T ~ 20 °C (70 °F).

is followed by heat transfer (without deformation) for an identical time increment Δt.[7] As the time increment $\Delta t \to 0$, more and more accurate predictions of the temperature field are calculated for various total times t. Nevertheless, a rough estimate of the temperature field can be obtained for the present experiments by assuming that all the reduction is imposed in a single step at time t = 0, i.e., adiabatically, and then heat transfer takes place during a single time interval of 0.09 sec. Estimates of T and $\partial T/\partial x$ made in this way using the proper material properties (Table 4.1) and Equations (4.4) and (4.5) were compared with more accurate finite difference computer simulations.[1, 2] This comparison demonstrated that the single-step temperature gradient calculation based on Equation (4.5) with t = 0.09 is close to the more accurate one, even though the predicted temperatures themselves are lower. When still more accurate computer simulations were carried out employing finite heat transfer coefficients for the lubricant interface characteristics, the thermal gradients estimated by this means remained very close to those predicted using Equation (4.5), even though the heat transfer coefficient in the latter case was assumed to be infinite.

The thermal gradient calculated from Equation (4.5) for the case T_S = 954 °C (1750 °F), T_D = 191 °C (375 °F), t = 0.09 sec., and zero dwell time is given in Table 4.2. The other item of information needed to apply Equation (4.3) (i.e., to calculate the strain-rate gradients from the temperature gradients) is the value of η, the ratio of the normalized thermal softening rate to the strain-rate sensitivity. For α + β microstructure Ti-6242Si, plots such as the one depicted in Figure 3.31 show that the η parameter is fairly constant and equal to 0.05 ± 0.01 C^{-1} for temperatures between 816 and 982 °C (1500 and 1800 °F) and strain rates between 0.1 and 10 $sec.^{-1}$.[2] Once a value of η is available, Equation (4.3) can be integrated to produce an es-

Table 4.2.
Estimated Temperature and Strain Rate Gradients at Fifty Percent Reduction of α + β Microstructure Ti-6242Si*[1]

x** (mm)	$\dfrac{dT}{dx}\left(\dfrac{°C}{mm}\right)$	$\dfrac{d\log_{10}\dot{\varepsilon}}{dx}$ (mm^{-1})	$\dfrac{\dot{\varepsilon}(x)}{\dot{\varepsilon}(x = 3.505 \text{ mm})}$
0.5	342.7	7.44	<0.01
1.0	202.3	4.39	<0.01
1.5	84.0	1.82	<0.01
2.0	24.6	0.53	0.05
2.5	5.1	0.11	0.47
3.0	0.7	0.02	0.88
3.5	0.1	~0.00	1.00

*Initial specimen temperature: 954 °C (1750 °F); initial die temperature: 191 °C (375 °F); time of deformation: 0.09 sec.
**x ≡ Distance from die-workpiece interface.

timate of the strain-rate gradients. For the specific case described in Table 4.2, the strain-rate gradients, as well as the strain rates relative to the strain rate at the center of the upset specimen (which does not see the effects of chilling under the chosen deformation conditions), have been calculated. From these results, it can be concluded that a nearly rigid zone extending into the upset specimen a distance of approximately 2.0 mm (0.08 in.) can be expected. At this location, the calculated strain rate is only one twentieth of that at the center. This result agrees quite favorably with the experimental observations pertaining to this case (Figure 4.1a).

For a β microstructure specimen deformed under the same conditions as the α + β one described above, a still greater degree of flow localization can be expected because of the additional influence of flow softening. In this case, the overall σ-T dependence (Figure 4.4) and m values are similar to those for the α + β microstructure.[8] Thus, chilling alone (i.e., in the absence of flow softening) should lead to nearly rigid chill zones extending inward some 2.0 mm (0.08 in.) from the die-workpiece interfaces, as in the previous case. However, in addition to the chilling effects, allowance must be made for the flow softening effects that were eliminated in the derivation of Equation (4.3). Once this correction is made, it is apparent that the flow should localize still further in the 3.5 mm (0.14 in.) region between the chill zones. This is exactly what is observed on metallographic cross sections (Figure 4.1c), in which the flow is seen to be confined to a narrow region approximately 1 mm (0.04 in.) wide (when measured along the central, or specimen, axis).

Flow Localization During the Nonisothermal Sidepressing of Ti-6242Si

The mode of flow localization during nonisothermal plane-strain metalworking operations is often quite different from that pertaining to the axisymmetric modes of deformation. This is not surprising in view of the discussion of flow localization under isothermal metalworking conditions given in the previous chapter. Here, it was seen that localized bulging is favored in axisymmetric deformation and shear band formation in plane-strain deformation modes. The nonisothermal analog of localized bulges in upsetting, namely the formation of nearly rigid chill zones, has just been analyzed and described. In what follows, the nonisothermal counterpart of shear banding in plane-strain isothermal deformation will be discussed. In this case, though, the mode of flow localization, i.e., the formation of shear bands, appears to be basically the same as that observed in isothermal plane-strain operations.

An understanding of the mode of flow localization under nonisothermal plane-strain conditions may be obtained from the research of Semiatin and Lahoti, who investigated shear band formation during the nonisothermal sidepressing of Ti-6242Si.[2] In this work, long, round (1.02 cm, or 0.4 in. diameter) bars of $\alpha + \beta$ and β microstructure were sidepressed in either an Erie mechanical press or an HPM hydraulic press between flat H11 tool steel dies preheated to either 191 or 343 °C (375 or 650 °F). A few round bars were also forged between tool steel blade dies heated to 191 °C (375 °F). Coated with Deltaglaze 349M lubricant (manufactured by Acheson Colloids Co., Port Huron, Michigan), the specimens were heated to either 913 °C (1675 °F) or 982 °C (1800 °F) prior to forging. These preheat temperatures were selected on the basis of nonisothermal hot upset tests and the observation that one of these temperatures lies in the regime in which the flow stress dependence on temperature is great and one lies in a regime in which it is small (Figures 3.31 and 4.4).

In the mechanical press trials, Ti-6242Si specimens were reduced in height (relative to the initial diameter) between 15 and 80 percent. Because the press was operated at full speed during all tests, the average nominal strain rate varied between approximately 25 sec.$^{-1}$ for the light reductions and approximately 40 sec.$^{-1}$ for the heavy reductions. For the hydraulic press forgings, specimens were reduced at a constant crosshead speed of 0.5 cm/sec. (0.2 in./sec.) to reductions between 20 and 70 percent. Thus, the strain rates in the hydraulic press trials were of the order of 1 sec.$^{-1}$. In both sets of trials, the effect of dwell time on the bottom die (prior to deformation) on shear band development was also established. The dwell times were 0 or 10 sec. for the mechanical press trials and 4 or 14 sec. for the ones in the hydraulic press. The 4 sec. longer dwell times in the hydraulic press resulted primarily from the ram position at the commencement of testing, which was approximately 2 cm. (0.8 in.) above the top of the specimen.

FLOW LOCALIZATION DURING THE SIDEPRESSING OF α + β MICROSTRUCTURE Ti-6242Si—MECHANICAL PRESS DEFORMATION RATE

Flow localization in the form of shear bands was found to be very common in nonisothermally sidepressed specimens of Ti-6242Si.

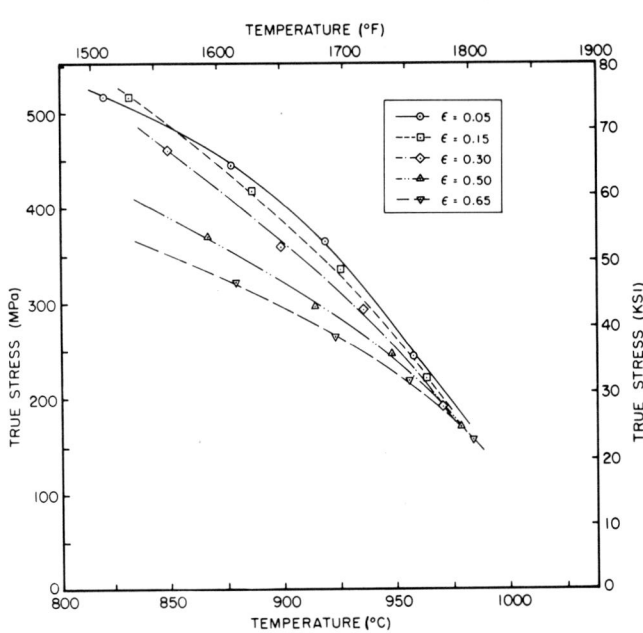

Figure 4.4. Flow stress versus temperature plot for β microstructure Ti-6242Si deformed at a strain rate of 10 sec.$^{-1}$. Data have been corrected for the effects of deformation heating.[6]

The severity of these shear bands was dependent on specimen preheat temperature, die temperature, dwell time, and working speed. However, the occurrence of shear bands in the two different microstructures was similar for identical specimen preheat temperatures and processing conditions. Thus, only the results for the α + β microstructure will be presented. For the die temperatures and dwell times used,

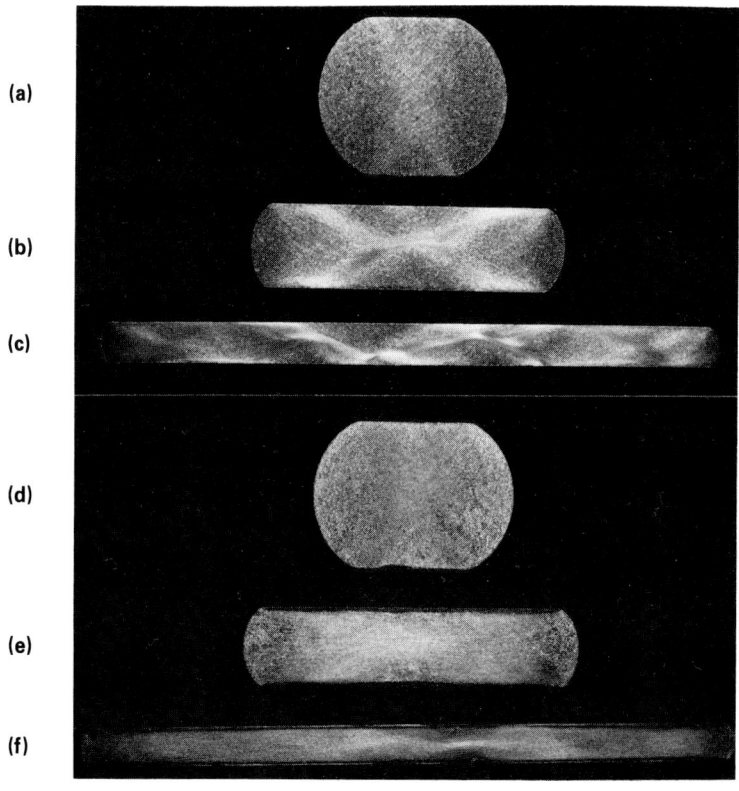

Figure 4.5. Transverse metallographic sections of α + β microstructure Ti-6242Si specimens nonisothermally sidepressed in a mechanical press ($\dot{\varepsilon} \approx 30$ sec.$^{-1}$).[2] Sample preheat temperatures, T_S, die temperatures, T_D, dwell times, t_D, and percent reductions, R, were the following: (a) T_S = 913 °C (1675 °F), T_D = 191 °C (375 °F), t_D = 0 sec., R = 14. (b) T_S = 913 °C (1675 °F), T_D = 191 °C (375 °F), t_D = 0 sec., R = 54. (c) T_S = 913 °C (1675 °F), T_D = 191 °C (375 °F), t_D = 0 sec., R = 77. (d) T_S = 982 °C (1800 °F), T_D = 191 °C (375 °F), t_D = 0 sec., R = 21. (e) T_S = 982 °C (1800 °F), T_D = 191 °C (375 °F), t_D = 0 sec., R = 57. (f) T_S = 982 °C (1800 °F), T_D = 191 °C (375 °F), t_D = 0 sec., R = 79.

it was found that certain preheat temperatures (e.g., 913 °C or 1675 °F) led to the occurrence of shear bands in sidepressings made in the mechanical press and the use of others (e.g., 982 °C or 1800 °F) did not (Figure 4.5). To understand this observation, it should be remembered that contact times are relatively short in this type of equipment and hence the amount of heat transfer is small. Furthermore, during the sidepressing of round bars between flat dies, the contact area is initially a line; it increases to substantial amounts only near the end of deformation. For these reasons, the temperature gradients that are generated are moderate to small, and by forging in the range where the flow stress is not too temperature sensitive (e.g., 982 °C or 1800 °F), both flow stress gradients and shear band formation can be avoided (Figures 4.5 d, e, and f). However, because no shear bands are observed when $\alpha + \beta$ microstructure Ti-6242Si is isothermally sidepressed at 913 °C (1675 °F), but they *are* observed when it is nonisothermally sidepressed using the same workpiece temperature but with a die temperature of 191 °C (375 °F), the localization of plastic flow in the latter case must be attributed to the temperature (and flow stress) gradients developed. Furthermore, in nonisothermal sidepressing, the flow can be expected to localize in the form of shear bands for the same reason that shear bands, rather than localized bulges, form in isothermal sidepressing (i.e., because a plane-strain deformation path is followed). Because of this and the fact that the die-workpiece contact area is small at the beginning of deformation, well-defined chill zones like those seen in nonisothermal *upsetting* are not found in specimens nonisothermally sidepressed.

Metallography on specimens deformed different amounts has also established that the detailed mode of flow localization in shear bands in nonisothermal sidepressing is indeed identical to the manner in which they develop in isothermal sidepressing. This mechanism is illustrated in Figures 4.5 a, b, and c and is shown schematically in Figure 3.16. In both nonisothermal and isothermal sidepressing, shear bands began as regions of intense, localized deformation in the form of *x*'s, patterns that are of the same form as the slip lines or velocity discontinuities in the slip-line field solutions for plane-strain sidepressing. Also, as in the isothermal case, the legs of the *x*'s rotate away from the forging axis, and flat regions of intense deformation are formed at the center of the sidepressings. With still further deformation, these "flats" bow toward one of the die surfaces.

The effect of the various process variables on shear band development can also be discerned from the metallographic sections. Increasing the die temperature decreases the amount of heat transfer between the dies and workpiece and thus decreases the severity of the observed shear bands (Figure 4.6). In contrast, increasing the dwell time on the dies (prior to deformation) tends to slightly increase the severity of localization of the observed shear bands (Figure 4.7). This effect is most striking when the specimen is preheated to a temperature, such as 982 °C (1800 °F), at which shear banding can be avoided with a short dwell time (Figure 4.5) and at which shear banding is noticeable with a long dwell time (Figure 4.7). Although the load-stroke data are not significantly affected by times as long as 10 sec.,[2] for an alloy such as Ti-6242, with such a sharply temperature-dependent flow stress at typical forging temperatures, the small amount of localized chilling prior to deformation sets up sufficient temperature and flow stress gradients to cause shear bands to form in specimens preheated to 982 °C (1800 °F).

FLOW LOCALIZATION DURING THE SIDEPRESSING OF α + β MICROSTRUCTURE Ti-6242Si—HYDRAULIC PRESS DEFORMATION RATE

Shear bands were also common in α + β microstructure sidepressings forged nonisothermally at low working speeds in a hydraulic press. At low reductions, the morphology of the shear bands was analogous to that observed for mechanical press forgings (Figure 4.8). At moderate to large reductions, however, the hydraulic press

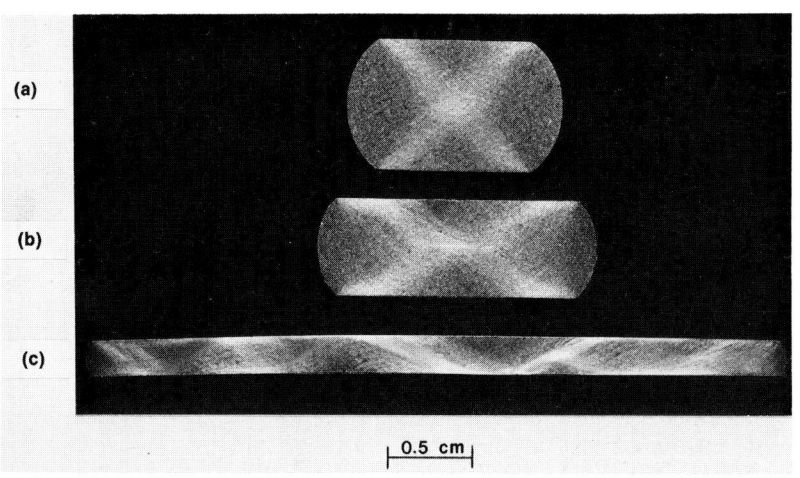

Figure 4.6. Transverse metallographic sections of α + β microstructure Ti-6242Si specimens nonisothermally sidepressed in a mechanical press ($\dot{\varepsilon} \approx 30$ sec.$^{-1}$).[2] Sample preheat temperature: 913 °C (1675 °F), die temperature: 343 °C (650 °F), dwell time: 0 sec. Reductions are (a) 30 percent, (b) 48 percent, and (c) 80 percent.

forgings developed cracks along the shear bands. Moreover, unlike the mechanical press forgings, the shear bands (and shear cracks) could not be avoided by preheating the samples to 982 °C (1800 °F) and using short dwell times (Figure 4.9).

A comparison of the load-stroke data for hydraulic and mechanical press forging makes it apparent that much higher loads are required for the slower equipment. This effect can be ascribed to the

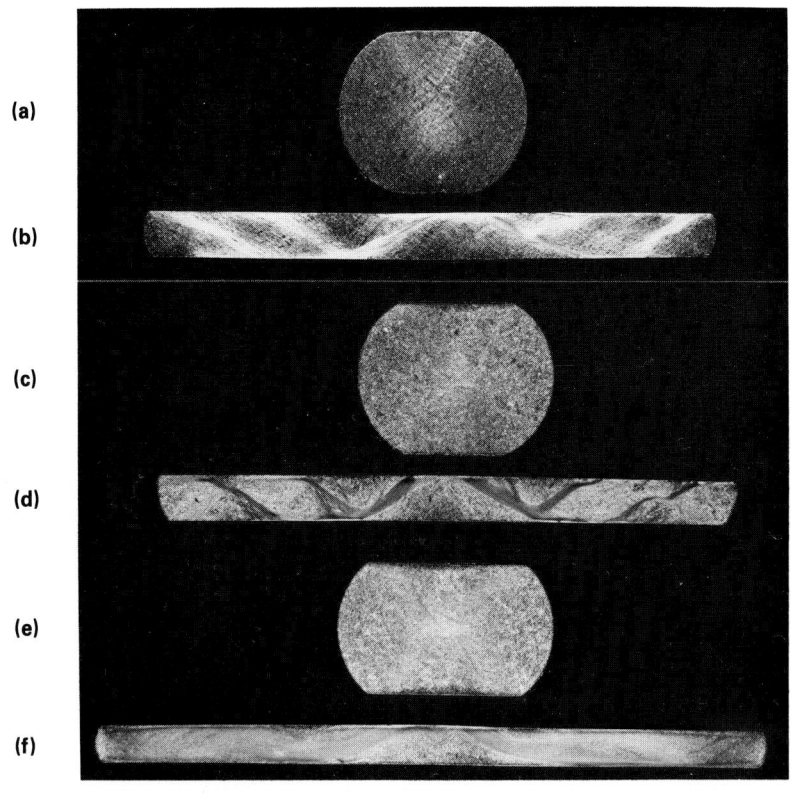

Figure 4.7. Transverse metallographic sections of $\alpha + \beta$ microstructure Ti-6242Si specimens nonisothermally sidepressed in a mechanical press ($\dot{\varepsilon} \approx 30$ sec.$^{-1}$).[2] Sample preheat temperatures, T_S, die temperatures, T_D, dwell times, t_D, and percent reductions, R, were the following: (a) $T_S = 913$ °C (1675 °F), $T_D = 191$ °C (375 °F), $t_D = 10$ sec., R = 13. (b) $T_S = 913$ °C (1675 °F), $T_D = 191$ °C (375 °F), $t_D = 10$ sec., R = 75. (c) $T_S = 982$ °C (1800 °F), $T_D = 191$ °C (375 °F), $t_D = 10$ sec., R = 18. (d) T_S 982 °C (1800 °F), $T_D = 191$ °C (375 °F), $t_D = 10$ sec., R = 76. (e) $T_S = 982$ °C (1800 °F), $T_D = 343$ °C (650 °F), $t_D = 10$ sec., R = 29. (f) $T_S = 982$ °C (1800 °F), $T_D = 343$ °C (650 °F), $t_D = 10$ sec., R = 79.

greater amount of chilling taking place in the hydraulic press combined with the sharp temperature dependence of the flow stress. Furthermore, when the effects of working speed and dwell time are compared, it appears that the former has a much larger influence on working load. Thus, it is evident that most of the heat transfer and chilling occurs during deformation and not during the dwell time. If this were not the case, the working load and shear band severity for hydraulic press forging with a 4 sec. dwell (deformation time = 0 to 1.5 sec.) would be expected to be less (because of the lower strain rate) than for mechanical press forging with a 10 sec. dwell (deformation time < 0.5 sec.).

A somewhat more quantitative explanation of the more severe shear banding and shear cracking in slow hydraulic press forming of

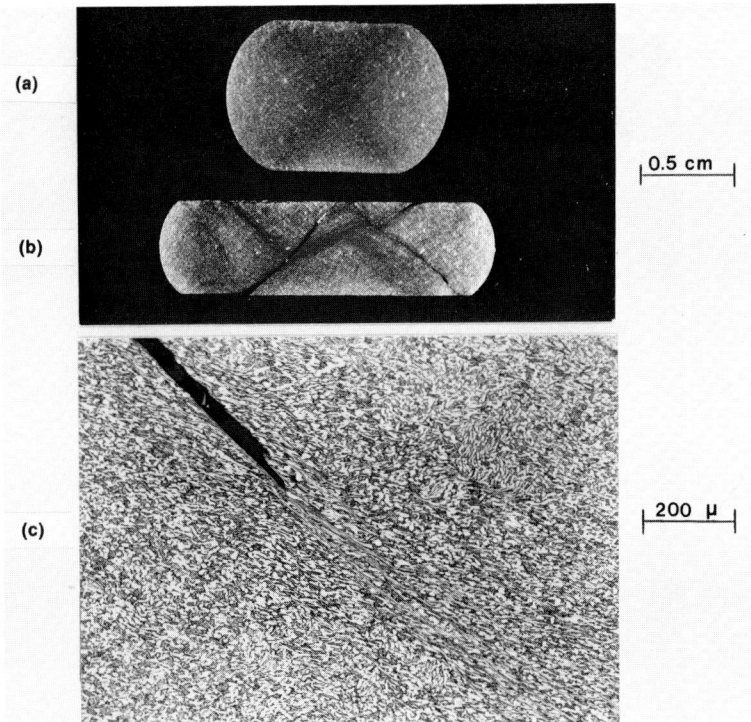

Figure 4.8. (a, b) Transverse metallographic sections and (c) micrograph of region with shear band and crack from section shown in (b) of α + β microstructure Ti-6242Si specimens nonisothermally sidepressed in a hydraulic press ($\dot{\varepsilon} \approx 1$ sec.$^{-1}$).[2] Preheat temperature: 913 °C (1675 °F), die temperature: 191 °C (375 °F), dwell time: 14 sec. Reductions are (a) 25 percent and (b) 53 percent.

α + β microstructure Ti-6242Si can be obtained from process simulations. Such simulations corroborate the conclusion that working at the low rates typical of hydraulic press forging leads to larger temperature gradients in the workpiece and that these larger gradients develop at lower reductions.[2] Moreover, the simulations show that the chilling in hydraulic press forging can lower the temperature of the workpiece into the regime of inherently low workability, namely T < 760 °C (1400 °F).[9] Thus, workpiece chilling, largely during the deformation interval, is the principal cause of the cracking observed in hydraulic press forgings (Figures 4.8 and 4.9).

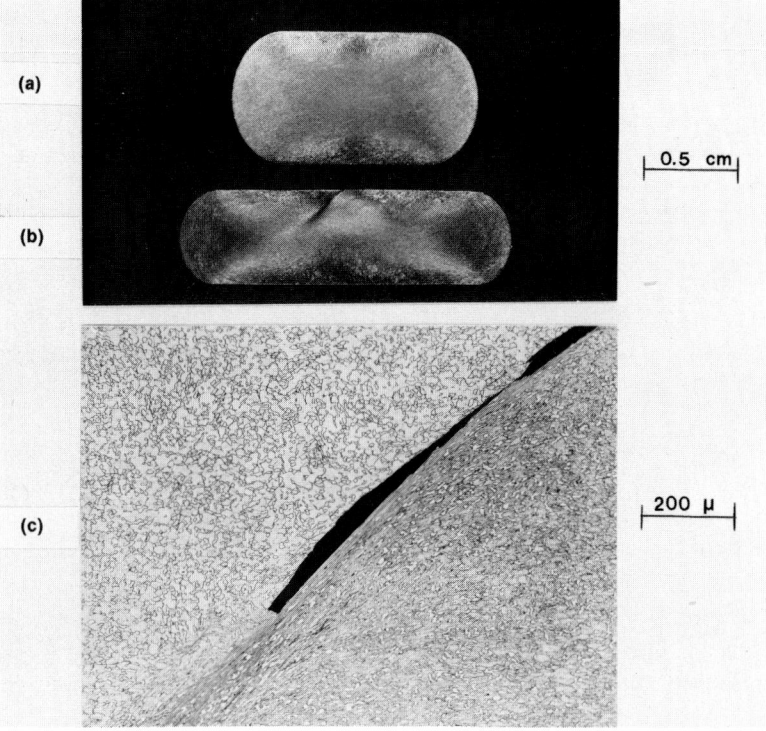

Figure 4.9. (a, b) Transverse metallographic sections and (c) micrograph of region with shear band and crack from section shown in (b) of α + β microstructure Ti-6242Si specimens nonisothermally sidepressed in a hydraulic press ($\dot{\varepsilon} \approx$ 1 sec.$^{-1}$).[2] Sample preheat temperature: 982 °C (1800 °F), die temperature: 343 °C (650 °F), dwell time: 4 sec. Reductions are (a) 33 percent and (b) 52 percent.

OTHER SHEAR BAND OBSERVATIONS—α + β MICROSTRUCTURE BLADE FORGING[10]

The following example also illustrates the effect of nonisothermal working conditions on the generation of shear bands in plane-strain forming operations. This concerns the occurrence of shear bands in nonisothermally forged blades of α + β microstructure Ti-6242Si. It demonstrates the continued importance of heat transfer when the forging geometry is somewhat more complicated. It should be noted that the shear bands illustrated in Figure 4.10 for blade forging (α + β microstructure, T_S = 913 °C or 1675 °F, T_D = 191 °C or 375 °F, dwell time 0 sec., equipment-mechanical press) are very similar to those shown in Figures 4.5 a, b, and c for a sidepressing operation in which the processing conditions (T_S, T_D, dwell time, and speed) are otherwise identical. The differences in the exact shapes of the shear bands are related to the geometrical differences through their effects on heat transfer and on the orientation of the zero-extension directions. The gross effects of the die-workpiece temperature difference on heat

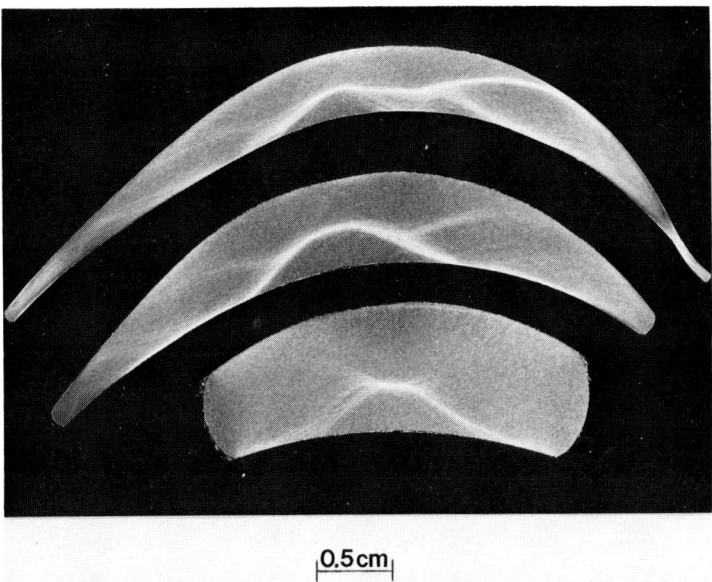

Figure 4.10. Transverse metallographic sections of nonisothermally forged α + β microstructure Ti-6242Si blades using cylindrical preforms. Forgings were done in a mechanical press ($\dot{\varepsilon} \approx 20$ sec.$^{-1}$). Preheat temperature: 913 °C (1675 °F), die temperature: 191 °C (375 °F), dwell time: 0 sec.[10]

transfer and thus on flow localization are nevertheless apparent in this case, as they are in sidepressing.

Flow Localization in Torsion

ANALYSIS

In Chapter 3, flow localization during the torsion of round bars was discussed in the context of the flow localization parameter and isothermal deformation conditions. In other words, it was assumed that the tendency towards strain concentration could be estimated without regard to any heat transfer effects. Such an assumption is most likely to be valid at very high and very low strain rates. At moderate strain rates, however, heat generation and transfer effects must be taken into account because of the axial temperature (and hence flow stress) gradients that are established as a result of uneven deformation heating (due to the presence of defects), as well as the conduction of deformation heat into the colder shoulders of a torsion specimen. The analysis for torsion, therefore, follows along lines similar to that presented for nonisothermal upsetting earlier in this chapter. It involves the development of an equilibrium equation, based on axial *torque* in the case of torsion, and the derivation of a relation to describe heat transfer. Approaches of this type have been studied extensively by Canova and Jonas, Rauch, Merzer, Litonski, and Costin et al.[11-15]

The torque equilibrium equation was presented before (Equation 3.45). A slightly modified form, which gives insight into the development of flow localization in the presence of variations in the outer radius $r_s = R = R(z)$ (i.e., geometric imperfections), can be derived very easily. At a fixed time, it is

$$\left(\frac{\partial \ln M}{\partial z}\right)\bigg|_t = \left(\frac{\partial \ln M}{\partial \theta}\right)\bigg|_{\dot\theta,T,R} \left(\frac{\partial \theta}{\partial z}\right)\bigg|_t + \left(\frac{\partial \ln M}{\partial \ln \dot\theta}\right)\bigg|_{\theta,T,R} \left(\frac{\partial \ln \dot\theta}{\partial z}\right)\bigg|_t$$

$$+ \left(\frac{\partial \ln M}{\partial T}\right)\bigg|_{\theta,\dot\theta,R} \left(\frac{\partial T}{\partial z}\right)\bigg|_t$$

$$+ \left(\frac{\partial \ln M}{\partial \ln R}\right)\bigg|_{\theta,\dot\theta,T} \left(\frac{d\ln R}{dz}\right) = 0 \quad . \tag{4.6}$$

The quantities M, θ, $\dot\theta$, and T have the same definitions as before, namely, torque (or moment), twist, twist rate, and temperature, respectively. All except torque are functions of the axial coordinate, taken to be z here. Equation (4.6) can be simplified somewhat by defining (1) $(\partial \ln M/\partial \theta)|_{\dot\theta,T,R} \equiv G_i$, (2) $(\partial \ln M/\partial \ln \dot\theta)|_{\theta,T,R} = m_i \approx m$, the conventional strain-rate sensitivity index, (3) $(\partial \ln M/\partial T)|_{\theta,\dot\theta,R} = \phi$, and (4) $(\partial \ln M/\partial \ln R)|_{\theta,\dot\theta,T} = \Delta$. Further, the quantities G_i, $m_i \approx m$, and ϕ, although material properties, are functions of deformation, deformation rate, and temperature, and thus are functions of θ, $\dot\theta$, and T, which vary during a torsion experiment. The value of Δ is rigorously equal to 4 during elastic deformation and decreases to between 3 and 3.5 during plastic flow. It will be assumed that it is equal to 3, which is sufficiently precise for the present purpose. Equation (4.6) thus becomes:

$$0 = m\left(\frac{\partial \ln \dot\theta}{\partial z}\right)\bigg|_t + G_i\left(\frac{\partial \theta}{\partial z}\right)\bigg|_t + \phi\left(\frac{\partial T}{\partial z}\right)\bigg|_t + 3\frac{d\ln R}{dz} \qquad (4.7)$$

Defining $\lambda_t = (\partial\theta/\partial z)|_t$, and noting that

$$\left(\frac{\partial \ln \dot\theta}{\partial z}\right)\bigg|_t = \frac{1}{\dot\theta}\left(\frac{\partial \dot\theta}{\partial z}\right)\bigg|_t = \frac{1}{\dot\theta}\left(\frac{\partial \theta}{\partial t \partial z}\right)\bigg|_{z,t} = \left(\frac{\partial(\partial\theta/\partial z)|_t}{\partial \theta}\right)\bigg|_z = \lambda'_t \qquad (4.8)$$

the governing equilibrium/differential equation reduces to

$$0 = m\lambda'_t + G_i\lambda_t + \phi u + 3\delta \quad, \qquad (4.9)$$

where $\mu \equiv (\partial T/\partial z)|_t$ and $\delta = d\ln R/dz$.

The rigorous heat transfer equation should include conduction and convection effects. However, for the twist rates at which flow localization usually occurs and for typical specimen geometries, convection may be overlooked. Insofar as conduction is concerned, the treatment may be either strictly axial or three-dimensional (axial and radial). Rauch, Canova, and Jonas have shown, however, that the application of the simpler one-dimensional axial heat conduction analysis provides results very close to the more rigorous two-dimensional one. In this instance, the temperature T which is calculated is an average over the cross section. By analogy with Equation (3.64), the rate at which heat is generated is given by

$$\frac{dT}{dt}(r) = \frac{0.95\,[\tau(r)]\dot\Gamma(r)}{\rho c} = \frac{0.95\,[\tau(r)](r\dot\theta)}{\rho c\,\ell} \quad, \qquad (4.10)$$

where ρ, c, τ, Γ, and ℓ have the same definitions as in Chapter 3. By multiplying by $2\pi r dr$ and integrating the last expression, a relation for the average rate of temperature change at a given axial position, due to deformation heating, is obtained:

$$\frac{dT}{dt} = \frac{0.95\,\dot{\theta}\,M}{\pi R^2 \rho c\,\ell} \quad , \tag{4.11}$$

in which the following relation between M and τ has been used:

$$M = 2\pi \int_0^R \tau r^2 dr \quad . \tag{4.12}$$

With Equation (4.11), the one-dimensional heat-conduction relation can be stated as:[16]

$$\left(\frac{\partial T}{\partial t}\right)\bigg|_z = \frac{0.95\,\dot{\theta}M}{\pi R^2 \rho c\ell} + \frac{k}{\rho c}\left(\frac{\partial^2 T}{\partial z^2}\right)\bigg|_t \quad . \tag{4.13}$$

Equations (4.9) and (4.13) can be used to study the kinetics of flow localization with the aid of an evolutionary law for the torque and the specification of boundary conditions. The evolutionary law determines dlnM/dt and is the temporal version of Equations (4.6) and (4.7):

$$\frac{d\ln M}{dt} = m\left(\frac{\partial \ln\dot{\theta}}{\partial t}\right)\bigg|_z + G_i\,\dot{\theta} + \phi\left(\frac{\partial T}{\partial t}\right)\bigg|_z \quad , \tag{4.14}$$

where dlnR/dt is assumed equal to zero. Boundary conditions consist of the specification of the initial temperature, or temperature field T(z), and the imposed twist rate (in revolutions per second), denoted by RPS:

$$RPS = \frac{1}{2\pi}\int_0^z \frac{\dot{\theta}(z)}{\ell} dz \quad , \tag{4.15}$$

which is usually assumed to be constant.

APPLICATION OF FLOW LOCALIZATION ANALYSIS FOR TORSION

The set of equations (4.9), (4.13), (4.14), and (4.15) specify completely the boundary-value problem for the torsion of round bars with (or without) a geometric defect in terms of a radius deficiency. Canova and Jonas described a simple numerical procedure by which the coupled equations can be solved.[11] It consists of dividing the torsion specimen into a number of slices N (each of thickness Δz); some of these slices are used to characterize the initial radius defect, as well as the nondeforming shoulders. Assuming that the temperature field is uniform prior to deformation, both μ (equal to $\partial T/\partial z$) and λ_t (equal to $\partial \dot\theta/\partial z$) are equal to zero at time t = 0. Because of this, the equilibrium equation (Equation 4.9) gives the twist rate gradient. In terms of $\dot\theta$ and R for the ith and (i + 1)st slice, this equation is:

$$\ln(\dot\theta_{i+1}/\dot\theta_i) = -\frac{3}{m}\ln(R_{i+1}/R_i) \quad , \quad (4.16)$$

or

$$\dot\theta_{i+1} = \dot\theta_i \left(\frac{R_{i+1}}{R_i}\right)^{-3/m} . \quad (4.17)$$

The finite difference formulation of Equation (4.15) is now applied:

$$\text{RPS} = \frac{1}{2\pi}\left[\frac{\dot\theta_1}{\ell}\Delta z + \frac{\dot\theta_1}{\ell}\left(\frac{R_2}{R_1}\right)^{-3/m}\Delta z + \frac{\dot\theta_1}{\ell}\left(\frac{R_3}{R_1}\right)^{-3/m}\Delta z \right.$$
$$\left. + \ldots + \frac{\dot\theta_1}{\ell}\left(\frac{R_N}{R_1}\right)^{-3/m}\Delta z\right] .$$

Alternatively, the above can be expressed as an integral:

$$\text{RPS} = \frac{\dot\theta_1}{2\pi\ell}\int_0^\ell \left(\frac{R(z)}{R_1}\right)^{-3/m} dz \quad , \quad (4.18)$$

a relation which specifies $\dot\theta$ for the first slice and hence $\dot\theta$ for the remaining slices.

Once the initial $\dot\theta$ distribution is calculated, the initial heating rate distribution and thus temperature change during a time increment dt can be estimated from Equation (4.13), with $\partial^2 T/\partial z^2$ set to zero and using a torque M that introduces a small but finite amount of plastic flow at the imperfection site. This M can be estimated from simple relationships between M and τ, such as Equation (2.29) and knowledge of the calculated twist rate and initial specimen temperature. By these means, the initial temperature and twist and twist rate gradients are estimated. The twist gradient also allows determination of the shear strain distribution along the specimen gage length.

The second and successive iterations are performed by estimating the change in torque from Equation (4.14) and then determining new twist rate and twist gradients from Equations (4.9) and (4.15) and a new temperature gradient from Equation (4.13). In this way, the development of twist, twist rate, shear strain, and temperature gradients can be determined from the knowledge of the material properties (m, G_i, ϕ, etc.) and the imposed boundary and initial conditions. The procedure is entirely similar when no initial imperfection is present in that, during the first time increment, θ is taken to be uniform, and the heat generation in the gage section is estimated from Equation (4.10). During the second time increment, a temperature gradient ($\equiv \mu$) is established along the gage length (due to heat conduction into the shoulders) using Equation (4.13). The corresponding twist gradient is determined from Equations (4.9) and (4.15), and the remainder of the procedure is carried out as in the case involving a geometric defect.

Although the application of the above procedure requires the use of a digital computer, the trends to be expected have been summarized by Jonas and his co-workers as well as by Merzer.[11-13] Jonas *et al.* treated the case of the torsion of a specimen with a geometric defect. In this instance, two extremes in behavior were analyzed—an isothermal case and a high-rate case. For the isothermal case, it was assumed that no temperature (or flow stress) gradient was developed because of either extremely high k, very low testing speeds, insensitivity of the flow stress to temperature, or a combination of these factors. Under these conditions, it was determined that no flow law could lead to *unbounded* flow localization. When a material exhibits flow softening (as in the case of Ti-6242Si with a β microstructure tested at substransus hot working temperatures), measurable strain concentrations occur but eventually stabilize when the flow softening disappears. In the high-rate case, temperature gradients are developed, which in conjunction with the temperature sensitivity, ϕ, promote unbounded flow localization.* The unbounded flow concentration may follow a period of quasi-stabilization at the defect, which results from the ability of increasing strain rate and rate sensitivity effects to offset initial thermal softening influences. By and large, Merzer confirmed these latter trends and established that flow localization can occur at high strain rates in the *absence* of a geometric

---

*The localization of flow during high-speed torsion is discussed further in Appendix C.

defect, merely as a result of temperature gradients set up by heat transfer from the gage section to the shoulders of test specimens. Such a finding is analogous to the effect of shoulder and fillet deformation on the localization of flow during the tension testing of round bars without defects,[17] which is discussed in the next chapter.

The above trends were verified in the detailed experimental and theoretical investigation of Rauch.[12] Two materials were tested in torsion—304 stainless steel (deformed at room temperature) and Ti-6242Si (deformed at hot working temperatures). The 304 was used as a model material to verify the validity of analyses that incorporate solely axial conduction on the one hand and axial and radial conduction on the other. The initial torsion tests were run on "perfect" cy-

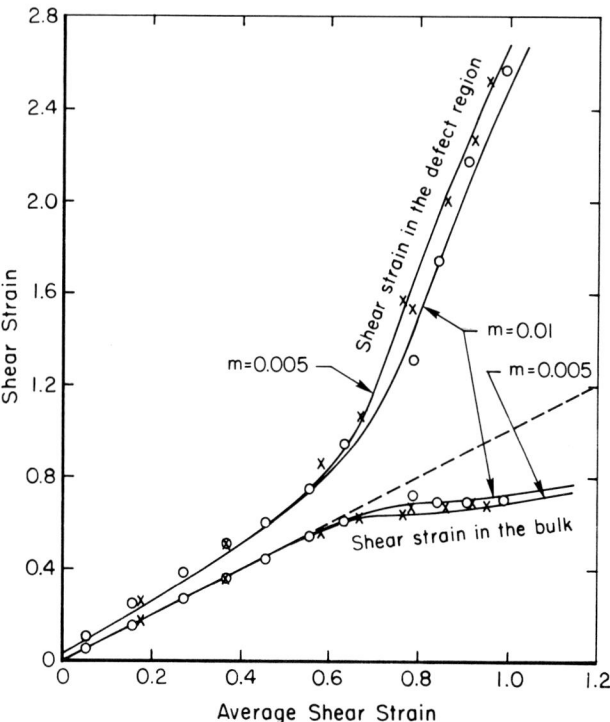

Figure 4.11. Comparison of experimentally observed localization (data points) in 304 stainless steel torsion tests at room temperature with results of the simulation corrected for radius change (solid lines). The simulations were run with two rate sensitivities, $m = 0.01$ and $m = 0.005$, whose values bounded those measured in torsion tests on specimens without geometric defects. Average surface shear strain rate was approximately 0.05 sec.$^{-1}$ in both experiments and simulations.[12]

lindrical samples, and the flow behavior results were analyzed to obtain analytic expressions to approximate the material parameters. Then, localization during torsion was simulated using these material parameters for samples displaying an initial 8 percent area defect at the center of the specimen. Torsion tests were run on specimens of the same design (i.e., with an identical geometric defect) for comparison with the predicted results. After correcting for radius and length changes during torsion, the two sets of results were found to agree very well (Figure 4.11). The effect of including radial heat transfer in the calculation was shown to have a negligible influence on the development of the localization.

The titanium alloy was twisted at temperatures between 840 °C (1545 °F) and 940 °C (1725 °F) and at strain rates of 0.001 to 1 sec.$^{-1}$. Both the equiaxed alpha ($\alpha + \beta$) and transformed beta (β) microstructures were investigated. The Ti-6242Si simulations revealed

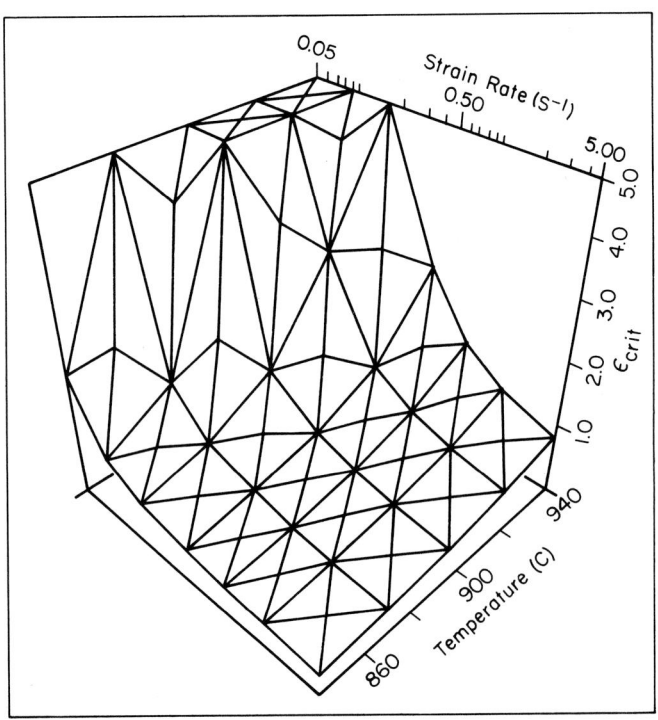

Figure 4.12. Dependence of the critical condition (defined in terms of ε_{crit}) on testing temperature and strain rate for a 15 °C (27 °F) initial gradient in temperature in torsion tests on Ti-6242Si with β microstructure.[12]

the sharply detrimental effect of temperature gradients on the homogeneity of the deformation. Also, it was concluded that relatively low forming temperatures promoted instabilities, but to a lesser extent than high strain rates. The effect of the former was related to the greater amount of deformation heating, while the decrease in the rate sensitivity with increasing strain rate, as well as the lack of time for temperature equalization, was used to explain the influence of the latter on the rate of localization. These dependences were illustrated with workability maps that depict the critical level of deformation for localization as a function of strain rate and temperature. Critical strains were defined as those at which the rate of change of strain outside the region of localization with respect to that within the localization is small (e.g., 0.05). Figure 4.12 shows a typical map for β microstructure Ti-6242Si in which the "defect" initiating the localization process was a temperature gradient of 15 °C (27 °F) over the gage length. The simulation formalism, however, allows for the construction of such workability maps for specimens containing other kinds of defects (e.g., strength and geometric) as well.

Summary

The discussion in this chapter has focused on the localization of plastic flow in nonisothermal hot working operations. In this type of situation, heat transfer between the tooling and workpiece sets up temperature gradients in the latter. The amount of heat transfer is determined primarily by the difference in temperature between the tooling and workpiece and by the time of intimate contact. Since, for a given deformation, the contact time depends on the working speed, the choice of equipment for performing a particular shaping operation has a strong effect on the degree of flow localization or even on the ability to form the desired part without fracture.

The analysis of flow localization in nonisothermal metalworking operations requires knowledge of the workpiece mechanical and thermal properties and the availability of a heat transfer model to predict the temperature fields that are generated during deformation. These heat transfer models are fairly easy to develop for straightforward deformation geometries (e.g., simple upsetting), but generally require sophisticated finite-difference or finite-element computer codes for greater accuracy, or when more complex geometries are under investigation.

The effect of heat transfer on flow localization in nonisothermal metalworking operations can be studied via the torsion test. In this test, deformation heat generated in the gage section can cause thermal gradients as the heat is dissipated into the nondeforming shoulders. The rate of flow localization therefore depends on the deformation rate, specimen geometry, and thermal and mechanical properties of the specimen. Although the rate of localization can be increased by the presence of geometric or other kinds of defects, it has been found that strain concentrations can still be developed in nominally perfect specimens solely because of heat transfer and temperature gradient effects.

References

[1] S.L. Semiatin, G.D. Lahoti, and S.I. Oh: *Material Behavior Under High Stress and Ultrahigh Loading Rates*, Plenum Press, New York, 1983, p. 119.
[2] S.L. Semiatin and G.D. Lahoti: *Met. Trans. A*, 1983, vol. 14A, p. 105.
[3] E.W. Collings: Unpublished Research, Battelle Columbus Laboratories, Columbus, OH, 1980.
[4] T. Altan, F.W. Boulger, J.R. Becker, N. Akgerman, and H.J. Henning: *Forging Equipment, Materials, and Practices*, Ch. 1, Metals and Ceramics Information Center, Battelle Columbus Laboratories, Columbus, OH, 1973.
[5] M.N. Janardhana and S.K. Biswas: *Inter. J. Mech. Sci.*, 1979, vol. 21, p. 699.
[6] S.L. Semiatin, G.D. Lahoti, and T. Altan: *Process Modeling: Fundamentals and Applications to Metals*, T. Altan, H. Burte, H. Gegel, and A. Male, eds., p. 387, ASM, Metals Park, OH, 1980.
[7] J.F.W. Bishop: *Quart. J. Mech. and Appl. Math.*, 1956, vol. 9, p. 236.
[8] S.L. Semiatin and G.D. Lahoti: *Met. Trans. A*, 1981, vol. 12A, p. 1705.
[9] C.C. Chen: Report RD-77-110, Wyman-Gordon Company, North Grafton, MA, October, 1977.
[10] S.L. Semiatin: Unpublished Research, Battelle Columbus Laboratories, Columbus, OH, 1982.
[11] G. Canova and J.J. Jonas: Unpublished Research, McGill University, Montreal, Canada, 1981.
[12] E. Rauch: M. Eng. Thesis, Department of Mining and Metallurgical Engineering, McGill University, Montreal, Canada, 1983.
[13] A.M. Merzer: *J. Mech. Phys. Solids*, 1982, vol. 30, p. 323.
[14] J. Litonski: *Bull. Polish Acad. of Sci.*, 1977, vol. 25, p. 7.
[15] L.S. Costin, E.E. Crisman, R.H. Hawley, and J. Duffy: Technical Report NSF 18532/7, Division of Engineering, Brown University, Providence, RI, January, 1979.
[16] H.S. Carslaw and J.C. Jaeger: *Conduction of Heat in Solids*, Clarendon Press, Oxford, 1959.
[17] A.K. Ghosh: *Met. Trans. A*, 1977, vol. 8A, p. 1221.

INSTABILITY AND FLOW LOCALIZATION IN UNIAXIAL TENSION

In the previous chapters, the occurrence of flow localization in bulk forming operations was discussed in some detail. The most common forms of strain concentration under such compressive loading conditions are localized bulges and shear bands. In this chapter, flow localization under tensile loading conditions is introduced through the analysis of the necking process in round bars and sheets during uniaxial tension testing. In these cases, the development of necks controls the amount of useful deformation that can be imposed prior to failure, provided fracture does not intercede. The discussion will concentrate on the material properties that control necking behavior and will serve as an introduction to the analysis of flow localization under biaxial tensile conditions. The latter occurs in sheet forming, for example, and will be reviewed in the next chapter. For simplicity, the effects of deformation heating on flow stability and flow localization will be neglected throughout this chapter.

Tension Testing of Round Bars—Instability

The oldest and most common test for the characterization of workability or formability, the round bar tension test, is an appropriate starting point for the analysis of flow localization under tensile loading conditions. The necking phenomenon in this test has come under extensive experimental and theoretical investigation. Probably the first treatment of tensile instability, Considère's analysis[1] in the nineteenth century is fundamental to the understanding of necking in materials that exhibit negligible rate and temperature sensitivity.

CONSIDÈRE'S ANALYSIS[1]

The basic premise of the Considère analysis is that the onset of necking occurs at the point of load instability, which corresponds to the attainment of a load maximum. In a rate and temperature insensitive material, i.e., one whose flow curve is independent of deformation rate or temperature, the net axial load P is simply $P = \sigma A$, where σ is the axial true stress (σ_1), and A is the instantaneous cross-sectional area. Thus, the instability occurs when

$$dP = 0 = d(\sigma A) = \sigma dA + A d\sigma \quad . \tag{5.1}$$

Since $dA/A = -d\varepsilon_1$, or simply $-d\varepsilon$ for conciseness, the moment of instability corresponds to the point at which

$$\frac{d\sigma}{d\varepsilon} = \sigma \quad . \tag{5.2}$$

For a material whose stress-strain curve follows the power-hardening form, $\sigma = K\varepsilon^n$, it is easy to verify that this condition is satisfied at a true axial strain of n. The fact that the n coefficients for most materials at cold working temperatures lie between 0.01 and 0.50 explains why cold working under tensile loading conditions is usually limited to small strains relative to those employed in bulk forming. At hot working temperatures, the rates of strain hardening, as represented by n, are frequently negligible or even negative, and the typical presence of a moderate to large rate sensitivity makes the Considère analysis inapplicable.

Considère also proposed a graphical means of establishing the instability strain. This alternative method employs the definition of the nominal axial strain, e

$$e = \frac{\ell - \ell_o}{\ell_o} \quad , \tag{5.3}$$

where ℓ and ℓ_o are the instantaneous and original lengths of the tensile bar, respectively. Inserting this into Equation (2.35) for ε, the following are obtained:

$$\varepsilon = \ln(1 + e) \quad , \tag{5.4}$$

or

$$d\varepsilon = \frac{de}{1 + e} \quad . \tag{5.5}$$

Thus, the other form for the instability condition (Equation 5.2) is

$$\frac{d\sigma}{de} = \frac{\sigma}{1 + e} \quad , \tag{5.6}$$

and a simple graphical construction on the σ-e plot, which involves drawing a subtangent from the point (ε = −1, σ = 0), enables the instability strain, e_c, to be determined (Figure 5.1).

HART'S ANALYSIS[2]

For a material that exhibits strain hardening *and* strain-rate hardening, an extension of the Considère analysis can be used to predict the strain at maximum load, as well as the strain at the onset of

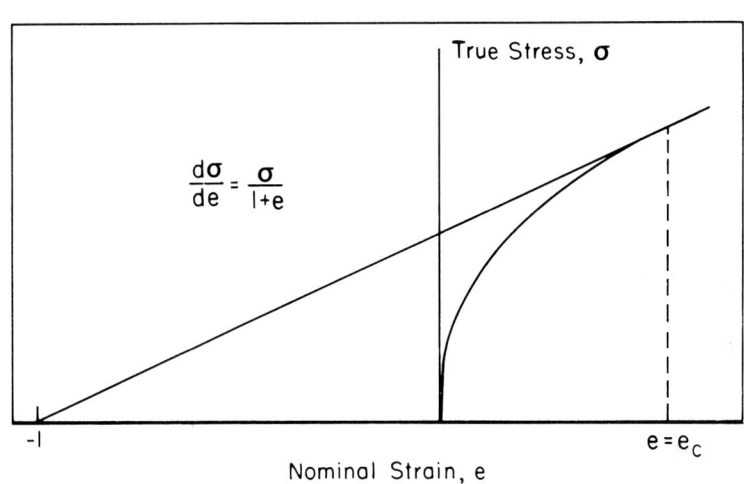

Figure 5.1. Considère construction for determination of the nominal strain at the maximum load in a tensile test, e_c.[1]

Instability and Flow Localization in Uniaxial Tension 151

flow localization. Although these two strains are identical for a rate-insensitive material, the strain associated with the load maximum changes slightly, depending on the crosshead law employed, and the strain for the onset of flow localization is no longer unique, but depends on the parameter (i.e., local extension, strain, or area of cross section) being followed. The effect of introducing the rate sensitivity into the analysis of instability has been discussed in some detail in Chapter 3. Only selected features of this treatment will be summarized here for illustrative purposes.

The practical effect of large positive rate sensitivity is not so much to modify the *onset* of nonuniform flow, but rather to stabilize the deformation that follows the onset, thus enabling substantial useful deformations beyond the load maximum to be attained. Thus, the influence of rate sensitivity when geometric softening is involved (i.e., in tensile deformation) is analogous to its effect during the compressive straining of materials that exhibit flow softening. The analysis that follows is similar to that originally developed by Hart and others,[2-4] but assumes initially that the tensile bar is perfectly homogeneous.*

The starting point of the Hart analysis is Equation (5.1), which, assuming $\sigma = \sigma(\varepsilon, \dot{\varepsilon})$, leads to

$$dP = 0 = \sigma dA + A d\sigma \tag{5.1}$$

or

$$0 = \sigma dA + A\left\{\left(\frac{\partial \sigma}{\partial \varepsilon}\right)\bigg|_{\dot{\varepsilon}} d\varepsilon + \left(\frac{\partial \sigma}{\partial \dot{\varepsilon}}\right)\bigg|_{\varepsilon} d\dot{\varepsilon}\right\} \tag{5.7}$$

Dividing by $A\sigma d\varepsilon$ and defining the strain-hardening coefficient γ to be:

$$\gamma = \frac{1}{\sigma}\left(\frac{\partial \sigma}{\partial \varepsilon}\right)\bigg|_{\dot{\varepsilon},T} , \tag{5.8}$$

Equation (5.7) becomes

$$0 = -1 + \gamma + m\alpha . \tag{5.9}$$

Note that the above definition of γ is equivalent to that given in

---

*This condition is adequate for determining the strains associated with the *load maximum*. Later, for the determination of the onset of rapid *flow localization,* various defects and inhomogeneities will be introduced.

Equation (3.16), but is for isothermal conditions. The parameter $\alpha = \mathrm{dln}\dot{\varepsilon}/\mathrm{d}\varepsilon$ is also the negative of the one given previously, because ε and $\dot{\varepsilon}$ are positive here.

In a constant strain rate tensile test, during which the flow is uniform, the parameter α is identically equal to zero. Hence, the maximum load occurs at $\gamma = 1$, i.e., at the strain defined by Equation (5.2). By contrast, in the more common tensile test run at constant extension rate, $\mathrm{d}\ell/\mathrm{d}t = \dot{\ell} = $ constant, and the load maximum is attained sooner at a larger value of γ. During uniform flow at constant crosshead speed, the value of α is obtained by noting that

$$\alpha = \frac{1}{\dot{\varepsilon}}\frac{\mathrm{d}\dot{\varepsilon}}{\mathrm{d}\varepsilon} = \frac{\ell^2}{\dot{\ell}}\left(\frac{\mathrm{d}\dot{\varepsilon}}{\mathrm{d}\ell}\right) = \frac{\ell^2}{\dot{\ell}}\frac{(-\dot{\ell}\ell^{-2})\mathrm{d}\ell}{\mathrm{d}\ell} = -1 \quad , \tag{5.10}$$

since

$$\mathrm{d}\dot{\varepsilon} = \mathrm{d}(\dot{\ell}\ell^{-1}) = -\dot{\ell}\ell^{-2}\,\mathrm{d}\ell + \ell^{-1}\mathrm{d}\dot{\ell} = -\dot{\ell}\ell^{-2}\mathrm{d}\ell \quad . \tag{5.11}$$

When $\alpha = -1$, Equation (5.9) for the load maximum is

$$\gamma = 1 + m \quad . \tag{5.12}$$

For a power-law hardening material, $\gamma = n/\varepsilon$, so that the strain at load instability is

$$\varepsilon_H = n/(1 + m) \quad . \tag{5.13}$$

Note that this is *smaller* in materials with $m > 0$ than the instability strain for a material with $m = 0$.

Yet a third critical strain can be associated with the load maximum under conditions of constant rate of area reduction $\dot{A}$. In this case, $\mathrm{d}\dot{A}/\mathrm{d}A = 0$, or

$$\frac{\mathrm{d}\dot{A}}{\mathrm{d}A} = \left\{\frac{\mathrm{d}\dot{\varepsilon}}{\mathrm{d}\varepsilon} - \dot{\varepsilon}\right\} = 0 \quad . \tag{5.14}$$

Thus, $\alpha = +1$, and from Equation (5.9), the result

$$\gamma = 1 - m \tag{5.15}$$

is obtained for the maximum load condition. For a power-law hardening material, this relation corresponds to

$$\varepsilon_H = n/(1 - m) \quad , \tag{5.16}$$

or a strain *greater* than the one pertaining to rate-insensitive materials.

Tension Testing of Round Bars—Flow Localization

It should be realized that the simple load instability analyses reviewed above do not give insight into the total useful amount of deformation (e.g., the total elongation) in a round bar tensile test. This is partly because the flow does not generally begin to localize perceptibly into a neck at the point of the load instability as described above. Furthermore, as the neck forms, the strain and strain rate within the neck usually exceed those outside the neck. However, the amount by which the neck strain rate exceeds the bulk strain rate, and therefore the rate of localization, depends on the inherent strain and strain-rate hardening capacities of the material. As demonstrated earlier, necking actually begins in the weakest cross section of the specimen at the initiation of straining.[4] Nevertheless, the rate of necking is very slow and not readily visible until the strain associated with the maximum load is exceeded. In addition, the rate of localization following the maximum load may be slow, leading to large amounts of quasistable flow, whose magnitude is a strong function of the rate sensitivity of the material (Figure 5.2), the size of the imperfection at which the neck grows, and, to a lesser extent, a function of strain-hardening capacity.[5]

The analysis of neck growth in a tensile bar can take a variety of forms. Most of them assume that the length of the neck in the axial direction is much greater than the diameter of the bar. This basic premise forms the basis of the so-called "long wavelength" approximation.[6] With this approximation, the complications inherent in the development of a triaxial stress state within the necked region are avoided, and the entire analysis can be performed in terms of uniaxial stress conditions within, as well as outside, the neck. This assumption is most useful and appropriate in materials with large m (m ≥ 0.1), in which the post-load maximum deformation is large and necking is a rather gradual process. Nevertheless, by performing the full triaxial analysis, it has been shown that a short wavelength neck (i.e., where the axial length of the neck < bar diameter and in which appreciable triaxial tensile stresses are developed) leads to *slower* neck growth than a long wavelength neck, so that the latter are likely to produce failure before the former.[7] Furthermore, as the long wavelength necks in the full triaxial analysis have the same behavior as the simple necks in the uniaxial analysis, the descriptions given in the sections that follow will be restricted to the results of the long wavelength or uniaxial analyses.

LOCALIZATION IN THE PRESENCE OF DEFORMATION DEFECTS—HART/DUNCOMBE/NICHOLS NECKING STRAIN[2, 6, 8]

The analyses of Hart,[2] Duncombe[8] and Nichols[6] provide several useful formulas for the prediction of the total elongation or, more precisely, the limit strain outside the necked region. These analyses begin with a tensile test on a round bar with an initial deformation defect (as may be caused by a "hammer blow"). The most readily understood of these treatments and a good starting point for discussion is Hart's analysis of flow localization in a constant load, constant temperature creep test. Since $P = \sigma A$, $\dot{P} = dP/dt$ (where $t \equiv$ time) is given by

$$0 = \dot{P} = \sigma\dot{A} + A\dot{\sigma} \quad . \tag{5.17}$$

Dividing by P and assuming $\sigma = \sigma(\varepsilon, \dot{\varepsilon})$, the following relation is obtained:

$$0 = \frac{\dot{P}}{P} = \frac{\dot{A}}{A} + \left(\gamma\dot{\varepsilon} + \frac{m\ddot{\varepsilon}}{\dot{\varepsilon}}\right) \quad . \tag{5.18}$$

Further, since $A\ell =$ constant, we have

$$\dot{A}\ell + A\dot{\ell} = 0 \quad , \tag{5.19}$$

and

$$\dot{\varepsilon} = \frac{\dot{\ell}}{\ell} = -\frac{\dot{A}}{A} \quad . \tag{5.20}$$

Differentiating Equation (5.20) with respect to time, we obtain the further relation

$$\ddot{\varepsilon} = \frac{\ddot{\ell}}{\ell} - \left(\frac{\dot{\ell}}{\ell}\right)^2 = -\frac{\ddot{A}}{A} + \frac{\dot{A}^2}{A} \quad . \tag{5.21}$$

With Equations (5.20) and (5.21), Equation (5.18) reduces to

$$0 = \frac{\dot{A}}{A}(1 - \gamma - m) + \frac{\ddot{A}}{\dot{A}} m \quad , \qquad (5.22)$$

or

$$\frac{d\ln\dot{A}}{d\ln A} = \frac{(\gamma - 1 + m)}{m} \quad . \qquad (5.23)$$

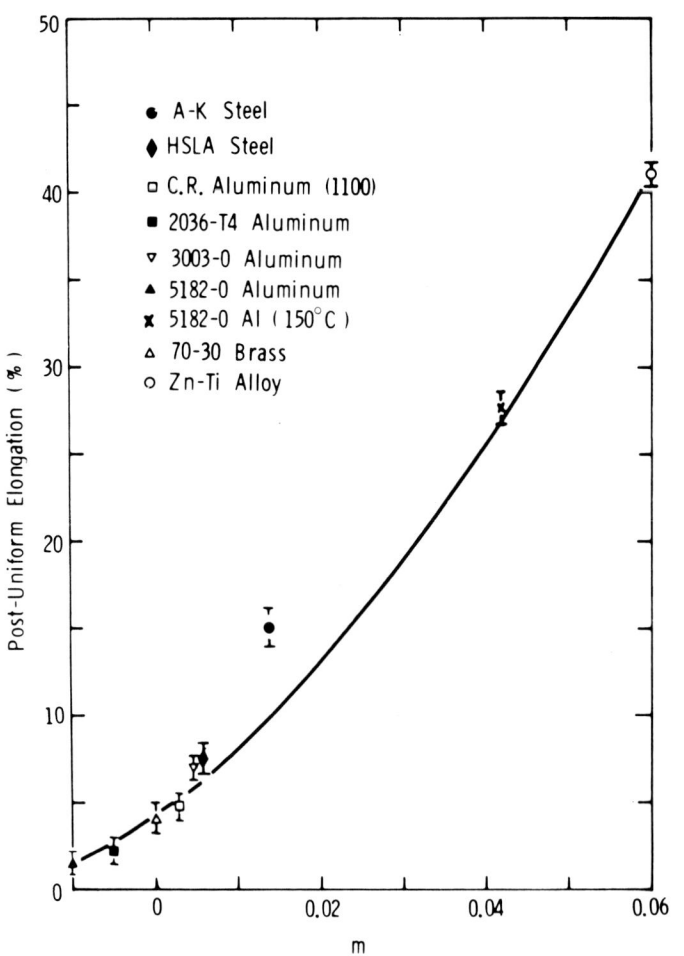

Figure 5.2. Post-uniform elongation (i.e., nominal strain beyond maximum load) for sheet tensile tests as a function of the strain-rate sensitivity parameter, m.[5]

If m is now assumed to be constant and γ is set equal to zero, Equation (5.23) can be integrated to yield

$$\frac{\dot{A}}{\dot{A}_o} = \left(\frac{A_o}{A}\right)^{(1/m)-1} , \qquad (5.24)$$

where A_o and $\dot{A}_o$ represent the initial values of the uniform cross section and rate of change of cross section, and A and $\dot{A}$ are the values of these quantities at some subsequent time t.

The growth of an initial hammer blow inhomogeneity represented by a variation in cross-sectional area δA_o can be followed using Hart's method. This is done by noting that the variation in cross section due to the imperfection can be considered equal to the time rate of change of cross sectional area in the uniform section multiplied by an imaginary time variation δt. This is equivalent to treating the inhomogeneity as a region whose cross section is smaller than that of the uniform part, because it is "ahead" of the latter on the curve $A = A(t)$ by a time interval δt. At a subsequent point in the experiment, the inhomogeneity is assumed, as an approximation, to remain on the *same* $A = A(t)$ curve as the homogeneous region and therefore "ahead" of the uniform part by the same fictitious time interval δt. Under these conditions, $\delta A_o = \dot{A}_o \delta t$, $\delta A = \dot{A} \delta t$, and

$$\frac{\delta A}{\delta A_o} = \frac{\dot{A}}{\dot{A}_o} . \qquad (5.25)$$

Inserting this in Equation (5.24), we obtain an expression that relates successive values of the cross-sectional area imperfection to previous ones and to the imposed evolution of the area $(A_o \to A)$ in the uniform region outside the imperfection:

$$\delta A = \left(\frac{A_o}{A}\right)^{(1/m)-1} \delta A_o . \qquad (5.26)$$

This is an important result and demonstrates the first-order influence of m on the growth of imperfections in cross-sectional area brought about by hammer blows.

A more general relationship relating δA and δA_o, which does away with the $\dot{P} = 0$ and $\gamma = 0$ assumptions in the Hart model, was obtained by Duncombe[8] and Nichols.[6] Not surprisingly, it is similar to Equation (5.26):*

---

*Note that it is only valid over time or strain intervals during which the value of γ can be taken as approximately constant.

$$\delta A = \left(\frac{A_o}{A}\right)^{[(1-\gamma)/m]-1} \delta A_o \quad . \tag{5.27}$$

From this relation, it is seen that a small variation in cross-sectional area will not grow rapidly until

$$\left(\frac{1-\gamma}{m}\right) > 1 \quad ,$$

or

$$\gamma < 1 - m \quad . \tag{5.28}$$

By comparing this to Equation (5.15), which defines the strain at the load maximum, it is evident that deformation imperfections have little effect on the distribution of strain until the Hart strain (Equation 5.15) has been exceeded.

With the aid of Equation (5.27), the cross-sectional area *outside* the necked region, and hence the uniform elongation, can be estimated. This is done by applying Equation (5.27) to the deformation as the uniform cross section goes from $A_o \to A_1 \to A_2 \to \ldots A_f$. We obtain, assuming $\gamma =$ constant,

$$\delta A_1 = \left(\frac{A_o}{A_1}\right)^{[(1-\gamma)/m]-1} \delta A_o \quad , \tag{5.29}$$

$$\delta A_2 = \left(\frac{A_1}{A_2}\right)^{[(1-\gamma)/m]-1} \delta A_1 = \left(\frac{A_o}{A_2}\right)^{(1-\gamma/m)-1} \delta A_o \tag{5.30}$$

$$\vdots$$

$$\delta A_f = A_f = \left(\frac{A_o}{A_f}\right)^{[(1-\gamma)/m]-1} \delta A_o \quad . \tag{5.31}$$

In the last expression, it is assumed that the material necks to a point; thus $\delta A_f = A_f - 0$.* If the definition of the imperfection factor f_o is used,

---

*The choice of zero for the cross-sectional area of the neck at its fracture, rather than some non-zero value, leads to small errors in the predicted value of A_f because of the exponential growth rate of the neck.[6, 9]

$$f_o = \frac{A_o - \delta A_o}{A_o} = 1 - \frac{\delta A_o}{A_o} \quad , \qquad (5.32)$$

or

$$(1 - f_o) A_o = \delta A_o \quad , \qquad (5.33)$$

and an average value of γ (say, the average of γ in the post-uniform elongation region) is used in the above equations, Equation (5.31) reduces to

$$1 = \left(\frac{A_o}{A_f}\right)^{[(1-\gamma)/m]} (1 - f_o) \quad . \qquad (5.34)$$

From volume constancy, the nominal (engineering) strain outside the neck, e_f, which is a good measure of the total elongation, can be deduced from the above to be

$$e_f = (1 - f_o)^{-m} - 1 \qquad (5.35)$$

for a non-strain hardening material. This relation can be used to estimate the total elongation of materials with varying initial imperfection sizes and m values. A similar expression can be derived from Equation (5.34) and evaluated when the material shows power-law strain hardening:

$$e_f = \exp[n - m\ln(1 - f_o)] - 1 \quad . \qquad (5.36)$$

The correlation of expressions such as (5.35) and (5.36) with experimental data employing various values of f_o (e.g., 0.995, 0.999) and various n's has demonstrated the success of the above formulation in an approximate sense (Figure 5.3).

LOCALIZATION IN THE PRESENCE OF GEOMETRIC DEFECTS—GHOSH AND AYRES/MARCINIAK/HUTCHINSON AND NEALE NECKING STRAIN[9-12]

A straightforward method of predicting the total elongation in a tensile bar containing a geometric defect involves a simple examination of the equilibrium between the necked and uniform regions of the tensile bar. This method has been utilized in a number of investigations.[9-12] Again, assuming uniaxial stress conditions, force equilibrium requires that

$$\sigma_h A_h = \sigma_i A_i \quad , \tag{5.37}$$

where the subscripts h and i refer to the homogeneous and imperfect regions, respectively. If we assume power-law strain and strain-rate hardening ($\sigma \sim \varepsilon^n \dot{\varepsilon}^m$) and noting that $A = A_o \exp(-\varepsilon)$, Equation (5.37) becomes

$$\varepsilon_h^n \dot{\varepsilon}_h^m A_{o_h} \exp(-\varepsilon_h) = \varepsilon_i^n \dot{\varepsilon}_i^m A_{o_i} \exp(-\varepsilon_i) \quad , \tag{5.38}$$

or

$$\varepsilon_h^{n/m} \dot{\varepsilon}_h \exp(-\varepsilon_h/m) = f_o \varepsilon_i^{n/m} \dot{\varepsilon}_i \exp(-\varepsilon_i/m) \quad , \tag{5.39}$$

since $f_o = (A_{o_h} - \delta A_o)/A_{o_h} = (A_{o_i}/A_{o_h})$. Noting further that $\dot{\varepsilon} = d\varepsilon/dt$,

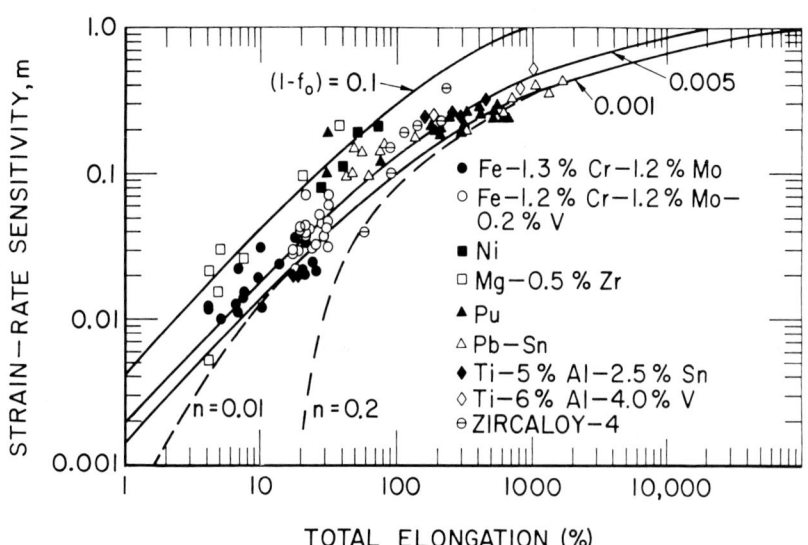

Figure 5.3. Relationship between total elongation and strain-rate sensitivity for round bar tensile tests on a number of engineering materials. Data are those of Woodford.[13] Solid lines are predictions of Equation (5.35); broken lines are from Equation (5.36).[6]

the following formula relating the strain away from and at the imperfection (where necking occurs) can be obtained:

$$\int_0^{\varepsilon_h} \varepsilon_h^{n/m} \exp(-\varepsilon_h/m)\, d\varepsilon_h$$
$$= f_o^{1/m} \int_0^{\varepsilon_i} \varepsilon_i^{n/m} \exp(-\varepsilon_i/m)\, d\varepsilon_i \quad . \quad (5.40)$$

Because n and m are arbitrary numbers, the above equation cannot be integrated directly. However, it should be noted that it does not contain an explicit strain-rate dependence, except as $\dot{\varepsilon}$ may affect m or n.

By evaluating Equation (5.40) numerically, Ghosh[10] has demonstrated the effect of variations in n, m, and f_o on the rate of strain localization in a tensile bar. The effect is particularly strong with regard to m (Figure 5.4). This dependence can also be seen from Equation (5.40), with n set equal to zero. In this case, the equation is integrable with the result:

$$\exp(-\varepsilon_h/m)\Big|_0^{\varepsilon_h} = f_o^{1/m} \exp(-\varepsilon_i/m)\Big|_0^{\varepsilon_i} \quad . \quad (5.41)$$

Letting $\varepsilon_i \to \infty$, as was assumed in deriving Equation (5.31), we obtain an expression for the true limit strain ε_f in the nominally uniform region of the tensile bar

$$\exp(-\varepsilon_f/m) = 1 - f_o^{1/m} \quad , \quad (5.42)$$

or

$$\varepsilon_f = -m\ln(1 - f_o^{1/m}) \quad . \quad (5.43)$$

Conversion of this to engineering strain leads to

$$e_f = (1 - f_o^{1/m})^{-m} - 1 \quad . \quad (5.44)$$

It should be noted that Equation (5.44) differs considerably from Equation (5.35), except for m → 1. Such differences may be ascribed to the fact that the two expressions for ductility are for specimens with two different types of defects. However, Equation (5.44) has been shown to be just as successful, with the proper choice of f_o, in correlating experimental results (Figure 5.5), particularly in materials with large values of m. The fact that the two analyses (Equations 5.35 and 5.44) lead to poor agreement at high and low m's, respectively, suggests that they may be somewhat oversimplified (either in the basic analysis or in the description of the material properties), or perhaps that more work needs to be done in characterizing the adjustable parameter f_o. For this reason, some more detailed treatments will be considered later in this chapter.

CRITICAL ASSESSMENT OF THE SIMPLIFIED NECKING THEORIES

At this point, the necking strains predicted by the hammer blow (HB), or deformation defect, analyses[2, 6, 8] will be compared with

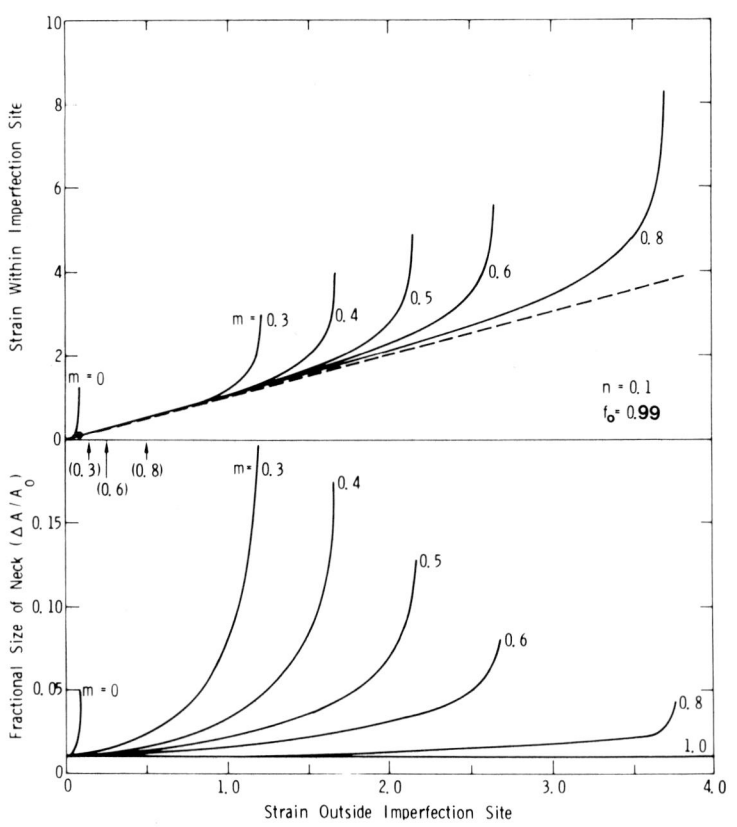

Figure 5.4. Influence of strain-rate sensitivity, m, on the growth of geometric (machining) imperfections. Strain within the imperfection as well as neck size increase from the outset. Considère strain (i.e., strain for $\gamma = 1$) is indicated by the solid circle, and the Hart strains for various values of m (Equation 5.16) are indicated by the vertical arrows.[10]

those obtained from treatments of the geometric defect (GD) type (Ghosh and Ayres,[9] Marciniak,[11] Hutchinson and Neale[12]), and both types of estimates will be measured against the experimental results compiled by Woodford.[13] For this purpose, Equations (5.35) and (5.44), which were derived above by employing the deformation defect (i.e., hammer blow) and geometric defect approaches, respectively, are the important results:

$$e_f(HB) = (1 - f_o)^{-m} - 1 \qquad (5.35)$$

$$e_f(GD) = (1 - f_o^{1/m})^{-m} - 1 \qquad (5.44)$$

These two relations represent the sample behavior in the *absence* of strain hardening. When strain hardening is taken into account in an approximate manner,* the following modified expressions are obtained (see Equation 5.34):

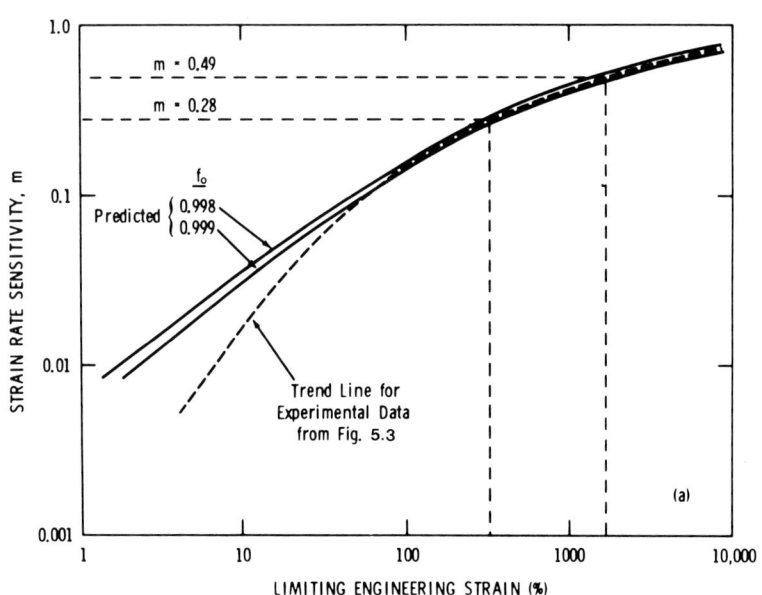

Figure 5.5 Limiting value of engineering strain as a function of m, predicted from Equation (5.44) for two different inhomogeneity factors, $f_o = 0.998$ and $f_o = 0.999$. Comparison with trend line of experimental data from Figure 5.3 is shown.[9]

---

*The coefficient γ normally decreases with strain. The relations that follow are based on an approximate "average" value of γ, denoted by $\bar{\gamma}$.

Table 5.1.
Predicted e_f of Tensile Specimens with Hammer Blow (HB) Defect and Geometric Defect (GD)

m	e_f (HB) (Equation 5.35)*	e_f (GD) (Equation 5.44)*	$\dfrac{e_f \text{ (HB)}}{e_f \text{ (GD)}}$	$\left.\dfrac{[1-f_o](\text{HB})}{[1-f_o](\text{GD})}\right|_{e_f(\text{GD})}$
0.01	0.047	0.005	10.31	63.4
0.05	0.259	0.089	2.91	18.2
0.2	1.512	0.828	1.83	4.90
0.5	9.000	6.089	1.48	1.99

*Assuming $f_o = 0.99$ and $\bar{\gamma} = 0$.

$$e_f(\text{HB} - \text{SH}) = (1 - f_o)^{-m/(1-\bar{\gamma})} - 1 \quad (5.45)$$

$$e_f(\text{GD} - \text{SH}) = (1 - f_o^{1/m})^{-m/(1-\bar{\gamma})} - 1 \quad (5.46)$$

For purposes of illustration of the above relations, the e_f for $f_o = 0.99$ and four values of m—0.01, 0.05, 0.2, and 0.5—have been calculated; these cover most of the experimental range. Under these conditions, the predictions shown in Table 5.1 are obtained for e_f according to Equations (5.35) and (5.44) (no strain hardening).

It is evident from the ratios e_f (HB)/e_f (GD) that the hammer blow predictions of e_f are consistently *higher* than those derived from the machining defect analysis by a considerable margin. This can be readily attributed (as has already been suggested in Chapter 3) to the stabilizing characteristics of the deformation defect. Because of the high resistance to flow localization of this type of flaw, much larger defects are needed to attain a given fracture strain than when there is an initial flaw of metallurgical or geometric origin. This is indicated in the last column of Table 5.1, from which it can be seen that, for the same* rate sensitivity and fracture strain e_f, the defect ratio $[1 - f_o]$ (HB)/$[1 - f_o]$ (GD) falls in the range of 1.99 to 63.4. Thus, a hammer blow must be about one order of magnitude larger than a geometric or metallurgical defect to have the same effect on the necking behavior.[4]

It now remains to compare the predictive accuracy of the two types of analysis. This can be deduced from Figures 5.3 and 5.5. In Figure 5.3, taken from the work of Nichols,[6] predictions based on

---

*The comparison is based on the e_f (GD) values shown in Table 5.1.

Equations (5.35) and (5.45) are compared with the data compiled by Woodford.[13] For the present purpose, the comparisons will be carried out for defects in the size range of 1 to 2 percent and not 0.1, 0.5, and 10 percent, as shown in the diagram. This is because metallurgical nonuniformities equivalent to strength variations of $\pm 1/2$ percent are considered to be normally present in conventional materials, together with diameter variations of about $\pm 1/4$ percent ($\pm 1/2$ percent on area). Taking into account possible overlaps, the difference in strength between the strongest and weakest parts of the sample can therefore be expected to fall quite generally in the range 1 to 2 percent. By comparison, the defect sizes of 0.1 and 0.5 percent employed in the preparation of Figure 5.3 are too small and unrealistic, and 10 percent is too large. The work of Azrin and Backofen[14] supports this conclusion. These workers found that a defect of at least 1.3 percent was needed to attract the failure to the imperfect region during in-plane stretching. Similar remarks apply to the defect sizes of 0.1 and 0.2 percent employed by Ghosh and Ayres[9] in Figure 5.5, which are again considered to be unrepresentative of "real" materials.

Although not represented directly on the figure, the behavior of a 1.5 percent defect can be estimated visually from Figure 5.3. The full lines (Equation 5.35, n = $\bar{\gamma}$ = 0) extrapolated to 1.5 percent can be seen to lead to elongations that are *too small* at values of m > 0.15 and marginally too small for values of m < 0.03. When the more realistic Equation (5.45) is used instead (n ≠ 0, $\bar{\gamma}$ ≠ 0), the predicted fracture strains are much *too large* at low rate sensitivities, in keeping with the stabilizing properties of the hammer blow defect (see broken lines in Figure 5.3 for n = 0.01 and n = 0.2). By contrast, the "acceptable" predictions of Equation (5.35) (no strain hardening) in this range can be attributed to the compensation of errors in this simplified analysis, according to which the neglect of work hardening compensates for the overstabilizing effect of using a hammer blow for a defect.

Somewhat similar conclusions can be drawn from Figure 5.5. Here it can be seen that the "no strain hardening" relation (Equation 5.44) employed for visualizing the effect of 1 to 2 percent defects leads to predictions that are *too low* (with respect to the Woodford compilation) over the entire range of m, but particularly at low rate sensitivities. It is also evident, as suggested by the authors, that an allowance for work hardening is likely to improve the fit. Such a correction could be carried out by using Equation (5.46), in which a strain-hardening term $(1 - \bar{\gamma})$ is included, and by making appropriate assumptions about the mean "effective" value of $\bar{\gamma}$.

From the above, the conclusion may be reached that, at low rate sensitivities (m < 0.05) and on the basis that *defects of 1 to 2 percent are present* (which are more realistic), a geometric defect analysis including strain hardening (along the lines of Equation 5.46) probably leads to the best agreement with experimental results. Similar remarks are also likely to apply to the fracture behavior at higher rate sensitivities (m > 0.05). To give further support to these assertions, it will be useful to call on evidence from the following types of investigation:

(i) More detailed analyses, in which the material characteristics are specified more completely and employed more precisely;

(ii) Further computer simulations, similar to those of Ghosh described above,[10] in which the full boundary conditions are included (neck length, bulk length, defect magnitude and shape, material properties, etc.); and

(iii) Experiments in which the material characteristics, defect geometry, and necking behavior are followed and analyzed simultaneously.

DIFFERENTIAL EQUATION FOR FLOW LOCALIZATION IN ENGINEERING MATERIALS

When the material behavior obeys either of the simple engineering flow laws (Equations 3.38 or 3.40), a useful differential equation can be derived to establish the influence of the material properties on the development of strain concentrations during tensile testing. These flow laws are the parabolic one,

$$\sigma = K\dot{\varepsilon}^m \varepsilon^n \quad , \tag{3.38}$$

where K, m, and n are constant (equal to the strength coefficient, strain-rate hardening exponent, and strain-hardening exponent) and the simple exponential one,

$$\sigma = B\dot{\varepsilon}^m [1 - \exp(-\varepsilon/\varepsilon_o)] \quad , \tag{3.40}$$

where B and ε_o are constants for a given temperature. The differential equation is obtained from the force equilibrium equation for uniaxial deformation, viz., Equation (3.18),

$$m\left(\frac{\partial \ln\dot{\varepsilon}}{\partial x}\right)\bigg|_t = \left(\frac{\partial \varepsilon}{\partial x}\right)\bigg|_t (1-\gamma) - \frac{d\ln A_o}{dx} - \frac{d\ln K}{dx} \quad , \tag{3.18}$$

in which the strength defect term (last term on the right-hand side) has been added for completeness, and γ' has been replaced by γ, because temperature effects are being neglected.

Differentiation of Equation (3.18) with respect to ε leads to the following relation:[15]

$$m\lambda'' + B\lambda' - C\lambda = 0 \quad . \quad (5.47)$$

Here $\beta = \gamma - 1$ is a strain hardening coefficient, and $C = -(\partial^2 \ln\sigma/\partial\varepsilon^2)|_{\dot\varepsilon}$ is the negative of the second derivative of the $\ln\sigma$ versus ε curve and is thus related to the curvature of the semi-log flow curve. Also, $\lambda = (\partial\varepsilon/\partial x)|_t$ denotes the strain gradient, $\lambda' = (\partial\ln\dot\varepsilon/\partial x)|_t = (\partial\lambda/\partial\varepsilon)|_x$ is the *strain rate* gradient (as well as the strain derivative of λ), and $\lambda'' = (\partial(\ddot\varepsilon/\dot\varepsilon^2)/\partial x)|_t = (\partial\lambda'/\partial\varepsilon)|_x$ is the strain derivative of λ', the acceleration gradient, as well as the second derivative of λ with respect to strain. The definitions of λ' and λ'' follow from:

(i) $\left(\dfrac{\partial\ln\dot\varepsilon}{\partial x}\right)\bigg|_t = \left(\dfrac{1}{\dot\varepsilon}\dfrac{\partial\dot\varepsilon}{\partial x}\right)\bigg|_t = \left(\dfrac{dt}{d\varepsilon}\dfrac{\partial^2\varepsilon}{\partial t\partial x}\right)\bigg|_t$

$\qquad = \left(\dfrac{\partial\lambda}{\partial\varepsilon}\right)\bigg|_x = \lambda' \quad , \quad (5.48)$

and

(ii) $\left[\dfrac{\partial}{\partial\varepsilon}\left(\dfrac{\partial\ln\dot\varepsilon}{\partial x}\right)\right]\bigg|_t = \left(\dfrac{\partial\lambda'}{\partial\varepsilon}\right)\bigg|_x = \lambda'' \quad (5.49a)$

or

$\left[\dfrac{\partial}{\partial\varepsilon}\left(\dfrac{\partial\ln\dot\varepsilon}{\partial x}\right)\right]\bigg|_t = \left[\dfrac{\partial}{\partial x}\left(\dfrac{\partial\ln\dot\varepsilon}{\partial\varepsilon}\right)\right]\bigg|_t = \left[\dfrac{\partial}{\partial x}\left(\dfrac{\ddot\varepsilon}{\dot\varepsilon^2}\right)\right]\bigg|_t \quad . \quad (5.49b)$

Equation (5.47) is also valid for other types of flow laws, in addition to the parabolic (Equation 3.38) and exponential (Equation 3.40) relations, as long as the work-hardening coefficient $\gamma = (\partial\ln\sigma/\partial\varepsilon)|_{\dot\varepsilon}$ is independent of strain rate.

Before considering the solutions to Equation (5.47), two particular features of this relation must be underlined. The first is that, in the axial gradient $(\partial/\partial x)|_t$, the coordinate x refers to the location of a *material* element and not to a laboratory coordinate. Thus, the strain and strain-rate gradients λ and λ' simply refer to differences in ε and $\ln\dot\varepsilon$ between neighboring elements in a sample; that is, Δx remains equal to 1 and does not need to be updated in a given calculation even though the actual *lengths* of individual elements increase during an experiment. The second important feature is the resemblance of Equation (5.47) to the well-known "spring-mass-damper" relation, with differentiation taking place, however, with respect to *strain* rather than time (hence the use of primes to signify differentiation rather than dots). Thus, the rate sensitivity m plays the role of the "mass" or inertia, $\beta = \gamma - 1$ that of the "viscous damping factor," and C that of the "spring constant." In contrast to the harmonic oscillator relation, the third term is negative, not positive, so the "restoring force" is negative and therefore *de*-stabilizing; moreover, the values of the various coefficients do not, unfortunately, remain constant, but vary gradually with strain. The usual solution, given below, is only valid, therefore, over the strain interval over which the coefficients themselves can be taken as constant:

$$\lambda = a \exp(\varepsilon/\varepsilon_u) + b \exp(-\varepsilon/\varepsilon_s) \qquad (5.50)$$

Here $\varepsilon_u = (2m/\beta)/(\sqrt{1+\psi} - 1)$, $\varepsilon_s = (2m/\beta)/(\sqrt{1+\psi} + 1)$, and $\psi = 4mC/\beta^2$. The coefficients a and b depend on the initial conditions and on the material coefficients as follows:

$$a = (\lambda_i + \varepsilon_s \lambda_i')/(1 + \varepsilon_s/\varepsilon_u) \qquad (5.51)$$

$$b = (\lambda_i - \varepsilon_u \lambda_i')/(1 + \varepsilon_u/\varepsilon_s) \qquad (5.52)$$

λ_i is the initial value of the strain gradient* when a deformation defect is present (otherwise $\lambda_i = 0$), and λ_i' is the initial value of the strain rate gradient, as given by:

$$\lambda_i' = -\frac{\beta \lambda_i}{m} - \frac{d\ln A_o}{dx} \cdot \frac{1}{m} - \frac{d\ln K}{dx} \cdot \frac{1}{m}$$

$$= -\frac{1}{m}\left[\frac{d\ln A_o}{dx} + \frac{d\ln K}{dx}\right] \qquad (5.53)$$

for combined geometric and metallurgical defects.

The solution consists of two branches; initially the stable one is $b \cdot \exp(-\varepsilon/\varepsilon_s)$, and the unstable one is $a \cdot \exp(\varepsilon/\varepsilon_u)$. Plastic flow is currently stable as long as the root containing the *negative* exponential predominates; conversely, it is unstable when the root containing the *positive* exponential predominates. An interesting feature of expression (5.50) is that the two terms exchange their roles some distance beyond the Considère strain (defined by $\gamma = 1$). This is be-

---

*In the notation employed here, the machining defect $d\ln A_o/dx$ is introduced *before* the hammer blow $d\lambda_i/dx$ is applied.

cause, when $\beta = (\gamma - 1) < 0$, ε_s becomes negative, and the $\exp(-\varepsilon/\varepsilon_s)$, with $(-\varepsilon/\varepsilon_s) > 0$, becomes the "unstable" exponential. The exchange of roles between the two roots can be seen from the various simplified forms of ε_u and ε_s pertaining to the cases where:
  (i) $\psi \gg 1$ (γ just less than or just greater than 1);
  (ii) $\psi \approx 1$ ($\gamma = 1 \pm 2\sqrt{mC}$); and
  (iii) $\psi \ll 1$ (some combination of $m \ll 1$, $C \approx 0$, and $\gamma \ll 1$).

These conditions are satisfied in sequence as the Considère strain is first approached and then exceeded:

(i) $\psi \gg 1$ ($\gamma \approx 1$)

$$\varepsilon_u \simeq \frac{m}{\sqrt{mC}}, \quad \varepsilon_s \simeq \frac{m}{\sqrt{mC}} \qquad (5.54)$$

(ii) $\psi \approx 1$ (and $\gamma < 1$)

$$\varepsilon_u = -\frac{m}{0.207\,(1-\gamma)}, \quad \varepsilon_s = -\frac{m}{1.207\,(1-\gamma)} \qquad (5.55)$$

(iii) $\psi \ll 1$ (and $\gamma \ll 1$)

$$\varepsilon_u = -\frac{(1-\gamma)}{C}, \quad \varepsilon_s = -\frac{m}{(1-\gamma)} \qquad (5.56)$$

For each of these forms of ε_u and ε_s, the two exponentials take the following respective forms:

(i) $\psi \gg 1$

$$\exp\left(+\frac{\varepsilon}{m} \cdot \sqrt{mC}\right), \exp\left(-\frac{\varepsilon}{m} \cdot \sqrt{mC}\right) \qquad (5.57)$$

(ii) $\psi \approx 1$ and $\gamma < 1$

$$\exp\left(-\frac{\varepsilon}{m}[0.207\,(1-\gamma)]\right),$$
$$\exp\left(+\frac{\varepsilon}{m}[1.207\,(1-\gamma)]\right) \qquad (5.58)$$

(iii) $\psi \ll 1$ and $\gamma \ll 1$

$$\exp\left(-\frac{\varepsilon C}{(1-\gamma)}\right), \exp\left(+\frac{\varepsilon(1-\gamma)}{m}\right) \qquad (5.59)$$

Instability and Flow Localization in Uniaxial Tension

The important point is that the unstable term (increasing exponential) in each case is proportional to $\exp(\varepsilon/m)$, in conformity with the results of the simplified analyses described above.* Furthermore, once the value of ψ decreases to the vicinity of 1 (at $\gamma \approx 1 - 2\sqrt{mC}$) or less, the relevant factor becomes $\exp(\varepsilon(1-\gamma)/m)$.

The importance of the above results can be seen from the following approximation of Equation (5.50). Here, for simplicity, we drop the "stable" root; we also assume that $-d\ln A_o/dx = (1 - f_o) = 0.01$ (a typical value for a machining defect), that the metallurgical defect $-d\ln K/dx = 0$ (i.e., that it is included in the geometric term), and finally that failure occurs when the strain gradient $\lambda_f = (\partial \varepsilon_f/\partial x)|_t$ attains the value $+ 0.1$. Under these conditions:**

$$\lambda \simeq b \cdot \exp(-\varepsilon/\varepsilon_s)$$

$$\simeq \left[\frac{-d\ln A_o}{dx}\right] \cdot \frac{1}{(1-\gamma)} \cdot \exp\left[\frac{\varepsilon(1-\gamma)}{m}\right] \quad (5.60)$$

where the term mC has been neglected with respect to $(1-\gamma)^2$. Thus,

$$\lambda_f = \left[\frac{1-f_o}{1-\gamma}\right] \exp\left[\frac{\varepsilon_f(1-\gamma)}{m}\right] = +0.1 \quad . \quad (5.61)$$

The failure criterion can therefore be written as:

$$\exp\left[\frac{\varepsilon_f(1-\gamma)}{m}\right] = \left[\frac{\lambda_f(1-\gamma)}{1-f_o}\right] \quad (5.62)$$

or

$$\varepsilon_f = \frac{m}{(1-\gamma)} \ln\left[\frac{\lambda_f(1-\gamma)}{(1-f_o)}\right] \quad . \quad (5.63)$$

To estimate the value of the logarithmic term, one can assume $(1-\gamma)$ to be on the order of 1 when $\psi \ll 1$. Thus,

$$\varepsilon_f \approx \frac{m}{1-\gamma} \ln[\lambda_f/(1-f_o)] \quad . \quad (5.64)$$

---

*For example, Equation (5.27) can be rewritten as $\delta A = \delta A_o[\exp(\varepsilon(1-\gamma)/m)]$, since $A_o/A = \ell/\ell_o = \exp(\varepsilon)$.

**Equation (5.60) represents the case where $\psi \ll 1$; when $\psi \approx 1$, the preexponential term is multiplied by 0.707, and the strain factor within the exponential is multiplied by 1.207.

For the values of λ_f and f_o given above, the failure strain is

$$\varepsilon_f = 2.3 \, m/(1 - \gamma) \tag{5.65}$$

or

$$e_f = [10]^{m/(1-\gamma)} - 1 \tag{5.66}$$

in terms of engineering strain.

An alternate means of evaluating Equation (5.60), and one that assumes no critical value of λ at failure, is through the technique employed by Nichols[6] and others. This involves transforming the expression to variational terms:

$$\delta\varepsilon = -\delta A/A \simeq (-\delta A_o/A_o)\left(\frac{1}{1-\gamma}\right) \exp\left[\varepsilon(1-\gamma)/m\right] \tag{5.67}$$

Assuming $\delta A_f = A_f$ as before and making use of the relation between δA_o and f_o (see Equations 5.31 through 5.34), Equation (5.67) leads to

$$\varepsilon_f \simeq [m/(1-\gamma)]\ln\left(\frac{1-\gamma}{1-f_o}\right), \tag{5.68}$$

and

$$e_f \simeq [(1-\gamma)/(1-f_o)]^{m/(1-\gamma)} - 1 \tag{5.69}$$

in terms of engineering strain.

When $\psi \gg 0$, procedures similar to the above result in

$$\varepsilon_f = \frac{m}{\sqrt{mC}} \ln\left(\frac{2\lambda_f \sqrt{mC}}{1-f_o}\right). \tag{5.70}$$

This expression is most useful for materials that fail at strains near the Considère strain. The above relations (e.g., Equation 5.64) should be compared with the relevant simplified hammer blow and machining defect expressions:

Hammer Blow:

$$\varepsilon_f(HB) = -m\ln(1 - f_o) \tag{5.71}$$

$$e_f(HB) = (1 - f_o)^{-m} - 1 \tag{5.35}$$

Geometric Defect:

$$\varepsilon_f(GD) = -m\ln(1 - f_o^{1/m}) \tag{5.43}$$

$$e_f(GD) = (1 - f_o^{1/m})^{-m} - 1 \tag{5.44}$$

as well as the ones including strain-hardening effects (Equations 5.45 and 5.46).

It is evident that, in the solutions on which the above expressions are based, the strain is consistently normalized by m, as in exp (ε/m), underlining the primary importance of the rate sensitivity as the "inertia" term. The role of the work hardening or "damping" term is not as straightforward, unfortunately, in part because γ varies with strain (which prevents integration) and in part also because, even when average values of γ are used, the appropriate simplifications are different in different ranges of behavior. Nevertheless, the damping factor $(1 - \gamma)$ (when positive and greater than $\sqrt{mC}$) participates in the strain normalization, as in exp $(\varepsilon(1 - \bar{\gamma})/m)$, indicating that non-zero values of $\bar{\gamma}$ can significantly affect the post-uniform elongation.

APPROXIMATE GRAPHICAL SOLUTION TO THE INSTABILITY RELATIONS

The effect of different experimental values of m, average γ or $\bar{\gamma}$, and $(1 - f_o)$ on the fracture strain predicted by the various formulas described above can be readily evaluated from the graph shown in Figure 5.6. Here, the "normalized" true strain $[\varepsilon(1 - \bar{\gamma})/m]$ is plotted as a function of strain ε for the usual ranges of m and $(1 - \bar{\gamma})$. Fracture can be considered to occur when:

$$\frac{\varepsilon_f(1 - \bar{\gamma})}{m} = \ln\left[\frac{\lambda_f(1 - \bar{\gamma})}{(1 - f_o)}\right] \tag{5.63}$$

The parallel expressions derived from the classical hammer blow and geometric defect approaches, when these are modified to include the effects of work hardening, are:

$$\frac{\varepsilon_f(HB)(1 - \bar{\gamma})}{m} = -\ln(1 - f_o) \tag{5.72}$$

and

$$\frac{\varepsilon_f(GD)(1 - \bar{\gamma})}{m} = -\ln(1 - f_o^{1/m}) \quad . \tag{5.73}$$

Thus, the fracture strain ε_f is specified by the intersection of the $[\varepsilon(1 - \bar{\gamma})/m]$ locus corresponding to the experimental conditions with the horizontal line appropriate to the failure criterion selected, i.e., $-\ln(1 - f_o)$, $-\ln(1 - f_o^{1/m})$, or $-\ln[(1 - f_o)/(1 - \bar{\gamma}) \lambda_f]$. Note that, as dis-

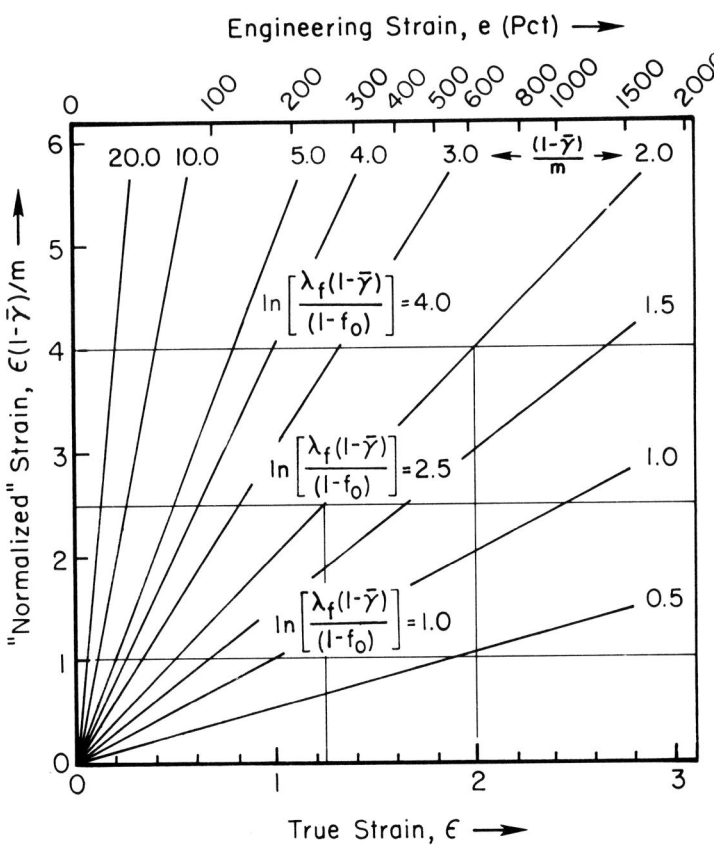

Figure 5.6. Diagram for determination of fracture strain given by Equation (5.63). The fracture strain is given by the intersection of the horizontal line representing the value of $\ln[\lambda_f (1 - \bar{\gamma})/(1 - f_o)]$ with the locus $(1 - \bar{\gamma})/m = 0.5, 1.0, 2.0$, etc. For example, $(1 - \bar{\gamma})/m = 2.0$ can correspond to $\bar{\gamma} = 0$ and $m = 0.5$, $\bar{\gamma} = 0.25$ and $m = 0.38$, or $\bar{\gamma} = 0.5$ and $m = 0.25$. The intersections with the horizontals $\ln[\lambda_f (1 - \bar{\gamma})/(1 - f_o)] = 2.5$ and 4.0 correspond to fracture strain predictions of 1.25 and 2.0 (nominal strains of 250 and 640 percent, respectively). Note that for materials that fracture near the Considère strain, i.e., for low m metals tested at ambient temperatures, $\psi \gg 1$, so that the normalized strain must be replaced by $\varepsilon\sqrt{mC}/m$ and the logarithmic term by $\ln[\lambda_f \sqrt{mC}/(1 - f_o)]$. Near ε_f, $\sqrt{mC}$ is generally less than 1 but greater than $(1 - \bar{\gamma})$ in such materials.

Instability and Flow Localization in Uniaxial Tension

cussed above, for a given defect size $(1 - f_o)$, the hammer blow analysis always predicts the greatest ε_f.

FLOW LOCALIZATION UNDER SUPERPLASTIC FLOW CONDITIONS

We return at this point to Figures 5.3 and 5.5 and to the predictions of Equations (5.35) (hammer blow) and (5.44) (geometric defect) in the superplastic range of rate sensitivities. The point was made above that these two relations, which do not allow for work hardening, predict fracture strains that are too low, particularly if realistic defect sizes are incorporated into the calculations. This deficiency can be greatly reduced, if not eliminated, through the use of the appropriate work hardening expressions and the use of Figure 5.6. Such an estimate, however, requires the availability of material coefficients that are more suitable than those given by the classical parabolic or exponential representations. These can only be obtained by carrying out tensile tests, preferably at constant *local,* but at least at constant *overall* true strain rates. An assessment of the data obtained from experiments performed in the latter manner is given in Reference 16, and only the conclusions that affect the use of Figure 5.6 will be reviewed here.

Characteristics of Superplastic Flow Curves Determined at Constant Overall True Strain Rates. The attributes of superplastic flow that must be taken into consideration for the proper prediction of tensile ductility include the following:

1. Superplastic flow curves generally pass through the Considère strain (where $d\sigma/d\varepsilon = \sigma$) at very low strains, e.g., less than 10 percent, particularly when flow softening is involved, or when a steady state of flow is achieved. When significant grain coarsening is taking place, so that flow *hardening* is observed, the Considère strain may be delayed to strains larger than 10 percent. Nevertheless, in all cases, the bulk of the specimen extension occurs in the strain regime beyond the maximum load and therefore well beyond the onset of detectable flow localization. Thus, the large experimental extensions are principally attributable to the very slow defect *growth* kinetics.
2. In cases where grain coarsening is taking place, the *current* value of the rate sensitivity m gradually diminishes with strain (Figure 5.7). Thus, the rate sensitivity can decrease from the vicinity of 0.5 to values as low as 0.25.
3. During flow softening, which is frequently observed at strain rates *above* the superplastic range, the flow curve

is concave upwards (see Figure 5.7). Thus, the curvature term as defined here $(C = -(\partial^2 \ln \sigma/\partial \varepsilon^2)|_{\dot{\varepsilon}})$ can be negative. During steady-state flow, also shown in the diagram, $C = 0$, whereas when grain coarsening is taking place, $C > 0$, because, although $(\partial \sigma/\partial \varepsilon)|_{\dot{\varepsilon}}$ may be approximately constant, the $\ln \sigma$ versus ε curve is concave downwards. Whether positive or negative, $|C|$ is generally well below 1, once the Considère strain has been exceeded.

4. Although steady-state flow can sometimes be observed under constant $\dot{\varepsilon}$ conditions, at the low $\dot{\varepsilon}$'s of interest in superplastic forming, the flow stress generally *increases with strain,* leading to *positive* values of γ, which are generally in the range 0.2 to 0.5. The dependence of such flow hardening on deformation-induced grain growth is considered in more detail below. The aspect of interest here is that γ values cannot be estimated from either the parabolic or the exponential flow laws, but are a function of the kinetics of grain coarsening. Their basic effect is to introduce $(1 - \bar{\gamma})$ factors in the range 0.5 to 0.8 and therefore to modify significantly the value of the $(1 - \bar{\gamma})/m$ term in Equation (5.63), which serves to normalize the

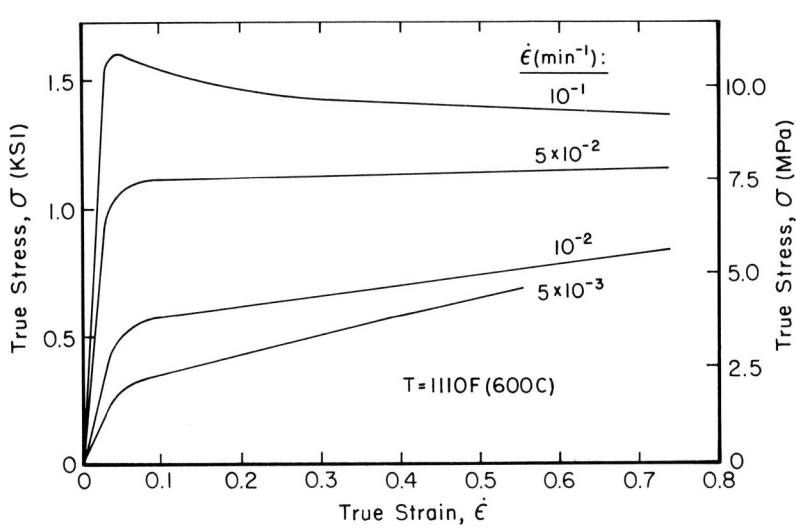

Figure 5.7. Constant strain rate flow curves for 60/40 brass determined at 600 °C (1110 °F) showing strain hardening due to grain growth at low strain rates and flow softening due to evolution of an equiaxed microstructure at the higher strain rates.[17]

Instability and Flow Localization in Uniaxial Tension   175 strain in the fracture relation. In effect, flow hardening increases the "apparent" rate sensitivity from m to $m/(1 - \bar{\gamma})$.

5. Given the values of m, $\beta = \bar{\gamma} - 1$, and C described above, the parameter $\psi = 4mC/\beta^2$ can be expected to fall largely in the categories of $\psi \approx 1$ and $\psi \ll 1$. In both cases, the relevant strain exponential (see Equation 5.60 above) is proportional to $\exp[\varepsilon(1 - \bar{\gamma})/m]$, so that the flow hardening attributable to grain coarsening cannot be omitted from consideration.

Prediction of Fracture Strain from Figure 5.6. If fracture is now assumed to occur when:

$$\frac{\varepsilon_f(1 - \bar{\gamma})}{m} = \ln\left[\frac{(1 - \bar{\gamma})\lambda_f}{(1 - f_o)}\right] \tag{5.62}$$

and $\ln\{[\lambda_f(1 - \bar{\gamma})]/(1 - f_o)\}$ for a carefully prepared sample is set equal to 4.0 for simplicity (although other values, such as 3.0 or 3.5, could also be justified), it is evident from Figure 5.6 that fracture strains well in the superplastic range (e.g., $\varepsilon_f = 2$ to 3) can be attained with the following combinations of material coefficients:

$[(1 - \bar{\gamma})/m] = 1.5$:

m = 0.5 and $\bar{\gamma}$ = 0.25

or

m = 0.34 and $\bar{\gamma}$ = 0.5

$[(1 - \bar{\gamma})/m] = 2.0$:

m = 0.5 and $\bar{\gamma}$ = 0

or

m = 0.25 and $\bar{\gamma}$ = 0.5

The important role of flow hardening in preventing strain localization is evident from these examples. In particular, it is apparent that non-zero $\bar{\gamma}$ raises the "effective" rate sensitivity from m to $[m/(1 - \bar{\gamma})]$, i.e., by 20 to 100 percent. Thus, the flow hardening that accompanies grain coarsening plays *two* roles:

(i) It compensates for the gradual decrease in m that generally occurs during superplastic straining.

(ii) It is probably responsible for increasing the experimental elongations well above the values predicted by the "no work hardening" relations described above.[16]

Constitutive Relation for Grain Coarsening. It remains to consider the type of constitutive relation that applies to grain coarsening and whether or not it is of a form that is consistent with the defect analysis presented here, which requires that $\sigma = \sigma(\varepsilon,\dot{\varepsilon})$ and therefore that $\gamma = \gamma(\varepsilon)$. All the relations referred to here assume isothermal conditions, of course. The detailed experiments of Suery and Baudelet[18, 19] have clearly shown that the rate of grain coarsening depends on strain rate. It also depends on temperature and on the initial or current grain size. This is also indicated by the results of Ghosh and Hamilton,[20] which show that the rate of grain coarsening (with respect to *strain*) *decreases* as the strain rate is increased (whereas the *time* rate of coarsening *increases* with strain rate). It therefore seems probable that the flow stress can be described in terms of the dependence $\sigma = \sigma(\dot{\varepsilon}, T, D)$. Here, the grain size D is a "hardness state" parameter and is the equivalent, in superplastic materials, of the dislocation density $\rho_\perp$ or threshold stress in work hardening materials. In an ideal material obeying such a relationship, $\gamma = \gamma(\dot{\varepsilon}, T, D)$ and, at constant temperature and D, $\gamma = \gamma(\dot{\varepsilon})$, in contrast to the dependence $\gamma = \gamma(\varepsilon)$ for "engineering" materials, and $\gamma = \gamma(\dot{\varepsilon}, \rho_\perp)$ or $\gamma = \gamma(\dot{\varepsilon})$ at constant state for work hardening materials. Note, however, that γ *decreases* with $\dot{\varepsilon}$ in superplastic materials, whereas it *increases* with $\dot{\varepsilon}$ under the dynamic recovery conditions that are rate controlling in work hardening materials.

As $\gamma = \gamma(\dot{\varepsilon})$, Equation (5.47) above, which is based on $\gamma = \gamma(\varepsilon)$, is not strictly speaking applicable. It remains a very good approximation only because the rate dependence of γ, as given by

$$B_\sigma = (\partial\gamma/\partial\ln\dot{\varepsilon})|_\sigma \tag{5.74}$$

is generally small ($|B_\sigma| \ll 1$). When this dependence is no longer negligible (i.e., when $|B_\sigma| \approx \pm 1$), the more detailed analysis described below must be employed.

INSTABILITY ANALYSIS INCLUDING RATE SENSITIVITY OF THE WORK HARDENING RATE

The "engineering" flow laws, which include the parabolic and simple exponential relations, are based on the simplifying assumption that the individual work hardening contributions associated with a series of deformation operations depend only on the applied strain increments and are independent of the strain *rates* at which the increments are imposed.* Under these conditions, γ is either constant or, more generally, a function of *strain alone*. This simplification works reasonably well in the cold working or ambient temperature range of metal behavior, in which the amount of work hardening can therefore be taken to depend only on the total strain. As already suggested in the superplasticity section, such an approximation becomes less and less valid as the temperature is increased into the hot working range. Under superplastic conditions, the simplification breaks down, because the amount of grain growth taking place during deformation does not depend on strain alone, but is influenced by the strain rate and temperature of the operation. Thus, the rate of flow hardening (which is linked to the rate of grain coarsening) depends on the strain rate and temperature, as well as on the strain.

Similar remarks apply to the amount of work hardening accomplished during high-temperature deformation. In this case, the "flow" hardening is due to the increase in dislocation density, which through the rate of dynamic recovery (with respect to *strain,* not time) is also a function of the strain rate and temperature at which the operation is performed. This dependence of $\gamma = (\partial \ln\sigma/\partial\varepsilon|_{\dot{\varepsilon}})$ on strain rate is illustrated in Figure 5.8.[21] The dependence can be expressed quantitatively in terms of the coefficient:

$$B_\sigma = (\partial\gamma/\partial\ln\dot{\varepsilon})|_\sigma \tag{5.74}$$

the physical significance of which is illustrated in Figure 5.9.[21] Also defined in the latter diagram is the curvature term C*, which is related to the previous curvature coefficient C as follows:

$$C^* = -(\partial\gamma/\partial\ln\sigma)|_{\dot{\varepsilon}} = -\left(\frac{\partial\gamma}{\partial\varepsilon}\right)\bigg|_{\dot{\varepsilon}} \cdot \left(\frac{\partial\varepsilon}{\partial\ln\sigma}\right)\bigg|_{\dot{\varepsilon}} = C/\gamma \tag{5.75}$$

It can be seen from Figure 5.8b that the current description of the flow curve reproduces the transient in flow stress observed after a strain rate change much better than the parabolic or exponential representation (Figure 5.8a), in which the flow stress passes directly from one continuous curve to the next. Here, the "short" transient associated with rapid adjustments in the density and distribution of mobile dislocations, shown as a broken line in Figure 5.8b, is never-

---

*In a more complete nonisothermal analysis, the work hardening increments would also be assumed to be independent of the *temperature* at which the strains are applied.

theless neglected. The type of transient illustrated in Figure 5.8b also involves a different definition of the rate sensitivity than that of Figure 5.8a. The sensitivity associated with the engineering flow laws (which only recognize instantaneous and complete transitions in flow behavior when the strain rate is changed) is necessarily the one as-

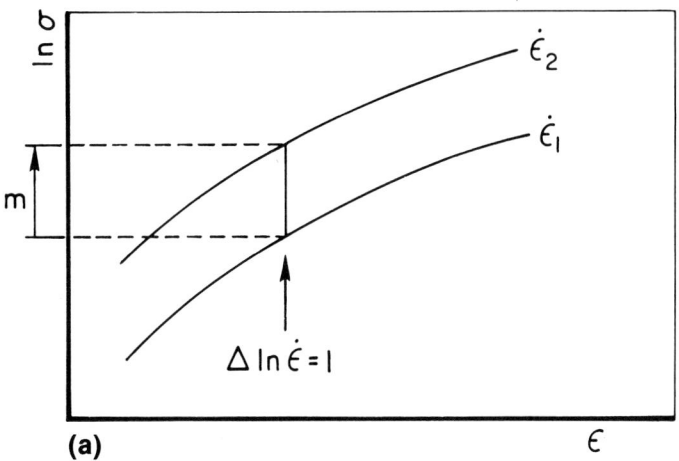

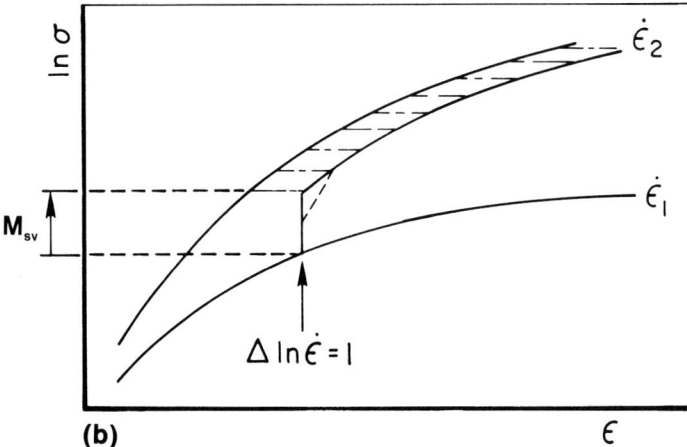

Figure 5.8. Two definitions of the strain-rate sensitivity index. (a) m, based on continuous flow curves measured at constant true strain rates and (b) M_{sv}, the state variable description based on strain-rate change tests.[21] Note the difference between the two definitions arises because strain is not a state variable.

sociated with the dependence of the *continuous* flow curves on strain rate. This is referred to as m here. By contrast, the rate sensitivity involved in the "state variable" description of work hardening[21] is referred to as $M_{sv} = (\partial \ln\sigma/\partial \ln\dot\varepsilon)|_{state}$, where the "state" controlling the

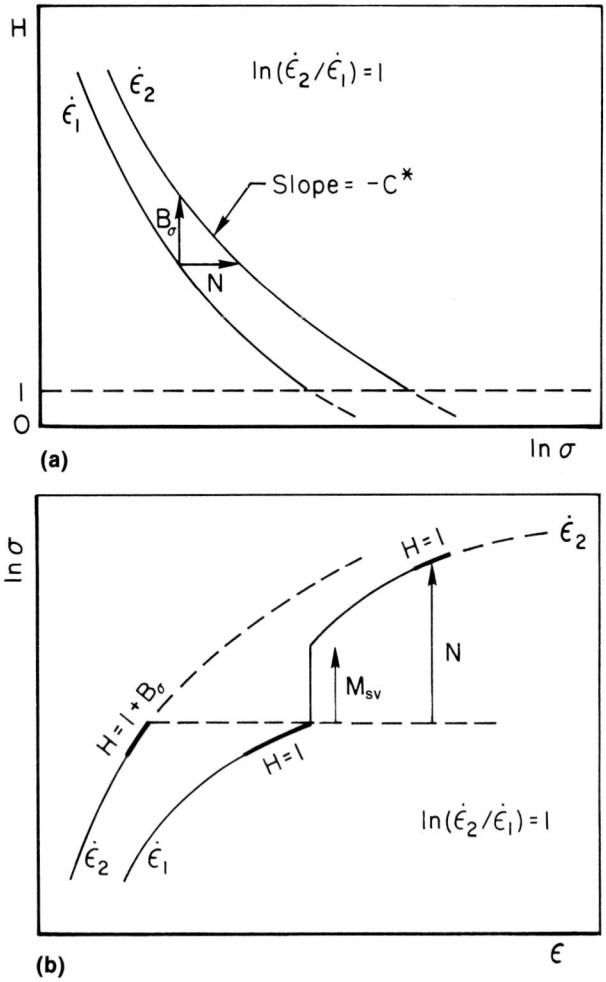

Figure 5.9. (a) The strain-hardening parameter $H \equiv (\partial \ln\sigma/\partial \varepsilon)|_{\dot\varepsilon}$ as a function of stress and strain rate and the relation between B_σ, C^*, and N. Note that H in this figure is equivalent to the coefficient γ employed in the present text. Also $N \equiv (\partial \ln\sigma/\partial \ln\dot\varepsilon)|_H = -(\partial \ln\sigma/\partial H)|_{\dot\varepsilon} \cdot (\partial H/\partial \ln\dot\varepsilon)|_\sigma = B_\sigma/C^*$. (b) Strain-rate change at the load maximum (H = 1) illustrating the definitions of the rate sensitivities: M_{sv} (of the flow stress at constant state), N (of the flow stress at constant H), and B_σ (of the strain-hardening coefficient H at constant σ).[21]

flow stress is the dislocation density, grain size, etc., as required. This "constant hardness state" rate sensitivity is determined by back extrapolation through the "short" transient of Figure 5.8b.

Under the conditions described above, the differential equation specifying the growth of strain and strain-rate gradients is the following:[21]

$$M_{sv}Y'' + (\gamma + B_\sigma - 1) Y' - C^* Y = 0 \qquad (5.76)$$

Here Y, Y', and Y'' are based on the *area* gradient $Y = (\partial \ln A/\partial x)|_t$ rather than on the strain gradient $\lambda = (\partial \varepsilon/\partial x)|_t$. As before, x is a *material element* coordinate and does not change with strain, as it does not refer to the laboratory coordinate system. The definitions of the above quantities follow:

$$Y = \left(\frac{\partial \ln A}{\partial x}\right)\bigg|_t = \frac{d \ln A_o}{dx} - \left(\frac{\partial \varepsilon}{\partial x}\right)\bigg|_t = \frac{d \ln A_o}{dx} - \lambda \qquad (5.77)$$

$$Y' = \left(\frac{\partial Y}{\partial \varepsilon}\right)\bigg|_x = \frac{1}{\dot\varepsilon}\frac{\partial}{\partial x}\bigg|_t\left(\frac{\partial \ln A}{\partial t}\right)\bigg|_x = -\left(\frac{\partial \ln \dot\varepsilon}{\partial x}\right)\bigg|_t = -\lambda' \qquad (5.78)$$

$$Y'' = \left(\frac{\partial Y'}{\partial \varepsilon}\right)\bigg|_x = \left(\frac{\partial^2 Y}{\partial \varepsilon^2}\right)\bigg|_x = -\left(\frac{\partial(\ddot\varepsilon/\dot\varepsilon^2)}{\partial x}\right)\bigg|_t = -\lambda'' \qquad (5.79)$$

As before, the solution to Equation (5.76) takes the form:*

$$Y = a_u \exp(\varepsilon/\varepsilon_u) + b_s \exp(-\varepsilon/\varepsilon_s) \qquad (5.80)$$

where

$$\varepsilon_u = 2 M_{sv}/\beta^*(\sqrt{1 + \psi} - 1) \qquad (5.81)$$

$$\varepsilon_s = 2 M_{sv}/\beta^*(\sqrt{1 + \psi} + 1) \qquad (5.82)$$

$$\beta^* = \gamma + B_\sigma - 1 \qquad (5.83)$$

$$\psi = 4 M_{sv} C^*/\beta^{*2} \qquad (5.84)$$

$$a_u = (Y_i + \varepsilon_s Y_i')/(1 + \varepsilon_s/\varepsilon_u) \qquad (5.85)$$

---

*Note that, in the Y notation,[21] hammer blows are applied *before* machining defects, whereas the reverse convention was adopted in the simpler λ analysis.[4, 22]

$$b_s = (Y_i - \varepsilon_u Y_i')/(1 + \varepsilon_u/\varepsilon_s) \qquad (5.86)$$

$$Y_i = d\ln A_o/dx \qquad (5.87)$$

and

$$Y_i' = \frac{Y_i}{M_{sv}} + \frac{\gamma}{M_{sv}} \frac{d\varepsilon_i}{dx} = -\frac{d\ln \dot{\varepsilon}_i}{dx} \qquad (5.88)$$

Equation (5.80) can be further simplified by taking into account the magnitude of $\psi = 4 M_{sv} C^*/\beta^{*2}$ and dropping the stable term, i.e., the term containing the *diminishing* exponential. For a geometric defect, all the large strain solutions take the form:

$$Y \simeq b_s \exp(-\varepsilon/\varepsilon_s) \qquad (5.89)$$

$$Y \simeq (Y_i/K_1) \exp\left(\frac{\varepsilon}{M_{sv}} \cdot K_2\right) \qquad (5.90)$$

where K_1 and K_2 have the following values:

$\psi \gg 1$ $(\gamma + B_\sigma \approx 1)$:

$$\left. \begin{array}{l} K_1 = 2 K_2/(\sqrt{M_{sv} C^*} + 1) \\ K_2 = \sqrt{M_{sv} C^*} \end{array} \right\} \qquad (5.91)$$

$\psi \approx 1$ $([\gamma + B_\sigma] \approx 1 - 2\sqrt{M_{sv} C^*})$:

$$\left. \begin{array}{l} K_1 = 1.171 K_2 \\ K_2 = 1.207 (1 - \gamma - B_\sigma) \end{array} \right\} \qquad (5.92)$$

$\psi \ll 1$:

$$K_1 = K_2 = (1 - \gamma - B_\sigma) \qquad (5.93)$$

Identifying the occurrence of fracture, as before, with the moment that the area gradient Y attains the critical value Y_f, say equal to 0.1, and replacing Y_i by $(1 - f_o)$, we can write that:

$$Y_f = (Y_i/K_1) \exp(\varepsilon_f \cdot K_2/M_{sv}) \qquad (5.94)$$

and therefore that

$$\exp\left(\frac{\varepsilon_f \cdot K_2}{M_{sv}}\right) = \frac{Y_f \cdot K_1}{1 - f_o} \tag{5.95}$$

so that

$$\varepsilon_f = \frac{M_{sv}}{K_2} \cdot \ln\left[\frac{Y_f \cdot K_1}{(1 - f_o)}\right] \tag{5.96}$$

In terms of engineering strain, the above expression is:

$$e_f = \left[\frac{Y_f \cdot K_1}{(1 - f_o)}\right]^{M_{sv}/K_2} - 1 \tag{5.97}$$

These relations are similar to the ones derived earlier, and an approximate solution (based either on the material coefficients remaining constant, or on their average values) can therefore be obtained graphically from Figure 5.6. Although the "inertia" term in this representation $M_{sv} < m$, some compensation is provided because the "damping" term $K_2 = (1 - \gamma - B_\sigma) < (1 - \gamma)$ in the earlier form. A more important difference arises from the change in the definition of the strain associated with the onset of rapid flow concentration through the introduction of the additional damping factor B_σ. As rapid defect growth cannot begin until $\beta^* = (\gamma + B_\sigma - 1) < 0$, the previous critical condition $\gamma \leq 1$ (achieved at the Considère strain ε_c) is transformed into $(\gamma + B_\sigma) \leq 1$. Thus, when $B_\sigma > 0$, which is the normal situation at elevated temperatures, the strain associated with the onset of detectable necking is increased *beyond* the classical value corresponding to $\gamma = 1$. This phenomenon is discussed in more detail in the section that follows.

EXPERIMENTAL OBSERVATIONS RELATING TO THE DETAILED ANALYSES OF FLOW LOCALIZATION

The analyses of neck development described above have obtained support from three complementary types of experiments. These involve:

(i) The accurate determination of the evolving values of the material coefficients m, γ, and C, or M_{sv}, γ, B_σ and C*, as appropriate, using a constant *local* experimental strain rate.

(ii) The simulation of tensile testing by means of computer programs employing these detailed coefficients, together with the appropriate geometric boundary conditions.
(iii) The quantitative investigation of the kinetics of necking, using initial defects of known geometry and a suitable experimental technique for following their development.

Such studies were carried out by Christodoulou and his coworkers[23-25]; their principal findings will now be reviewed briefly.

When OFHC copper is deformed at room temperature (0.22 T_{MP}) and at 698 K (0.51 T_{MP}), the value of $B_\sigma = (\partial \gamma / \partial \ln \dot{\epsilon}|_\sigma)$ is about 0.10 and 0.19, respectively, at the Considère strain, and then decreases with continuing deformation.[23] Thus, the parabolic law description of the flow curve is adequate for purposes of necking simulation. As a result, there is satisfactory quantitative agreement between the experimental measurements and the predictions regarding the rate of neck growth calculated using Equation (5.47).[24] This representation takes into account the presence of a geometric defect and also employs the *evolving* values of the material coefficients. However, once significant localization is underway, good agreement can only be obtained when the *effective stress* in the neck is employed, which corrects for the presence of transverse stresses in the highly curved regions. For this purpose, both the Bridgman correction and the Bridgman correction gradient were utilized.

When 99.99 percent aluminum is deformed at room temperature (0.32 T_{MP}) and at 200 °C (0.51 T_{MP}), the value of B_σ at the Considère strain ($\gamma = 1$) increases to 0.35 and 0.44, respectively.[23] Thus, the parabolic law description of flow is no longer adequate for high stacking fault energy materials at these homologous temperatures. The employment of the alternative "state variable" description of flow, which involves Equation (5.76), leads to a good quantitative agreement between measurement and predictions.[24] This approach is also based on a *geometric* defect and takes into account the evolving values of the material coefficients. As in the case of the copper, agreement at large strains requires the use of the *effective* stress and *effective* stress gradient in the neck regions. Because B_σ is no longer negligible at these homologous temperatures, the instability condition $\gamma + B_\sigma = 1$ is not satisfied until about 0.2 strain beyond the point of maximum load ($\gamma = 1$) (see Figure 5.10). Only *after* this condition is met does the rate of flow localization attain a practically significant level. The effect of finite B_σ on delaying instability and enabling larger useful deformation beyond the Considère strain (in titanium and zirconium alloys) has also been reported by Reed-Hill, Cetlin, and their co-workers,[26, 27] who proposed a simple model to describe the influence of the rate dependence of strain hardening on necking behavior.

The exact solutions to the instability analyses depend on the *evolving* values of the material coefficients, as indicated above. The results of Christodoulou's detailed experiments[24] show that even M_{sv} changes with strain, first decreasing (at low homologous temperatures) and then increasing. The average values of M_{sv} under the four conditions investigated are shown in Table 5.2. The evolving values of C^*, as well as of $\gamma = H$ and B_σ, are displayed in Figure 5.11. Here, it is evident that, once the Considère strain is exceeded ($\gamma = H = 1$), $C^* \lesssim 3$. Thus, the factor $\sqrt{M_{sv}C^*}$ in Equation (5.90) has values in the range 0.1 to 0.5, and $\sqrt{M_{sv}C^*}$ is generally $<\sqrt{mC}$. As the ratio M_{sv}/m is about 0.5, it can be seen that the use of the state variable or instantaneous definition of the rate sensitivity *decreases* the strain normalization factor by about 2. This destabilizing effect is compensated, in part *within* the normalization factor by values of B_σ (see Figure 5.11) in the range 0.1 to 0.5 (which decreases $-\beta^* = (1 - \gamma - B_\sigma)$ in the exp ($\varepsilon (1 - \gamma - B_\sigma)/M_{sv}$)), and in part by the increase in the *strain* at which the exp ($\varepsilon \sqrt{M_{sv}C^*}/M_{sv}$) and the exp ($\varepsilon (1 - \gamma - B_\sigma)/M_{sv}$) terms become significant.

The fracture strain has also been predicted *solely* from computer simulations (without direct experimental measurement of the

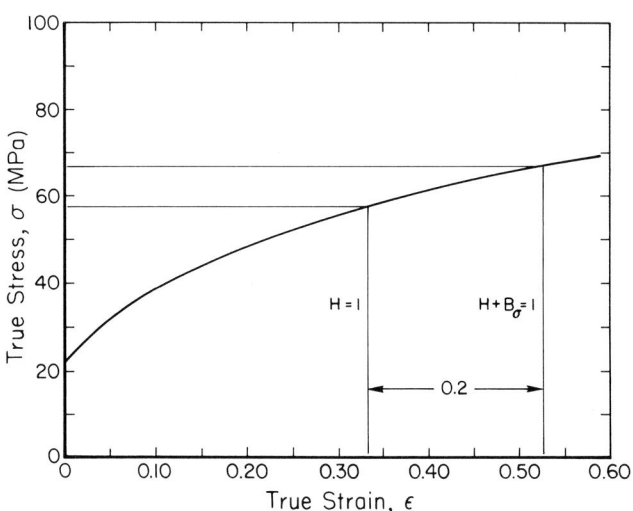

Figure 5.10. The initial part of a true stress-strain curve for aluminum at $\dot{\varepsilon} = 5 \times 10^{-4}$ sec.$^{-1}$. Note that the condition $H = 1$ (maximum load) is separated from the condition $H + B_\sigma = 1$ (onset of flow localization) by a true strain of 0.2.[23]

Table 5.2.
Rate-Sensitivity Coefficients for Copper and Aluminum[24]

Material	Temperature, K	M_{sv}	m	M_{sv}/m
Copper	273 (0.22 T_{MP})	0.006	0.010	0.60
Copper	698 (0.51 T_{MP})	0.038	0.061	0.62
Aluminum	273 (0.32 T_{MP})	0.013	0.032	0.40
Aluminum	473 (0.51 T_{MP})	0.045	0.090	0.50

necking kinetics or of the material coefficients). Under these conditions, the following approximate relation has been obtained:[25]

$$\varepsilon_f = 2.5m + n - 0.05 \quad . \tag{5.98}$$

Here a geometric defect of 1.5 percent was assumed, and the gradual decrease in the work hardening coefficient γ, as based on the parabolic law, was taken into account. When this relation is compared with the Woodford compilation, it is evident that the fracture strain is *underestimated* in the superplastic range and *overestimated* in the low m range. In terms of the present analysis, the discrepancy in the superplastic region can be ascribed to the influence of non-negligible γ's at large strains. These are associated with the occurrence of grain coarsening and the flow hardening that it entails, as described above; they are not foreseen by the usual engineering flow laws and are thus omitted from conventional analyses. The overestimate in the low m range, on the other hand, requires a different explanation. The simplest interpretation is based on the gradual increase in the critical strain gradient λ_f with rate sensitivity m. Because of the influence of increasing m in retarding flow localization and promoting strain equalization, higher λ_f values are associated with "failure" in the high, as opposed to the low, m regions.[25] In the use of Figure 5.6, or in the use of Equations (5.63, 5.70, and 5.96), this signifies that λ_f increases from, say, 0.1 at low to 0.15 at high rate sensitivities. It should also be remarked that the *actual* values of λ_f corresponding to catastrophic flow localization are *less* than 0.1 to 0.15 and are in the range 0.01 to 0.1 instead.[25] However, in calculations based on the *final* (and lowest) rather than on *evolving* values of γ, the use of higher than realistic λ_f values compensates for the employment of γ coefficients that are lower than the effective average value.

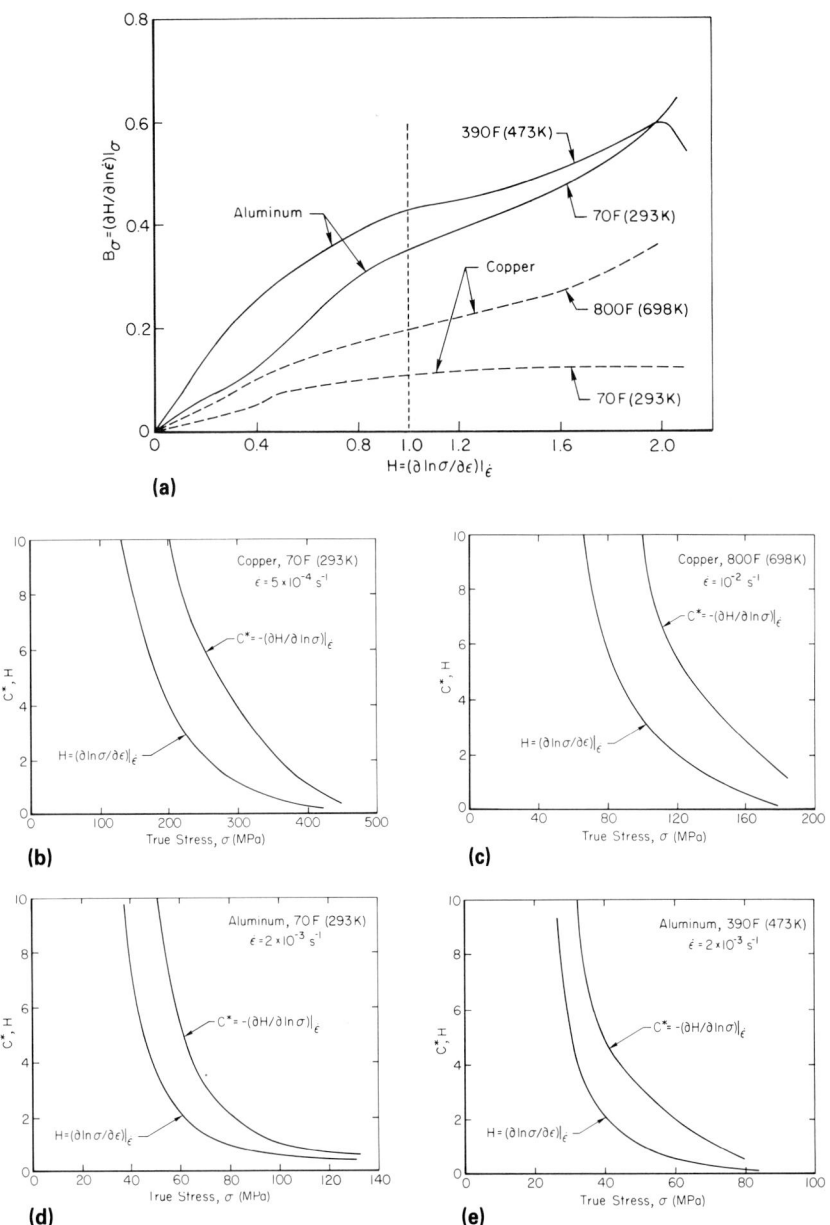

Figure 5.11. Dependence of (a) B_σ on the work hardening coefficient H ($\equiv \gamma$) in the vicinity of the load maximum and (b, c, d, e) C^* and H on σ for copper and aluminum at various temperatures.[24] Note the decrease of C^* with stress. C^* always remains higher than H.

Instability and Flow Localization in Uniaxial Tension

Tension Testing of Sheet Metals

As with round tensile bars, the failure of ductile sheet tensile specimens (whose width >> their thickness) is generally controlled by the onset of load instability followed by flow localization via necking. Unlike the tensile bar case, however, two types of necking process (Figure 1.4) are possible.[28] The first is *diffuse* instability, which leads to a neck that is symmetric about the tensile axis. This mode of unstable flow is the sheet tensile test analogue to the necks formed in the round bar tensile test. Because the axial extent of the neck produced following diffuse instability is on the order of the sheet width, the neck appears rather diffuse, and thus the instability process and necking associated with it are termed diffuse. This necking process may be terminated by fracture or, as is the case for many metals used in sheet forming, by another instability and necking process. In the latter case, the geometric softening in the diffuse neck reaches such a level that localized through-thickness necking is favored over continued diffuse necking. In the following sections, these various processes are discussed.

DIFFUSE INSTABILITY AND DIFFUSE NECKING IN SHEET METALS

The conditions for diffuse instability and the onset of diffuse necking are identical to those derived for load instability and the onset of flow localization for round tensile bars. Thus, Equations (5.2), (5.12), and (5.15) can be employed to predict the effect of material properties on the load maximum. For the particular example of an isotropic material that exhibits power-law strain and strain-rate hardening, the load instability strains are given by Equations (5.13) and (5.16). Note that these results are valid even when the material exhibits normal plastic anisotropy (i.e., R ≠ 1).

The *localization* of strain in the diffuse necking process is, however, affected by normal plastic anisotropy when it is present. This occurs as a result of shifts in the stress and strain states within the neck away from those associated with uniaxial tension. These effects have been treated in a semiempirical manner and with the aid of a numerical simulation procedure in two papers by Ghosh.[29, 30]

In the first of these papers, Ghosh concentrates on the hardening effects of increased strain rate and the development of a biaxial stress state in the neck on flow stabilization. He assumes that the flow instability relation (Equation 5.2) does not change much with the small changes in stress state in the diffuse neck. Then he rearranges the expanded form of this instability relation in terms of $\bar{\sigma}$,

$\bar{\epsilon}$, $\dot{\bar{\epsilon}}$, and ρ^*, where ρ^* is the ratio of the in-plane principal strain ϵ_2 (width strain) to ϵ_1 (axial strain), to give:

$$\frac{1}{\bar{\sigma}}\frac{d\bar{\sigma}}{d\bar{\epsilon}} = 1 = \frac{1}{\bar{\sigma}}\left(\frac{\partial\bar{\sigma}}{\partial\bar{\epsilon}}\right)\bigg|_{\dot{\bar{\epsilon}},\rho^*} + \frac{1}{\bar{\sigma}}\left(\frac{\partial\bar{\sigma}}{\partial\dot{\bar{\epsilon}}}\right)\bigg|_{\bar{\epsilon},\rho^*}\frac{d\dot{\bar{\epsilon}}}{d\bar{\epsilon}}$$

$$+ \frac{1}{\bar{\sigma}}\left(\frac{\partial\bar{\sigma}}{\partial\bar{\rho}^*}\right)\bigg|_{\bar{\epsilon},\dot{\bar{\epsilon}}}\frac{d\rho^*}{d\bar{\epsilon}} \quad , \tag{5.99}$$

from which the following flow stability parameter, s, is obtained:

$$s = \frac{\dfrac{1}{\bar{\sigma}}\left(\dfrac{\partial\bar{\sigma}}{\partial\dot{\bar{\epsilon}}}\right)\bigg|_{\bar{\epsilon},\rho^*}\dfrac{d\dot{\bar{\epsilon}}}{d\bar{\epsilon}} + \dfrac{1}{\bar{\sigma}}\left(\dfrac{\partial\bar{\sigma}}{\partial\rho^*}\right)\bigg|_{\bar{\epsilon},\dot{\bar{\epsilon}}}\dfrac{d\rho^*}{d\bar{\epsilon}}}{1 - \dfrac{1}{\bar{\sigma}}\left(\dfrac{\partial\bar{\sigma}}{\partial\bar{\epsilon}}\right)\bigg|_{\dot{\bar{\epsilon}},\rho^*}} \quad . \tag{5.100}$$

For a power-law strain and strain-rate hardening material, Equation (5.100) becomes

$$s \approx \frac{\dfrac{m}{\theta}(\Delta\dot{\epsilon}_1/\dot{\epsilon}_1) + \dfrac{p}{\theta}\Delta\rho^*}{\dfrac{\theta}{n}} \quad , \tag{5.101}$$

where $\theta = \epsilon_1 - n$ and $p = (1/\sigma_1)(\partial\sigma_1/\partial\rho^*)|_{\epsilon_1,\dot{\epsilon}_1}$. The derivation of Equation (5.101) assumes small θ's and $\bar{\sigma} \approx \sigma_1$, $\bar{\epsilon} \approx \epsilon_1$ and $\dot{\bar{\epsilon}} \approx \dot{\epsilon}_1$. Moreover, $\Delta\dot{\epsilon}_1$ and $\Delta\rho^*$ are the changes in axial strain rate and ρ^* in the neck. Assuming a linear variation of $\dot{\epsilon}_1$ along the length of neck, Ghosh uses the approximation that $\Delta\dot{\epsilon}_1 = \dot{\epsilon}_1$. Arbitrarily setting $\Delta\rho^* = 0.005$, the flow stability parameter, Equation (5.101), for a set θ is

$$s \propto n\,(m + 0.005\,p) \quad . \tag{5.102}$$

For strains $\epsilon_1 \approx n$, p is given by

$$p = \frac{(1 + R)^3}{3(1 + 2R)} \quad . \tag{5.103}$$

With Equations (5.102) and (5.103) and the measured material properties n, m, and R, the parameter s can be determined and used to rank the relative flow stability of different materials at given fixed θ's or strains beyond n. One estimate of such flow stability is the axial extent of the diffuse neck. By making specimen profile measurements at various strains beyond maximum load for a variety of materials, Ghosh found a correlation between the s parameter and the neck length (Figure 5.12). In this way, the important effects of m and R (which tend to increase p and the level of transverse tensile stress, and hence delay neck growth) on flow localization were established.

In the second of Ghosh's papers on the sheet tensile test, the results of a finite-difference computer simulation were described. Here, he shows that flow localization in a sheet tensile test may occur even in the absence of an imperfection because of the nonuniformity of the deformation caused by the change in cross-sectional area in going from the gage section to the grip ends. It is demonstrated, however, that the presence of even mild geometric imperfections considerably enhances the growth of the diffuse neck and decreases the amount of quasistable post-uniform elongation. In addition, the simulation results confirmed the previous conclusions based on the s parameter that increasing the rate sensitivity (m) can substantially increase to-

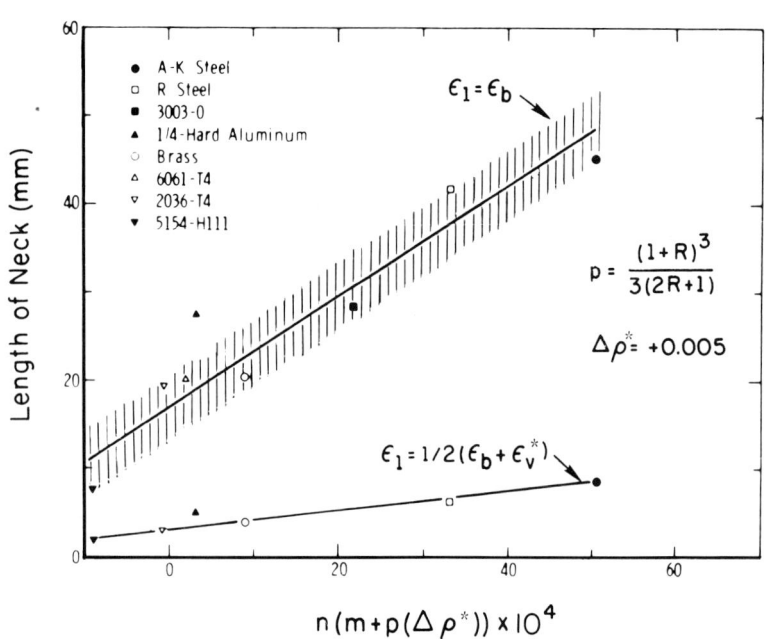

Figure 5.12. Neck length at $\varepsilon_1 = \varepsilon_b$ (or the "base" strain outside the neck) and at $\varepsilon_1 = 0.5 (\varepsilon_b + \varepsilon_v^*)$ ($\varepsilon_v^* \equiv$ strain at the boundary of a visually observed localized neck), plotted as a function of $n (m + p (\Delta\rho^*))$. $\Delta\rho^*$ is arbitrarily assumed to be +0.005.[29]

tal elongation, particularly when it is combined with moderate to large n. For example, in the presence of a small imperfection $(1 - f_o = 0.004)$, the post uniform strain for m = 0.02, n = 0.2 is estimated to be 27 percent, whereas that for m = 0.02, n = 0.05 is predicted to be reduced to only 15 percent. In the extreme case, negative m was shown to lead to serrations in the engineering stress-strain curve (much like those observed experimentally in various aluminum alloys with negative m's) and reduced uniform and post-uniform strains.

LOCAL INSTABILITY AND LOCALIZED NECKING IN SHEET METALS

The growth of the diffuse neck is terminated by fracture or by the development of a localized, through-thickness neck, as mentioned previously. In the case of localized necking, a criterion was developed by Hill[31, 32] to describe the onset of instability and the orientation of the necking direction relative to the tensile axis. An estimate of the effect of material properties on the onset of local instability will now be described. Although the criterion developed below is limited to rate-insensitive materials, its generalization is not difficult.

As with the condition for the load instability, the local instability can be assumed to occur when the current rate of strain hardening in the diffuse neck is just balanced by the rate of geometric softening (i.e., of decrease in cross-sectional area perpendicular to the load) in a possible *localized* neck. Such a localized neck can only form in plane strain; under these conditions, the longitudinally oriented principal strain is equal to the negative of the through-thickness strain, and the principal strain in the appropriate width direction is equal to zero. Thus, the localized neck is constrained to form along a zero width-strain direction.

Again, as with diffuse instability, the rate of strain hardening can be derived from the increase in axial force P with strain by holding the area term constant. It is:

$$\frac{1}{A}\left(\frac{\partial P}{\partial \varepsilon_1}\right)\bigg|_A = \frac{1}{A}\left(\frac{\partial (\sigma_1 A)}{\partial \varepsilon_1}\right)\bigg|_A = \frac{d\sigma_1}{d\varepsilon_1} \quad , \tag{5.104}$$

where the 1's denote quantities in the axial direction. The rate of strain-induced softening due to geometry changes is obtained by holding the *flow stress* constant and is similarly:

$$\frac{1}{A}\left(\frac{\partial P}{\partial \varepsilon_1}\right)\bigg|_{\sigma_1} = \sigma_1 \frac{dA/A}{d\varepsilon_1} \quad . \tag{5.105}$$

At this point, it is necessary to determine the quantity dA/A pertaining to the (possible) localized neck. This can be done by referring to the Mohr's circle for strain (Figure 5.13). Under *uniaxial* stress conditions, the principal strain increments are those associated with the axial strain, the width strain, and the thickness strain, $d\varepsilon_1$, $d\varepsilon_2$, and $d\varepsilon_3$, respectively. Because of the definition of the R value (R = $d\varepsilon_2/d\varepsilon_3$) and using volume constancy, $d\varepsilon_2$ and $d\varepsilon_3$ can be expressed in terms of $d\varepsilon_1$ and R as follows:

$$\left. \begin{array}{l} d\varepsilon_2 = -\left(\dfrac{R}{1+R}\right) d\varepsilon_1 \\[2mm] d\varepsilon_3 = -\left(\dfrac{1}{1+R}\right) d\varepsilon_1 \end{array} \right\} \quad (5.106)$$

The center of the Mohr's circle is thus at:

$$d\varepsilon = \frac{d\varepsilon_1 + d\varepsilon_2}{2} = \left(\frac{1}{2(1+R)}\right) d\varepsilon_1 \quad (5.107)$$

If the axis system that contains the zero-width strain direction (the xx, yy, zz axis system in Figure 5.13) is now examined, the normal

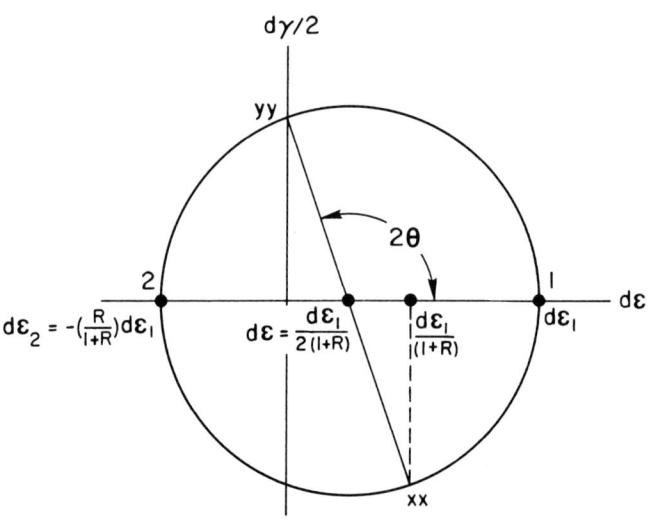

Figure 5.13. Mohr's circle representation of strain state during uniaxial tension testing of anisotropic sheet metals.

strain increments in this orientation are evident from the Mohr's circle:

$$d\varepsilon_{xx} = \left(\frac{1}{1+R}\right) d\varepsilon_1 \quad ,$$

$$d\varepsilon_{yy} = 0 \quad , \quad\quad\quad\quad\quad\quad\quad\quad (5.108)$$

and

$$d\varepsilon_{zz} = -d\varepsilon_{xx} = -\left(\frac{1}{1+R}\right) d\varepsilon_1 \quad .$$

Note that there is also a shear strain in this axis system. Along the zero-width strain (yy) direction, dA/A is simply

$$\left.\frac{dA}{A}\right|_{\substack{xx,yy,zz\\ \text{system}}} = d\varepsilon_{zz} = -\left(\frac{1}{1+R}\right) d\varepsilon_1 \quad . \quad\quad (5.109)$$

Inserting Equation (5.109) into Equation (5.105), the rate of geometric softening with respect to the incipient local instability direction is found to be:

$$\frac{1}{A}\left.\left(\frac{\partial P}{\partial \varepsilon_1}\right)\right|_{\sigma_1} = -\frac{\sigma_1}{(1+R)} \quad . \quad\quad\quad\quad (5.110)$$

By summing the results given in Equations (5.110) and (5.104) and recognizing that $\sigma_1 = \sigma(\varepsilon)$ is the uniaxial flow curve determined under uniaxial stress conditions, the following condition is obtained for the local instability:

$$\frac{d\sigma}{d\varepsilon} = \frac{\sigma}{1+R} \quad . \quad\quad\quad\quad\quad\quad (5.111)$$

For a power-hardening material, Equation (5.111) yields as the axial local instability strain, ε_ℓ:

$$\varepsilon_\ell = (1+R)n \quad . \quad\quad\quad\quad\quad\quad (5.112)$$

It is seen that large R and n delay the onset of local instability and thus local necking and failure. Another important result can be obtained if proportional loading (i.e., $d\varepsilon_1:d\varepsilon_2:d\varepsilon_3$ = constant) is assumed. Under these conditions, the differential signs may be dropped from Equations (5.106), and with Equation (5.112), the through-thickness strain at the onset of local instability, ε_{3_ℓ}, is given by:

$$\varepsilon_{3_\ell} = -\left(\frac{1}{1+R}\right)\varepsilon_\ell = -n \qquad (5.113)$$

Various measurements on failed sheet tensile specimens of low-carbon steels and several titanium alloys have verified the predictive capability of Equations (5.112) and (5.113).[33, 34] These measurements, using circle grids placed on tensile specimens prior to testing, have tended to give higher strains than those predicted by the above relationships, probably because the localized neck does not develop instantaneously following the onset of local instability. However, because the rate sensitivities of these materials were only on the order of 0.005 to 0.015, the difference was small (on the order of 15 percent or less). Although no analyses have been done to predict these strain differences, a dependence on imperfection size, n, and m can be expected, similar to those given in Equations (5.36), (5.44), and (5.69).

It should be added that measurements of the angle θ between the tensile axis and the localized neck have also agreed fairly well with that predicted from the Mohr's circle (Figure 5.13):

$$\cos(180 - 2\theta) = -\cos 2\theta = (1 + 2R)^{-1}$$

or

$$\tan \theta = \sqrt{(1+R)/R} \quad . \qquad (5.114)$$

For isotropic materials, $\tan \theta = \sqrt{2}$, yielding $\theta = 54.7°$.

Bifurcation Theory

In the analysis described above regarding the onset and growth of necks in round bar and sheet tensile specimens, the presence of some imperfection or inherently inhomogeneous strain state was assumed as a triggering mechanism for flow localization. Although a great deal of experimental data seems to support the conclusions drawn from such theories, a totally different approach to the necking problem has been put forward in the last fifteen years. This approach is based on the mathematical concept of bifurcation, which can be used to demonstrate that a necking mode of deformation may be possible, regardless of the presence of an imperfection or imposed strain gradient.

The simplest application of bifurcation theory is that for the analysis of the necking of a homogeneous round tensile bar whose ends are subject to an axial extension and zero shear tractions.[35, 36] Under these conditions, two deformation modes or mathematical solutions can be visualized beyond the maximum load (Figure 5.14). The first, termed the fundamental mathematical solution, involves the continued homogeneous deformation after the load maximum under slowly falling load. In this case, the velocity field is uniform throughout the body. Also, it should be noted that, under constant extension rate conditions, the energy input rate per unit volume, $\dot{E}$ (equal to

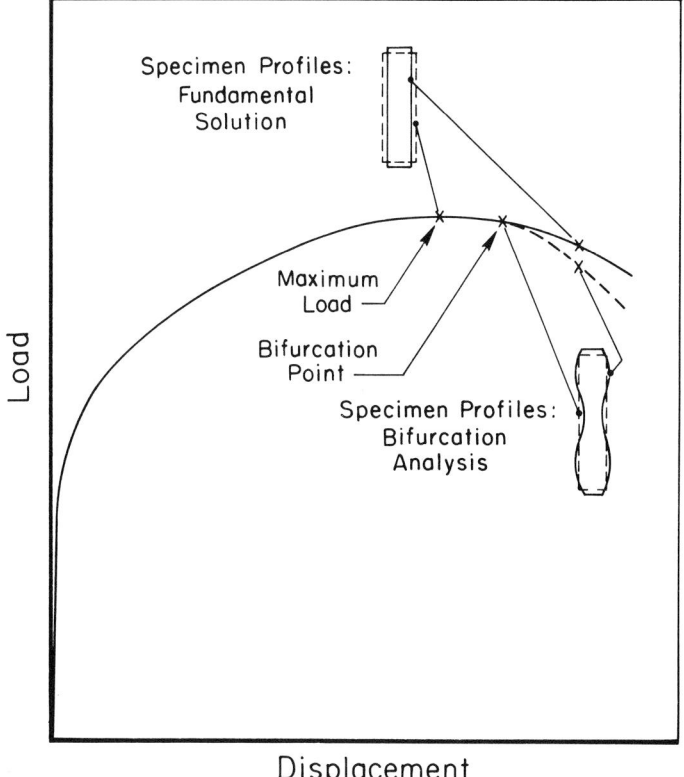

Figure 5.14. Fundamental and bifurcation (necking) modes for tension of a round bar with shear free ends.[35, 36]

Instability and Flow Localization in Uniaxial Tension

σέ), passes through a maximum at maximum load in the fundamental solution.

A bifurcation is said to exist if another deformation mode (or modes) is possible that also gives rise to a maximum in the energy input rate and that satisfies the same set of boundary conditions and stress equilibria throughout the body. For the uniaxial tension of a round bar, the bifurcation mode is necking. If necking were to be initiated *at* the load maximum, the shear energy involved would increase the energy input rate so that $\dot{E}$ would not pass through a maximum here. Thus, bifurcation cannot occur at this point. On the other hand, if necking were to be initiated at a somewhat greater extension, at which the fundamental solution exhibits a *decreasing* energy input rate, the development of a neck and the accompanying need for shear energy input could in fact give rise to an overall energy input rate that is still decreasing and that therefore has passed through a maximum. It is this particular extension that signals the point of bifurcation and the onset of necking.

The exact displacement and hence axial strain at which bifurcation occurs is a function of the length-to-diameter (L_o/D_o) ratio of the tensile specimen. The most easily accommodated necking bifurcation involves a velocity distribution disturbance whose wavelength is equal the length of the specimen. Thus, because the shear energy term increases with decreasing wavelength of the neck, bifurcation occurs at larger and larger strains as the length-to-diameter ratio (L_o/D_o) of the specimen decreases. At an infinite value of this ratio, bifurcation via necking may be expected to occur at maximum load. For finite values of this ratio, calculations on rate-insensitive elastic-plastic materials, such as those carried out by Needleman,[36] show that the bifurcation strain can be merely a few percent greater than the maximum load strain for L_o/D_o equal to 4, or as large as several times the maximum load strain for L_o/D_o equal to 2, the exact numbers depending on the choice of constitutive relation.

Unfortunately, little experimental confirmation of the bifurcation theory of necking in uniaxial tension has been attempted. This may be because of the difficulty of imposing the required boundary conditions. Nevertheless, research of this type is needed before a judgment regarding the validity or practical value of the theory can be made.

Summary

Most analyses of the onset and growth of necks in the uniaxial tension test have employed one of two methods. The preponderance of the analyses have centered on the effect of imperfections on strain localization. The imperfections are generally in the form of either a deformation defect or a geometric defect. The latter type of imperfection leads to much more rapid rates of flow localization and thus smaller total elongations in tension. Moreover, the analyses have shown that the imperfection does not grow appreciably to form a neck until *after* the load instability strain is reached. Following this strain, the analyses have demonstrated the important influence of large rate sensitivity in quasistabilizing the deformation and allowing total elongations much larger than the maximum load strain. The predictions of these models are backed by a large amount of experimental verification.

The strain associated with the onset of necking can be estimated through another technique involving a search for bifurcations in the mathematical solution of the plasticity boundary value problem. Using this technique, the strain at the onset of necking in tension testing is predicted to occur at strains *exceeding* the maximum load strain, the exact amount depends on the geometry of the test specimen. However, the bifurcation theory of necking onset requires experimental verification before it can be applied with confidence.

References

[1] A. Considère: *Ann. des Ponts et Chaussées*, 1885, vol. 9, ser. 6, p. 574.
[2] E.W. Hart: *Acta Met.*, 1967, vol. 15, p. 351.
[3] J.D. Campbell: *J. Mech. Phys. Solids*, 1967, vol. 15, p. 359.
[4] J.J. Jonas, R.A. Holt, and C.E. Coleman: *Acta Met.*, 1976, vol. 24, p. 911.
[5] A.K. Ghosh: *J. Eng. Mat. Techn., Trans. ASME*, 1977, vol. 99H, p. 264.
[6] F.A. Nichols: *Acta Met.*, 1980, vol. 28, p. 663.
[7] J.W. Hutchinson and H. Obrecht: *Proc. Fourth Inter. Conf. on Fracture, Vol. 1*, D.M.R. Taplin, ed., University of Waterloo Press, Waterloo, Ontario, 1977, p. 101.
[8] E. Duncombe: *Inter. J. Mech. Sci.*, 1972, vol. 14, p. 325.
[9] A.K. Ghosh and R.A. Ayres: *Met. Trans. A*, 1976, vol. 7A, p. 1589.
[10] A.K. Ghosh: *Acta Met.*, 1977, vol. 25, p. 1413.
[11] Z. Marciniak: *Aspects of Material Formability*, Ch. 1, McMaster University, Hamilton, Ontario, 1974.
[12] J.W. Hutchinson and K.W. Neale: *Acta Met.*, 1977, vol. 25, p. 839.
[13] D.A. Woodford: *Trans. ASM*, 1969, vol. 62, p. 291.
[14] M. Azrin and W.A. Backofen: *Met. Trans.*, 1970, vol. 1, p. 2857.
[15] N. Christodoulou and J.J. Jonas: *Res Mechanica*, 1982, vol. 5, p. 49.
[16] J.J. Jonas: *Superplastic Forming of Structural Alloys*, N. Paton and C.H. Hamilton, eds., p. 57, TMS-AIME, Warrendale, PA, 1982.
[17] M. Suery and B. Baudelet: *Rev. de Phys. Appl.*, 1978, vol. 13, p. 53.

[18] B. Baudelet and M. Suery: *J. Mat. Sci.*, 1972, vol. 7, p. 512.
[19] M. Suery and B. Baudelet: *J. Mat. Sci.*, 1973, vol. 8, p. 363.
[20] A.K. Ghosh and C.H. Hamilton: *Met. Trans. A*, 1979, vol. 10A, p. 699.
[21] U.F. Kocks, J.J. Jonas, and H. Mecking: *Acta Met.*, 1979, vol. 27, p. 419.
[22] J.J. Jonas and B. Baudelet: *Acta Met.*, 1977, vol. 25, p. 43.
[23] N. Christodoulou, J.J. Jonas, and G. Canova: *Mechanical Testing for Deformation Model Development, ASTM STP 765*, R.W. Rohde and J.C. Swearengen, eds., p. 51, American Society for Testing and Materials, Philadelphia, 1982.
[24] N. Christodoulou: Ph.D. Thesis, Department of Metallurgical Engineering, McGill University, 1982.
[25] N. Christodoulou and J.J. Jonas: *Can. Met. Quart.*, 1983, vol. 22, p. 379.
[26] A.T. Santhanam and R.E. Reed-Hill: *Met. Trans.*, 1971, vol. 2, p. 2619.
[27] F.J.M. Boratto, P.R. Cetlin, and J.T. Veado: *Scripta Met.*, 1973, vol. 7, p. 1031.
[28] W.A. Backofen: *Deformation Processing*, Ch. 10, Addison-Wesley, Reading, MA, 1972.
[29] A.K. Ghosh: *Met Trans.*, 1974, vol. 5, p. 1607.
[30] A.K. Ghosh: *Met. Trans. A*, 1977, vol. 8A, p. 1221.
[31] R. Hill: *Proc. Roy. Soc. London,* 1948, vol. 193, ser. A, p. 281.
[32] R. Hill: *The Mathematical Theory of Plasticity*, Oxford University Press, London, 1950.
[33] S.L. Semiatin: Unpublished research, Armco, Inc., Middletown, OH, 1978.
[34] K.S. Chan, K.J. Weinmann, and D.A. Koss: *Proc. NAMRC-X,* R.S. Hahn, ed., p. 116, Society of Manufacturing Engineers, Dearborn, MI, 1982.
[35] J.P. Miles: *J. Mech. Phys. Solids*, 1971, vol. 19, p. 89.
[36] A. Needleman: *J. Mech. Phys. Solids*, 1972, vol. 20, p. 111.

INSTABILITY AND FLOW LOCALIZATION DURING SHEET FORMING

The formability of flat-rolled thin sheet metals is often controlled by flow localization processes in much the same way as the total elongation is in a flat sheet or round bar tensile test. That is to say, the occurrence of tensile instability, due to geometric softening and the concentration of strain at material imperfections, often determines the amount of plastic deformation that can be imposed prior to failure. This failure is influenced by necking geometries that take two basic forms. The first of these, the diffuse neck, corresponds to a very gradual and mild thinning of the sheet, the extent of which is many times the sheet thickness. Because, in many sheet forming operations such as stretching, the sheet is clamped around its entire periphery, the symmetric profile radius observed during diffuse necking in a sheet tensile test is often not detectable. Moreover, substantial amounts of deformation are frequently obtainable even after the onset of diffuse necking. For this reason, the process of diffuse necking is considered as merely a precursor to the second necking mode, that of the localized neck, which actually determines the formability of the sheet metal. During this necking process, plastic flow concentrates into a through-thickness neck along a zero-extension direction, the extent of which is approximately equal to the sheet thickness. When this occurs, deformation outside the neck ceases, determining the so-called forming limit strain levels.

In this chapter, the Swift and Hill instability criteria for diffuse and local instability, respectively, will be summarized.[1-3] These criteria provide insight into the gross limits of sheet metal formability in much the same way as the Considère criterion for instability and necking in the uniaxial tensile test. However, they are incapable of describing the rate of flow localization following instability. For this purpose, analyses such as that due to Marciniak and his co-workers are required.[4-6] Such analyses are particularly important for imposed deformation states that consist of two positive in-plane strains. In these instances, Hill's local instability criterion cannot be applied, and the presence of a material or geometric imperfection must often be postulated to account for the development of a local strain state that includes a zero-extension direction.

Swift's Diffuse Instability Criterion

In the previous chapter, the onset of diffuse instability in the tensile test was associated with the attainment of a load maximum. Under conditions of *biaxial* tensile loading, such a criterion is not applicable. In these situations, a more general condition is needed. Although a number of criteria have been developed (e.g., instability is initiated when one or the other of the loads associated with the principal stresses passes through a maximum),[7] the one due to Swift[1], which is restricted to von Mises rate and temperature independent materials, appears to be the most reasonable on physical grounds.

The Swift criterion states that an instability is initiated when the increment in applied effective stress due to geometric softening exceeds that which can be produced by strain hardening. It defines the strain at which a function of the principal stresses passes through a maximum. To obtain the increment in effective stress due to changes in the applied strains, use will be made of the von Mises effective stress (Equation 2.14a). Attention will be restricted to the plane stress case involving the principal stresses σ_1 and σ_2 (and principal strains ε_1 and ε_2). In most sheet forming applications, the thickness stress is usually quite small anyway. In this case, the effective stress is:

$$\bar{\sigma} = (\sigma_1^2 - \sigma_1\sigma_2 + \sigma_2^2)^{1/2} \quad . \tag{6.1}$$

Differentiating this expression, the increment in effective stress is found to be

$$d\bar{\sigma} = \frac{(2\sigma_1 - \sigma_2)d\sigma_1 + (2\sigma_2 - \sigma_1)d\sigma_2}{2\bar{\sigma}} \quad . \tag{6.2}$$

Defining the stress ratio $X = \sigma_2/\sigma_1$:

$$d\bar{\sigma} = \frac{(2 - X)d\sigma_1 + (2X - 1)d\sigma_2}{2\sqrt{1 - X + X^2}} \quad . \tag{6.3}$$

Further reduction of this equation relies on the load maxima conditions, the definition of effective strain, and the flow rule. A load maximum along the "1" principal direction requires

$$0 = dP_1 = d(\sigma_1 A_1) = \sigma_1 dA_1 + A_1 d\sigma_1$$

or

$$d\sigma_1 = \sigma_1 d\varepsilon_1 \quad . \tag{6.4}$$

Similarly, the condition for the "2" principal direction is:

$$d\sigma_2 = \sigma_2 d\varepsilon_2 \quad . \tag{6.5}$$

Inserting Equations (6.4) and (6.5) into (6.3) results in

$$d\bar{\sigma} = \left\{\frac{(2 - X) + (2X - 1)(X)(d\varepsilon_2/d\varepsilon_1)}{2\sqrt{1 - X + X^2}}\right\} \sigma_1 d\varepsilon_1 \quad . \tag{6.6}$$

Next, use is made of the definition of effective strain (Equation 2.16a), the incompressibility condition, and the flow rule (Equation 2.15a) to obtain:

$$d\bar{\varepsilon} = \frac{2}{\sqrt{3}} \left\{1 + \frac{d\varepsilon_2}{d\varepsilon_1} + \left(\frac{d\varepsilon_2}{d\varepsilon_1}\right)^2\right\}^{1/2} d\varepsilon_1 \quad . \tag{6.7}$$

and

$$\frac{d\varepsilon_2}{d\varepsilon_1} = \frac{1 - 2X}{X - 2} \quad . \tag{6.8}$$

Putting these into Equation (6.6), employing the definition of effective stress (Equation 6.1), and performing a small amount of algebraic manipulation, the following is obtained:

$$d\bar{\sigma} = \frac{\bar{\sigma} d\bar{\varepsilon}}{Z_d} \quad . \tag{6.9a}$$

Instability and Flow Localization During Sheet Forming

where

$$Z_d = \frac{4(1 - X + X^2)^{3/2}}{(4 - 3X - 3X^2 + 4X^3)} \quad . \tag{6.9b}$$

The increment in effective stress $d\bar{\sigma}_H$ due to strain hardening (in a rate and temperature-independent material) is easily found to be

$$d\bar{\sigma}_H = \left(\frac{\partial \bar{\sigma}}{\partial \bar{\varepsilon}}\right)\bigg|_{\dot{\bar{\varepsilon}},T} d\bar{\varepsilon} = \frac{d\bar{\sigma}}{d\bar{\varepsilon}} d\bar{\varepsilon} \quad . \tag{6.10}$$

Equating (6.9) and (6.10) leads to the condition for the onset of diffuse instability:

$$\frac{d\bar{\sigma}}{d\bar{\varepsilon}} = \frac{\bar{\sigma}}{Z_d} \quad . \tag{6.11}$$

Note that this equation defines a critical subtangent for instability, which is analogous to that obtained from the Considère analysis. This subtangent is, however, a function of the applied stress ratio.

The application of Equation (6.11) is quite straightforward once the strain-hardening behavior of a material is known. If it is assumed that a power-law hardening formulation ($\bar{\sigma} = K\bar{\varepsilon}^n$) is valid for all strain paths and if attention is further restricted to proportional straining ($d\varepsilon_2/d\varepsilon_1$ = constant = ρ^*), Equation (6.11) yields the effective strain at the onset of diffuse instability, $\bar{\varepsilon}_d$:

$$\bar{\varepsilon}_d = nZ_d \quad . \tag{6.12}$$

The principal in-plane strains associated with this effective strain are found using Equations (6.7), (6.8), and (6.9b):

$$\left.\begin{array}{l} \varepsilon_{1_d} = \dfrac{(4 - 2X)(1 - X + X^2)}{(4 - 3X - 3X^2 + 4X^3)} n \\[2mm] \varepsilon_{2_d} = \dfrac{(1 - 2X)}{(X - 2)} \varepsilon_{1_d} \end{array}\right\} \tag{6.13}$$

For the stress states of uniaxial tension ($X = 0$, $\rho^* = -1/2$), plane strain tension ($X = +0.5$, $\rho^* = 0$), and balanced biaxial tension ($X = \rho^* = 1$), instability is initiated at $\varepsilon_{1_d} = n$ for an isotropic power-law hardening material. The behavior of such a material deformed proportionally along other paths is shown in Figure 6.1. For a metal sheet that possesses some normal anisotropy R, Moore and Wallace[8] have shown that the critical subtangent is defined through a Z_d equal to

$$Z_d = \sqrt{\frac{2(2+R)}{3}}$$
$$\cdot \left\{ \frac{[(1+R) - 2RX + (1+R)X^2]^{3/2}}{(1+R)^2 - (2+R)RX - (2+R)RX^2 + (1+R)^2 X^3} \right\} \cdot$$
(6.14)

Note that this reduces to Equation (6.9b) when R = 1. The effect of R ≠ 1 on the strain levels at diffuse instability is well illustrated in the paper by Moore and Wallace.

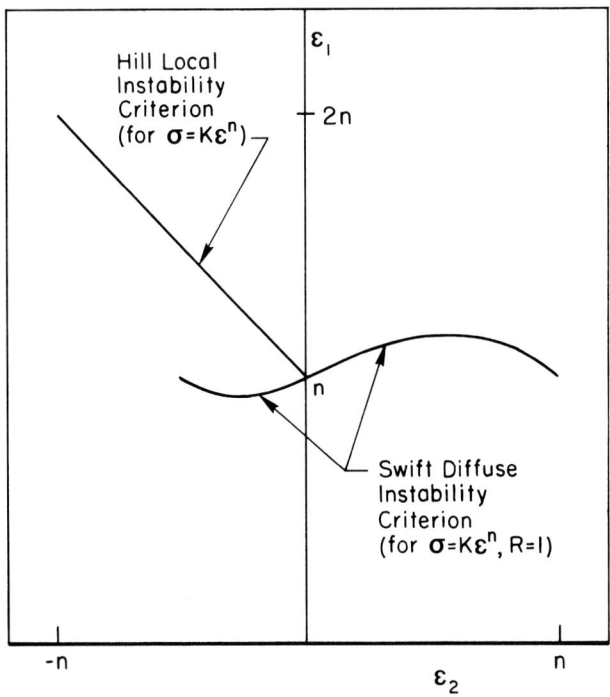

Figure 6.1. Principal surface strains, ε_1 and ε_2, that satisfy the Swift (diffuse instability) and Hill (local instability) criteria for a rate-insensitive material exhibiting power-law strain hardening.[1, 2]

Instability and Flow Localization During Sheet Forming 203

Hill's Local Instability Criterion

Although the Swift criterion gives a very gross approximation of the forming limits of many metals whose rate sensitivities are minimal, other conditions are needed to predict precisely the shift in localization mode from diffuse to localized, or through-thickness, necking and hence the onset of failure. A criterion due to Hill[2] is applicable when one of the two principal in-plane strains describing the deformation state is negative and the other is positive. In these cases, a direction of zero extension (i.e., a direction along which the normal strain is zero) exists and is the most probable site for through-thickness necking.

Hill's criterion for the onset of local instability along a zero-extension direction is derived in a manner quite analogous to the way in which local instability in a sheet tensile test is predicted (Chapter 5). The derivation is begun by postulating proportional straining, i.e., it is assumed that the ratio of the principal in-plane strains remains constant, even after the onset of diffuse instability. With proportional straining, $d\varepsilon_2/d\varepsilon_1 = \varepsilon_2/\varepsilon_1 = $ a constant, ρ^*. Local instability is said to arise when the rate of strain-induced hardening associated with the larger in-plane principal stress is just balanced by the rate of geometric softening. As for tensile testing, the rate of strain-induced hardening is that given by Equation (5.104):

$$\frac{1}{A}\left(\frac{\partial P_1}{\partial \varepsilon_1}\right)\bigg|_A = \frac{d\sigma_1}{d\varepsilon_1} \quad . \tag{6.15}$$

The rate of geometric softening along the zero-extension direction, yy, is found from:

$$\frac{1}{A}\left(\frac{\partial P_1}{\partial \varepsilon_1}\right)\bigg|_{\sigma_1} = \sigma_1 \frac{(dA/A)|_{yy}}{d\varepsilon_1} \tag{6.16}$$

and the Mohr's circle for strain (Figure 6.2). The quantity $(dA/A)|_{yy}$ is equal to the thickness normal strain $d\varepsilon_{zz}$ (see Chapter 5), which is equal to $-d\varepsilon_{xx}$,

$$-d\varepsilon_{xx} = -2\left(\frac{d\varepsilon_1 + d\varepsilon_2}{2}\right) = -(d\varepsilon_1 + d\varepsilon_2) \quad . \tag{6.17}$$

Hence, the rate of strain-induced, or geometric, softening is

$$\frac{1}{A}\left(\frac{\partial P_1}{\partial \varepsilon_1}\right)\bigg|_{\sigma_1} = -\sigma_1\left(1 + \frac{d\varepsilon_2}{d\varepsilon_1}\right) = -\sigma_1(1 + \rho^*) \quad , \tag{6.18}$$

and local instability is induced when

$$\frac{d\sigma_1}{d\varepsilon_1} + \left(-\sigma_1(1+\rho^*)\right) = 0 \quad . \tag{6.19}$$

Rearranging Equation (6.19), the local instability condition is

$$\frac{d\sigma_1}{d\varepsilon_1} = \sigma_1(1+\rho^*) \quad . \tag{6.20}$$

Before proceeding, it should be pointed out that a local instability cannot occur in strain states characterized by ρ^* equal to -1 (a state of pure shear) or less, i.e., strain states in which the thickness strain is everywhere zero or positive. For $\rho^* > -1$, the assumption of proportional straining leads to relations between $\bar{\sigma}$ and σ_1 and $\bar{\varepsilon}$ and ε_1 of the form

$$\left.\begin{array}{c} \sigma_1 = C_\sigma \bar{\sigma} \\ \\ \text{and} \\ \\ \varepsilon_1 = C_\varepsilon \bar{\varepsilon} \quad , \end{array}\right\} \tag{6.21}$$

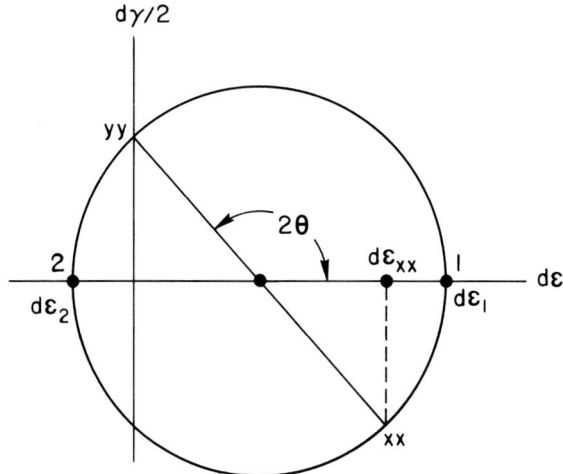

Figure 6.2. Mohr's circle for strain states characterized by $\varepsilon_2 \leq 0$ and $\varepsilon_1 > 0$.

where C_σ and C_ε are constants equal to $(1 - X + X^2)^{-1/2}$ and $(X - 2)/2\sqrt{1 - X + X^2}$, respectively, in a von Mises material. The stress ratio X is determined from the value of ρ^* and Equation (6.8). Substituting Equations (6.21) into (6.20) results in

$$\left(\frac{1}{C_\varepsilon}\right)\frac{d\bar{\sigma}}{d\bar{\varepsilon}} = \bar{\sigma}(1 + \rho^*) \qquad . \tag{6.22}$$

In the case of a power-law hardening material, $\bar{\sigma} = K\bar{\varepsilon}^n$, this expression gives

$$\frac{n}{C_\varepsilon \bar{\varepsilon}_\ell} = \frac{n}{\varepsilon_{1_\ell}} = (1 + \rho^*) = \left(1 + \frac{\varepsilon_{2_\ell}}{\varepsilon_{1_\ell}}\right) \quad ,$$

or

$$n = \varepsilon_{1_\ell} + \varepsilon_{2_\ell} \quad , \tag{6.23}$$

where the subscript ℓ refers to conditions at the onset of local instability. This last equation is the very simple condition for local instability in a power-law hardening material. On a plot of ε_1 versus ε_2, the locus of strains satisfying this condition lies in the second quadrant along a line, at 45° to the abscissa, whose intercept is equal to n (Figure 6.1). Viewed differently, local instability sets in at a true thickness strain ε_{3_ℓ} of $-n$ ($= -(\varepsilon_{1_\ell} + \varepsilon_{2_\ell})$) because of volume constancy.

It should be noted that the simple result of Equation (6.23) is independent of the normal plastic anistropy parameter, R. The effect of R enters only through the various stress ratios that correspond to particular imposed values of ρ^*. From the flow rule (Equation 2.15b), ρ^* and X for an anisotropic material are related through:

$$\rho^* = \frac{d\varepsilon_2}{d\varepsilon_1} = \frac{R - (1 + R)X}{RX - (1 + R)} \tag{6.24}$$

It should also be observed that the angle between the principal direction 1 and the zero-extension direction of local instability, from the Mohr's circle, is

$$\theta = \tan^{-1}(1/\sqrt{-\rho^*}) \quad , \tag{6.25}$$

and depends on X only through its dependence on ρ^*.

As with tensile instability and necking, an additional strain increment beyond the strains defined by Equation (6.23) must be imposed before a localized neck is observed. The amount of this strain increment is dependent primarily on the rate sensitivity of the material. For materials that show negligible rate sensitivity, localized necking can be expected soon after the local instability strain. One such material that confirms this conclusion is the sandwich sheet material stainless steel clad aluminum, both of whose components (304 stainless steel and 1100 aluminum) display rather low rate sensitivity.[9] This material has an effective n value of 0.33 and R ≈ 1, and localized necking observations that formed the basis of the $\rho^* \leq 0$ forming limit diagram (Figure 6.3) were found to follow the same trend as the predicted local instability strains from Equation (6.23). In fact, the average strain increment, $\Delta\varepsilon_1$, between the local instability strain and the forming limit strain was only approximately 0.07.

Flow Localization for $\rho^* > 0$

MARCINIAK-KUCZYNSKI ANALYSIS

For strain paths characterized by $\rho^* > 0$ (i.e., those in the so-called stretching regime of the forming limit diagram), no zero-extension direction exists along which local instability and localized necking can occur. Thus, since through-thickness necking is still frequently observed to precede fracture, some other process that allows for the flow localization to develop must be hypothesized. Such a process was put forward by the Polish researchers Marciniak and Kuczynski in pioneering work first published in English in 1967.[4-6, 10, 11] The model by Marciniak and his co-workers postulates the presence of a material imperfection at which a shift in strain state from $\rho^* > 0$ to $\rho^* = 0$ occurs and thence permits a localized neck to form. Such a process and model were discussed in Chapter 3 with regard to flow localization and surface fracture during bulk forming at cold working temperatures.

Although the Marciniak and Kuczynski (M-K) model allows for the consideration of imperfections whose origin may be material related (e.g., variations in hardness, strain hardening index, etc.), the growth of an imperfection that is *geometric* in nature is most easily formulated and visualized. This geometric imperfection was taken to be a thickness variation or groove perpendicular to the maximum principal stress σ_1 (Figure 6.4). It will be assumed that, in the region outside the imperfection (i.e., region A), the loading is uniform and proportional, i.e., $(d\varepsilon_2/d\varepsilon_1)|_A$ = a constant, ρ^*. This uniformity assumption is a good one when the sheet is stretched in plane, but not when it is punch stretched. Hence, the forming limits predicted from the M-K analysis are strictly applicable only in the former case.

From the definitions of effective stress, effective strain, and the flow rule (Equations 2.14b, 2.16b, and 2.15b), the following can be defined in terms of the principal stresses, σ_1, σ_2, principal strains, ε_1, ε_2, and the strain ratio, ρ^*:

$$X_A = \frac{\sigma_{2_A}}{\sigma_{1_A}} = \frac{R + \rho^*(1 + R)}{R\rho^* + (1 + R)} \quad , \tag{6.26}$$

$$\bar{\sigma}_A = \sigma_{1_A} \sqrt{\frac{3(1 + R)}{2(2 + R)}} \left(1 - \frac{2R}{1 + R} X_A + X_A^2\right)^{1/2} \quad , \tag{6.27}$$

and

$$d\bar{\varepsilon}_A = d\varepsilon_{1_A} \sqrt{\frac{2(2 + R)(1 + R)}{3(1 + 2R)} \left(1 + \frac{2R}{1 + R} \rho^* + \rho^{*2}\right)} \tag{6.28}$$

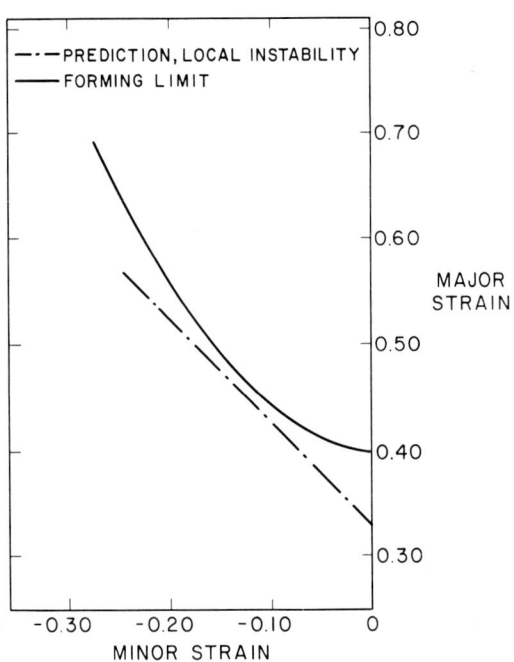

Figure 6.3. Forming limit measurements and local instability predictions for stainless steel clad aluminum sheet deformed under strain paths characterized by $\rho^* \leq 0$.[9]

Note that X_A and ρ^* ($= d\varepsilon_2/d\varepsilon_{1_A}$) are assumed to remain constant during the entire deformation.

In the region with the imperfection (region B), the stress and strain state can be obtained from considerations of force equilibrium and strain compatibility. Force equilibrium leads to

$$\sigma_{1_B} = \sigma_{1_A} (t_A/t_B) = \sigma_{1_A}/f \quad , \tag{6.29}$$

where t_A and t_B are the thicknesses in regions A and B (the grooved region), respectively, and f is the inhomogeneity or imperfection parameter, which is assumed to have a value of f_o (less than unity) at the onset of deformation and which gradually decreases during flow localization.

The stress component σ_{2_B} is obtained from the fact that $d\varepsilon_{2_B} = d\varepsilon_{2_A} = \rho^* \, d\varepsilon_{1_A}$. To obtain an expression for $d\varepsilon_{2_B}$, we start by defining the stress ratio in the B region, X_B. With this stress ratio, the effective stress σ_B is given by

$$\bar{\sigma}_B = \sigma_{1_B} \sqrt{\frac{3(1+R)}{2(2+R)}} \left(1 - \frac{2R}{1+R} X_B + X_B^2 \right)^{1/2} . \tag{6.30}$$

The two effective stresses $\bar{\sigma}_A$ and $\bar{\sigma}_B$ can now be used to relate $\bar{\varepsilon}_A$ and

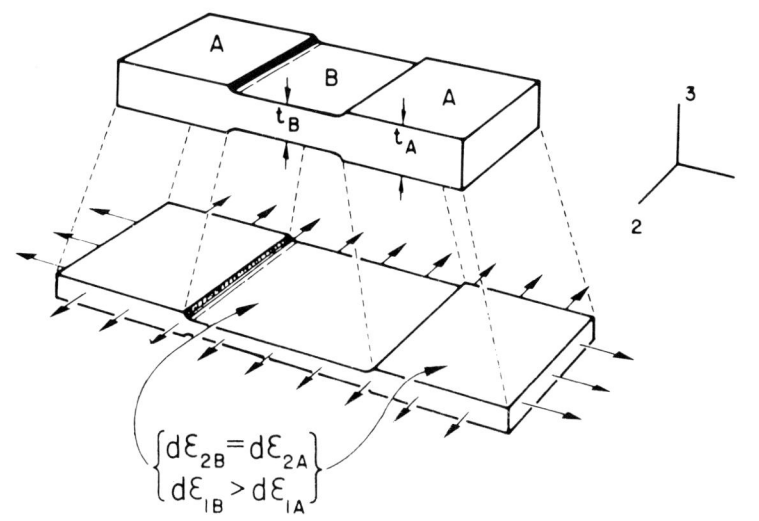

Figure 6.4. Schematic view of how the strain state in the region of a thickness imperfection (region B) can approach plane strain while proportional straining is maintained outside (region A).[13]

$\bar{\varepsilon}_B$ if a constitutive relation is postulated. For this purpose, let us assume that $\bar{\sigma} = K\bar{\varepsilon}^n$. Thus, from Equations (6.27), (6.29), and (6.30),

$$\bar{\varepsilon}_B = \bar{\varepsilon}_A \left\{ \frac{1}{f} \cdot \frac{\left(1 - \frac{2R}{1+R} X_B + X_B^2\right)^{1/2}}{\left(1 - \frac{2R}{1+R} X_A + X_A^2\right)^{1/2}} \right\}^{1/n}$$

$$= \bar{\varepsilon}_A \cdot F(f, X_A, X_B) \quad . \tag{6.31}$$

From Equation (6.31), the *increments* in effective strain $d\bar{\varepsilon}_B$ can be evaluated during a strain localization process defined by the independent variables $\bar{\varepsilon}_A$ and $d\bar{\varepsilon}_A$ and the instantaneous values of f. The increments in the principal strain components in the B region can then be determined from the flow rule and the definition of effective strain (Equations 2.15b and 2.16b):

$$d\varepsilon_{1_B} = d\bar{\varepsilon}_B \sqrt{\left(\frac{3(1 + 2R)}{2(2 + R)(1 + R)}\right) \left(1 + \frac{2R}{1 + R} \rho_B^* + \rho_B^{*2}\right)^{-1/2}} ,$$
(6.32a)

$$d\varepsilon_{2_B} = \rho_B^* d\bar{\varepsilon}_B \sqrt{\frac{3(1 + 2R)}{2(2 + R)(1 + R)}} \left(1 + \frac{2R}{1 + R} \rho_B^* + \rho_B^{*2}\right)^{-1/2}$$
(6.32b)

$$d\varepsilon_{3_B} = -d\varepsilon_{1_B} - d\varepsilon_{2_B} \quad , \tag{6.32c}$$

where

$$\rho_B^* = \frac{R - (1 + R)X_B}{RX_B - (1 + R)} \quad . \tag{6.33}$$

Since $d\varepsilon_{2_B} = d\varepsilon_{2_A}$, Equations (6.31) and (6.32b) represent two equations in two unknowns, X_B and $d\bar{\varepsilon}_B$ (or $\bar{\varepsilon}_B$). Hence, all of the strain components in the B region can be evaluated. The change in f due to the imposed strain increment is found easily from

$$df = d(t_B/t_A) = f(d\varepsilon_{3_B} - d\varepsilon_{3_A}) \quad . \tag{6.34}$$

With the above equations, the strain localization in the groove is readily determined. Initially $d\varepsilon_{1_A}$, ρ^*, and f_o (the initial value of f) are selected. From this, X_A, σ_{1_A}, $\bar{\sigma}_A$, $d\bar{\varepsilon}_A$, and $\bar{\varepsilon}_A$ are found from Equations (6.26), (6.27), and (6.28) and the constitutive relation. Then Equations (6.31) and (6.32b) are applied to estimate $d\bar{\varepsilon}_B$ (and $\bar{\varepsilon}_B$) and X_B, from which the strain components $d\varepsilon_{1_B}$ and $d\varepsilon_{3_B}$ are derived and hence a new value for f (Equations 6.32c and 6.34). The procedure is then repeated with the new value of f by "applying" another strain increment $d\varepsilon_{1_A}$ under the same imposed ρ^*. When this is done a sufficient number of times, the strain state in the groove, as characterized by ρ_B^*, approaches plane strain ($\rho_B^* = 0$). When ρ_B^* is sufficiently close to zero (e.g., 10^{-4}), the strains ε_{1_A} and ε_{2_A} are taken as the limit strains. This approach and sample results are given in Appendix D.

Marciniak and his co-workers have extended this analysis to materials with various constitutive behaviors and degrees of normal plastic anisotropy. They have also treated materials that exhibit rate sensitivity and planar plastic anisotropy. The general trends are that limit strains increase as ρ^* increases for given material properties and a fixed imperfection size f_o; for fixed ρ^*, they increase with increasing f_o, decreasing R, and increasing strain and strain-rate hardening rates. The original M-K papers should be reviewed for the details of these trends.

SOWERBY-DUNCAN INTERPRETATION OF THE M-K ANALYSIS

In a paper that followed shortly after the original M-K publication in 1967, two Canadian workers, Sowerby and Duncan, described the thrusts of the M-K analysis in a graphical manner employing the yield locus.[6] Their method, which was also discussed in a U.S. Army report by Azrin and Wonsiewicz,[12] shows the effects of ρ^* on forming limits very well and is therefore reviewed here.

Assuming, as in the M-K analysis, that the stretched sheet has a thickness imperfection perpendicular to the larger in-plane principal stress, σ_1, the states of stress and strain increment in region A and the grooved region B can be represented on a set of yield loci (Figure 6.5). As the sheet is loaded initially, region B reaches the yield locus first, because its cross-sectional area is lower; σ_{1_A} and σ_{1_B} are related through f_o. Prior to yielding, the stress states pertaining to the two regions are characterized by points A and B in Figure 6.5. As loading in region A is increased just to the point of yield, A_0, but not beyond, σ_{1_B} increases, but the stress state characterizing region B (point B_0) must stay on the initial yield locus, because no plastic strain increment has yet been imposed. When a strain increment, $d\bar{\varepsilon}_A$, is imposed in region A, however, a strain increment of greater magnitude, $d\bar{\varepsilon}_B$, must take place in region B because of the condition $d\varepsilon_{2_A} = d\varepsilon_{2_B}$ and the normality rule. After this strain increment, the stress state in region A goes from A_0 to A_1 along a proportional (constant X_A) stress path to a new yield locus. The material in region B, though, has undergone a larger amount of deformation ($d\bar{\varepsilon}_B > d\bar{\varepsilon}_A$) and thus lies on a larger yield surface. Further, since f has decreased, X_B, the stress ratio in region B, decreases. The overall result in B is therefore a movement from B_0 to B_1 in $\sigma_1 - \sigma_2$ space (Figure 6.5). With increasing deformation, the process is repeated, until finally $\rho_B^* \approx 0$.

From the above discussion, it is apparent that f_0 has a large effect on the amount of deformation that can be imposed prior to $\rho_B^* \approx 0$. In addition, and more importantly, it is obvious that the amount of deformation that can be imposed during the gradual flow localization process prior to $\rho_B^* \approx 0$ is a strong function of the X_A or ρ_A^* ratio imposed in the uniform region of the sheet. As ρ_A^* increases (up to a maximum of 1), the stress state in the region of imperfection *starts* at stress states that are farther and farther away from $\rho_B^* = 0$. Hence, more strain can be imposed in the imperfection, as well as in the uniform region, prior to failure. For this reason, forming limits can be

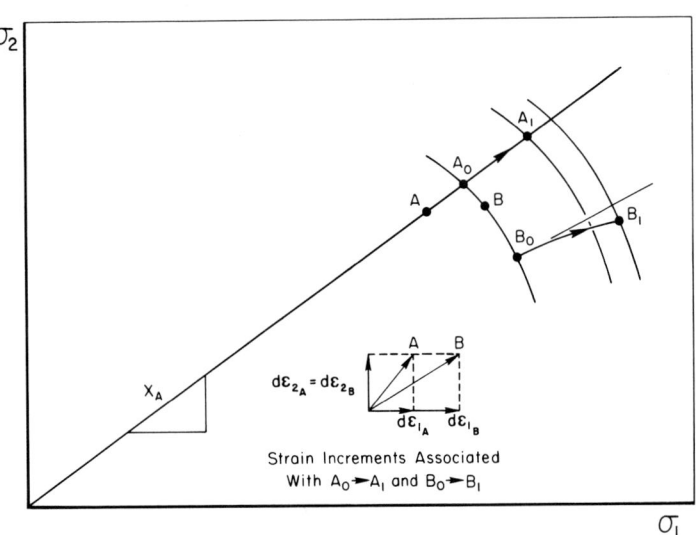

Figure 6.5. Sowerby and Duncan[6] interpretation of the stress and strain states involved in the Marciniak and Kuczynski analysis of flow localization.

expected to increase with ρ^*. Experimental findings in regard to this conclusion are described in the next section.

In their papers, Sowerby and Duncan and Azrin and Wonsiewicz also briefly discuss several special cases in the analysis of flow localization. One of these involves the forming limits in a sheet deformed under plane-strain conditions. This deformation mode can be expected to give the minimum forming limit and is the easiest to analyze to determine the gross effects of strain-hardening capacity and initial imperfection size. In particular, the forming limit in this case is controlled simply by the onset of tensile instability at the load maximum (assuming that the rate sensitivity and temperature effects are negligible). This load maximum in a power-law hardening material is reached under plane-strain conditions when $\varepsilon_{1_B} = n$, the strain-hardening exponent. Noting the facts that in plane strain

$$\bar{\sigma} = \sigma_1 \sqrt{\frac{3(1 + 2R)}{2(2 + R)(1 + R)}} \quad , \tag{6.35}$$

and

$$\bar{\varepsilon} = \varepsilon_1 \sqrt{\frac{2(2 + R)(1 + R)}{3(1 + 2R)}} \quad , \tag{6.36}$$

an axial force balance yields at $\varepsilon_{1_B} = n$

$$\sigma_{1_A} A_A = \sigma_{1_B} A_B \quad , \tag{6.37}$$

$$\bar{\sigma}_A \sqrt{\frac{2(2 + R)(1 + R)}{3(1 + 2R)}} [\exp(-\varepsilon_1^*)](A_{A_o})$$

$$= \bar{\sigma}_B \sqrt{\frac{2(2 + R)(1 + R)}{3(1 + 2R)}} [\exp(-n)]A_{B_o} \quad , \tag{6.38}$$

or

$$\bar{\sigma}_A \exp(-\varepsilon_1^*) = f_o \bar{\sigma}_B \exp(-n) \quad . \tag{6.39}$$

ε_1^* denotes the limit strain in region A. Since $\bar{\sigma} \propto \bar{\varepsilon}^n \propto \varepsilon_1^n$, we obtain

$$\varepsilon_1^{*n} \exp(-\varepsilon_1^*) = f_o n^n \exp(-n) \quad , \tag{6.40}$$

and therefore, the limit strain ε_1^* is defined by

$$\varepsilon_1^* \exp[(n - \varepsilon_1^*)/n] = n f_o^{1/n} \quad . \tag{6.41}$$

Table 6.1.
Limit Strains in Plane-Strain Deformation

f_o	n	ε_1^*
0.99	0.40	0.315
0.99	0.20	0.143
0.99	0.05	0.025
0.96	0.40	0.246
0.96	0.20	0.098
0.96	0.05	0.010

Table 6.1 lists estimates of ε_1^* for various f_o's and n's based on Equation (6.41). It should be noted that, in all cases, ε_1^* is less than n. The percentage difference between ε_1^* and n is seen to increase rapidly with f_o and to decrease with n.

EXPERIMENTAL CORRELATIONS WITH THE M-K THEORY

Research by Azrin and Backofen and Ghosh and Backofen brought into question the details of the M-K analysis of the forming limits for sheet metals stretched in plane.[13, 14] In their papers, the $\rho^* > 0$ forming limits (ε_1^* versus ρ^*) were presented for a number of materials. However, the ε_1^*'s did not always increase with ρ^* as predicted by the M-K model. Only in the cases of an aluminum-killed low-carbon steel and 1100-0 aluminum did ε_1^* versus ρ^* show a positive slope (Figure 6.6). Further, only for these materials was ε_1^* under plane-strain conditions approximately equal to the uniform elongation in uniaxial tension, a trend that is predicted by both the Swift-Hill instability criteria and the M-K analysis for $f_0 \approx 1$. In contrast, for materials such as 70 percent copper–30 percent zinc (alpha brass), ETP copper, and type 301 austenitic stainless steel, $d\varepsilon_1^*/d\rho^*$ was either zero or negative (Figure 6.6). In addition, these materials exhibited plane strain ε_1^*'s considerably less than the uniform elongation in uniaxial tension. Further doubt on the M-K analysis was shed when the forming limits of sheets with relatively deep premachined thickness imperfections failed to substantiate the predicted effect of f_o on the limit strain.

The work of Ghosh and Backofen[14] went a long way in explaining these shortcomings. In their paper, a strain-path dependence of strain-hardening rate was found. This was substantiated by new measurements and by a collection of literature data. Thus, the use of

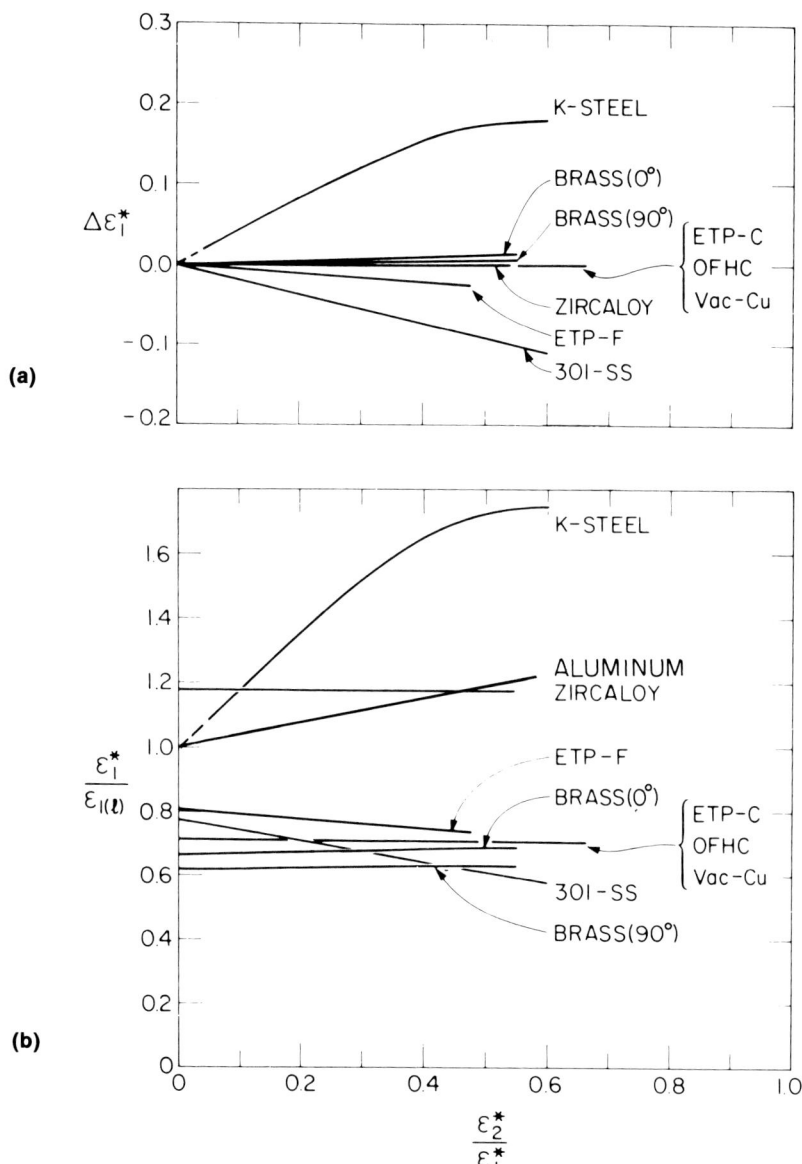

Figure 6.6. Strain path dependence of the (a) quasistable flow increment, $\Delta\varepsilon_1^*$ and (b) normalized limit strain $\varepsilon_1^*/\varepsilon_{1(\ell)}$ for a variety of engineering alloys. $\Delta\varepsilon_1^*$ is defined as the difference between the limit strain ε_1^* and the load instability strain in plane strain ($\rho^* = 0$). The normalization factor $\varepsilon_{1(\ell)}$ is the Swift load instability strain in uniaxial tension. Data are from Azrin and Backofen[13] and Ghosh and Backofen.[14]

Instability and Flow Localization During Sheet Forming

a $\bar{\sigma} \sim \bar{\varepsilon}^n$ relationship would require n to be a function of ρ^*. For example, Ghosh and Backofen's aluminum-killed, low-carbon steel exhibited a strain-hardening exponent that *increased* with biaxiality. The forming limits for this material could therefore be expected to be in excess of the M-K predictions based on the uniaxial tension n value. On the other hand, alpha brass was found to have a strain-hardening exponent under biaxial tension conditions much lower than that in uniaxial tension, an exponent which, moreover, tended to *decrease* with increasing biaxiality.

The changes in strain-hardening rates noted by Ghosh and Backofen may be attributable to effects arising from (1) a change in deformation mode with stress state (e.g., slip versus twinning), (2) the development of deformation textures and latent hardening that could be stress-state dependent, (3) the occurrence of stress-state dependent phase transformations (such as occur in certain austenitic stainless steels), or (4) other metallurgical processes that could be influenced by stress state. That such metallurgical effects can indeed have an influence on the forming limits was well illustrated by Ghosh and Backofen's measurements on heavily cold rolled aluminum-killed low-carbon steel, alpha brass, and aluminum. After such cold rolling, a strong, stable deformation texture and a microstructure with little, if any, strain-hardening capacity might have been expected to have been produced in all three materials. The forming limits of *all* three of these materials showed positive $d\varepsilon_1^*/d\rho^*$, in support of the M-K analysis (Figure 6.7). These and other measurements were employed to

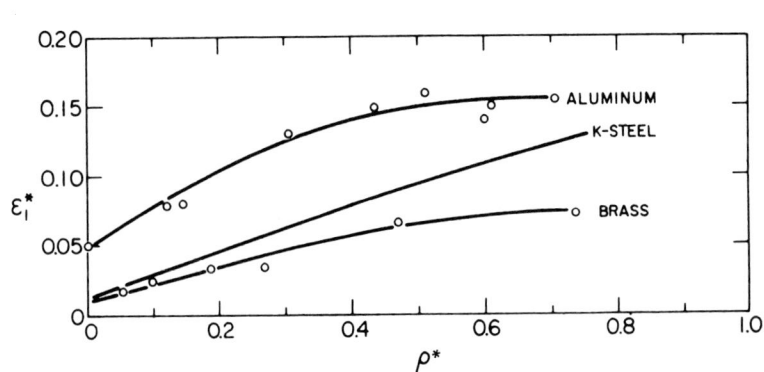

Figure 6.7. Strain ratio dependence of the in-plane limit strain ε_1^* for aluminum-killed steel (K-Steel),[13] aluminum,[14] and 70-30 brass[14] deformed in plane following reductions of 30, 20, and 45 percent, respectively, by cold rolling. Cold rolling axis coincided with original rolling direction of the sheet materials, as well as the major principal strain axis during stretching.

conclude that the $\rho^* > 0$ forming limit diagram consists of two parts. One is the increment of stable deformation that occurs prior to diffuse instability and diffuse necking, which is largely determined by the Swift instability condition and the strain-hardening rate of the material. It is the part that is most affected by the stress-state dependence of strain hardening. The other part is a quasistable deformation increment whose magnitude is dependent upon the rate of growth of imperfections (which may actually include the diffuse neck itself) following diffuse instability according to the M-K theory.

Further work by Ghosh illustrated the effects of variable n and rate sensitivity on the forming limit diagram for sheet metals stretched in plane. For instance, with an n that decreases from the uniaxial value of 0.56 to 0.43 in the biaxial tensile mode of deformation, alpha brass M-K forming limits in much closer agreement with measurements were predicted.[15] Also, Ghosh has shown that fracture can sometimes intercede prior to localized thinning and should be considered in the interpretation of FLD data.[16] In particular, it was demonstrated that the aluminum-killed low-carbon steel forming limit near balanced biaxial tension is controlled by fracture rather than by localized thinning prior to fracture. As far as rate sensitivity is concerned, Ghosh has verified that rather small m's, m ≈ 0.01, can substantially increase the $\rho^* > 0$ forming limits much like the effect of m on uniaxial tensile elongation. In the case of aluminum-killed low-carbon steel, a substantial portion of the large $d\varepsilon_1^*/d\rho^*$ is attributable to the stabilizing influence of rate sensitivity. The interested reader is referred to the original papers referenced below for further details on these subjects.

FORMING LIMITS FOR OUT-OF-PLANE STRETCHING

As mentioned in Chapter 2, the FLD's for sheet metals deformed out-of-plane, by rigid punches for example, tend to be somewhat higher than the corresponding in-plane measurements (Figure 6.8).[17, 18] Since out-of-plane FLD's are easier to measure and can be related more closely to material performance in industrial sheet metal stamping operations, it is worth explaining briefly the source of these differences.

According to Ghosh and Hecker,[17, 19] the primary sources of the higher forming limits are the nonuniform strain distributions and geometrical and frictional effects inherent to out-of-plane forming. In hemispherical punch forming of a sheet clamped around its edges, for instance, the strain state varies from one near plane strain close to the so-called flange region where the sheet is clamped to one of balanced biaxial tension at the pole of the deformed sheet. Because of this strain gradient, no material imperfection need be postulated to explain the occurrence of localized through-thickness necking. This conclusion is analogous to that drawn by Ghosh, who demonstrated that no imperfection need be present to explain necking of sheet tensile specimens (Chapter 5), as well as that of Semiatin and Lahoti, whose process simulations of shear band formation in the isothermal hot sidepressing of Ti-6242Si required no initiation site to generate flow localization (Chapter 3). In a similar manner, Wang and his coworkers have been able to simulate the formation of strain localizations during punch stretching on a computer.[20, 21] This is not to say, though, that some form of load instability does not occur, for load-

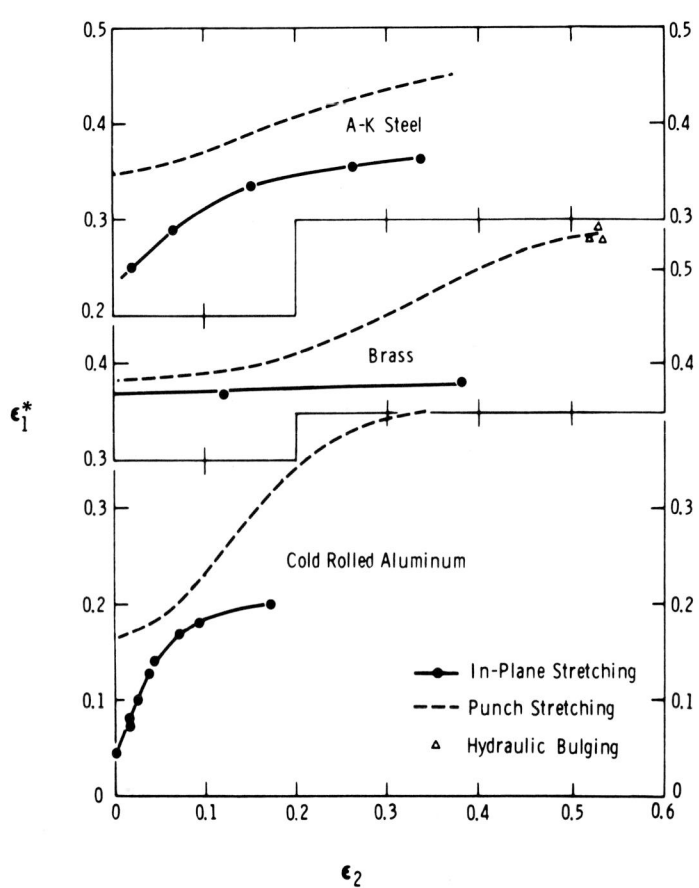

Figure 6.8. Forming limit data for in-plane and out-of-plane stretching of aluminum-killed steel, alpha brass, and aluminum.[17]

stroke curves from punch stretching tests show inflection points that are indeed attributable to localizations developing at particular points in the deformed sheet.

The important influence of geometric and frictional factors comes into play with regard to their tendency to shift the site of strain localization away from the point at which it is first initiated. The shift occurs partly because of strain and strain-rate hardening and also because it is impossible to maintain $d\varepsilon_2 = 0$ in the region where localized thinning is initiated under punch forming conditions. The latter effect is a result of the deformation brought about by punch displacement subsequent to the initiation of localized necking, which requires that $d\varepsilon_2 \neq 0$ in the surrounding material. It has also been found that the direction of the shift over the surface of the punch-formed cup is toward the flange, or plane-strain region (Figure 6.9). This can be rationalized by recalling that localized necking is favored by plane-strain deformation and that the punch-sheet interface friction is greatest at the pole and less or zero away from it. Because of the foregoing, the greatest difference between the in-plane and out-of-plane FLD's is expected to occur for $\rho^* = 1$. This is indeed what is found for alpha brass and cold rolled aluminum (Figure 6.8), but not for aluminum-killed low-carbon steel. Such a discrepancy can be attributed to the occurrence of fracture-controlled failure rather than necking-controlled failure, as mentioned previously.

OTHER ANALYSES OF SHEET METAL FORMING LIMITS FOR $\rho^* > 0$

There have been several other noteworthy approaches to the prediction of the $\rho^* > 0$ forming limit diagram. By and large, these have addressed the problem of in-plane stretching. One of these is the analysis of Parmar and Mellor.[22] These researchers have applied an M-K type of analysis, employing a modified yield locus and flow rule recently proposed by Hill. For rotationally isotropic material, the yield locus takes the form

$$2(1 + R)\sigma_o^q = (1 + 2R)|\sigma_1 - \sigma_2|^q + |\sigma_1 + \sigma_2|^q \qquad (6.42)$$

in principal stress space, where R is again the normal plastic anisotropy parameter, σ_o is the yield stress in uniaxial tension, and q is a constant that must be determined experimentally. For q = 2, the yield locus reduces to Equation (2.13). By using this yield locus with q < 2, the authors show how forming limits, especially near $\rho^* \approx 1$, are substantially lower compared to those for q = 2 in materials with R < 1. In support of the formulation, they have shown how the FLD for soft aluminum sheet is much better predicted by the M-K theory with $q = 1.8$ in Equation (6.42). This value of q was derived from uniaxial tensile and bulge-type tests.

Another major analysis for the prediction of FLD's, one which is totally different from M-K theory, is that due to Stören and Rice.[23] This analysis invokes no material imperfection as the source of localized necking. Rather, it assumes the development of a corner or vertex on the yield locus. Such an occurrence is suggested by various

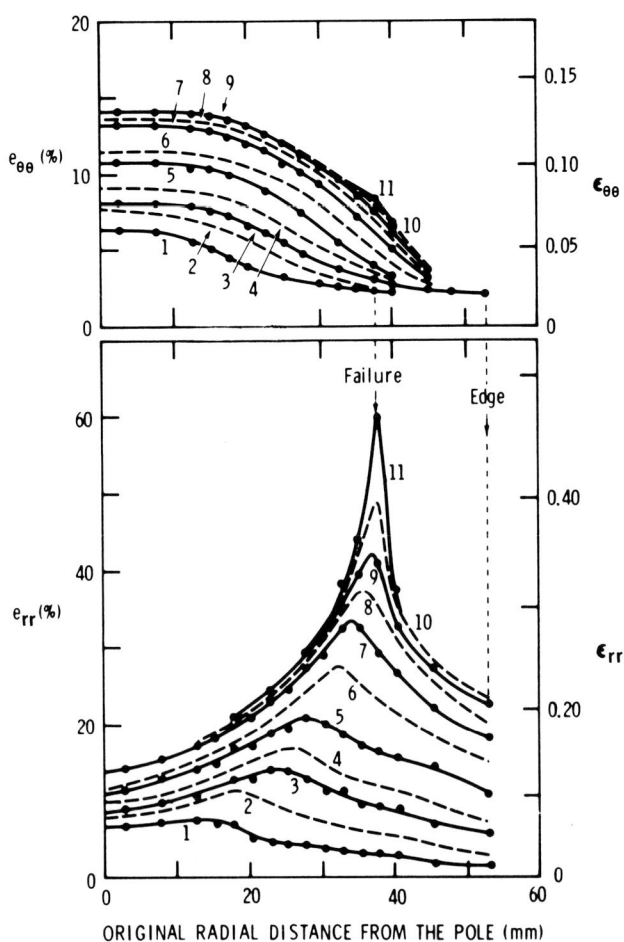

Figure 6.9. Radial (e_{rr}, ε_{rr}) and circumferential ($e_{\theta\theta}$, $\varepsilon_{\theta\theta}$) strain distributions over the surface of an unlubricated 70-30 brass sheet stretched out-of-plane by a hemispherical punch.[19] Numbers indicate successive loading interruptions made in order to take data.

theories of crystal plasticity for polycrystalline aggregates, although only very limited experimental confirmation has been attempted. With the assumption of a yield locus vertex, however, a bifurcation in the possible strain and strain-rate increments in a body undergoing plastic deformation occurs, because the normality condition can only be applied to a smooth yield surface. It is this bifurcation that Stören and Rice examine, and this allows regions to follow different deformation modes, such as a groove undergoing localized thinning in an otherwise homogeneously deforming sheet. From this theory, bifurcation and the onset of localized necking are found to occur in a power-law hardening material at $\varepsilon_1(\rho^*)$ given by

$$\varepsilon_1 = [3\rho^{*2} + n(2 + \rho^*)^2]/[2(2 + \rho^*)(1 + \rho^* + \rho^{*2})] \quad , \quad (6.43)$$

where n denotes the strain-hardening exponent. Assuming that these bifurcation strains are about equal to the limit strain ε_1^*, it may be deduced from Equation (6.43) that materials with small n's (≤ 0.25) will show $d\varepsilon_1^*/d\rho^* > 0$ for $\rho^* > 0$ and those with large n's (>0.33) will exhibit $d\varepsilon_1^*/d\rho^* < 0$ along these strain paths. Experimental measurements for alpha brass and hard aluminum follow the predicted trends, but those for aluminum-killed low-carbon steel and type 301 austenitic stainless steel do not. From this, Stören and Rice surmise that both bifurcation and the growth of imperfections have an effect on the FLD. However, a final determination of the magnitude of each effect awaits careful experimental documentation.

Summary

The analytical results presented in this chapter can be used to establish the forming limits of sheet metals that are deformed by tensile loads under conditions of plane stress. For the most part, they have dealt with material constitutive relations that include only the influence of strain hardening in order to simplify the approach that must be taken to predict flow localization rates. The generalization of the results to materials that are rate and temperature sensitive is discussed in cited references.

When the imposed strain path is such that $\rho^* \leq 0$, the forming limit is determined by the onset of local instability and localized necking along a zero-extension direction. Under these conditions, the criterion due to Hill is useful in predicting the forming limit strain levels of rate and temperature-independent materials. It is of interest to note that, in a power-law strain-hardening material, the forming limit diagram for $\rho^* \leq 0$ is determined solely by the value of the strain-hardening exponent and is independent of the normal plastic anisotropy.

In the case of $\rho^* > 0$, no zero-extension direction exists along which a through-thickness neck may be initiated naturally, and the problem of predicting forming limits becomes somewhat more difficult than for $\rho^* \leq 0$. Two approaches can be taken. One is to postulate the existence of a geometric (e.g., thickness) or material imperfection in the sheet and analyze the local shift in strain path due to this imperfection during proportional straining in the bulk of the material. This approach, first proposed by Marciniak and Kuczynski, employs the plasticity equations without resorting to an instability criterion for analyzing the flow localization process and is valid only when the strain state outside the imperfection is uniform, as can be obtained during frictionless in-plane stretching. The other approach, due to Stören and Rice, does not postulate an imperfection, but treats the onset of localized necking for $\rho^* > 0$ as a bifurcation problem that occurs as a result of the development of a corner or vertex on the yield locus. This vertex or corner gives rise to an indeterminacy in the plastic strain increments and thus permits bifurcation modes that can include localized necking. As for the Marciniak-Kuczynski analysis, that due to Stören and Rice is strictly applicable only to in-plane stretching. With certain modifications, both theories are capable of predicting forming limit trends for a variety of materials, but more careful experimental research is needed before firm conclusions about them can be made, particularly for the Stören and Rice model.

When sheet metals are stretched out-of-plane, the $\rho^* > 0$ forming limits tend to be higher than the in-plane limits. In these circumstances, both the Marciniak and Kuczynski and Stören and Rice theories are inapplicable. Ghosh and Hecker have explained the higher forming limits in punch forming, for example, as resulting from the unavoidable strain gradients and geometric and friction effects that produce regions of higher than average deformation. Their quasi-empirical model and various computer simulations have indeed verified that neither a material imperfection nor a bifurcation is required to explain the forming limits observed for punch stretching.

References

[1] H.W. Swift: *J. Mech. Phys. Solids,* 1952, vol. 1, p. 1.
[2] R. Hill: *J. Mech. Phys. Solids,* 1952, vol. 1, p. 19.
[3] R.D. Venter and M.C. de Malherbe: *Sheet Metal Industries,* 1971, vol. 48, p. 656.

[4] Z. Marciniak and K. Kuczynski: *Inter. J. Mech. Sci.*, 1967, vol. 9, p. 609.
[5] Z. Marciniak, K. Kuczynski, and T. Pokora: *Inter. J. Mech. Sci.*, 1973, vol. 15, p. 789.
[6] R. Sowerby and J.L. Duncan: *Inter. J. Mech. Sci.*, 1971, vol. 13, p. 217.
[7] F. Negroni, S. Kobayashi, and E.G. Thomsen: *J. Eng. Ind., Trans. ASME*, 1968, vol. 90B, p. 387.
[8] G.G. Moore and J.F. Wallace: *J. Inst. Metals*, 1964-1965, vol. 93, p. 33.
[9] S.L. Semiatin and H.R. Piehler: *Met. Trans. A*, 1979, vol. 10A, p. 1107.
[10] Z. Marciniak: *Aspects of Material Formability*, McMaster University, Hamilton, Ontario, 1974.
[11] B.C. Wonsiewicz, M. Azrin, and W.A. Backofen: *Met. Trans.*, 1972, vol. 3, p. 1322.
[12] M. Azrin and B.C. Wonsiewicz: Technical Report AMMRC TR 73-20, Army Materials and Mechanics Research Center, Watertown, MA, April, 1973.
[13] M. Azrin and W.A. Backofen: *Met. Trans.*, 1970, vol. 1, p. 2857.
[14] A.K. Ghosh and W.A. Backofen: *Met. Trans.*, 1973, vol. 4, p. 1113.
[15] A.K. Ghosh: *Mechanics of Sheet Metal Forming: Material Behavior and Deformation Analysis*, D.P. Koistenen and N.M. Wang, eds., p. 287, Plenum Press, New York, 1978.
[16] A.K. Ghosh: *Met. Trans. A*, 1976, vol. 7A, p. 523.
[17] A.K. Ghosh and S.S. Hecker: *Met. Trans.*, 1974, vol. 5, p. 2161.
[18] P.L. Charpentier: *Met. Trans. A*, 1975, vol. 6A, p. 1665.
[19] A.K. Ghosh and S.S. Hecker: *Met. Trans. A*, 1975, vol. 6A, p. 1065.
[20] N.M. Wang and B. Budiansky: *J. Appl. Mech., Trans. ASME*, 1978, vol. 45, p. 73.
[21] N.M. Wang and M.L. Wenner: *Mechanics of Sheet Metal Forming: Material Behavior and Deformation Analysis*, D.P. Koistenen and N.M. Wang, eds., p. 367, Plenum Press, New York, 1978.
[22] A. Parmar and P.B. Mellor: *Inter. J. Mech. Sci.*, 1978, vol. 20, p. 385.
[23] S. Stören and J.R. Rice: *J. Mech. Phys. Solids*, 1975, vol. 23, p. 421.

7
RELATED PROBLEMS OF FLOW LOCALIZATION

The ideas discussed in this monograph have other important applications related to metal deformation outside the specific area of deformation processing or metalworking. These areas include those of flow localization during metalcutting, shear band formation and shear plugging during ballistic impact, and aseismic shear zone formation in the field of geology. The objective of this chapter is to briefly review how the flow localization ideas presented in previous chapters can be extended to these areas and to present experimental results that have been used to validate the accuracy of the models presented.

Flow Localization During Metalcutting

Metalcutting is one of the other areas in which flow localization processes have been observed. In actuality, metalcutting does not consist of the *cutting* of metal per se, but rather of the *shearing* of metal back upon itself to form what are commonly known as chips. The morphology of the chips depends on a number of material properties and process variables. Two of the most common chip morphologies are the continuous chip (common for many steels cut at moderate speeds) and the serrated or cyclic chip (Figure 7.1). Under the latter category come chips that are serrated because of the localization of plastic flow by shear (Figure 7.1b), which occurs periodically along the length of the chips. Such shear localized chips may be desirable from the standpoint of chip disposal, but are usually detrimental because their formation often leads to increased tool wear and poor control of final machined geometry. This type of chip is formed when titanium alloys are cut at all speeds and when some steels are cut at high speeds;[1-4] it arises when strain-hardening tendencies are outweighed by the effects of deformation heating. In addition, it has been suggested that, when this occurs at low-to-moderate cutting speeds, the rate at which the cutting force decreases during the localization process must be compatible with the rate at which the machine-tool structure itself can unload.[5] An estimate of the tendency for the formation of shear-localized chips that is based solely on the flow localization analysis is therefore of only approximate validity. This simple analysis will be discussed next.

FLOW LOCALIZATION ANALYSIS FOR ORTHOGONAL CUTTING[6, 7]

The flow localization analysis that is presented here is for the simple case of orthogonal cutting (Figure 7.2). In this operation, the cutting tool of rake angle α^* causes metal to deform under plane-strain conditions. In particular, the deformation consists of a certain thickness of metal, d (the depth of cut), undergoing shear through the action of the cutting tool, so that the final thickness is t_c (the chip thickness). If the angle of the shear zone is denoted by ϕ, it may be shown[8] that the shear strain Γ_{max} imposed upon the metal for a continuous chip is given by

$$\Gamma_{max} = \tan(\phi - \alpha^*) + \cot\phi \quad . \tag{7.1}$$

Rake angles α^* are typically between $-10°$ and $+10°$; Figure 7.2 shows a positive rake angle. Thus, for large shear angles ($\phi \sim 30°$ to $40°$), the shear strains are on the order of 2. For small shear angles ($\phi \sim 10°$), shear strains in excess of 5 are obtained.

Under the plane-strain conditions of orthogonal cutting, shear localization in chips may be expected to be initiated along zero-extension directions. To a first approximation, these directions correspond to the y' directions in Figure 7.2, which form angles of ϕ with the cutting direction. Assuming that the cross-sectional area in the shear zone does not vary with position, force equilibrium requires that the gradient of shear stress τ along the x' direction (i.e., the direction perpendicular to y') vanish, or that

$$\frac{d\tau}{dx'} = 0 \quad . \tag{7.2}$$

Unlike the non-steady-state flow localization problems that have been discussed previously, however, the shear stress and shear strain Γ vary with x', even prior to flow localization. As a first approximation, it will be assumed that the shear strain varies linearly with x':

$$\Gamma = \Gamma_{max} x' \quad , \tag{7.3}$$

for x' between zero and the maximum extent of the shear zone. Since $\tau = \tau(\Gamma, \dot{\Gamma}, T)$, Equation (7.2) becomes

$$0 = \left(\frac{\partial \tau}{\partial \Gamma}\right)\bigg|_{\dot{\Gamma},T} \Gamma_{max} + \left(\frac{\partial \tau}{\partial \dot{\Gamma}}\right)\bigg|_{\Gamma,T} \frac{d\dot{\Gamma}}{d\Gamma} \Gamma_{max}$$

$$+ \left(\frac{\partial \tau}{\partial T}\right)\bigg|_{\Gamma,\dot{\Gamma}} \frac{dT}{d\Gamma} \Gamma_{max} \quad . \tag{7.4}$$

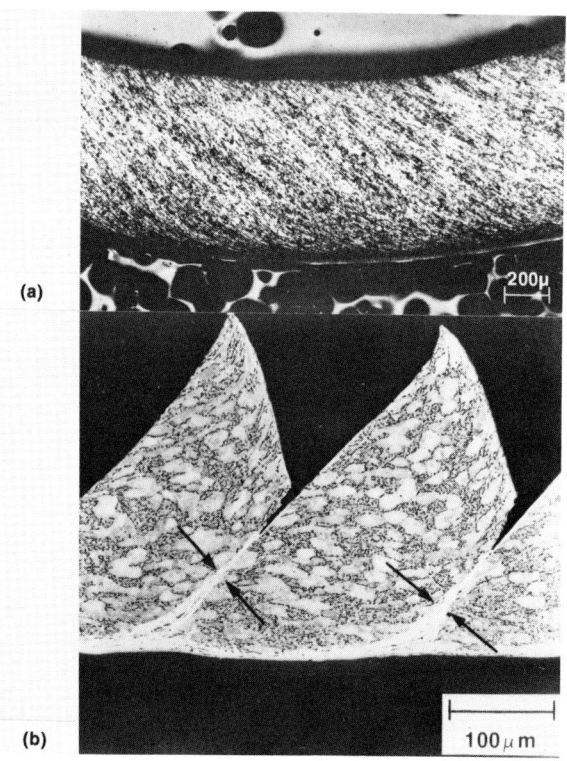

Figure 7.1. Micrographs of chips formed during metalcutting. (a) Continuous AISI 4340 chip and (b) shear-localized Ti-6Al-4V chip. (Photographs courtesy of R. Komanduri, General Electric Corporate R&D, Schenectady, New York).

After multiplying by $(1/\tau\Gamma_{max})$ and rearrangement, this equation reduces to an expression for the flow localization parameter α:

$$\frac{1}{\dot{\Gamma}}\frac{d\dot{\Gamma}}{d\Gamma} = \frac{\alpha}{\sqrt{3}} = -\left\{\left(\frac{\partial \ln\tau}{\partial \Gamma}\right)\bigg|_{\dot{\Gamma},T} \right.$$
$$\left. + \left(\frac{\partial \tau}{\partial T}\right)\bigg|_{\Gamma,\dot{\Gamma}} \left(\frac{1}{\tau}\frac{dT}{d\Gamma}\right)\right\}\bigg/ m \quad , \tag{7.5}$$

which is identical to Equation (3.43). All of the terms in this expression, except $(1/\tau)(dT/d\Gamma)$, are material properties that are functions of Γ, $\dot{\Gamma}$, and T and thus must be measured in conventional mechanical property tests. Moreover, inspection of Equation (7.5) demonstrates that the flow localization tendency increases with Γ, since the strain-hardening term decreases with Γ. For this reason, flow localization is most likely to be initiated in the material elements just leaving the shear zone, which have undergone the most shear strain. To apply Equation (7.5), though, we need to estimate the rate of temperature change during deformation, $dT/d\Gamma$. If the deformation were adiabatic, this would be rather straightforward. However, this is not the case. The temperature change with Γ is controlled by the coupled effects of heat generation (due to deformation), heat conduction, and heat transport (because the chip is moving). Thus, it depends on material and process variables. Because of this, α (Equation 7.5) is a function of the process variables as well, the most important of which is the cut-

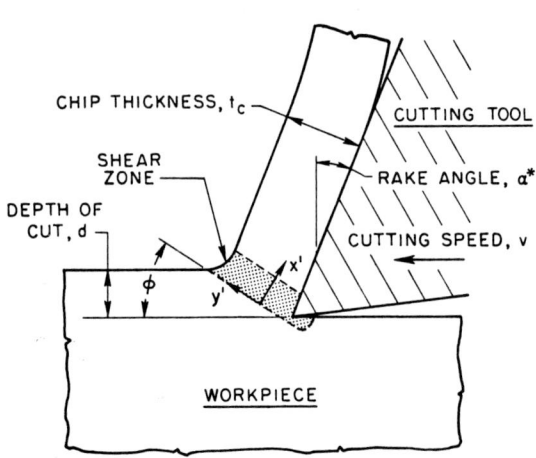

Figure 7.2. Schematic illustration of orthogonal cutting operation.

ting speed. If we postulate a critical α for shear localization (e.g., α = 5 as in Chapter 3), it is apparent that a critical cutting speed is obtained for shear localization.

The magnitude of $(1/\tau)(dT/d\Gamma)$ may be obtained from a variety of models for the temperature in the shear zone.[9-11] Two such models are of Loewen and Shaw and that of Weiner. According to the Loewen and Shaw model, the temperature T in the shear zone (which is assumed to be infinitesimally thin), relative to the ambient temperature T_{amb}, is given by

$$T - T_{amb} = \frac{0.95 \int_0^\Gamma \tau d\Gamma}{\rho c} \left[1 + 1.328 \sqrt{\frac{\Delta \Gamma}{vd}}\right]^{-1}, \quad (7.6)$$

or

$$T - T_{amb} = \frac{0.95 \int \tau d\Gamma}{\rho c} [1 - \beta]. \quad (7.7)$$

In these expressions, Δ, v, and β represent the thermal diffusivity of the workpiece, the cutting speed, and the fraction of heat lost to the chip and workpiece due to heat conduction and transport (convective heat loss). Again, it has been assumed that 95 percent of the deformation work is converted to heat. The model of Weiner gives a similar result with a β factor defined by

$$\beta = \frac{1}{4Y_L} \operatorname{erf} \sqrt{Y_L} + (1 + Y_L) \operatorname{erfc} \sqrt{Y_L}$$
$$- \frac{e^{-Y_L}}{\sqrt{\pi}} \left(\frac{1}{2\sqrt{Y_L}} + \sqrt{Y_L}\right), \quad (7.8)$$

where $Y_L = (vd/4\Delta)\tan\phi = (R^* \tan\phi/4)$. The quantity R^* is commonly called the thermal number in metalcutting research.

The accuracy of the two models may be judged by comparison with Boothroyd's measurements[12] of β using an infrared technique during metalcutting operations at 600 °C (1112 °F). Boothroyd presented his data in terms of β versus log ($R^* \tan\phi$). Hence, a direct comparison with Weiner's prediction (Equation 7.8) is straightforward (Figure 7.3). This is not true for Loewen and Shaw's model, since their β is a function of $R^*/\Gamma = R/(\tan(\phi - \alpha^*) + \cot\phi)$, use having been made of Equation (7.1) for Γ. Examination of Boothroyd's data shows, however, that $\tan(\phi - \alpha) \ll \cot\phi$ for his cutting trials. Thus, Loewen and Shaw's factor of $(\Delta\Gamma/vd) \approx (\cot\phi/R^*) = (R^* \tan\phi)^{-1}$, and their model can then be compared to Boothroyd's measurements (Figure 7.3). It is seen that the Loewen and Shaw model overestimates β, and the Weiner model underestimates β. However, both predict approximately the right $d\beta/d(\log R^* \tan\phi)$. Therefore, because of its relative simplicity and the fact that it includes the explicit dependence of T on Γ, the Loewen and Shaw model will be used to estimate $(1/\tau)(dT/d\Gamma)$. From Equation (7.6), we find this quantity easily (assuming a power-law hardening material, $\tau = G\Gamma^n$):

$$\frac{1}{\tau}\frac{dT}{d\Gamma} = \frac{0.95}{\rho c}\left\{\left[1 + 1.328\sqrt{\frac{\Delta\Gamma}{vd}}\right]^{-1} - \frac{0.664}{(1+n)}\sqrt{\frac{\Delta\Gamma}{vd}}\left[1 + 1.328\sqrt{\frac{\Delta\Gamma}{vd}}\right]^{-2}\right\} . \quad (7.9)$$

Equation (7.9) in conjunction with Equation (7.5) may be employed to obtain estimates of the flow localization parameter.

FORMATION OF SHEAR-LOCALIZED CHIPS—COMPARISON OF MEASUREMENTS AND PREDICTIONS

The applicability of the analysis just presented will be illustrated with data obtained by Komanduri et al.[3] for the cutting of AISI 4340 steel (tempered to R_c 35). In Komanduri's cutting experiments on 4340, cutting speeds of 30 to 60 m/min gave rise to continuous chips. Above 60 m/min, serrated chips, which formed apparently as a result of a flow localization process, were obtained. The other cutting parameters were d = 0.05 cm and $\alpha^* = -5°$. From chip thickness measurements, it was found that $\phi = 30°$ and $\Gamma = 2.5$. Physical properties for 4340 (Table 7.1) were obtained from the literature.[13, 14] Pertinent mechanical properties for the alloy (Table 7.1) were obtained from References 15 (m values at $\dot\varepsilon \approx 10^3$ sec.$^{-1} \approx \dot\varepsilon$ in metalcutting), 16 and 17 $(\partial\ln\tau/\partial\Gamma)$, and 16 and 18 $(\partial\tau/\partial T)$. Also, an approximate value of n (for use in Equation 7.9) was obtained from Reference 16. All of these data except $\partial\tau/\partial T$ were for room-temperature deformation. Despite the fact that Equation (7.6) shows that chips can attain temperatures as high as approximately 350 °C (660 °F), it is thought that using room-temperature data for these quantities does not introduce significant errors for the quenched and tempered 4340 steel.

Inserting the data in Table 7.1 (plus the previously mentioned cutting parameters) into Equations (7.5) and (7.9), estimates of the flow localization parameter α as a function of cutting speed can be obtained (Table 7.2). It should be emphasized that these α's are for material points just leaving the shear zone, i.e., at the elastic-plastic boundary. From the data in Table 7.2, it is seen that α reaches a value of 5 at a cutting speed of 60 m/min and higher values at higher speeds (at which more of the deformation heating is retained to thermally soften the material in the shear zone). Since it is reasonable to expect that flow localization will occur only when $\alpha \geq 5$ over a non-negligible portion of the shear zone, serrated chips exhibiting shear localization should start to form only at cutting speeds *exceeding* 60 m/min. This is indeed what was observed during Komanduri's cutting experiments on 4340 (R_c 35).

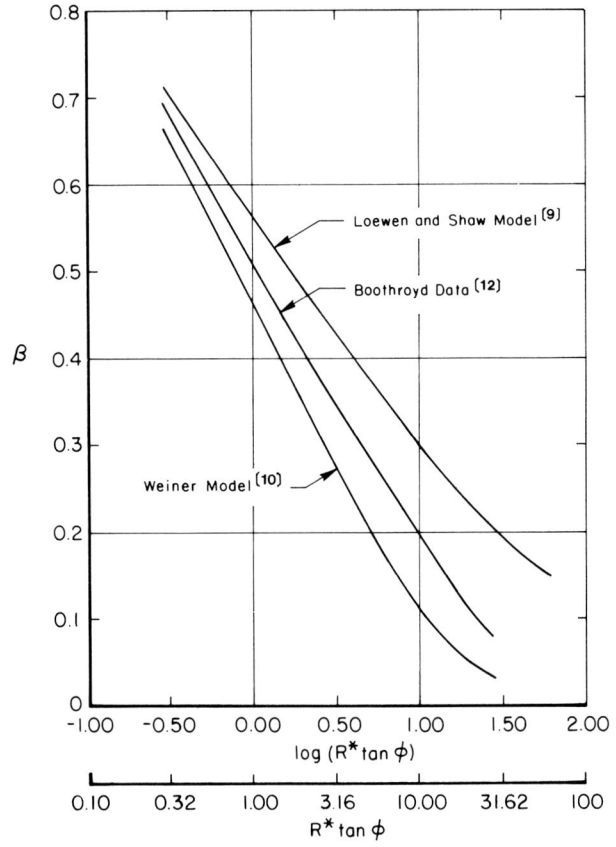

Figure 7.3. Comparison of model predictions of β factor to experimental measurements.[7]

Related Problems of Flow Localization

Table 7.1.
Physical and Mechanical Properties of AISI 4340 (R_c 35)

Density, ρ (g./cm^3)	7.83
Specific Heat, c (cal./g. °C)	0.11
Thermal Diffusivity, Δ (cm^2/sec.)	0.0925
Rate Sensitivity at $\Gamma = 2 \times 10^3$ sec.$^{-1}$	0.040
$(\partial \ln \tau / \partial \Gamma)|_{\dot{\Gamma},T}$ at $\Gamma = 2.5$	0.062
$(\partial \tau / \partial T)|_{\Gamma,\dot{\Gamma}}$ (kPa/°C)	968
n	0.07

Table 7.2.
α Parameter Predictions for AISI 4340 Steel (R_c 35)

Cutting Speed, v		
m/min.	(ft./min.)	α
12	(40)	2.8
30	(100)	4.1
60	(200)	5.0
90	(300)	5.5
120	(400)	5.8
150	(500)	6.0
180	(600)	6.2
240	(800)	6.4
300	(1000)	6.6
∞	(∞)	8.4

Flow Localization During Impact Loading of Metals

In recent years, the deformation and failure of metal structures due to impact-type loading has come under increasingly closer examination. Particular areas on which attention has been focused include those related to automotive impact and the collision of meteorites with space vehicles. Both of these situations involve large stresses and high rates of deformation ($\dot{\varepsilon} \geq 10^3$ sec.$^{-1}$) that usually proceed by wave propagation. Another, and perhaps the most highly researched, area among those involving impact, is that of ballistic impact. The most common form of this type of deformation is comprised of a projectile traveling at subsonic (or nowadays hypersonic) velocity impacting an armored target. An understanding of the materials and mechanics interactions in such situations is of great importance to the development of new types of ordnance and armor. Unfortunately, however, there exists only limited data for the correlation of material properties and armor failure mechanisms. These failure mechanisms include (for homogeneous armor): shear localization and failure, spalling, and petalling. In this section, it will be shown how material property data can be used to estimate the onset of shear localization in ballistic impact environments.

STAKER'S CONTAINED CYLINDER EXPERIMENTS

Recently, Staker at the U.S. Army Mechanics and Materials Research Center has performed a large number of experiments involving a "quick-stop" of explosively expanded cylinders of 4340 steel that had been tempered to various strength levels prior to testing.[16] The basis of this so-called "contained fragmenting round" technique[19, 20] consists of a hollow right circular cylinder expanded (largely radially) under the action of a high explosive (HE). Surrounding the test cylinder, there are other cylinders of a "buffer" (of polymeric composition), as well as of mild steel and lead. The outermost lead cylinder carries momentum away after detonation, preventing damage to the test cylinder. By varying the thickness of the buffer as well as by tapering it, different controllable amounts of deformation may be imposed from test to test as well as in a given test.

In Staker's tests, two failure modes predominated. One was macroscopic shear banding followed by shear failure, and the other was ductile fracture. In the specimens that showed shear banding, it was found that flow localization was initiated at the I.D. of the cylinders and consisted of bands of intense deformation forming angles of 45° ± 3° to the I.D. tangent plane at the initiation point. These findings are reasonable in view of the following considerations: (1) the plastic waves that result from the explosive loading initiate at the HE-I.D. interface; and (2) the deformation is largely one of plane strain, the axial strain being small relative to the radial and circumferential strains. Since friction is absent, the maximum shear and shear strain planes coincide with each other and also with the planes at 45° to the I.D. tangent plane.

Because the strain rates involved in the test program were on the order of 10^4 sec.$^{-1}$, Staker's data can be analyzed employing the simple model for flow localization under adiabatic heating conditions, presented in Chapter 3. In other words, it can be applied to determine the flow localization tendency (i.e., value of the α parameter) associated with the maximum imposed strain, whose average magnitude was measured after explosive expansion of the cylinders. Since the deformations involved wave propagation, the actual strain state through the thickness of the cylinders was not uniform. However, we will assume that a substantial portion of the cylinder cross section underwent the maximum plastic deformation associated with the impact speed imposed at the I.D. by the explosive. Therefore, the deformation mechanics can be analyzed to a first order using the previous methods developed for predicting flow localization in an initially uniform deformation field.

Staker's data are reported in terms of Γ and τ, the maximum shear strain and shear stress in the deformation field. The quantity Γ is equal to 0.5 ($\varepsilon_T - \varepsilon_R$), where ε_T and ε_R denote the hoop and radial normal strains, respectively. If a power-law hardening material is assumed, a behavior that Staker's 4340 steels do follow, it can be shown[16] that, because of adiabatic heating, the τ-Γ curve will show a maximum at a critical Γ_c given by

$$\Gamma_c = -\frac{\rho c\, n}{0.95\left(\dfrac{\partial \tau}{\partial T}\right)\bigg|_{\Gamma,\dot{\Gamma}}} , \qquad (7.10)$$

Here, ρ and c have their usual definitions of density and specific heat. Note that Equation (7.10) is the τ-T equivalent of Equation (3.62). Under adiabatic conditions, Equation (3.67) defines α. Assuming that the von Mises criterion applies, $\Gamma = \sqrt{3}\,\bar{\varepsilon}$, and the following is obtained

$$\alpha = \sqrt{3}\left(\frac{n}{\Gamma_c} - \frac{n}{\Gamma}\right)\bigg/ m . \qquad (7.11)$$

Employing the above relations for Γ_c and α, a detailed analysis of the kinetics of adiabatic shear banding will now be presented and will be validated using Staker's data.

TWO-SLICE MODEL FOR ADIABATIC FLOW LOCALIZATION IN SIMPLE SHEAR

The occurrence of adiabatic shear bands, such as those observed by Staker, generally involves the localization of plastic flow under a state of simple shear. Thus, a two-dimensional model is sufficient to describe this phenomenon. For this purpose, a "two-slice" analysis analogous to that described in Appendix A for the problem of flow localization during uniaxial compression will be developed. The two-slice model consists of the simple shear of a plate that has a nominally perfect, or uniform, region (or slice) and a region (or slice) that contains an initial defect of geometric or strength origin.

As discussed in Chapter 3, an initial geometric defect (δA_o) is equivalent to a variation in the strength coefficient (δK). We shall focus attention on the case involving a defect of strength origin. Taking the breadth of the plate to be unity, equilibrium requires that the shear load supported by the two slices be equal, or $\delta F_\tau = 0$, resulting in

$$\delta(A\tau) = A\delta\tau + \tau\delta A = 0 \qquad (7.12a)$$

or

$$\delta\tau/\tau = 0 \qquad (7.12b)$$

since $\delta A = 0$. Here τ and A denote shear stress and cross-sectional area, respectively.

Assuming an engineering material, such that $\tau = \tau(K, \Gamma, \dot\Gamma, T)$, where K, Γ, $\dot\Gamma$, and T are the strength coefficient, shear strain, shear strain rate, and temperature, as before, Equation (7.12b) can be expanded as follows:

$$\delta\ln\tau = \left(\frac{\partial\ln\tau}{\partial\Gamma}\right)\bigg|_{\dot\Gamma,T}\delta\Gamma + \left(\frac{\partial\ln\tau}{\partial\dot\Gamma}\right)\bigg|_{\Gamma,T}\delta\dot\Gamma$$
$$+ \left(\frac{\partial\ln\tau}{\partial T}\right)\bigg|_{\Gamma,\dot\Gamma}\delta T + \delta\ln K \quad . \qquad (7.13)$$

For a power-law strain-hardening and strain-rate hardening material characterized by n and m, respectively, the above becomes

$$\delta\ln\tau = n\delta\ln\Gamma + m\delta\ln\dot\Gamma + \left(\frac{\partial\ln\tau}{\partial T}\right)\bigg|_{\Gamma,\dot\Gamma}\delta T + \delta\ln K \quad . \qquad (7.14)$$

The temperature term in this expression can be expressed as follows:

$$\left(\frac{\partial\ln\tau}{\partial T}\right)\bigg|_{\Gamma,\dot\Gamma}\delta T = \left(\frac{\partial\tau}{\partial T}\right)\bigg|_{\Gamma,\dot\Gamma}\frac{\delta T}{\tau} = \left(\frac{\partial\tau}{\partial T}\right)\bigg|_{\Gamma,\dot\Gamma}\left(\frac{0.95}{\rho c}\delta\Gamma\right) \qquad (7.15)$$

in which an expression analogous to Equation (3.64) has been employed due to the assumed adiabatic conditions. If we now assume that $(\partial \tau/\partial T)|_{\Gamma,\dot{\Gamma}}$ is a constant, Equation (7.15) can be further reduced through the application of Equation (7.10) to yield

$$\left(\frac{\partial \ln \tau}{\partial T}\right)\bigg|_{\Gamma,\dot{\Gamma}} \delta T = -\frac{n}{\Gamma_c} \delta \Gamma \quad , \tag{7.16}$$

where Γ_c is the critical value of Γ associated with the shear stress maximum. Combining Equations (7.12b), (7.14), and (7.16), the final result is

$$\left(\frac{n}{\Gamma} - \frac{n}{\Gamma_c}\right) \delta \Gamma + m \delta \ln \dot{\Gamma} + \delta \ln K = 0 \tag{7.17}$$

Hence, for the two-slice model, we obtain

$$\delta \ln \dot{\Gamma} = \left\{\left(\frac{n}{\Gamma_c} - \frac{n}{\Gamma}\right) \delta \Gamma - \delta \ln K\right\}\bigg/m \tag{7.18}$$

or

$$\dot{\Gamma}_{def} = \dot{\Gamma}_{unif} (K_{unif}/K_{def})^{1/m} \left\{\exp\left[\left(\frac{n}{\Gamma_c} - \frac{n}{\bar{\Gamma}}\right) \cdot (\Gamma_{def} - \Gamma_{unif})/m\right]\right\} \tag{7.19}$$

Here $\bar{\Gamma}$ is a suitable average of Γ_{def} and Γ_{unif} which ensures equilibrium. Usually, a simple arithmetic mean provides sufficiently accurate results.

In actual calculations, the values of n, m, Γ_c (Equation 7.10), and f_o (K_{def}/K_{unif} in the case of a strength defect) are specified, and Equation (7.19) is applied incrementally, provided a boundary condition (e.g., $\dot{\Gamma}_{unif}$ = constant) is supplied. At t = 0, $\Gamma_{unif} = \Gamma_{def} = 0$, and Equation (7.19) defines $\dot{\Gamma}_{def}$. After a time increment Δt, $\Gamma_{unif} = \dot{\Gamma}_{unif} \Delta t$ and $\Gamma_{def} = \dot{\Gamma}_{def} \Delta t$, thereby defining a new $\dot{\Gamma}_{def}$. The procedure is repeated to trace out the course of strain concentration.

The specification of the strain rate boundary condition in the above can be shown to have no influence on the actual development of the strain-rate concentration, provided that the material properties n, m, and Γ_c do not depend on strain rate. As a result, the relation between Γ_{def} and Γ_{unif} in Equation (7.19) can be expressed in the form*

$$\int_0^{\Gamma_{def}} f(\Gamma_{def}) \, d\Gamma_{def} = \int_0^{\Gamma_{unif}} g(\Gamma_{unif}) \, d\Gamma_{unif} \quad , \tag{7.20}$$

where f and g are functions of Γ_{def} and Γ_{unif}, respectively.

The above point is illustrated more clearly perhaps when the problem is formulated in terms of the force equilibrium equation. For a two-slice model, this requires

$$\tau_{def} = \tau_{unif} \tag{7.21}$$

Bearing in mind that $\tau = K\Gamma^n \dot{\Gamma}^m h(T)$, where h(T) is a function of temperature

$$K_{def} \, \Gamma_{def}^n \, \dot{\Gamma}_{def}^m \, h(T_{def}) = K_{unif} \, \Gamma_{unif}^n \, \dot{\Gamma}_{unif}^m \, h(T_{unif}) \quad . \tag{7.22}$$

Assuming as before that $(\partial \tau / \partial T)|_{\Gamma, \dot{\Gamma}}$ is constant, h(T) can be found by integration of the differential form of Equation (7.16) to obtain

$$\ln \tau = -\frac{n}{\Gamma_c} \Gamma + \text{fcn}(\Gamma, \dot{\Gamma}) \tag{7.23}$$

Therefore, under adiabatic conditions, the temperature dependence of τ is implicitly included in Γ, or $h(T) = \exp[-(n/\Gamma_c)\Gamma(T)]$. Putting this into Equation (7.22),

$$K_{def} \, \Gamma_{def}^n \, \dot{\Gamma}_{def}^m \left[\exp\left(-\frac{n}{\Gamma_c} \gamma_{def} \right) \right]$$
$$= K_{unif} \, \Gamma_{unif}^n \, \dot{\Gamma}_{unif}^m \left[\exp\left(-\frac{n}{\Gamma_c} \gamma_{unif} \right) \right] \quad , \tag{7.24}$$

an expression that can be rearranged to define $\dot{\Gamma}_{def}$ as a function of Γ_{unif}, Γ_{def}, $\dot{\Gamma}_{unif}$, the strength defect, and the material properties.

Comparing Equations (7.19) and (7.24), it is evident that the latter eliminates the need to define $\bar{\Gamma}$. Also, the forms of $f(\Gamma_{def})$ and $g(\Gamma_{unif})$ in Equation (7.20) are apparent from inspection of Equation (7.24). Hence, the lack of influence of the strain-rate boundary condition on the predicted values of strain concentration is confirmed.

---

*Note that a similar procedure can be used in the tensile necking case. See, for example, Equations (5.37) through (5.43).

This conclusion would be identical if a *multiple*-slice model were developed based on force equilibrium considerations and if the strain in the most highly deformed region were compared to that in the uniform region. This is especially true in the case of simple shear because of the absence of stress triaxialities due to necking.

TWO-SLICE MODEL CALCULATIONS FOR STAKER'S FRAGMENTING SHELL EXPERIMENTS[16]

Equations (7.19) or (7.24) can be used to study the kinetics of flow localization under conditions of adiabatic simple shear. This has been done for the problem of shell fragmentation via adiabatic shear banding, and the simulation results obtained are compared below to measurements on explosively loaded 4340 steel cylinders made by Staker.[16] Although Staker's experiments involved a deformation mode change from pure shear (plane strain) to simple shear, the simulation is based solely on simple shear in view of the importance of the final, i.e., simple shear, stage of adiabatic shear band formation.

Material Properties for Simulation. Inputs for the localization simulation consist of values of n, m, Γ_c, and f_o (K_{def}/K_{unif}). Values of n for the various hardness levels of the 4340 material used by Staker are given in his paper.[16] Although these are based on low speed tests, it will be assumed that they are applicable to high-rate deformation as well. An m value of 0.04 for 4340 at high rates of deformation was taken from the work of Nicholas.[15] With regard to the value of f_o, it was assumed that a strength defect of 1.5 percent, resulting in $f_o = 0.985$, was appropriate. This conclusion is supported by the findings of Azrin and Backofen,[21] who found that a 1.3 percent geometric defect was required to attract the failure site away from regions with strength defects during the in-plane sheet forming of low-carbon steel.

This leaves only the values of Γ_c to be determined for the various hardness levels. Equation (7.10) shows that Γ_c is a function of n, ρ, c, and $(\partial\tau/\partial T)|_{\Gamma,\dot{\Gamma}}$. The values of ρ and c were obtained from material property handbooks. Staker also lists values of $(\partial\tau/\partial T)|_{\Gamma,\dot{\Gamma}}$ for the different lots of 4340. Unfortunately, these data were extracted from low-speed tests as well. Because of this and the fact that rate appears to have a strong effect on this quantity,[22] particularly at $\dot{\Gamma}$'s above about 10 sec.$^{-1}$, another source of this type of data was found. Flow curves determined by Wulf[23] on a series of 4130 steels quenched and tempered to various hardness levels and tested at a rate of $\sim 10^4$ sec.$^{-1}$ were found to be useful for this purpose. Using Staker's n values and the initial portions of Wulf's curves, the 10^4 sec.$^{-1}$ "isothermal" flow curves were constructed.† The difference $\Delta\bar{\sigma}^*$ between the isothermal and adiabatic flow stresses at $\bar{\varepsilon} = 0.7$ was estimated. The ΔT^*'s for the adiabatic flow curves were then calculated from the area under the adiabatic flow curves from $\bar{\varepsilon} = 0$ to 0.7. The value of $\Delta\bar{\sigma}^*/\Delta T^*$ so obtained thus gave an average value of the temperature sensitivity of the flow stress. These temperature sensitivities were converted to values of $(\partial\tau/\partial T)|_{\Gamma,\dot{\Gamma}}$ by multiplying by $1/\sqrt{3}$, since $\bar{\sigma} = \sqrt{3}\tau$ under simple shear conditions for a von Mises material. For n's of 0.055 (R_c 41 ≈ 400 HV) and 0.10 (R_c 23.5 ≈ 257 HV), $(\partial\tau/\partial T)|_{\Gamma,\dot{\Gamma}}$'s of 645 and 572 kPa/°C were derived this way. Values for other strain-hardening coefficients and hardness levels were established by linear interpolation between these values.

A self-consistent check of the values of $(\partial\tau/\partial T)|_{\Gamma,\dot{\Gamma}}$ obtained as described above was made by estimating the $\bar{\varepsilon}_c$ strains for Wulf's flow curves using Equation (3.62) and the estimated values of $\Delta\bar{\sigma}^*/\Delta T^*$. These predictions showed excellent agreement with the reported strains at the flow stress maxima.

Simulation Results. Since it was assumed that m and f_o were independent of hardness level, only n and Γ_c were varied in the simulations of flow localization that were performed. Use was made of both Equations (7.19), with $\bar{\Gamma} = 0.5$ ($\Gamma_{def} + \Gamma_{unif}$), and (7.24). The results were almost identical; thus, only those from the latter equation will be discussed.

Figure 7.4 shows the predicted rates of localization in terms of Γ_{def} versus Γ_{unif} for four hardness levels or n values. Localization begins slowly and eventually accelerates rapidly until $d\Gamma_{def}/d\Gamma_{unif}$ approaches ∞, i.e., until the catastrophic localization typical of adiabatic situations occurs. The "uniform" or bulk strains at which this takes place can be considered good estimates of the fragmentation strains.

Also plotted in Figure 7.4 is a series of closed and open circles corresponding to observations of the presence or absence of shear bands in Staker's exploded cylinder tests.[16] The circles have been plotted on the appropriate curve (depending on the n value of the material in the particular experiment) and at the imposed bulk shear strain. (These shear strains are twice those reported by Staker, since an error was made in Reference 16 in converting from measured normal strains to shear strain.) It can be seen that the open circles lie in regions where the predicted localization is small and the closed ones where it is large.

The observations can also be interpreted with regard to the loci corresponding to the magnitude of the instantaneous alpha pa-

---

†The isothermal flow curves are those that would be expected under isothermal conditions at high strain rates (i.e., without deformation heating).

rameter. The bulk strains at which $\alpha = 3$ and $\alpha = 4$ were determined from Equation (7.11) and are also shown in Figure 7.4. It appears that for small n's (0.054, 0.061) an $\alpha = 4$ criterion for shear bands is applicable. By contrast, an $\alpha = 3$ criterion appears sufficient for larger n's (0.072, 0.093).

The relation between the values of α and the occurrence of shear banding is further illustrated in Figure 7.5, which contains all

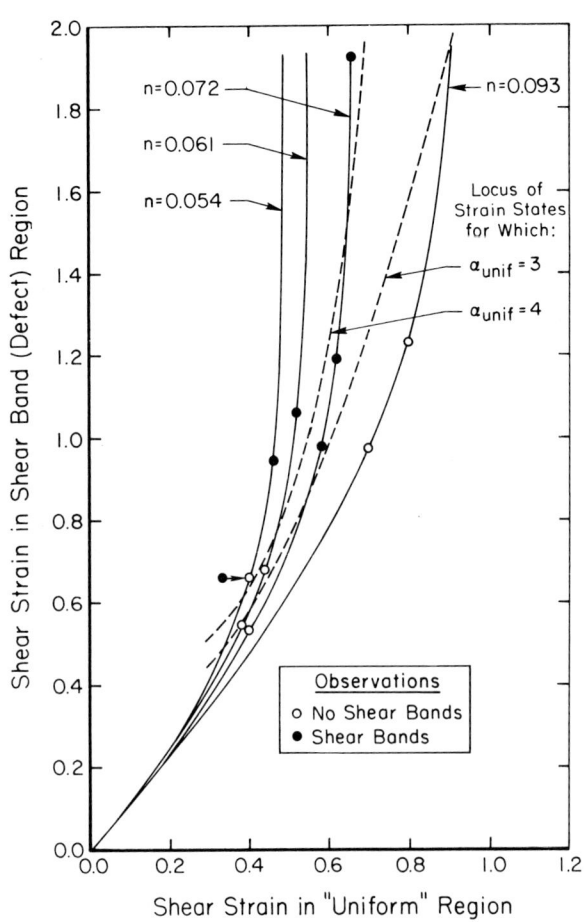

Figure 7.4. Predicted kinetics of flow localization during formation of adiabatic shear bands in 4340 steel tempered to different hardness levels. The dashed curves represent the loci of bulk strains at which $\alpha = 3$ or 4 in the "uniform" region of the two-slice model employed. The open and closed circles correspond to observations made by Staker.[16]

of Staker's data. The observations are plotted in terms of imposed bulk shear strain as a function of n value. The lines in this figure correspond to the bulk strains at which $\alpha = 0$, 3, or 4 and were derived from Equation (7.11). It is apparent that all of Staker's observations are consistent with a criterion based on $\alpha = 3$ to 4.* These results and those in Figure 7.4 provide strong support for the usefulness of the flow localization model developed earlier.

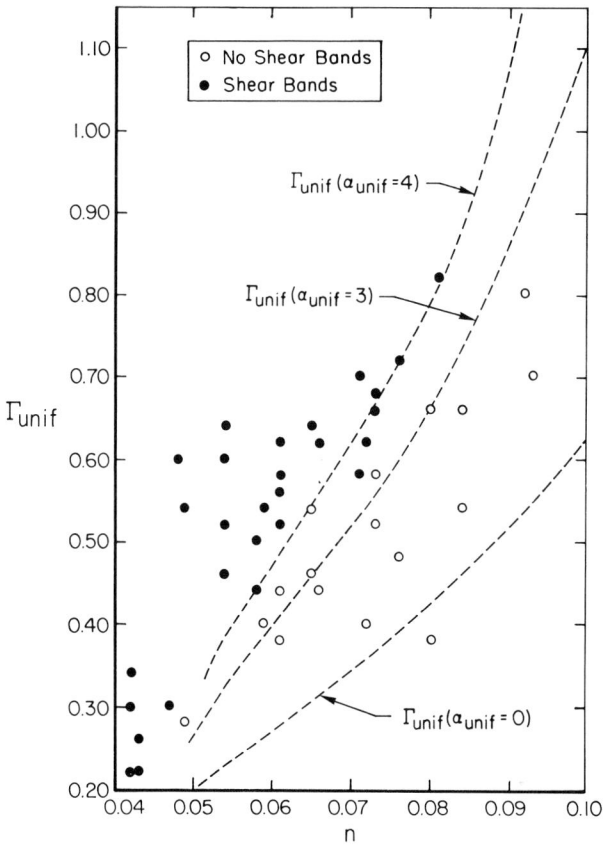

Figure 7.5. Staker's shear band observations[16] plotted in terms of the imposed bulk strain (strain in the "uniform" region) as a function of strain-hardening exponent. Bulk strains at which $\alpha = 0$, 3, and 4 are shown as broken lines.

---

*Although these values of α are somewhat lower than those applicable to torsion, tension, or compression (see Chapter 3), they may be a feature of the *path change* involved in adiabatic shear experiments.

Geological Shear Zones

The flow localization analysis of torsion testing, described in Chapter 4, can also be applied to geological shear processes, i.e., to situations in which there is no change of area term to increase (as in tension) or decrease (as in compression) the tendency toward strain concentration. One example of this kind is the development of ductile shear zones in the earth's crust. This problem was analyzed by Poirier and co-workers,[24] who came to a number of conclusions that are consistent with the present treatment of these problems. Their findings can be summarized below.

Under isothermal conditions, an initial strength defect is required to initiate localization. In the case of the geological materials studied, this can be due to composition gradients. It can also result from the occurrence of dynamic recrystallization, or of some other microstructural process that leads to flow softening.

When an exponential flow law is assumed, leading to saturation or steady-state creep, there is a relatively brief transition period, followed by an extended period of linear growth. During the latter, the ratio of the strain rate within the shear zone $\dot{\Gamma}_{sz}$ to that in the uniform region outside the zone $\dot{\Gamma}_u$ is given by:

$$\dot{\Gamma}_{sz}/\dot{\Gamma}_u = 1 + \frac{\Delta K/K}{m} \quad . \tag{7.25}$$

Here $\Delta K/K$ is the relative magnitude of the strength defect, K is the strength coefficient (see Chapter 3), and m is the rate sensitivity of the material. It is of interest that this steady-state solution can be readily deduced from the integrated version of Equation (5.47) (which is the form used by Poirier *et al.*) when the area decrease term (-1) is removed. Then

$$m\lambda' + G^*\lambda + \frac{d\ln K}{dz} = 0 \quad . \tag{7.26}$$

Here $G^* = (\partial \ln \tau/\partial \Gamma)|_{\dot{\Gamma}}$ is the work-hardening coefficient in shear, $\lambda' = (\partial \ln \dot{\Gamma}/\partial z)|_t$ is the shear strain rate gradient, $\lambda = \partial \Gamma/\partial z$ is the shear strain gradient, and $d\ln K/dz$ is the gradient in the relative strength. At saturation, $G^* = 0$, so that

$$\lambda' = \ln(\dot{\Gamma}_{sz}/\dot{\Gamma}_u) = -\frac{1}{m} \cdot \frac{d\ln K}{dz} \tag{7.27}$$

$$\approx \frac{\Delta K/K}{m} \quad (7.28)$$

Thus

$$\dot{\Gamma}_{sz}/\dot{\Gamma}_u = \exp\left(\frac{\Delta K/K}{m}\right) \quad (7.29)$$

and, when $(\Delta K/K)/m \ll 1$, this solution can be replaced by relation (7.25) above. The magnitudes of $(\Delta K/K)/m$ estimated from laboratory measurements for a certain type of granite led to differences in shear strain inside and outside the shear zone in reasonable agreement with geological observations.

The occurrence of dynamic recrystallization or of some other dynamic softening process sharpens the shear zone and delays the disappearance of the transient regime; however, its effect eventually dies out, leading to a steady-state solution similar to Equation (7.25) above.

The occurrence of mild shear heating also sharpens the shear zone. However, under the conditions investigated by Poirier et al., such deformation heating did *not* produce unbounded flow localization. This contrasts sharply with the unbounded flow localization that develops when titanium alloys are deformed in torsion under somewhat different heat transfer conditions.

References

[1] H.C. Rogers: *Ann. Rev. Mat. Sci.*, 1979, vol. 9, p. 283.
[2] R. Komanduri and R.H. Brown: *J. Eng. Ind., Trans. ASME*, 1981, vol. 103, p. 33.
[3] R. Komanduri, T. Schroeder, J. Hazra, B.F. von Turkovich, and D.G. Flom: *J. Eng. Ind., Trans. ASME*, 1982, vol. 104, p. 121.
[4] R. Komanduri and B.F. von Turkovich: *Wear*, 1981, vol. 69, p. 179.
[5] J.C. Lemaire and W.A. Backofen: *Met. Trans.*, 1972, vol. 3, p. 477.
[6] S.L. Semiatin, G.D. Lahoti, and S.I. Oh: *Material Behavior Under High Stress and Ultrahigh Loading Rates*, Plenum Press, New York, 1983, p. 119.
[7] S.L. Semiatin and S.B. Rao: *Mat. Sci. Eng.*, 1983, vol. 61, p. 185.
[8] M.E. Merchant: *J. Appl. Phys.*, 1945, vol. 16, p. 267, p. 318.
[9] E.G. Loewen and M.C. Shaw: *Trans. ASME*, 1954, vol. 76, p. 217.
[10] J.H. Weiner: *Trans. ASME*, 1955, vol. 77, p. 1331.
[11] B.T. Chao and K.J. Trigger: *Trans. ASME*, 1953, vol. 75, p. 109.
[12] G. Boothroyd: *Proc. Inst. Mech. Engrs.*, 1963, vol. 177, p. 789.
[13] Y.S. Touloukian: *Thermophysical Properties of High Temperature Solid Materials*, Macmillan Company, New York, 1967.

[14] T. Lyman: *Metals Handbook, Vol. 1: Properties and Selection of Metals*, Eighth Edition, American Society for Metals, Metals Park, OH, 1961.

[15] T. Nicholas: Technical Report AFWAL-TR-80-4053, Materials Laboratory, Air Force Wright Aeronautical Laboratories, Wright-Patterson Air Force Base, OH, 1980.

[16] M.R. Staker: *Acta Met.*, 1981, vol. 29, p. 683.

[17] T.B. Cox and J.R. Low, Jr.: "An Investigation of the Plastic Fracture of High Strength Steels," NASA Technical Report No. 5 under Research Grant NGR 39-087-003, Carnegie-Mellon University, Pittsburgh, PA, 1973.

[18] Anon.: *Aerospace Structural Metals Handbook*, Mechanical Properties Data Center, Battelle Columbus Laboratories, Columbus, OH, 1982.

[19] M.R. Staker: *Scripta Met.*, 1980, vol. 14, p. 677.

[20] D.A. Shockey and D.C. Erlich: *Shock Waves and High Strain Rate Phenomena*, M.A. Meyers and L.E. Murr, eds., p. 249, Plenum Press, New York, 1981.

[21] M. Azrin and W.A. Backofen: *Met. Trans.*, 1970, vol. 1, p. 2857.

[22] S.M. Doraivelu: Ph.D. Thesis, Metallurgy Department, Indian Institute of Technology, Madras, India, February, 1979.

[23] G.L. Wulf: *Inter. J. Mech. Sci.*, 1978, vol. 20, p. 843.

[24] J.P. Poirier, J.L. Bouchez, and J.J. Jonas: *Earth and Planetary Science Letters*, 1979, vol. 43, p. 441.

APPENDIX A
KINETICS OF FLOW LOCALIZATION IN UNIAXIAL COMPRESSION

In Chapter 3, the localization of plastic flow during the uniaxial compression of specimens containing geometric (i.e., machining) and hammer blow (i.e., deformation) defects was discussed at length. The purpose of this Appendix is to illustrate the procedures by which expressions such as Equation (3.18b) can be evaluated to obtain a first-order insight into the kinetics of the flow localization process itself.

Relations such as Equation (3.18b) represent the necessary differences in strain and strain rate (between regions in a specimen that contain a defect and that are defect-free) that are required to maintain force equilibrium at any given instant during the deformation. To apply such expressions, however, boundary and initial conditions must be specified. For purposes of illustration, the boundary condition of a constant true strain rate in the defect-free region will be assumed.[1]* Further, the specimen will be cut into merely two slices, corresponding to the two regions with and without a defect.[1] By using more realistic boundary conditions (e.g., a constant *overall* true strain rate) and dividing the specimen into many slices, more accurate results may be obtained.[2] This is partly because when the difference in strain between adjacent slices is small (e.g., in the many-slice model), there is little ambiguity in selecting the value of γ' (or

---

*This corresponds to a specimen of "infinite" length being tested under constant overall strain rate conditions.

γ) for use in equations such as (3.18b). On the other hand, when a two-slice model is chosen, it is usually best to evaluate γ' at some strain between that of the uniform and defect regions, say the average strain. The present approximate method is therefore presented primarily for heuristic purposes.

Equation (3.18b) can be used to gage the growth of strain and strain-rate gradients in the simple two-slice model, since

$$m\delta \ln \dot{\varepsilon} = (1 - \gamma)\delta\varepsilon - \delta \ln A_o \tag{3.18b}$$

reduces to

$$m \ln\left(\frac{\dot{\varepsilon}_{unif}}{\dot{\varepsilon}_{def}}\right) = (1 - \gamma)(\varepsilon_{unif} - \varepsilon_{def}) - \ln\left(\frac{A_{o_{unif}}}{A_{o_{def}}}\right) . \tag{A.1}$$

Here γ' has been replaced by γ, since temperature effects are being neglected, and the subscripts "unif" and "def" denote quantities pertaining to the defect-free (uniform) and imperfect (defect) regions, respectively. The solution to Equation (A.1) depends on whether a geometric or a deformation defect is being considered.

For the case of a *geometric* defect, Equation (A.1) in the form

$$\dot{\varepsilon}_{def} = \dot{\varepsilon}_{unif} \left\{ \left(\frac{A_{o_{def}}}{A_{o_{unif}}}\right)^{(1/m)} \right\}^{-1} \exp\left[-(1-\gamma)(\varepsilon_{unif} - \varepsilon_{def})/m\right]$$

$$\tag{A.2}$$

can be used. At time $t = 0$, $\varepsilon_{unif} = \varepsilon_{def} = 0$, so that

$$\dot{\varepsilon}_{def}(t=0) = \dot{\varepsilon}_{unif} \left\{ \left(\frac{A_{o_{def}}}{A_{o_{unif}}}\right)^{(1/m)} \right\}^{-1} . \tag{A.3}$$

In other words, the initial strain-rate gradient is specified totally by the magnitude of the geometric defect, the rate sensitivity m, and the (constant) strain rate in the uniform region, $\dot{\varepsilon}_{unif}$. After a sufficiently small time increment, the strain in the two regions is calculated from the strain rates at $t = 0$. This defines $\lambda = \delta\varepsilon = \varepsilon_{unif} - \varepsilon_{def}$, which, in conjunction with a suitable value of γ, can be used to define a new $\dot{\varepsilon}_{def}$ with Equation (A.2). After subsequent time increments, new values of ε_{unif}, ε_{def}, and γ are obtained that are used to establish $\dot{\varepsilon}_{def}$ and λ over the course of the deformation, thereby describing the kinetics of flow localization (or flow stabilization) in compression of materials with geometric defects.

For the case of an initial *deformation* defect, Equation (A.2) is also applied, after noting that the term in the braces is identically equal to unity. However, $\delta\varepsilon \neq 0$ at the onset of deformation, but is determined by the magnitude of the hammer blow itself, which gives rise to an initial ε_{def}. Since $\varepsilon_{unif} = 0$ at $t = 0$, $\dot{\varepsilon}_{def}$ can be evaluated in this way. After a given time increment, ε_{unif} and ε_{def} are calculated from the known strain rates yielding a new value of λ, and expression (A.2) is again used to estimate the difference in strain rate between the uniform and imperfect regions. The procedure is then repeated as before to map the entire flow localization process.

Procedures such as the above are readily performed on pocket calculators or with simple programs on digital computers. Such calculations are illustrated next; they are based on the flow curves pertaining to a variety of hypothetical materials, as well as to a titanium and a nickel-base alloy.

Simulation Results for Hypothetical Materials

Since the geometric (or strength) defect is the more important of the two types of defect, results from a two-slice model for a material with this type of flaw will serve to illustrate the gross localization trends that can be expected. The defect size was chosen to be $f_o = A_{o_{unif}}/A_{o_{def}} = 0.985$, a value in the range typically found in practice.

From Equation (A.2), it is seen that the material properties of importance are the rate sensitivity m and the flow softening rate γ, or more precisely the rate sensitivity and the alpha parameter for compression, i.e., $\alpha = (\gamma - 1)/m$. Simulations employing Equation (A.2) were performed for materials with a variety of m's and α's, in each of which the value of α was held constant. The results are shown in Figure A.1 in terms of the strain in the defect part of the specimen versus that in the uniform part of the specimen. The dashed curve in the figure represents an average compressive strain of 0.69 (upset reduction = 50 percent) and was calculated assuming that the initial lengths of the two slices were equal. Thus, the intersections of the dashed and solid curves represent the approximate degrees of inhomogeneous deformation that can be expected in a compression test to 50 percent height reduction.

The results for m = 0.1, a typical rate sensitivity at hot working temperatures, demonstrate that little localization is observed at 50 percent reduction for materials characterized by $\alpha = -1.0, 0.0$, and 1.0. A slight amount is noted for m = 0.1, $\alpha = 3.0$ and large amounts for m = 0.1, $\alpha = 5.0$ or $\alpha = 10.0$, in agreement with the premise that α = 5.0 or greater is required for noticeable flow localization under typical forming conditions.

Three cases in Figure A.1 reveal that both the α parameter *and* m must be considered in gaging, at least qualitatively, the tendency for flow localization to occur. These are the curves for the three α = 5.0 materials with m = 0.01, m = 0.10, and m = 0.50. The first and second m values are typical for metals at cold and hot working

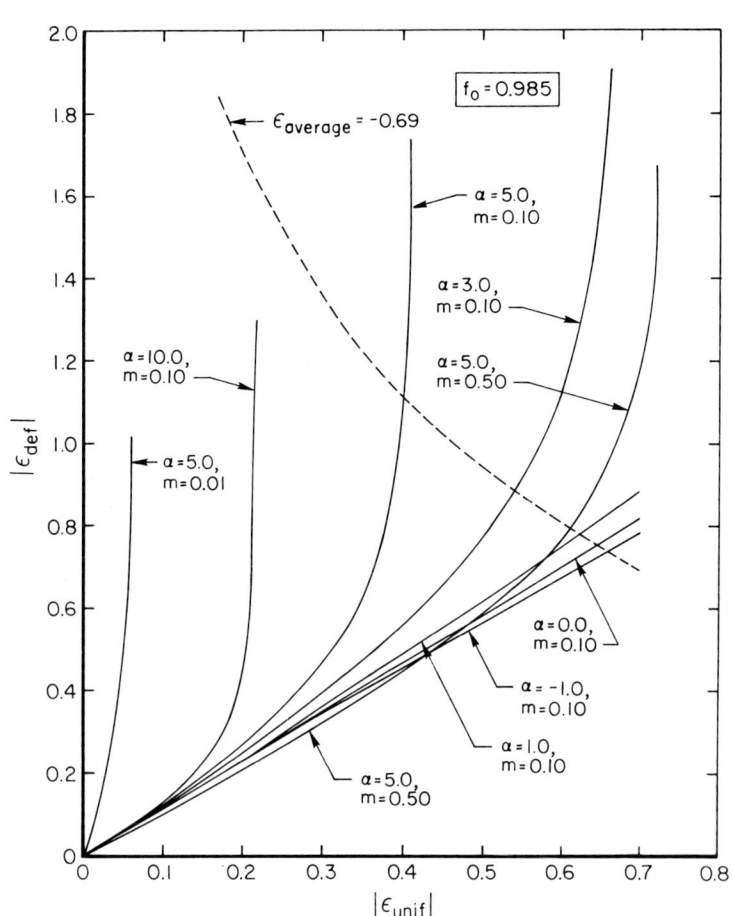

Figure A.1. Relationship between the strains in the "defect" and "uniform" regions of compression specimens containing an initial 1.5 percent geometric defect. Calculations are for hypothetical materials whose flow behavior is described by constant values of α and m. The intersections of the dashed and solid curves correspond to strain states at 50 percent reduction of specimens whose "defect" and "uniform" regions were initially of equal length.

temperatures, respectively, whereas the third is representative of superplastic materials. For the materials with $\alpha = 5$, the strain at which localization becomes marked is very small for m = 0.01, moderate for m = 0.10, and much larger for m = 0.5. The effect of large m on the stabilization of flow under flow softening conditions is evident from these calculations and is seen to be similar to the behavior of superplastic materials in tensile loading.

Simulation Results for Ti-10-2-3 and U-700

In the main body of this monograph, the $\alpha_{max} = 5.0$ criterion was applied successfully to predict the occurrence of nonuniform flow in simple compression tests. Inspection of Equation (A.1) or (A.2) shows, however, that the process of flow localization is a strong function of the *instantaneous* values of the material properties γ and m, which can vary during straining. Under these conditions, more rigorous flow localization calculations (such as those illustrated in Figures 3.13 and 3.14) are required to predict the kinetics of the entire process. Two cases for actual materials will serve to illustrate when approximate (e.g., Ti-10-2-3) or more detailed (e.g., U-700) calculations are necessary.

The first case is for Ti-10-2-3 isothermally compressed at 704 °C (1300 °F), $\dot{\varepsilon} = -10$ sec.$^{-1}$. Table 3.1 and Figure 3.11c reveal that the material deforms nonuniformly under these conditions. Although $\alpha_{max} = 5.0$, it was found that for the greater part of the deformation $\alpha = 0$ to a reasonable degree of approximation. For $\alpha = 0$, Equation (A.2) can be integrated directly to provide

$$\varepsilon_{def}/\varepsilon_{unif} = f_o^{-(1/m)} \quad . \tag{A.4}$$

If $f_o = 0.985$, the above expression with m = 0.08 leads to $\varepsilon_{def}/\varepsilon_{unif} = 1.21$. If $f_o = 0.980$, we obtain $\varepsilon_{def}/\varepsilon_{unif} = 1.29$. For the specimen shown in Figure 3.11c, diameter measurements at various circumferential locations in the bulged and non-bulged regions led to $\varepsilon_{def}/\varepsilon_{unif} \approx 1.29$, i.e., to a value in agreement with the $f_o = 0.98$ prediction.

In the case of U-700 tested at 1038 °C and a strain rate of 25 sec.$^{-1}$, conditions under which nonuniform flow also occurs (Table 3.1 and Figure 3.12), the flow curve between -0.1 and -0.7 was found to be fitted well by the expression

$$\sigma(MPa) = -574 - 430\varepsilon \quad , \tag{A.5}$$

resulting in

$$\gamma' = 430/(574 + 430\varepsilon) \quad . \tag{A.6}$$

Employing a two-slice model and Equation (A.2) (in which γ' replaces γ), with $f_o = 0.985$, $m = 0.12$, and the above relation for γ', the localization process was simulated to approximately 60 percent reduction, again assuming that the original lengths of the uniform and defect-containing slices were equal. At 50 percent reduction ($\varepsilon = -0.69$), A_{def}/A_{unif} was predicted to be equal to 1.14, and at 60 percent reduction ($\varepsilon = -0.92$) to be equal to 1.50. These values correspond to diameter ratios of 1.07 and 1.22. Comparison with specimens such as those shown in Figure 3.12 showed good agreement to 50 percent reduction, but that the predicted diameter ratio was in excess of that observed at 60 percent reduction. This can be attributed to the decrease in the observed flow softening rate γ' at compressive strains greater than -0.7, a trend that was not accounted for in the analytical expression for γ' used in the simulation, Equation (A.6).

The above results suggest that simple flow localization models are indeed capable of predicting the extent of bulging during the uniaxial compression of flow softening materials. Further work is warranted, however, in the development of multiple-slice models that include the effects of stress triaxiality, as well as on the experimental determination of reliable f_o values for use in such models.

References

[1] J.J. Jonas, R.A. Holt, and C.E. Coleman: *Acta Met.*, 1976, vol. 24, p. 911.
[2] N. Christodoulou and J.J. Jonas: *Res Mechanica*, 1982, vol. 5, p. 49.

APPENDIX B
EFFECT OF STRESS TRIAXIALITY ON THE PROPAGATION OF NECKS AND BULGES

The Effective Stress and the Bridgman Triaxiality Factor[1]

The analyses described in Chapters 3 and 5 are rigorously valid only when the state of stress is uniaxial; that is, when no radial or circumferential stresses are developed in the stretched or compressed bar. This assumption is reasonably valid as long as the deformation is homogeneous and the profile of the specimen remains fairly uniform. Conversely, if the stress tensor deviates from a uniaxial one, so that finite radial and circumferential stresses (σ_r and σ_θ, respectively) are induced in addition to the axial stress σ_x, the plastic behavior of the specimen must be described instead in terms of the local effective stress $\bar{\sigma}$ and effective strain $\bar{\varepsilon}$. According to this concept, $\bar{\sigma}$ is numerically equal to the uniaxial stress that would produce the same effective strain rate as the one generated by the complex stress field. The rate of plastic deformation is increased by the triaxiality effect if the transverse stresses are opposite in sign to the axial stress and conversely decreased if the hydrostatic term is of the same sign. When an axially symmetric specimen containing a defect is deformed, in tension for example, beyond the onset of strain localization, the profile becomes highly nonuniform, and transverse components of stress are developed. Since these components usually vary across a given cross section, it is useful to characterize the overall effect of triaxiality in the section by the mean effective stress $\langle \bar{\sigma} \rangle$. Following Bridgman,[2] we henceforth denote by the term "triaxiality factor" the ratio $F_T = \langle \bar{\sigma} \rangle / \langle \sigma_x \rangle$, where the mean axial stress $\langle \sigma_x \rangle = F/A$.

In a tension or compression specimen with a uniform cross section, the triaxiality factor is equal to 1. If, on the other hand, the specimen profile is curved, F_T is less than or greater than 1, depending on whether the external surface of the sample is concave or convex, respectively (see Figure B.1). Note that, following earlier authors, the curvature of the individual field of force lines is of the same sign as that of the outer profile. Thus, in the externally concave region, the stresses can only be balanced if σ_r and σ_θ are both of the same sign as σ_x, so that $F_T < 1$. Conversely, in the externally convex region, which is of greater interest to the present discussion, $F_T > 1$.

To date, no simple analytical expression for F_T has been proposed that is valid for arbitrary axisymmetric profiles. This is because F_T depends in a complex way not only on the first and second derivatives of the profile radius a(X), but also on the plastic properties of the material.[2]* Nevertheless, the effect of triaxiality can be expressed for the case in which the ratio a/R (of the specimen radius a to the radius of curvature of the profile R) is small and in which there is a transverse plane of symmetry, e.g., at the neck of a tensile bar. At the latter site, $da/dX = 0$, and the radius of curvature R, given by $R = 1/(d^2a/dX^2)$ when $da/dX = 0$, is positive. Under these conditions, F_T can be expressed as follows:

$$F_T = 1/[(1 + (2R/a)] \cdot \ln[(1 + (a/2R)] \quad (B.1)$$

It can be readily shown that the original assumptions of Bridgman remain valid for symmetrically *bulged* profiles (as well as for symmetrically necked profiles) as long as a *negative* value is attributed to R.

---

*As indicated in Chapter 3, the instability analyses are all expressed in terms of Lagrangian or *specimen* coordinates. That is, in the gradient $(\partial/\partial x)|_t$, x refers to a specimen coordinate that is fixed to a specific material element; it does not change during straining, even though the element itself is moving and changing its shape. This is because the constitutive laws describe the behavior of a particular sample element, and the evolution of the material coefficients associated with the element (e.g., γ and m) is only known with respect to the *material* cross section of interest. Conversely, the triaxiality effects depend on the current shape of the sample in Eulerian or *laboratory* space. They must, therefore, be evaluated in these coordinates, which are distinguished from the former by the use of capital X as opposed to lower case x.

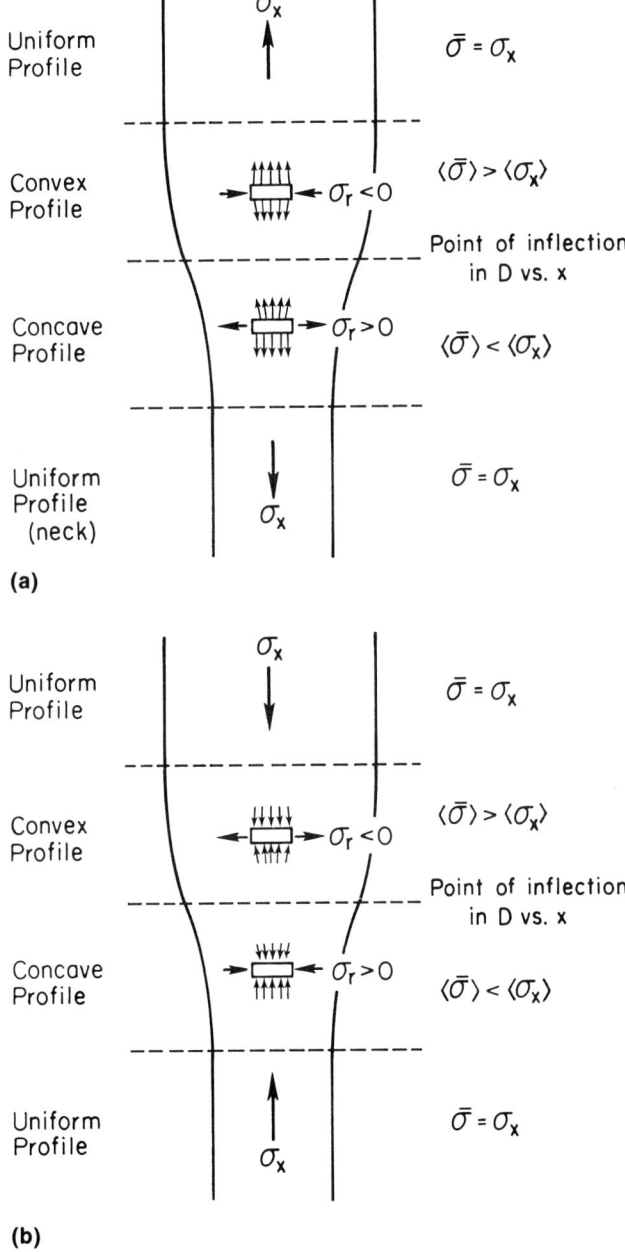

Figure B.1. Schematic representation of the transverse stresses generated in a sample of varying cross section. Note that $\langle \bar{\sigma} \rangle > \langle \sigma_x \rangle$ ($F_T > 1$) in externally convex regions. (a) Tension, (b) compression.[1]

The dependence of the Bridgman triaxiality factor F_T on the ratio a/R is illustrated in Figure B.2 for *negative* as well as positive values of a/R. When $da/dX \neq 0$, it is not immediately evident whether or not Equation (B.1) can continue to apply. In such parts of the sample, the expression for F_T could include, for example, terms in (da/dX). However, the Bridgman relation appears to be of at least approximate validity under these conditions, inasmuch as the work of Argon *et al.*[3] has shown, by means of a finite-element method, that the expressions for σ_r and σ_θ given by the Bridgman analysis continue to apply along the axis of symmetry. From their work, it can be concluded that Equation (B.1) is a good first approximation for the actual triaxiality factor, even when $da/dX \neq 0$.

Influence of The Triaxiality Factor on The Kinetics of Plastic Strain Localization

In the derivation of the differential equation (expression 3.18a) relating the strain and strain-rate gradients to the material coefficients and nonuniformities, the relevant stress was the uniaxial stress, as is normally the case for the so-called "long wavelength" approximations. However, in the present instance, the force per unit of current cross section must be expressed in terms of the longitudinal component σ_x of the axially oriented principal stress. In what follows, we will not be concerned with the radial variation in this quantity, but will consider only its average value, $\langle \sigma_x \rangle$. Recalling that $\langle \sigma_x \rangle = \langle \bar{\sigma} \rangle / F_T$, we can represent the effect of differences in F_T along the axis of an otherwise uniform sample, for example, by the expression:

$$\delta \ln \langle \sigma_x \rangle = \delta \ln \langle \bar{\sigma} \rangle - \delta \ln F_T \tag{B.2}$$

In order to extend the instability analysis to include the effect of triaxial stresses, the following assumptions now prove useful:
(i) The increment in the mean effective strain $d\langle \bar{\varepsilon} \rangle$ is taken as approximately equal to the increment in the mean longitudinal strain $d\langle \varepsilon_x \rangle$.
(ii) Although the strain-hardening (and rate sensitivity) properties of the material depend on the mean effective strain (and mean effective strain rate), these can be deduced to a sufficient degree of accuracy from the mean longitudinal strains (and strain rates).

Under these conditions, Equation (3.18a) can be replaced by:

$$m\lambda' = (1 - \gamma')\lambda - \frac{d\ln A_o}{dx} + \left(\frac{\partial(\ln F_T)}{\partial x}\right)\bigg|_t \qquad (B.3)$$

From the above relation, it can be seen that the triaxiality term $[\partial(\ln F_T)/\partial x]_t$ is formally equivalent to the other types of nonuniformities considered in turn above.* The magnitude and therefore the importance of this term can be estimated from Figure B.2.[1] For this purpose, we consider two neighboring regions of equal cross section, one of which is of uniform radius ($da/dX = 0$; $a/R = 0$; $F_T = 1.0$), and the other of which has a small negative curvature (e.g., $a/R = -0.12$; $F_T = 1.04$). It is evident that $\delta\ln F_T$ in this instance is equivalent to an area defect $\delta\ln A_o$ of 4 percent.

Thus, the triaxiality term in Equation (B.3) provides a ready explanation for the observation that a neck or bulge, once formed, generally propagates in an orderly fashion toward the ends of a specimen, instead of being reinitiated at small "strength" defects along the so-called "uniform" portion of the unconstricted parts of the spec-

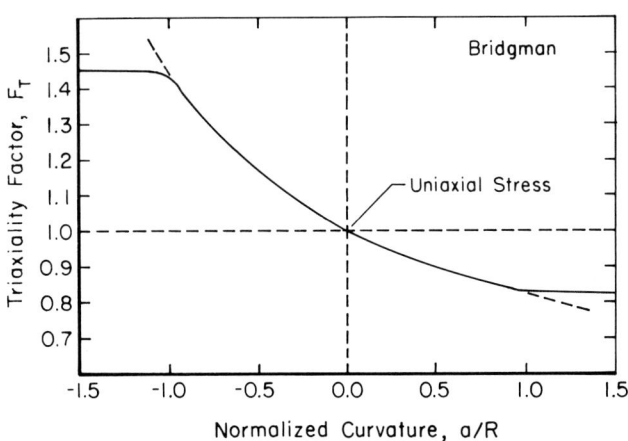

Figure B.2. Dependence of Bridgman triaxiality correction factor F_T on (a/R). The extension of Bridgman's relation for F_T into the region of negative (a/R) is limited to (a/R) ≥ −1 because of St. Venant's principle.

---

*Note, however, that the area and strength defects $d\ln A_o/dx$ and $d\ln K/dx$ are initial conditions that are independent of the time t, whereas the triaxiality gradient evolves with time and can eventually disappear.

imen. This is because the negative curvature at the ends of such regions has a large enough effect, according to the instability analysis, to provoke deformation at this location, rather than in the less inhomogeneous regions of the sample.

References

[1] C. G'Sell, N.A. Aly-Helal, and J.J. Jonas: *J. Mat. Sci.,* 1983, vol. 18, p. 1731.
[2] P.W. Bridgman: *Trans ASM,* 1944, vol. 32, p. 2024.
[3] A.S. Argon, J. Im, and A. Needleman: *Met. Trans. A,* 1975, vol. 6A, p. 815.

APPENDIX C
DEVELOPMENT OF ADIABATIC SHEAR BANDS IN TORSION

The occurrence of flow localization in torsion was discussed at some length in Chapters 3 and 4. In Chapter 3, the application of the α parameter to predict shear bands during the hot torsion testing of Ti-6242Si was described. Subsequently, an analysis of nonuniform flow that is driven by heat transfer phenomena was detailed in Chapter 4 and shown to be capable of predicting shear band formation in Type 304 stainless steel.[1]

In this Appendix, the development of strain localizations in very high-rate torsion tests will be discussed, concentrating on the work of Costin et al.[2] Their torque-twist observations will be interpreted in some detail, and the failure mode involved in these tests will also be described.

Experiments of Costin et al.[2]

Costin et al. performed torsion tests on short gage length, thin-walled tubes of a 1018 steel that had been cold rolled prior to testing, hereafter referred to as 1018 CRS, and a 1020 hot rolled steel, or 1020 HRS. The gage section of each specimen was 2.5 mm long with an internal diameter of 9.5 mm and a wall thickness of 0.4 mm. Using an apparatus capable of imposing static and dynamic strain rates,[3] they ran tests at shear strain rates of 5×10^{-4} sec.$^{-1}$ (to obtain material property data) and 500 sec.$^{-1}$ (1018 CRS) or 1000 sec.$^{-1}$ (1020

HRS) to investigate the occurrence of shear bands. An expression originally used by Litonski[4] was fitted to the material flow stress data:

$$\tau = c(1 - aT)(1 + b\dot{\gamma})^m \gamma^n \quad . \tag{C.1}$$

Here, τ, γ, and $\dot{\gamma}$ are the shear stress, strain, and strain rate, respectively. T is the absolute temperature, and c, a, b, m, and n are material constants, whose values for the two test materials are given in Table C.1.

Costin et al.[2] reported dynamic shear stress-strain data to overall engineering shear strains γ_{ov} of about 0.3, although photographs in their work suggest that the 1020 HRS was twisted to γ_{ov}'s as large as 0.8. At $\gamma_{ov} = 0.3$, the 1018 CRS had already developed shear bands, but the 1020 HRS steel showed no evidence of strain localization, even at γ_{ov}'s as high as 0.8. In order to rationalize these results, a flow localization analysis based on the torque equilibrium equation and a one-dimensional heat transfer model was performed. A 2 percent defect in cross section covering 20 percent of the gage length and a constant overall shear strain or twist rate were assumed for the simulation.* Model predictions taken to $\gamma_{ov} = 0.3$ confirmed the observations, in that shear bands were predicted for the 1018 CRS but not for the 1020 HRS. These results will be discussed in somewhat more detail in the next sections in which another set of simulations, for which *adiabatic* conditions were assumed to prevail, are described.

Analysis of The Torsion Test Under Adiabatic Conditions

The general analysis of flow localization in torsion is not straightforward when heat transfer effects must be taken into account. Nevertheless, at strain rates of 500 sec.$^{-1}$ and above and γ_{ov}'s on the order of 1.0, the deformation heating is essentially adiabatic, a condition which leads to considerable simplification. This can be shown in two ways. First, the characteristic diffusion distance for heat is $x_c = 2\sqrt{Dt^*}$, where D is the thermal diffusivity and t^* is the time avail-

---

*In Chapter 3, geometric defects were shown to be similar to strength defects in their effect on the process of flow localization. Further, it has been found that a 2 percent defect is reasonable for engineering materials.

Table C.1.
Material Properties for Test Materials of Costin et al.[2]

Material	c (MPa)	a ($10^{-3}K^{-1}$)	b (10^4 s)	m	n
1018 CRS	614	1.5	1	0.025	0.05
1020 HRS	531	1.2	1	0.034	0.20

able. For $\dot{\gamma}_{ov} = 500$ sec.$^{-1}$ and $\gamma_{ov} = 1$, $t^* = 2 \times 10^{-3}$ sec.$^{-1}$. Since D ≈ 0.15 cm^2/sec. for the carbon steels under investigation, x_c ≈ 0.35 mm, or a relatively small fraction of the 2.5-mm gage length. At 1000 sec.$^{-1}$, x_c is even smaller. A second means of gaging the degree of adiabaticity in torsion is through a complete thermal analysis of the type carried out by Johnson et al.[5] for a torsion specimen geometry almost identical to that used by Costin et al.[2] In this work, it was shown that, for deformation times below 0.01 sec., the temperature at the center of the gage section is not measurably influenced by conduction effects. Since the deformation times here are substantially less, it can be concluded that a large proportion of the gage length deforms under adiabatic or near adiabatic conditions at strain rates of 500 and 1000 sec.$^{-1}$.

With the adiabaticity assumption, the progress of strain localization in torsion can be followed by applying the torque equilibrium equation, which for a thin-walled tube is

$$\pi d_A^2 t_A \tau_A = \pi d_B^2 t_B \tau_B \quad . \tag{C.2}$$

Here A and B refer to the uniform (bulk) and defect regions, $d_A \approx d_B$ is the tube diameter, and t_A and t_B are the wall thicknesses in the two regions. From the definition of τ (Equation C.1), the above becomes

$$t_A(1 - aT_A)(1 + b\dot{\gamma}_A)^m \gamma_A^n$$
$$= t_B(1 - aT_B)(1 + b\dot{\gamma}_B)^m \gamma_B^n \quad , \tag{C.3}$$

an expression that can be rearranged to specify $\dot{\gamma}_B$ in terms of $\dot{\gamma}_A$, γ_A, γ_B, T_A, T_B, t_A, and t_B. Under adiabatic conditions, T is given by the $\tau - \Gamma$ equivalent of Equation (3.64). Hence, the development of nonuniform flow can be simulated using the methods discussed in Appendix A, provided a boundary condition on $\dot{\gamma}_A$ is chosen. Alternatively, if a fixed *overall* strain rate, $\dot{\gamma}_{ov}$, is specified, Equation (C.3) can be solved simultaneously using the condition

$$\dot{\gamma}_{ov} = \text{constant} = (L_a \dot{\gamma}_A + L_B \dot{\gamma}_B)/(L_A + L_B) \tag{C.4}$$

in which L_A and L_B are the (assumed) lengths of the uniform and defect regions, taken to be in the ratio of 4:1 in the present case, as was done by Costin et al.[2]

Simulation Results for Adiabatic Torsion Testing

The high-speed torsion deformation of tubes, assuming adiabatic conditions and $t_B/t_A = 0.98$, was simulated by Semiatin[6] for 1018 CRS (500 sec.$^{-1}$) and 1020 HRS (1000 sec.$^{-1}$) and compared to the simulation results and observations reported by Costin et al.[2] Two sets of runs were made, one in which $\dot{\gamma}_A$ was held constant at either 500 sec.$^{-1}$ (1018 CRS) or 1000 sec.$^{-1}$ (1020 HRS) and one in which the overall shear strain rate $\dot{\gamma}_{ov}$ was held constant at the same two strain rates. The temperature change taking place during each step of the numerical solution (in degrees Kelvin) was estimated from $dT = 0.289 \cdot \tau d\gamma$, where τ is in MPa and $d\gamma$ denotes the strain increment in the region of interest. The factor of 0.289 was calculated from handbook values of the density and specific heat for 1020 steel and the value of the mechanical equivalent of heat.

1018 CRS

The simulation results for the 1018 CRS are shown in Figure C.1. The lines represent the simulation results of Costin et al.,[2] which *include* the effects of heat transfer. Individual points in these plots came from the simulations based on the *adiabatic* heating assumption[6] and are seen to agree quite well in terms of γ_A and γ_B (Figure C.1a) and T_A and T_B (Figure C.1b), irrespective of whether a $\dot{\gamma}_A =$ constant or a $\dot{\gamma}_{ov} =$ constant boundary condition is used. The agreement between the results of Costin et al.[2] and those from the adiabatic solution confirm that heat transfer, taken into account in the former work, must have been negligible. All of these localization trends are also in good agreement with measurements of γ_A in 1018 CRS torsion specimens, which contained shear bands.

The fact that the choice of the boundary condition has a negligible effect on the γ_A, γ_B and T_A, T_B predictions can be understood

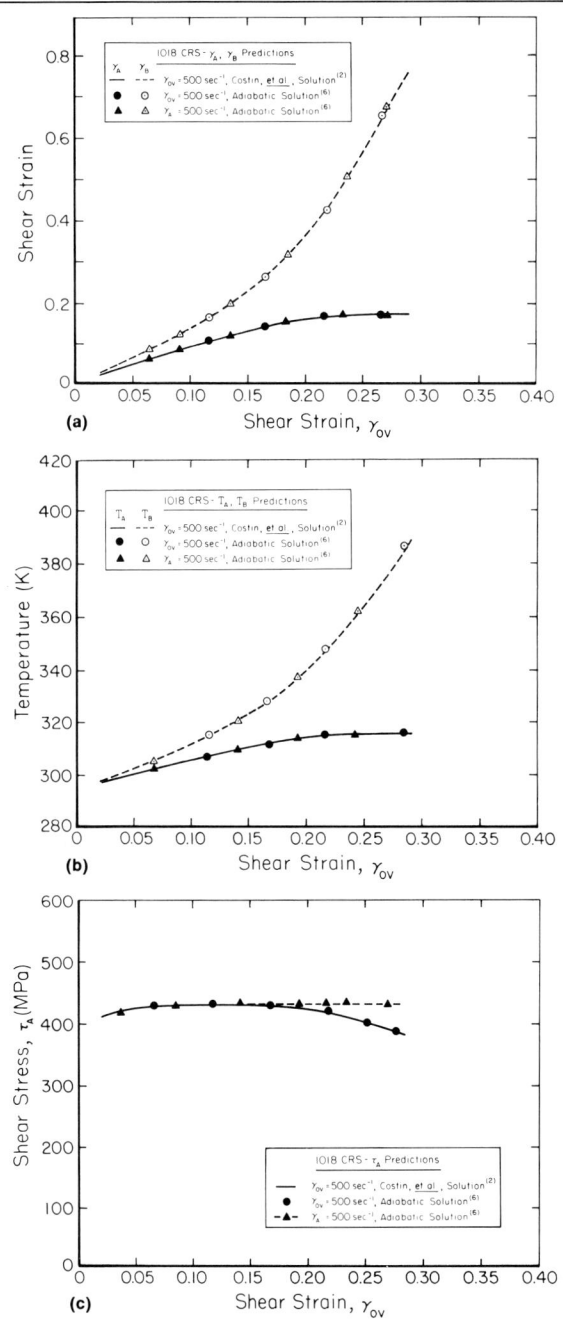

Figure C.1. Comparison of torsion simulation results for 1018 CRS based on (1) heat-transfer model (Costin *et al.*[2]) and (2) assumption of adiabatic heating.[6] Predictions are in terms of (a) γ_A and γ_B versus γ_{ov}, (b) T_A and T_B versus γ_{ov}, and (c) τ_A versus γ_{ov}.

through an examination of Equation (C.3), the equilibrium expression. Inasmuch as τ is relatively insensitive to γ (see Figure C.1c), $T \sim \int \tau d\gamma$ is a strong function of γ but only weakly dependent on τ. Further, $b\dot{\gamma} \gg 1$, so that Equation (C.3) can be written as

$$\int_0^{\gamma_A} \text{Fcn.} (\gamma_A) d\gamma_A \approx \int_0^{\gamma_B} \text{Fcn.} (\gamma_B) d\gamma_B \quad , \tag{C.5}$$

since $\dot{\gamma} = d\gamma/dT$, and the development of strain (and temperature) gradients is independent of the exact value of $\dot{\gamma}_A$ or $\dot{\gamma}_B$, as long as adiabaticity is maintained.*

The choice of boundary condition in the 1018 CRS simulations does, however, have an effect on the predicted value of τ_A.** When $\dot{\gamma}_A$ is held constant, τ_A versus γ_{ov} shows a maximum (at $\gamma_{ov} \approx 0.165$) and a *very small amount of softening* (which is not perceptible on the plot in Figure C.1c). Such a dependence of τ_A on γ_{ov} is very similar to the form of the constant strain rate τ_A versus γ_A curve (i.e., the flow curve represented by Equation C.1). However, since γ_{ov} in the present case is larger than γ_A (due to the fact that $\gamma_B > \gamma_A$), the actual τ_A versus γ_A (not γ_{ov}) curve is a version of the τ_A versus γ_{ov} curve which is slightly compressed along the γ_{ov} axis.

In contrast to the τ_A versus γ_{ov} behavior for $\dot{\gamma}_A$ = constant, the corresponding results for the $\dot{\gamma}_{ov}$ = constant boundary condition can be seen to exhibit a pronounced downward trend once localization sets in (i.e., for $\gamma_{ov} \geq 0.175$). This phenomenon is in agreement with the predictions of Costin and co-workers for $\dot{\gamma}_{ov}$ = constant and demonstrates an important point often over-looked in the literature on the torsion test. Conventionally, noticeable softening associated with the $\dot{\gamma}_{ov}$ = constant boundary condition is taken to be equivalent to appreciable *material flow softening*.† We have just remarked that, under constant $\dot{\gamma}_A$ conditions, the amount of softening is imperceptible. Under the constant $\dot{\gamma}_{ov}$ condition, the major portion of the softening must

---

*This conclusion is valid only as long as (1) the independent variables in Equation (C.1) can be taken as state variables and (2) the rate sensitivity m $(= (\partial \ln \tau/\partial \ln \dot{\gamma})|_{\gamma,T})$ is relatively constant.

**Note that for the thin-walled tube, τ is proportional to the torque M and the form of M versus γ_{ov} is similar to that of τ versus γ_{ov}. For the torsion of a solid bar, the dependence of γ, $\dot{\gamma}$, and T on radius rules out such a simple correspondence.[1]

†This fallacy is analogous to the assumption that a large load drop in a tensile test is due to flow softening, which is obviously incorrect. If necking could be prevented, the load-deflection curve in tensile tests on rate insensitive materials would show only a *very gradual* downward trend.

therefore be attributed to the sharp decrease in $\dot{\gamma}_A$, and therefore to the effect of decreasing $\dot{\gamma}_A$ on τ_A (Equation C.1) as the extent of flow localization increases. The above generalization also applies to tests carried out under *non*-adiabatic (i.e., heat transfer) conditions. This can be seen from the results of Rauch,[1] in which torsion data for 304 stainless steel specimens revealed substantial torque softening (Figure C.2) and flow localization (Figure 4.11) in specimens with large machining (i.e., geometric) defects, but neither of these effects in tests on specimens without such flaws.

1020 HRS

Similar simulations were carried out by Semiatin[6] on the 1020 HRS. These were also based on the adiabatic heating premise, but employed two slightly different boundary conditions ($\dot{\gamma}_A = 1000$ sec.$^{-1}$ and $\dot{\gamma}_{ov} = 1000$ sec.$^{-1}$). Comparison with the results of Costin et al. (which were only reported to $\gamma_{ov} = 0.30$) again showed excellent agreement. The simulations of Semiatin, however, were taken to much larger strains in an attempt to determine why shear bands were not observed in the torsion tests on 1020 HRS. As expected, the γ_A, γ_B, T_A, and T_B predictions were found to be unaffected by the choice of the strain-rate boundary condition. On the other hand, the τ_A versus γ_{ov} relation depended on the boundary condition (for the reasons discussed above) in a manner similar to that for 1018 CRS. There was

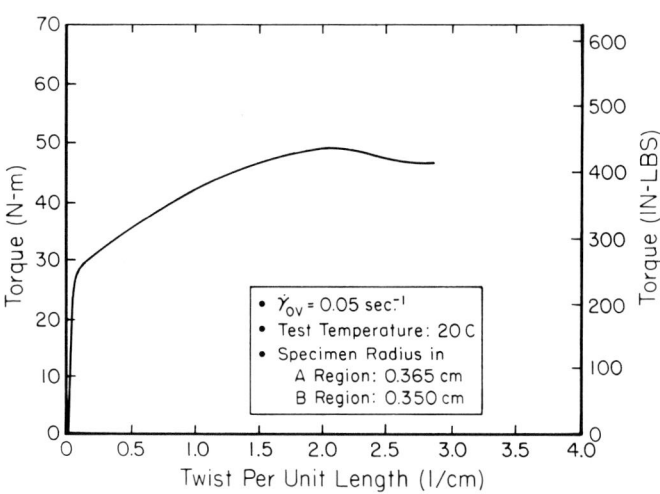

Figure C.2. Experimental torque-twist curve for AISI 304 samples displaying an initial geometric defect at their centers.[1]

an important difference in that the two values of τ_A only diverge appreciably at overall shear strains greater than about 0.7, whereas the divergence in the 1018 CRS is noticeable much earlier (e.g., ~0.17). As indicated above, the divergence in τ_A is linked to that of γ_A and γ_B. Thus, at large strains of the order of γ_{ov} = 0.9 to 1.0, localization is indeed predicted to occur (Figure C.3). These strains are considerably in excess of those imposed in the experiments of Costin et al.,[2] suggesting that further torsion tests are warranted. However, comparison of the 1018 CRS and 1020 HRS results demonstrates that flow localization is delayed a considerable amount in the latter material relative to the former because of the stabilizing influence of larger n and m and smaller temperature sensitivity (Table C.1).

The predicted occurrence of shear bands in torsion tests on 1020 HRS would not be observed if fracture were to intercede. According to the ASM Metals Handbook,[7] 1020 HRS has a tensile reduction in area of about 50 percent, or an axial fracture strain of $\bar{\varepsilon}_f$ = 0.70. The corresponding fracture strain for torsion γ_f can be estimated from the Cockcroft and Latham criterion.[8] Neglecting temperature and strain rate effects, the tensile flow curve can be taken to be given approximately by

$$\sigma = C\varepsilon^n \quad , \tag{C.6}$$

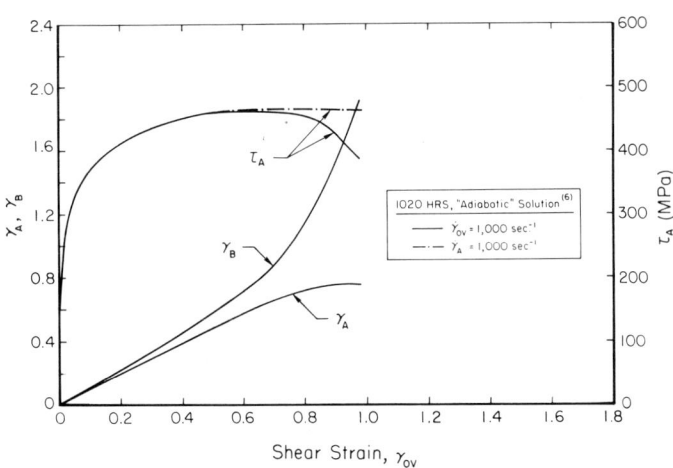

Figure C.3. Predictions of γ_A, γ_B, and τ_A for high-speed torsion of 1020 HRS using boundary conditions of $\dot{\gamma}_A$ = 1000 sec.$^{-1}$ and $\dot{\gamma}_{ov}$ = 1000 sec.$^{-1}$. Note that γ_A and γ_B are independent of the boundary condition.[6]

in which n = 0.2 for 1020 HRS. The corresponding curve for torsion, assuming a von Mises material, is:

$$\sqrt{3}\tau = C\,(\gamma/\sqrt{3})^n$$

or

$$\tau = G\gamma^n \qquad (C.7)$$

where G = 0.517 C for n = 0.2.

Applying the Cockcroft and Latham criterion, $\int_0^{\bar{\varepsilon}_f} \sigma^* d\bar{\varepsilon}$ = constant, in which σ^* is the maximum tensile stress ($\approx \sigma$ for tension* and = τ for torsion) and $\bar{\varepsilon} = \varepsilon$ for tension and $\gamma/\sqrt{3}$ for torsion, one obtains

$$\int_0^{\varepsilon_f} C\varepsilon^n d\varepsilon = \int_0^{\gamma_f} G\gamma^n \left(\frac{d\gamma}{\sqrt{3}}\right) = \frac{0.517}{\sqrt{3}} \int_0^{\gamma_f} C\gamma^n d\gamma \quad ,$$

or

$$\gamma_f = \left\{\frac{\sqrt{3}}{0.517}\right\}^{1/(1+n)} \varepsilon_f \qquad (C.8)$$

For n = 0.2 and ε_f = 0.70, γ_f = 1.92. This is appreciably in excess of the γ at which the initiation of localization is expected (Figure C.3). High strain rate torsion tests on 1020 HRS that are taken to higher strains than those of Costin et al. are therefore expected to give rise to flow localization *preceding* fracture.

References

[1] E. Rauch: M. Eng. Thesis, Department of Mining and Metallurgical Engineering, McGill University, Montreal, Canada, 1983.
[2] L.S. Costin, E.E. Crisman, R.H. Hawley, and J. Duffy: Technical Report NSF 18532/7, Division of Engineering, Brown University, Providence, RI, January, 1979. Report also published in *Proc. Second Oxford Conference on Behavior of Materials at High Rates of Strain,* J.

---

*In actuality, σ^* for tension is somewhat higher than the flow stress σ because of necking and triaxiality effects. The γ_f estimated from the Cockcroft and Latham criterion assuming $\sigma^* = \sigma$ for tension is therefore a conservative one.

Harding, ed., Inst. Phys. Conf. Series No. 47, p. 90, Institute of Physics, London, 1979.
[3] P.S. Senseny, J. Duffy, and R.H. Hawley: *J. Appl. Mech., Trans. ASME,* 1978, vol. 45, p. 60.
[4] J. Litonski: *Bull. Polish Acad. of Sci.,* 1982, vol. 30, p. 323.
[5] G. Johnson, J.M. Hoegfeldt, U.S. Lindholm, and A. Nagy: *J. Eng. Mat. Techn., Trans. ASME,* 1983, vol. 105, p. 42.
[6] S.L. Semiatin: Unpublished research, Battelle Columbus Laboratories, Columbus, OH, 1983.
[7] T. Lyman: *Metals Handbook, Vol. 1,* Eighth Edition, p. 188, American Society for Metals, Metals Park, OH, 1961.
[8] M.G. Cockcroft and D.J. Latham: N.E.L. Report No. 240, National Engineering Laboratory, East Kilbride, Glasgow, July, 1966.

APPENDIX D
M-K ANALYSIS FOR FLOW LOCALIZATION

In Chapters 3 and 6, analyses of flow localization under biaxial stress states were discussed. This was done for flow localization leading to surface fracture in bulk forming (Lee and Kuhn model[1] in Chapter 3) and for localized necking during the in-plane stretching of sheet metal (Marciniak-Kuczynski analysis[2] in Chapter 5). For the former problem, two possible modes of strain concentration ("R" and "Z", using Lee and Kuhn's terminology) were discussed. In both of these, σ_{zz} was assumed to be equal in the nominally uniform region ("A") and the region with an imperfection of geometric or strength origin ("B"). This assumption is probably valid for the R but not for the Z model. For the latter, an approach in which $d\varepsilon_{zz}$ continuity is enforced makes more sense on physical grounds. Such an approach would then make the localization formulation equivalent to the Marciniak-Kuczynski (M-K) analysis described in Chapter 6.

Because the M-K concept plays an important role in the development of modern flow localization theory, a simple computer program for carrying out the analysis is given in this Appendix. The application of this method to several sheet stretching operations is described and a modified Z model, in which $d\varepsilon_{zz}$ continuity is maintained, is presented and discussed.

M-K Problem Formulation

The formulation of the M-K analysis, assuming a geometric defect (t_b/t_A) of initial magnitude f_o, was presented in Chapter 6. There, it was assumed that the strain ratio in the uniform region $\rho^* = d\varepsilon_{2_A}/d\varepsilon_{1_A}$ and the corresponding stress ratio $X_A = \sigma_{2_A}/\sigma_{1_A} = (1 + 2\rho^*)/(2 + \rho^*)$ remain constant during the entire deformation. In addition, the material was considered to be plastically isotropic, i.e., $R = 1$. For a strain-rate insensitive material whose effective stress varies with effective strain, $\bar{\varepsilon}$, as $(\bar{\varepsilon} + \bar{\varepsilon}_o)^n$, where $\bar{\varepsilon}_o$ is the effective prestrain, the description of localized necking is obtained from the solution of the following two simultaneous equations in the two unknowns X_B and $d\bar{\varepsilon}_B$ (or $\bar{\varepsilon}_B$):

$$\bar{\varepsilon}_B = (\bar{\varepsilon}_A + \bar{\varepsilon}_o) \left\{ \frac{1}{f} \cdot \frac{(1 - X_B + X_B^2)^{1/2}}{(1 - X_A + X_A^2)^{1/2}} \right\}^{1/n} - \bar{\varepsilon}_o \qquad (D.1)$$

and

$$d\varepsilon_{2_A} - d\varepsilon_{2_B} = \frac{\sqrt{3}}{2} \rho_B^* d\bar{\varepsilon}_B (1 + \rho_B^* + \rho_B^{*2})^{-1/2} \qquad (D.2)$$

Here, $\rho_B^* = d\varepsilon_{2_B}/d\varepsilon_{1_B}$ and X_B is related to ρ_B^* by the expression

$$X_B = (1 + 2\rho_B^*)/(2 + \rho_B^*) \qquad (D.3)$$

The solution procedure consists of first specifying the material properties (ε_o, n), initial imperfection size (f_o), ρ^* (and thus X_A), and $d\varepsilon_{1_A}$. From this information, $d\bar{\varepsilon}_A$ (and thus $\bar{\varepsilon}_A$) are found through

$$d\bar{\varepsilon}_A = \frac{2}{\sqrt{3}} d\varepsilon_{1_A} (1 + \rho^* + \rho^{*2})^{1/2} \qquad (D.4)$$

In order to proceed, an initial estimate of X_B is made (Equation D.1), from which $\bar{\varepsilon}_B$ and thus $d\bar{\varepsilon}_B$ are obtained. With these values of X_B and $d\bar{\varepsilon}_B$ (and Equation D.3 to obtain ρ_B^*), $d\varepsilon_{2_B}$ is determined (Equation D.2). This procedure is repeated with successively better estimates for X_B until $d\varepsilon_{2_B}$ is found to be equal to $d\varepsilon_{2_A}$. Once this condition is met, a new value of f is found from

$$df = f(d\varepsilon_{3_B} - d\varepsilon_{3_A}) \qquad , \qquad (D.5)$$

in which the values of $d\varepsilon_{3_B}$ and $d\varepsilon_{3_A}$ are derived from the incompressibility relation. The procedure is then repeated (by incrementing $\bar{\varepsilon}_A$) until localization becomes catastrophic ($d\bar{\varepsilon}_B/d\bar{\varepsilon}_A$ and $d\varepsilon_{1_B}/d\varepsilon_{1_A}$ go to infinity or f goes to zero).

For the M-K version of the Z model, the problem formulation is similar. However, the 1, 2, and 3 principal directions associated

```
      PROGRAM MKANAL(INPUT,OUTPUT,TAPE5=INPUT,TAPE6=OUTPUT)
C     PROGRAM FOR FLOW LOCALIZATION IN BULK FORMING(SURFACE FRACTURE) AND
C     IN- PLANE STRETCHING OF SHEET METAL
   10 FORMAT(1X,I2)
   20 FORMAT(2(1X,F6.3),2(1X,F4.2),1X,F6.4)
   30 FORMAT(1H1,3X,#FNOUGHT=#,1X,F6.3,3X,#K VALUE=#,1X,F6.3,3X,#N VALUE
     1=#,1X,F4.2,3X,#EPZERO=#,1X,F4.2,3X,#DEPS THETA A=#,1X,F6.4)
   40 FORMAT(1H ,4X,#F VALUE#,4X,#EPSTTA#,4X,#EPSZZA#,4X,#EPSTTB#,4X,
     1#EPSZZB#,2X, #EPS BAR B#,5X,#XB#)
   50 FORMAT(2X,7(1X,F9.5))
   80 READ(5,10)NOK
   90 DO 600 J=1,NOK
  100 READ(5,20) XFO,XK,XNVAL,EPZERO,DEPTA
  110 WRITE(6,30)    XFO,XK,XNVAL,EPZERO,DEPTA
  120 WRITE(6,40)
  130 RHOA= -1.0*XK
  140 XA = (1.0+(2.0*RHOA))/(2.0+RHOA)
  145 XB = XA
  150 EPBRA = 0.0
  160 EPBRB1 = 0.0
  170 EPTA = 0.0
  180 EPZA = 0.0
  190 EPRA = 0.0
  200 EPTB = 0.0
  210 EPZB = 0.0
  220 EPRB = 0.0
  230 DEPBRA = ((2.0*DEPTA)/(3.0**0.5))*((1.0-(XK)+(XK*XK))**0.5)
  240 DEPZA = -1.0*XK*DEPTA
  245 DEPRA = -1.0*(DEPTA+DEPZA)
  250 F = XFO
  260 XNFAC = 1.0/(2.0*XNVAL)
  300 DO 590 I=1,4000
  310 EPTA = EPTA + DEPTA
  320 EPZA = EPZA+DEPZA
  330 EPBRA = EPBRA + DEPBRA
  345 XB1 = XB + 0.005
  350 EPBRB =((EPBRA+EPZERO)*(((1.0-XB1+(XB1*XB1))/(F*F*(1.0-XA+(XA*XA))
     1))**XNFAC))-EPZERO
  355 DEPBRB = EPBRB-EPBRB1
  360 RHOB = (1.0-(2.0*XB1))/(XB1-2.0)
  370 DEPZB = 0.866025404*RHOB*DEPBRB/((1.0+RHOB+(RHOB*RHOB))**0.5)
  380 DEL1 = DEPZA-DEPZB
  382 XB = XB1
  385 IF(ABS(DEL1).LE.0.000005) GO TO 500
  390 XB2 = XB1+0.005
  400 EPBRB =((EPBRA+EPZERO)*(((1.0-XB2+(XB2*XB2))/(F*F*(1.0-XA+(XA*XA))
     1))**XNFAC))-EPZERO
  405 DEPBRB = EPBRB-EPBRB1
  410 RHOB = (1.0-(2.0*XB2))/(XB2-2.0)
  415 DEPZB = 0.866025404*RHOB*DEPBRB/((1.0+RHOB+(RHOB*RHOB))**0.5)
  420 DEL2 = DEPZA-DEPZB
  422 XB = XB2
  425 IF(ABS(DEL2).LE.0.000005) GO TO 500
  430 SLOPE = (DEL2-DEL1)/(XB2-XB1)
  440 XB1 = XB2-(DEL2/SLOPE)
  460 GO TO 350
  500 EPBRB1 = EPBRB
  510 EPZB = EPZB + DEPZB
  520 EPTB = EPTB + (DEPZB/RHOB)
  530 WRITE(6,50) F,EPTA,EPZA,EPTB,EPZB,EPBR31,XB
  550 DEPRB = (-1.0*DEPZB)-((1.0*DEPZB)/RHOB)
  560 DF = F*(DEPRB - DEPRA)
  570 F = F+DF
  580 IF(F.LE.0.05) GO TO 600
  590 CONTINUE
  600 CONTINUE
  700 STOP
      END
```

Figure D.1. FORTRAN program MKANAL for M-K analysis.

Table D.1.
Variables Names in Program MKANAL

Program Variable Name	Stretching Formulation Variable	Z Model Formulation Variable
XFO, F, DF	f_o, f, df	f_o, f, df
EPZERO, XNVAL, XNFAC	$\bar{\varepsilon}_o$, n, $1/2$n	$\bar{\varepsilon}_o$, n, $1/2$n
EPBRA, DEPBRA	$\bar{\varepsilon}_A$, $d\bar{\varepsilon}_A$	$\bar{\varepsilon}_A$, $d\bar{\varepsilon}_A$
EPTA, EPZA, EPRA	ε_{1_A}, ε_{2_A}, ε_{3_A}	$\varepsilon_{\theta\theta_A}$, ε_{zz_A}, ε_{rr_A}
DEPTA, DEPZA, DEPRA	$d\varepsilon_{1_A}$, $d\varepsilon_{2_A}$, $d\varepsilon_{3_A}$	$d\varepsilon_{\theta\theta_A}$, $d\varepsilon_{zz_A}$, $d\varepsilon_{rr_A}$
EPBRB	Estimated value of $\bar{\varepsilon}_B$	Estimated value of $\bar{\varepsilon}_B$
EPBRB1, DEPBRB	$\bar{\varepsilon}_B$, $d\bar{\varepsilon}_B$	$\bar{\varepsilon}_B$, $d\bar{\varepsilon}_B$
EPTB, EPZB, EPRB	ε_{1_B}, ε_{2_B}, ε_{3_B}	$\varepsilon_{\theta\theta_B}$, ε_{zz_B}, ε_{rr_B}
DEPTB, DEPZB, DEPRB	$d\varepsilon_{1_B}$, $d\varepsilon_{2_B}$, $d\varepsilon_{3_B}$	$d\varepsilon_{\theta\theta_B}$, $d\varepsilon_{zz_B}$, $d\varepsilon_{rr_B}$
RHOA, RHOB	ρ^*, ρ_B^*	ρ^* $(-K^*)$,[†] ρ_B^*
XA, XB	X_A, X_B	$X_A(r^*)$,[††] X_B
XB1, XB2	Estimated values of X_B	Estimated values of X_B
XK	$-\rho^*$	$K^*(-\rho^*)^\dagger$

[†]See Equation (3.1).
[††]See Equation (3.3).

with sheet stretching (Figure 6.4) are associated instead with the θ, z, and r directions, respectively, pertaining to the bulk forming geometry (Figure 3.3), after which the solution procedure is identical.

Computer Code

A simple FORTRAN computer program MKANAL that performs the calculations described above is given in Figure D.1. The variable names in the program and their equivalents in the M-K stretching and Z models are given in Table D.1. Inputs to the program are the number of ρ^*'s or strain paths NOK (Statement 80) and the values of f_o, $-\rho^*$ (K^*), n, $\bar{\varepsilon}_o$, and $d\varepsilon_{1_A}$ (or $d\varepsilon_{\theta\theta_A}$) associated with each path (Statement 100). Statements 140 through 250 initialize the values of f, the stress ratios, effective strains, and strains in both regions (A and B), as well as the strain and effective strain increments in region A, which are fixed.

The actual strain localization analysis is performed in Statements 300 to 520 of MKANAL. Increments of strain in region A are applied first (Statements 310 to 330). Then, the opening value of X_B, XB1, is estimated, and $\bar{\varepsilon}_B$, $d\bar{\varepsilon}_B$, and ρ_B^* determined (Statements 350, 355, and 360), from which $d\varepsilon_{2_B}$ (or $d\varepsilon_{zz_B}$) is derived (Statement 370) and compared to the corresponding strain component in the A region. If the two are arbitrarily close to each other, DEL1 ≈ 0 (Statement 385), the appropriate value of X_B has been guessed. Otherwise another X_B, XB2, is tried and the previous procedure repeated to obtain DEL2 (Statements 390 to 425). The values of DEL1 and DEL2 are used to obtain a "new" value of X_B, XB1, which is the linear interpolation between the "old" XB1 and XB2 and which corresponds to "DEL" equal to zero. The procedure in Statements 350 to 460 is repeated until the strain increment compatibility condition is met. An alternate approach involves *overall* strain compatibility, a condition which can help to minimize the accumulation of approximation errors in the above numerical procedure.

Once $\bar{\varepsilon}_B$, $d\bar{\varepsilon}_B$, ρ_B^*, X_B, and $d\varepsilon_{2_B}$ (or $d\varepsilon_{zz_B}$) are known, the values of the other strain components in region B are derived together with

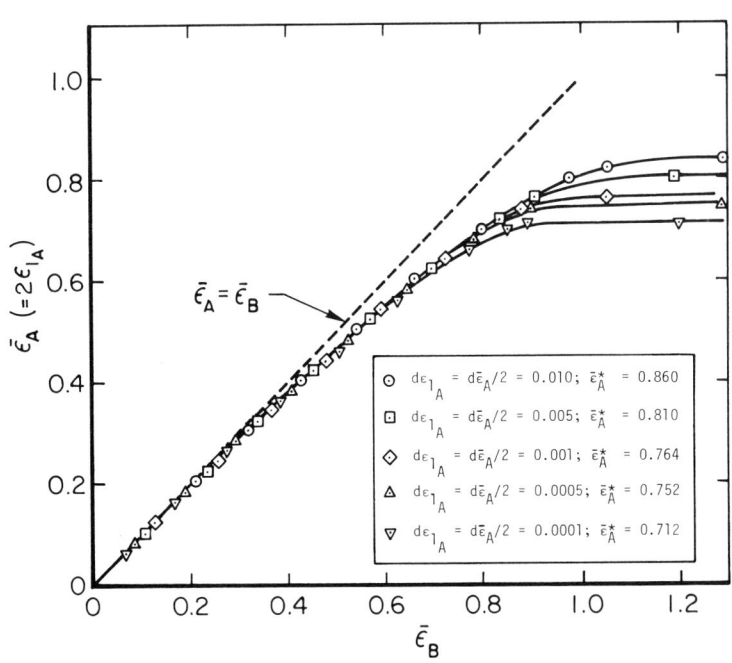

Figure D.2. Effective strains $\bar{\varepsilon}_A$ and $\bar{\varepsilon}_B$ during strain localization under conditions of balanced biaxial stretching ($\rho^* = 1$). Material characterized by n = 0.22, $\bar{\varepsilon}_0 = 0.01$, R = 1, and $f_0 = 0.98$.

a new value of f (Statements 510, 520, 550, 560, and 570), after which the entire procedure is repeated. When f is suitably small (typically f < 0.05, although catastrophic flow usually occurs once f drops below approximately 0.8), the strain in region A is taken to be equal to the forming limit.

Sample M-K Results

SHEET STRETCHING

Several sample calculations will serve to illustrate the type of behavior predicted by analyses such as that originated by Marciniak and Kuczynski. As a first example, the balanced biaxial stretching of a rate-insensitive material characterized by $n = 0.22$, $\bar{\varepsilon}_o = 0.01$, $R = 1$, and $f_o = 0.980$ is depicted in Figure D.2. These calculations

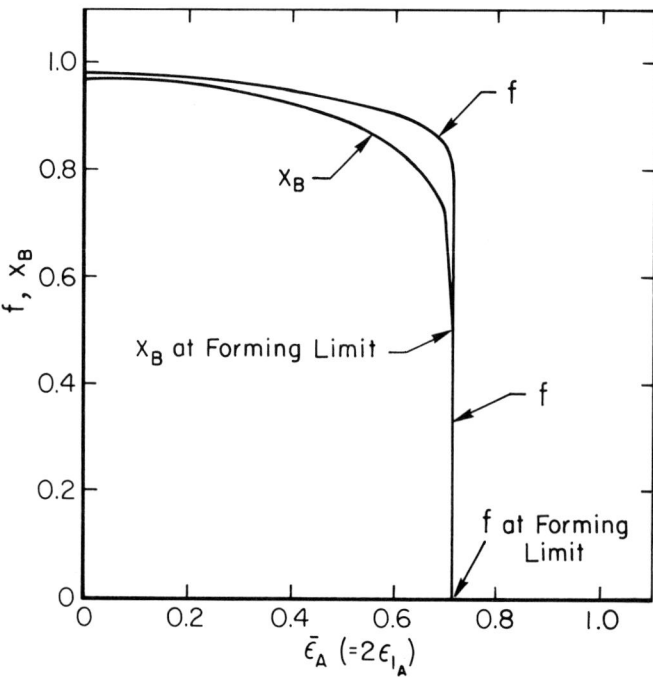

Figure D.3. Process of strain concentration in a biaxially stretched sheet ($\rho^* = 1$) as characterized by f and X_B as functions of $\bar{\varepsilon}_A$. Material properties were taken to be $n = 0.22$, $\bar{\varepsilon}_o = 0.01$, $R = 1$, and $f_o = 0.980$.

were carried out using a range of strain increments, as shown in the figure. All of the simulations reveal a regime of quasistable flow during which $\bar{\varepsilon}_B \approx \bar{\varepsilon}_A$. However, it is of interest that the actual value of the limit strain depends on the particular increment selected.* The detailed numerical results show that the limit strain reaches a stable value once the strain increment $d\varepsilon_{1_A}$ is decreased to 0.0002 or less.

The process of imperfection growth for this problem is illustrated further in Figure D.3, in which f and X_B are plotted as functions of $\bar{\varepsilon}_A$. The defect grows slowly (df/d$\bar{\varepsilon}_A$ is small) until f drops below 0.8, after which growth is very rapid. Note that this period of rapid defect growth corresponds to X_B approaching 0.5, i.e., to the stress ratio associated with plane-strain deformation in an isotropic sheet. This trend has been discussed in more detail in Chapter 6.

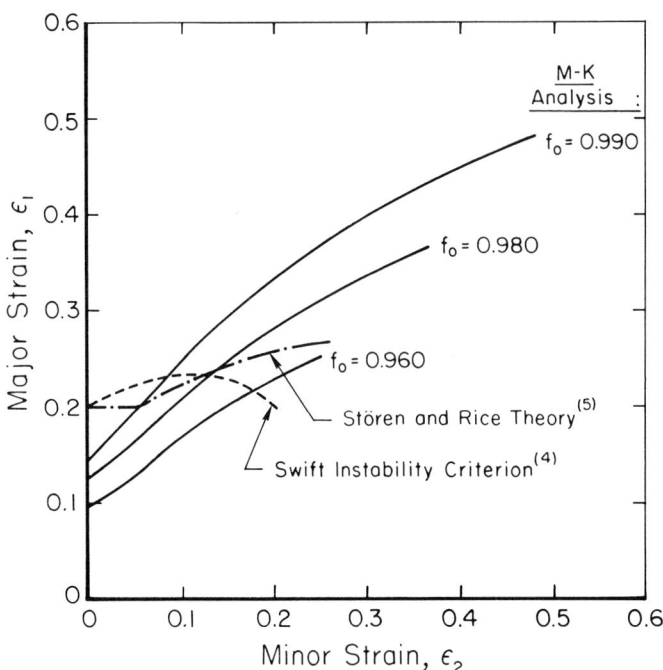

Figure D.4. M-K localization strains (for f_o = 0.960, 0.980, and 0.990) compared to forming limits based on the Swift instability criterion[4] (Equation 6.13), and Stören and Rice's bifurcation theory[5] (Equation 6.43).

---

*This problem was simulated in the 1973 paper of Marciniak, Kuczynski, and Pokora.[3] They obtained a limit strain $\bar{\varepsilon}_A^*$ of 0.754.

Another example of the application of the M-K analysis is shown in Figure D.4. Here the forming limits in the entire stretching regime have been determined for a material characterized by n = 0.20, $\bar{\varepsilon}_o = 0.00$, R = 1, and f_o = 0.96, 0.98, and 0.99. The dependence of the limit strain on the initial imperfection size is quite strong. Also shown in the figure are the strain states at which the Swift diffuse instability criterion (Equation 6.13)[4] and Stören and Rice's bifurcation theory (Equation 6.43)[5] are satisfied. Since typical materials have initial defect sizes on the order of 0.980 to 0.990, it is apparent that the latter two criteria lead to forming limit predictions that differ substantially from those of the M-K analysis, particularly for stress states near balanced biaxial stretching.

When the strain path dependence of the constitutive equation is taken into account, experimental measurements suggest that the

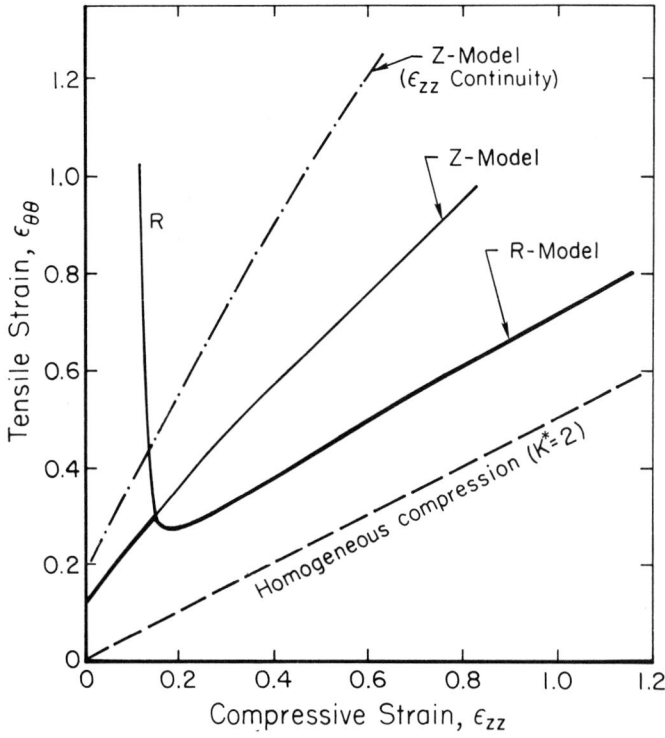

Figure D.5. Locus of limit strains for the R model and Z models based on σ_{zz} or ε_{zz} continuity. Calculations were based on f_o = 0.99, ε_o = 0.10, and n = 0.25.

M-K theory comes closest to modeling the physical processes which determine the forming limit.[6]

SURFACE FAILURE DURING BULK FORMING

As mentioned above, the M-K analysis can be employed to calculate a modified Z model failure locus, in which ε_{zz} compatibility is enforced, as opposed to the σ_{zz} constancy assumed in the Z model described in Chapter 3. The results of calculations for just such a model are compared to the ones presented previously (e.g., Figure 3.5) in Figure D.5. As before, the calculations were carried out for a material with a flow law of the form $\bar{\sigma} \sim (\bar{\varepsilon} + 0.10)^{0.25}$ with f_o equal to 0.99. From the figure, it is evident that the modified Z model, in which strain continuity is maintained, gives rise to substantially higher predictions than the original Z model. This effect is probably a consequence of $d\varepsilon_{zz_B}$ (and $d\varepsilon_{\theta\theta_B}$) growing much more rapidly in the original Z model than in the M-K analysis. The rapid growth, in turn, gives rise to larger effective strains and therefore the more rapid loss of the stabilizing influence of strain hardening than in the modified Z model.

The M-K based Z criterion described above may be of limited practical interest because the experimentally observed internal necking and failure processes strongly suggest that the R type of behavior actually controls the forming limit. In addition, it should be noted that R-type models give failure loci in better agreement with the trends observed experimentally (Figure 2.4).

References

[1] P.W. Lee and H.A. Kuhn: *Met. Trans.*, 1973, vol. 4, p. 969.
[2] Z. Marciniak and K. Kuczynski: *Inter. J. Mech. Sci.*, 1967, vol. 9, p. 609.
[3] Z. Marciniak, K. Kuczynski, and T. Pokora: *Inter. J. Mech. Sci.*, 1973, vol. 15, p. 789.
[4] H.W. Swift: *J. Mech. Phys. Solids,* 1952, vol. 1, p. 1.
[5] S. Stören and J.R. Rice: *J. Mech. Phys. Solids,* 1975, vol. 23, p. 421.
[6] A.K. Ghosh: *Mechanics of Sheet Metal Forming: Material Behavior and Deformation Analysis,* D.P. Koistenen and N.M. Wang, eds., p. 287, Plenum Press, New York, 1978.

Index

A

Activation energy
and strain dependence, 18
Adiabatic flow localization
in simple shear model, 234-238
two-slice model for, 234-235
Adiabatic heating
flow softening from, 109-116
Adiabatic shear bands
in 4340 steel during flow localization, 240
analysis of, 234-238
from deformation heating, 6
development in torsion, 257-266
shell fragmentation by, 238. See also *Shear band formation.*
Adiabatic torsion testing, simulation results for, 260-265
Aging processes, high temperature, 100
Alpha brass, $^{70}/_{30}$, M-K analysis for, 214, 215
Alpha microstructure, equiaxed
estimated temperature and strain rate gradients, 130
flow localization during sidepressing, 132-135
ALPID
large strain, for process modeling of shear band development, 76
plane-strain version, 77
sidepressing simulations, 80

Aluminum
99.99 percent, necking simulation, 184
forming limit data, 218
rate-sensitivity coefficients for, 186
von Mises effective stress-strain curves, 29, 30
Aluminum alloys, specific types
1100, diffuse and localized necking, 6, 207, 208
1100, elongation as function of strain-rate sensitivity, 156
1100, M-K theory for, 214, 215
2024-0, flow stress as function of homologous temperature, 8
2036-T4, elongation as function of strain-rate sensitivity, 156
3003-0, elongation as function of strain-rate sensitivity, 156
5182-0, elongation as a function of strain-rate sensitivity, 156
6061-0, flow localization under adiabatic shear band conditions, 111, 112
Aluminum-killed steel
forming limit data, 218
strain ratio dependence, 216. See also *Steel alloys.*
Anisotropic materials, Hill yield locus for, 19. See also *Plastic anisotropy.*
Annealing, completeness and metallurgical defects, 68

Area-rate gradient, dependence on strain in tensile testing, 63, 64
Area reduction, during tensile deformation, 2
Aspect ratio, initial, influence on flow localization and fracture, 46
Associated flow rule, 1
and yield function, defined, 18-23
Austenitic stainless steels, and M-K theory, 214, 215. See also *Stainless steels, specific types.*
Axial strain
and circumferential strain, dependence on overall height reduction, 44, 45
in flow localization parameter, 53
nominal, and instability, 150-151
Axial stress, and uniaxial stress, 19
Axial torque, equilibrium equation, 140
Axial true strain rate, in uniaxial compression testing, 24
uniaxial tension test, round bars, 31
Axial true stress
in uniaxial compression testing, 24
in uniaxial tension test, 31
Axisymmetric compression
tests based on, 13
work softening for flow localization in, 95. See also *Compression.*
Axisymmetric deformation, flow localization due to flow softening under, 51-69
Axisymmetric forming, and bulging, 9

B

Balanced biaxial stretching. See *Biaxial stretching.*
Ballistic impact environments, shear localization in, 233
Barreling
and friction, 44
and lubrication, 44-46
Bars
instability and tension testing of, 149-154
nonisothermal sidepressing, 131
tensile testing and flow localization, 154-177

torsion testing, 26-27
uniaxial tension testing, 31
Bauschinger transient, 96
Biaxial stretching
balanced, of rate-insensitive material, 271, 272
strain concentration in, 272, 273
strains during, 271
Biaxial tensile loading
Swift's diffuse instability criterion for, 200-203
Bifurcation theory, 194-196
Blade forging, shear banding in, 139-140
Block shearing
deformation, 128
in sidepressing test, 31
Boothroyd Model, for metalcutting, 231
Boundary-value problems, torsion, 142-143
Brasses
forming limit data, 218
strain ratio dependence, 216
Brasses, specific types
$^{60}/_{40}$, constant strain rate flow curves, 175
$^{70}/_{30}$, post-uniform elongation as a function of strain-rate sensitivity, 156
$^{70}/_{30}$, shear banding from texture softening, 108
Bridgman analysis, to estimate transverse principal stress, 33
Bridgman triaxiality factor
and the effective stress, 251-254
St. Venant's principle in, 255
Bulging
die heating for, 24
and dimensional variations, 4
due to flow softening, 52, 56-58, 65
and flow localization, 4, 52
free surface, 4, 25
by mechanical and geometric defects, 65-66
in oxidized uranium, isothermally upset, 55, 56
periods of formation, 66-69
plus shearing, 58, 60
by rapid flow softening, 65
vs shear bands in plane-strain deformation, 70
shearing leading to, 127

in upsetting, 128, 130-131
Bulk forming
at cold working temperatures, and friction, 2
compression test for workability data, 24-25
defined, 7
flow localization in, 43-119
flow localization under nonisothermal deformation, 121-148
surface failure during, 275
temperatures for deformation under, 2
under compressive loading, tests for, 13, 23-40
at warm working temperatures, 2
Bulk strains
during formation of adiabatic shear bands, 240
in fragmenting shell experiments, 239

C

Catastrophic strain, estimated, 54
Chill caps, effects on deformation, 124, 127
Chilling
as cause of flow localization, 4
die heating for, 24
effect on die-workpiece interface, 130
effect on loads for slower equipment, 136-137
effects on strain and strain rate gradients in nonisothermal deformation, 121
and heat transfer between workpiece and tooling, 7-8
higher working loads due to, 126
in hydraulic press forging, 136-137
nonuniform flow patterns from, 121
strain-rate gradients, 124
Chill zones
effects on deformation, 124-126
measured, 25
in nonisothermal upsetting/sidepressing, 134
Chip(s)
continuous, 225
control of machined geometry with, 226
and increased tool wear, 225-226

from localization of plastic flow, 225
in metalcutting, 225
morphology of, 225, 227
and rate of cutting force, 226
serrated, from deformation heating, 226
serrated, from titanium alloys, 226
serrated or cyclic, 225
thickness, in orthogonal cutting, 226, 228
Circle construction, Mohr's, 15-17, 192, 204, 205
Coarsening rate, in precipitation strengthening, 97, 98
Cockroft and Latham fracture criterion, $50n$
Cold working, instability in, 150
Cold working temperatures
flow localization at, 2-7, 44-50
surface fracture at, 44-50
workability at, 2, 3
Compression
axisymmetric, tests based on, 13
flow curves, 56
frictionless, homogeneous, 46
subtransus, 98, 99
uniaxial test for, 23-26
von Mises locus as yield stress in, 19. See also *Axisymmetric compression; Uniaxial compression.*
Compressive loading
at cold working temperatures, 2
flow instability under, 56
negative, in compression tests, $24n$
tests for bulk forming, 13, 23-40
at warm and hot working temperatures, 7
Compressive strains, in upset tests, $24n$
Compressive stresses, in upset tests, $24n$
Considère's analysis, of tensile instability, 150-151
Considère strains, 66-67
Constant hardness state, rate sensitivity, 181
Constant strain rate tensile test, 153
Contained cylinder experiment
adiabatic heating in, 234
deformation in, 233
ductile fracture in, 233

Contained cylinder experiment (continued)
flow localization in, 234
macroscopic shear banding and failure in, 233
by Staker, 233-234
Contained fragmenting round technique, with 4340 steel, 233
Conventional hot working
flow localization during bulk forming, 121. See also *Hot working.*
Copper, rate-sensitivity coefficients for, 186
Copper alloys, specific types
ETP, von Mises effective stress-strain curves, 29, 30
OFHC, necking simulation, 184
Cracking
grain-boundary, and workability, 7
shear, in slow hydraulic press forming, 136, 137-138
surface, failure loci, 25
triple point, 7
from workpiece chilling, 138
Creep test, constant load, constant temperature, 155
Critical strains
in torsion simulation, 147
Crosshead speed, in uniaxial compression testing, 24n
Cutting depth, in orthogonal cutting, 226, 228
Cutting speed
for AISI 4340 steel, 232
in flow localization parameters, 231
in shear localization, 229
Cylinders
nonisothermal upsetting of lubricated Ti-6242Si, 124-128
upset forging of, 122-124
upsetting temperature gradients, 123-124

D

Dead-metal zones, effect of friction during bulk forming, 4
Deep drawing
earing during, 34
tensile testing, 13
Defect growth kinetics, 174
Defects. See *Geometric defects; Mechanical defects; Metallurgical (strength) defects.*

Definitions, fundamental, 13-24
Deformation
bulging types of, 9
at cold working temperatures, flow curves, 5
defect analysis of, 162-166
defect vs flow localization, 65, 155
effect of necking in, 149
flow localization during, 13
isothermal, flow localization in bulk forming, 43-119
of metal structures during impact loading, 232
necking mode of, 195
nonisothermal, flow localization in bulk forming, 121-148
out-of-plane and flow localization, 7
plane-strain modes of, 9
positive rate sensitivity in, 152
processes, defined, 1
rate of development of nonuniformities during, 62-63
steps in nonisothermal upsetting, 128
temperature gradients on homogeneity of, 147
textures, and flow localization, 5
time, working speed as, 124
under primary or bulk forming conditions, 2
uniform, 24
useful, 154. See also *Axisymmetric deformation; Bifurcation theory; Plastic deformation.*
Deformation heating
adiabatic shear bands from, 6
effect on temperature gradients in torsion testing, 147
and flow localization, 3, 60, 61
and flow softening, 51, 109
Deformation modeling, aspects of, 1
Deformation rate
hydraulic press, 135-138
mechanical press, 132-135
slow, approximation, 27
Deformation resistance
as function of strain, strain rate, and temperature, 23-24
uniaxial compression test for, 23-24
Die(s)
effect of increasing dwell time, 127-128

materials, for uniaxial compression test, 24
temperature, effect on shear banding, 133-134
thermal properties, 124
Die-workpiece
in blade forging, 139-140
heat transfer between, 4
interface, chilling effect on, 130
temperature differences, 25-26, 123, 124
Diffuse instability
defined, 188
and necking in sheet metals, 188-191
Swift's criterion, 200-203
Diffuse necking, 6, 7
as basic necking geometry, 199
defined, 188
and diffuse instability in sheet metals, 188-191
Dimensional tolerances, effect of cold working on, 2
Dislocation
channeling in irradiated materials, 98-99
density, flow hardening due to, 178
in plane-strain compression/tension tests, 37
removal during straining, 96
removal of pairs by dynamic recovery, 96
softening due to channeling, 98-99
in torsion tests, 30
Dwell time
effect of increasing, 127
effect on shear band formation, 132
effect on working load, nonisothermal sidepressing, 137
Dynamic recovery, work softening at elevated temperatures by, 93-96
Dynamic recrystallization
in geological shear zone localization, 242-243
work softening (at elevated temperatures) from, 96-97

E

Earing, measured by uniaxial tension tests, 34

Effective strain
defined, 21-22
during strain localization of biaxial stretching, 271
increment in plane-strain compression test, 36
in necking (uniaxial tension), 33
and stress curves, 29, 30. See also *Effective stress-strain.*
Effective strain rate
contours, predicted, 83, 84
increment, for isotropic metals, 22
titanium alloy microstructures, 77-78
Effective stress
for anisotropic sheet loaded biaxially, 19, 20
and the Bridgman triaxiality factor, 251-254
defined, 19-23
due to changes in applied loads, 200
gradient, in necking simulation with aluminum, 184
in localization analysis, 48-49
in necking simulation with aluminum, 184
in plane-strain compression testing, 36
-strain curves, 29, 30. See also *Effective strain; Stress.*
Elastic strain, vs plastic strain, 16n
Elongation
effect in method of relaxed constraints, 104-105
as function of strain-rate sensitivity, 156
geometric defect effects, 190. See also *Total elongation.*
Engineering flow laws, 177
simple, 166
Engineering materials, flow localization in, 166-172
Engineering strain, limiting value, as function of m, 163. See also *Nominal engineering strain.*
Equiaxed alpha microstructure, shear banding in, 139-140
Equilibrium
equation of plasticity mechanics, 1
force, and flow localization parameter, 52
force, in M-K model, 209
in localization analysis, 48

Erie mechanical press, for nonisothermal sidepressing, 131
Eulerian axes, relative to strain, 16-17
Exponential strain, 68
Extrusion
  effects of chilling workpiece in, 121
  workability under hot working conditions, 2

F

Failure
  data from in-plane and punch-stretching tests, 39-40
  and deformation method, 40
  effect of necking on prior deformation, 149
  effects of tensile instability and necking geometries, 199
  locus, typical, 25, 45, 46
  and strain paths during upset testing, 45, 46. See also *Fracture.*
Failure strain
  defined, 171
  and geometric defect, 172
  and hammer blow and machining defects, 171-172
FEM techniques, for modes of flow localization, 76
Fields and Backofen relation, 28
Fixed and torsion, and simple shear, $107n$
FLCs. See *Forming limit curves.*
FLDs. See *Forming limit diagrams.*
Flow
  associated rule of. See *Associated flow rule.*
  behavior mechanisms, 1
  curves in fragmenting shell experiments, 238
  curves, for metals deformed in hot working regime, 79, 80
  hardening, due to dislocation density, 178
  instability, 2-4, 56
  nonuniform, development of, $55n$
  rate, as function of strain, strain rate, and temperature, 23-24
Flow law(s), 27
  engineering, 166, 177

Flow localization
  in adiabatic simple shear, 238
  analysis, 46-50, 183-187
  and area reduction during tensile deformation, 2
  boundary and initial conditions, 245
  and bulging, 4
  in bulk forming, isothermal deformation, 43-119
  in bulk forming, nonisothermal deformation, 121-148
  causes, 2-4
  at cold working temperatures, 2-7
  in compression of materials with deformation and geometric defects, 246-247
  condition for significant, 52
  in constant load, constant temperature creep test, 155
  controlled formability of sheet metals, 199
  defect and uniform regions of compression specimens in, 248
  definitions, 13-23
  driving force for, 44
  due to flow softening, in axisymmetric deformation, 51-69
  due to flow softening, under plane-strain deformation, 69-85
  due to flow softening, under torsion, 85-93
  during formation of adiabatic shear bands in 4340 steel, 240
  during impact loading of metals, 232-241
  during metalcutting, 225-232
  during nonisothermal compression, 128
  during nonisothermal sidepressing, 131-140
  during sidepressing with hydraulic press, 135-138
  effects of friction and lubrication, 44-46
  in engineering materials, differential equation for, 166-172
  estimation of, 1
  and flow softening, 3. See also *Flow softening.*
  as fracture modes, 1
  and fracture process, 45, 46
  of geological shear processes, 242-244

Hart's analysis, 155
and heat transfer, 4. See also *Heat transfer.*
at high strain rates, 144-145
in hot torsion tests, shear banding as, 90-91
and instability during sheet forming, 199-223
and instability in uniaxial tension, 149-198
and interaction between workpiece and tooling, 121
kinetics, in uniaxial compression, 64-68, 245-250
material influence in, 122
minimized by strain hardening and strain rate hardening, 122
M-K (Marciniak-Kuczynski) analysis for, 267-275
models in uniaxial compression of flow softening materials, 250
of nickel-base alloys, 249-250
in nonisothermal upsetting, model and experimental predictions compared, 128-131
onset, 62-63
for orthogonal cutting, 226-230
parameter, 52-55, 122
phenomenology, at cold working temperatures, 44-46
predicted rates of hardness in, 239
prediction criteria, 6
in presence of metallurgical (strength) defects, 68-69
as process, 84
rate of temperature change during, 228
related problems of, 225-244
in shear band form, 9, 132-135
Sowerby and Duncan stress and strain states, 212
in stainless steel, 263
strain at onset of, 151-152
and strain gradients, 2
in stretching regime of forming limit diagram, 207-221
and surface fracture at cold working temperatures, 44-50
in tensile loading conditions, 149-198
and tensile testing of round bars, 154-177
of titanium alloys, 249-250

in torsion, 140-147
trends in geometric defect material, 247-249
unbounded, 144
under adiabatic shear band conditions, 110-111, 112
under biaxial tensile conditions, 149
under superplastic flow conditions, 174-177
in upsetting of Ti-6242Si, observations, 124-128
at warm working temperatures, 7-9. See also *Localization.*

Flow localization parameter
during bulk forming under plane-strain conditions, 69-71
as function of cutting speed, 231
and observations, correlations, 55-61
and simulation predictions, compared, 84-85
for Ti alloys, 93, 94
for torsional deformation, 85-93

Flow rule, associated. See *Associated flow rule.*

Flow softening
from adiabatic heating, 109-116
as cause of flow instability and flow localization, 3, 5
as controlling strain and strain-rate gradients in nonisothermal upsetting, 122
defined, 93-94
deformation heating as common source, 51
as destabilizing influence, 123
due to reversal of strengthening mechanisms, 97-100
due to textural effects, 100-103
effect on strain concentrations, torsion, 144
flow localization due to plane-strain deformation, 69-85
flow localization due to torsion, 85-93
influence on strain concentration during uniaxial compression, 64-65
with isothermal hot working, 9
localization of strain in, 51
minimal, and flow localization resistance, 56
in oxidized uranium, 55, 56

Flow softening (continued)
  physical causes, 93-116
  rates, 81
  in strain-hardening materials, 109-112
  sources in metals, 93-116
  and temperature gradients, 122-123
  under axisymmetric deformation, 51-69
  and work softening, 93-94, 100
Flow stress
  dependence on strain, 79, 80
  dependence on temperature, 121, 126
  effect of hot working, 2, 8
  increasing with strain, 175
  maximum, effect on flow localization, 5
  measured by torsion test, 26
  measured by uniaxial tension test, 31-34
  negative dependence on temperature, 122-123
  rate, in texture softening, 101
  of solute-hardening materials, 97n
  steady-state, flow softening and, 113
  and strain, in flow localization, 6
  vs temperature, effects on shear band formation during adiabatic heating, 113, 114
  vs temperature, nonisothermal sidepressing, 131, 132
  temperature sensitive, and flow localization, 109
  uniaxial compression test for, 23-24
  uniaxial tension, and plane-strain compression, 37, 38
Flow theory of plasticity, and strain, 16
Force equilibrium
  in flow localization parameter, 52
  in M-K model, 209. See also *Equilibrium.*
Forging
  effects of workpiece chilling in, 121
  flow localization/surface fracture during, 44-46
  shear band formation, 73, 74
  sidepressing test as simulation of, 30-31
  workability under hot working conditions, 2

Formability
  determined by localized neck, 199
  of sheet metals, 199-200
  tests, 13, 23-40. See also *Flow localization; Workability.*
Forming
  axisymmetric modes of, 9
  limited by instability and flow localization, 1
  temperature, and flow localization, 2
Forming limit(s)
  measurements, and local instability predictions, 207, 208
  for out-of-plane stretching, 217-219
  for sheet metal, 213, 214, 219-221
  strain levels, defined, 199
Forming limit curves (FLC's), 39-40
Forming limit diagrams (FLD's), 39-40
  flow localization in stretching regime of, 207-221
FORTRAN program MKANAL, for M-K analysis of flow localization, 269, 270
Fracture
  criterion, Cockroft and Latham, 50n
  flow localization leading to, 44
  following necking, 7
  and localized thinning, plasticity analysis, 47
  process and flow localization, 1, 45, 46
  surface, and end of flow localization, 50. See also *Failure; Surface fracture.*
Fracture strain
  diagram for determination, 173
  predicted by computer simulations, 185-186
  prediction, 176-177, 185-186
  superplastic range, 176
  true axial, 33
Fragmenting shell experiments
  and 4340 steel cylinders compared, 238-239
  bulk strains in, 239
  shear banding in, 240-241
  two-slice model for, 238-241
  Wulf's flow curves in, 238-239
Free surface bulging, 4
  measured, 25

Friction
and barreling, 44
in bulk forming at cold working temperatures, 4
effects on flow localization at cold working temperatures, 2, 44-46
and lubrication, 44-46
nonuniform, 60, 61
Full constraints, method of, 103-104

G

Gamma-prime-strengthened superalloys, precipitation strengthening, 97
Gas, ideal constant for, 18. See also *R values.*
Geological shear processes, flow localization analysis of, 242-243
Geological shear zone localization, dynamic recrystallization in, 242-243
Geological shear zones
flow softening in, 242-243
shear heating in, 243
Geometric defects
analysis, experimental agreement with, 165
effects of diffuse necking growth, 190
kinetics of flow localization in uniaxial compression, 64-68
large strain solutions, 182
localization with, 159-162
and predicted nominal (engineering) strain, 164
radius/height, local irregularity in, 47-50
and strength defects, 69
as thickness variation and strain state, 207, 209
in torsion, 143-144, 146
Geometric imperfections. See *Geometric defects.*
Geometric softening
defined, 7
rate, in Hill's criterion, 204
Gosh and Ayres/Marciniak/Hutchinson and Neale necking strain, 159-162
Gradients, in cross-sectional area, as flow localization parameter, 61

Grain boundary, cracking, and workability, 7
Grain coarsening, constitutive relation for, 177
Grain growth, deformation-induced, dependence of flow hardening on, 175
Grain rotations, method of relaxed constraints to calculate, 104-105
Grain size, local variations as metallurgical defects, 68
Graphite, as compression test lubricant, 24
Grid distortions, and material property influences, 80, 81
Grid-length gradients, as flow localization parameter, 61

H

Hammer blow (HB)
defects, nominal (engineering) strain, predicted, 164
inhomogeneity, growth of, 157
necking strains predicted by, 162
variations in hardness due to, 54
Hardness
of 4340 steel during flow localization, 240
and effective strain, 21
Harmonic oscillator relation, 168
Hart/Duncombe/Nichols necking strain, 155-159
Hart's analysis, of tensile testing of instability, 151-154
Heat generation
effects as moderate strain rates, 140
rate, in torsion, 141-142
Heat transfer
amount determined, 147
analysis, 128-129
between workpiece and tooling, 7-8
effects on chilling, 8
effect in complex forging geometry, 139
effect on flow localization in bulk forming, 121
effects at moderate strain rates, 140
equation for torsion, 141
and flow localization, 4, 8, 121
measured by upset tests, 26

Heat transfer (continued)
in nonisothermal upsetting, 128
radial, effects in torsion testing, 146
Heat treatment
effect in texture softening, 103, 108-109
and metallurgical defects, 68
Hecker's punch-stretching technique, 13, 37-40
Hill's local instability criterion, 204-207
Hill's plastic anisotropy, 36
Hill yield locus, defined, 19
Hollomon equation, for strain dependence, 18
Homologous temperature
flow stress as function of, 8
workability as function of, 2, 3
workpiece, 2
Hot torsion tests, 90
Hot work die steels
for uniaxial compression test, 24
as upset test die material, 24
Hot working
advantages, 2
conventional, flow localization during bulk forming, 121
flow behavior, and stress dependence, 18
hypothetical flow curves, 79, 80
Hot working temperatures
flow softening at, 56, 57
von Mises stress-strain curves, 29
workability at, 2, 3. See also *Temperature(s)*.
HPM hydraulic press, for nonisothermal sidepressing, 131
Hydraulic press deformation rate, flow localization during sidepressing, 135-138
Hydraulic press forgings
chilling in, 138
and mechanical press forging, load-stroke data, compared, 136-137
shear cracking, 136, 137-138
Impact loading
and automotive impact, 232
and ballistic impact, 233
deformation of metal structures, 232
of metals in flow localization, 232-241
in space, 232
wave propagation in, 232

Imperfection. See *Geometric defect(s); Surface imperfection*.
Inclusion(s), and flow localization, 5
Infrared technique, during metal-cutting, 229
Inhomogeneity
estimation of growth, 49
and flow localization, 5
In-plane stretching
flow localization in, 7
test, 13
In-plane tests, 37-40
Instability
analysis, with rate of sensitivity of work hardening rate, 177-183
diffuse, and diffuse necking in sheet metals, 188-191
diffuse, Swift's criterion, 200-203
and flow localization during sheet forming, 199-223
and flow localization during sheet forming, summary, 221-222
and flow localization in uniaxial tension, 149-198
forming limited by, 1
load, simple analysis for, 154
local, and localized necking, sheet metals, 191-194
moment of, 150
and rate sensitivity, 152
relations, approximate graphical solution, 172-174
strain, defined, 150-151
summary, 196-197
and tension testing of round bars, 149-154. See also *Tensile instability*.
Irradiated materials, dislocation channeling in, 98-99
Isothermal deformation, flow localization in bulk forming, 43-119. See also *Deformation*.
Isothermal hot working, to reduce strain localization, 8-9. See also *Hot working; Hot working temperatures*.
Isothermal metalworking, upset test for strain localization, 25
Isothermal sidepressing, shear band formation, 71, 72, 134
Isostrain method
as flow softening, 103. See also *Method of full constraints*.

Isotropic materials
effective strain for, 22
von Mises yield locus for, 19

J

JBK-75 alloy, shear band formation in, 75-76

K

Keeler-Goodwin diagrams, 39-40
Kinetics, of flow localization in uniaxial compression, 55, 64-68, 245-250
Komanduri, metalcutting of AISI steel, 230
K-steel, strain ratio dependence, 216

L

Lagrangian strain measures, 16
Lamellar structure(s), 98, 99
spheroidization, softening due to, 98, 99
Lee and Kuhn upset cylinders, 44
Length-rate gradient, dependence on strain in tensile testing, 63, 64
Levy-Mises relations, 21. See also *Effective strain*.
Limit strain(s)
locus in R and Z models, 51, 274
and measured failure loci, 50
outside necking region, 155
in plane-strain deformation, 214
for R model, 274
for Z model, 274
Loading(s)
external (applied), 14
flow localization during, 13
specifications, textbooks treating, 13
as tractions within the body, 14
Load instability
analyses, simple, 154
necking at point of, 150
Load maximum
attainment, and onset of necking, 150
equation for, 153
Load-stroke
analysis by upset test, 25

data of chill zone or chill cap formation, 124
Local instability
Hill's criterion, 204-207
and localized necking, sheet metals, 191-194. See also *Instability*.
Localization
with deformation defects, 155
with geometric defects, 159-162
mode, shift from diffuse to localized, 204. See also *Flow localization*.
Localization strain, and failure loci, measured, 50
Localized necking, 6, 7, 199
and local instability, sheet metals, 191-194
Localized shear
and chill cap formation, 126-127. See also *Chilling; Shear; Shear band formation; Shear bands*.
Loewen and Show Model
for metalcutting, 231
for shear zone temperature, 229
Long wavelength approximation, 154
Low carbon steel, specific types
aluminum-killed, M-K theory for, 214, 215
aluminum-killed, plane-strain flow stress and uniaxial tension flow stress, 37, 38
DQAK, uniaxial tension testing, 34
Lubricant(s)
breakdown, 60-61
effects of contact time and heat transfer with, 8
interface and heat transfer, 26
interface thermal characteristics, 26, 121
in upset or uniaxial compression testing, 24
workpiece, and tooling interface, effects on flow localization, 121
Lubrication
effect on barreling, 44-46
effects on flow localization at cold working temperatures, 44-46

M

Machining defect analysis, 164. See also *Geometric defects*.

Marciniak-Kuczynski (M-K) analysis
experimental correlations with, 214-217
for flow localization, 267-275
of flow localization by computer program, 267, 269
of flow localization in FLD stretching regime, 207-221
Sowerby-Duncan interpretation, 211-214
of Z model failure locus, 275. See also *M-K localization strains; M-K stretching models; M-K Z models.*
Martensitic microstructures
break-up by spheroidization of lamellar structures in, 98
and texture softening, 101
Maximum external work, 22. See also *Maximum work.*
Maximum load
prediction of strain at, 151-154
rate of localization following, 154
Maximum work, and effective strain, 21. See also *Maximum external work.*
Mechanical damage, and hardness variations, 54
Mechanical defects, kinetics of flow localization in uniaxial compression with, 64-68
Mechanical press deformation rate, flow localization during sidepressing, 132-135
Mechanical press forgings, shear band morphology, 135
Metalcutting
Boothroyd, using infrared technique, 229
flow localization during, 225-232
models, compared, 231
shearing in, 225
shear-localized titanium chip, 227
steel alloys, 225, 227, 230
steel chip, 225, 227
titanium-alloy chip, 227
Metallographic measurement, of strain localization, 25
Metallurgical (strength) defects
causes, 68
effects of flow softening, $65n$
flow localization with, 68-69

Method of full constraints (isostrain method),
as texture softening, 103-104
Method of relaxed constraints, as flow softening, 104-105
Microstructural softening, of pearlite rapid spheroidization, 98
Microstructure blade forging, shear banding in, 139-140
M-K analysis. See *Marciniak-Kuczynski (M-K) analysis.*
M-K localization strains
compared to Stören and Rice bifurcation theory, 273
compared to Swift instability criterion, 273
M-K model. See *Marciniak-Kuczynski (M-K) analysis.*
M-K stretching models, variable names in MKANAL, 270
M-K Z models, variable names in MKANAL, 270
Mohr's circle construction, 15, 16
in Hill's criterion, 204, 205
and localized necking, 192
for two-dimensional strain-transformation problems, 17
Molybdenum alloys, specific types, TZM, in uniaxial compression testing, 24
Molybdenum disulfide, as uniaxial compression test lubricant, 24
Morphology, of chips, 225

N

Necking
analysis, experimental approaches, 183-184
analysis, and flow localization under tensile loading conditions, 149-198
analysis, in sheet stretching, 50
behavior, material properties controlling, 149
and bulging, effect of stress triaxiality on, 251-256
diffuse, 6, 7
diffuse, and diffuse instability in sheet metals, 188-191
effect on useful deformation, 149

flow following, in uniaxial tension, 33
geometries, basic forms, 199
growth of, analysis in tensile bar, 154
growth of, effect of triaxial tensile stresses on, 154
influence of rate dependence of strain hardening, 185
initiation, 154
localized, 6, 7
localized, and local instability, sheet metals, 191-194
at point of load instability, 150
rate, slow, 154
region, limit strain outside, 155
in round bars during uniaxial tension testing, 149
in sheet during uniaxial tension testing, 149
strain hardening and, 163
summary, 196-197
tensile, flow softening in, 52
theories, simplified, 162-166
through-thickness, 46-47. See also *Bulging; Necking strain.*
Necking strain
Ghosh and Ayres/Marciniak/ Hutchinson and Neale, 159-162
Hart/Duncombe/Nichols, 155-159
and localization with geometric defects, 159-162
rate, vs bulk strain rate, 154
Negative strain hardening, with isothermal hot working, 9
Negative work hardening, 51. See also *Flow softening.*
Nickel alloys, values for upsetting, 57
Nickel alloys, specific types
Inconel 718, flow stress as function of homologous temperature, 8
U-700, localized bulging to localized shearing, 57, 58
U-700, unstable flow of, 60-61
Nickel-base alloys, flow localization of, 249-250
Nickel-base superalloys, as upset test die material, 24. See also *Superalloys.*
Nominal axial strain, and instability, 150-151

Nominal (engineering) strain
as measure of total elongation, 159
predicted, of tensile specimens with hammer blow and geometric defects, 164. See also *Engineering strain.*
Nonhardening materials
flow softening from adiabatic heating in, 113-116. See also *Strain-hardening materials.*
Nonisothermal compression, flow localization during, 128
Nonisothermal deformation, flow localization in bulk forming, 121-148
Nonisothermal hot working, modes of flow localization in, 121-148
Nonisothermal plane-strain metalworking, mode of flow localization, 131
Nonisothermal sidepressing
flow localization in Ti-6242Si, 131-140
process simulations, 138
shear band initiation, 134
Nonisothermal upsetting
analysis of flow localization in, 122-124
flow localization predictions, compared, 128-131
and nonisothermal sidepressing, chill zones in, 134
Nonproportional straining, 23
Nonuniform flow, development of, 55n

O

Orthogonal cutting
chip thickness in, 226, 228
cutting speed in, 228-229
defined, 226
depth of cut in, 226, 228
flow localization analysis for, 226-230
plane-strain conditions of, 226
and rake angle, 226, 228
schematic, 228
shear localization in chips, 226
shear strains in, 226, 228
shear zone in, 228

Out-of-plane deformation, and flow localization, 7
Out-of-plane stretching, forming limits for, 217-219
Overaging, and yield drops, 100

P

Parmar and Mellor analysis, sheet metal forming limits, 219
Path changes, bulk-to-bulk, in texture softening, 107
Pearlite, rapid spheroidization, as microstructural softening, 98
Pinning, and yield drops, 99
Planar defects, shear bands as, 70
Planar isotropy, yield locus, 19
Plane strain
conditions in orthogonal cutting, 226
deformation, flow localization due to flow softening under, 69-85
deformation, limit strains, 214
operations, flow softening in, 5-6
tension loading, of sheetmetal, 36
Plane-strain compression
and tension tests, 34-37
tests based on, 13, 34-37
and uniaxial tension flow stress, 37, 38
Plane strain sidepressing
isothermal test for shear bands, 71
slip-line field solutions in, 134
tests, 13, 30-31
tests for bulk forming under compressive loading, 13
Plane stress
two-dimensional problems in, 15
yield loci for sheet metals, 19, 20
Plastic anisotropy
Hill's formulation, 19, 36
principle directions of stress/strain with, 17
rotationally symmetric, effective strain increment, 22
yield locus, 19-20
Plastic deformation
amount determined by tensile instability, 199
effects of arbitrary increment of, 21.

See also *Deformation*.
Plastic flow, localization in nonisothermal hot working operations, 121-148
Plasticity
analysis of localized thinning and fracture, 47
flow theory, and strain, 16
fundamental equations of, 1
mechanics, 1
Plastic potential, 22. See also *Effective stress; Yield locus*.
Plastic strain
vs elastic strain, $16n$
localization, mean longitudinal strains in, 254
localization, triaxiality factor of, 254-256
Polycrystalline hexagonal materials, texture softening, 101
Power-law hardening materials, under adiabatic conditions, 110, 112
Precipitate(s)
dissolution, and flow localization, 5
fineness, variations as metallurgical defects, 68
Precipitation strengthening, 97-98
softening due to, 97-98
Primary forming, workability at cold working temperatures, 2
Principal stresses, 15, 16
directions of, 15, 16
Process modeling
of shear band development in hypothetical materials, 79-85
of shear band development in Ti-6242Si, 76-79
tools, 79
Process simulations, of nonisothermal sidepressing, 138
Proportional straining, 204
PTFE (Teflon) film, as uniaxial compression test lubricant, 24
Punch stretching
flow localization during, 7
tests, 37-40
Pure shear, defined, 15
Pure titanium, flow localization under adiabatic shear band conditions, 111, 112

Q

Quenching, completeness, and metallurgical defects, 68

R

Rake angle, in orthogonal cutting, 226, 228
Rate sensitivity
  coefficients for aluminum and copper, 186
  and instability, 152, 177-183
  parameter, 54
  positive and large, as stabilizing deformation, 152
  of work hardening rate, 177-183
Relaxed constraints, method of, 104-105
Restoring force, 168
R model
  for flow localization analysis, 47-50
  locus of limit strains for, 51, 274
Rolled sheet, principle directions of anisotropy, 19
Rolling
  effects of workpiece chilling in, 121
  flow localization and surface fracture during, 44-46
  workability under hot working conditions, 2
Rolling direction, as axis in rolled sheet, 19
Room temperature, and workability, 2, 3
Rotations, of material elements, and strain, 16-17
Round bars
  instability and tension testing of, 149-154
  necking during uniaxial tension testing, 149
  tensile testing, and flow localization, 154-177
R values, 19-23
  defined, 19
  measurement, 22, 23
  and texture, 108-109
  in uniaxial tension test, 34
  and yield locus shape under uniaxial tension, 22, 23

S

Schmid factor, in texture softening, 100
Secondary forming operations
  sheet, workability at cold working temperatures, 2
  tensile testing during, 13
  uniaxial tension test in, 31
Shear
  block, in sidepressing test, 31, 32
  cracking, in slow hydraulic press forming, 136, 137-138
  instabilities, rate of work softening for, 95
  localized, and chill cap formation, 126-127
  in metalcutting, 225
  plus bulging, 58, 60
  pure, defined, 15
  simple, and fixed end torsion, 107n.
  See also *Shear band formation; Shear bands.*
Shear band formation
  analysis by torsion test, 30
  and chill cap formation, 126-127
  defined, 69
  during nonisothermal compression, 128
  effect of adiabatic heating on, 113-116
  effect of dwell time, 132
  effect of process variables, 134-135
  in equiaxed alpha microstructure blade forging, 139-140
  flow softening under plane-strain deformation, 69-71
  in fragmenting shell experiment, 240-241
  in hot torsion test, 90-91
  mechanism, in isothermal sidepressing, 71, 72
  morphology at low reductions, 135
  prediction of, 84
  process modeling in hypothetical materials, 79-85
  process modeling in Ti-6242Si, 76-79
  temperatures and strain rates for, 73, 74
  from texture softening, 108

Shear band formation (continued)
in upsetting, 131-140
workability maps, 74, 75. See also *Shear; Shear bands.*

Shear banding. See *Shear band formation.*

Shear bands
adiabatic, defined, 6
due to flow softening, 52
effects, 4
as flow localization, 9
and flow softening, plane-strain loading path, 52
from flow stress maximum, 5
initiation during hot plane-strain sidepressing, 113-116
sidepressing tests for, 30
in Staker's cylinder tests, 239
workability diagrams for, 71-76

Shearing deformation, described, 17

Shear localization
in ballistic impact environments, 233
cutting speed in, 229
in orthogonal cutting, 226

Shear-localized chips
comparison of measurements and predictions, 230-232
formation of, 230-232

Shear strain(s)
defined, 17
distribution, in torsion, 143-144
in orthogonal cutting, 226, 228
-shear stress, in torsion test, 27
in "uniform" region of two-slice model, 240

Shear stress
defined, 14
-shear strain, in torsion test, 27

Shear zone, in orthogonal cutting, 228

Shear zone temperature
Loewen and Shaw model for, 229
models, compared, 229-230
Weiner model for, 229

Sheet forming
flow localization during punch stretching, 7
flow localization effects, 7, 199-223
gross limits, 200
instability and flow localization during, 199-223
limits, 219-221
local instability and localized necking in, 191-194
necking during uniaxial tension testing, 149
secondary, 2
under biaxial tensile conditions, 149

Sheet metals
diffuse instability and diffuse necking in, 188-191
effective strain increment, 22
flat-rolled thin, formability, 199
formability, gross limits, 200
forming limits, 219-221
plane-strain compression and plane-strain tension loading, 36
plane-strain compression test, 35
plane-stress yield loci for, 19, 20
products, uniaxial tension test for, 31
rolled, principle directions of anistropy, 19
stretching. See *Sheet metal stretching.*
tension testing, 188-194. See also *Sheet forming; Sheet metal stretching.*

Sheet metal stretching
flow localization analysis, 46-47
necking analysis in, 50
operations, effect of material inhomogeneity, 7
in plane, M-K model for, 207-208

Sheet normal (S.N.), as axis in rolled sheet, 19

Short wavelength neck, 154-155

Sidepressing
of equiaxed alpha microstructure of Ti-6242Si, 132-135
flow localization during, 135-138
hot plane-strain, 113-116
isothermal and nonisothermal, 71, 72, 131-140
plane-strain, slip-line fields, 134
plane-strain, test, 13, 30-31, 71
shear band initiation, 32, 71, 113-116, 134
simulations, ALPID, 80
tests, 13, 30-31, 71

Silicon nitride, as uniaxial compression test die material, 24

Simple shear
adiabatic flow localization model in, 234-238

and fixed end torsion, 107n
Simplified necking theories, critical assessment, 162-166
Simulation(s), 13, 23-40
   localization during torsion, 145
   predictions and flow localization parameter, compared, 84-85
   process, nonisothermal sidepressing, 138
Slip
   accumulated, in texture softening, 101
   lines, in sidepressing test, 31
Softening
   microstructural, 98. See also *Flow softening; Geometric softening; Thermal softening.*
Solid solution, substitutional, in precipitation strengthening, 97
Solidus temperature, and workability, 2
Solute content, variations as metallurgical defects, 68
Sowerby-Duncan interpretation of M-K analysis, 211-214
Spatial axes, relative to strain, 16-17
Spheroidization, of lamellar structures, 98, 99
Spring-mass damper relation, 167-168
Staker, contained cylinder experiments, 233, 239
Stainless steels, austenitic, M-K analysis, 214, 215
Stainless steels, specific types
   304, annealed, flow localization under adiabatic shear band conditions, 110, 111, 112
   304, localized necking in, 207, 208
   304, tested in torsion, 145
   304, torque softening and flow localization in, 263
   304L, von Mises effective stress-strain curves, 29, 30
   316, annealed, flow localization under adiabatic shear band conditions, 111, 112
Steel alloys, specific types
   1006, flow localization under adiabatic shear band conditions, 110, 111, 112
   1015, flow stress as function of homologous temperature, 8
   1018 CRS, material properties for, 259
   1018 CRS, simulation results for, 260-263
   1018 CRS, torsion testing results compared, 264
   1020 HRS, high speed torsion using boundary conditions, 264
   1020 HRS, material properties for, 259
   1020 HRS, simulation results of torsion testing on, 263-265
   1020 HRS, torsion testing results, 264
   1043, normalized, flow localization under adiabatic shear band conditions, 111, 112
   1045, strain dependence on overall height reduction, 44, 45
   4340, adiabatic shear banding during flow localization, 240
   4340, chip, metalcutting, 227
   4340, contained fragmenting round technique, 233
   4340, cutting speed for, 232
   4340, density of, 232
   4340, flow localization under adiabatic shear band conditions, 111, 112
   4340, hardness levels, 238, 240
   4340, metalcutting, 230
   4340, metalcutting continuous chip, 227
   4340, parameter predictions for, 232
   4340, physical and mechanical properties of, 230
   4340, rate sensitivity of, 232
   4340, specific heat of, 232
   4340, thermal diffusivity of, 232
   A-K steel, elongation for sheet tensile tests as function of strain-rate sensitivity, 156
   aluminum-killed, 216, 218
Storen and Rice
   analysis for prediction of FLD's, 220
   bifurcation theory compared to M-K localization strains, 273
Strain
   axial, true, 24
   concentration in biaxially stretched sheet, 272

Strain (continued)
defined, 16-17
and deformation resistance, upset test for, 23-24
dependence on overall height reduction, 44, 45
elastic vs plastic, $16n$
exponential, 68
and flow localization parameter, 52
and flow stress, 6, 23-24, 79, 80
history, estimate by localization analysis, 48
Lagrangian measures of, 16
levels in necking, 7
localization, 25, 50
nonproportional, 23
normal, 17
principal directions, 17
state near plane strain, fracture at, 50
and strain-rate gradients, growth of, 181
-transformation problems, Mohr's circle for, 17. See also *Effective strain.*

Strain gradients
accentuation and flow localization, 2
growth and decay as overall strain, 65, 66

Strain hardening
capacity, exhaustion of, 3
as controlling strain and strain-rate gradients in nonisothermal upsetting, 122
and flow localization resistance, 56
as function of stress and strain rate, 180
materials, flow softening from adiabatic heating in, 109-112
minimizing effect on flow localization, 122
negative, with isothermal hot working, 9

Strain localization
reducing, 8-9
in torsion, 259
under balanced biaxial stretching, 271. See also *Flow localization.*

Strain path
change, and texture softening, 106-108
change, work softening from, 95-96

fixed and changing, in texture softening, 103
work softening and texture softening, 100

Strain rate
axial, 24
concentration, in adiabatic flow localization in simple shear, 236-237
and deformation resistance, upset test for, 23-24
and flow localization parameter, 52
flow softening at, 56, 57
and flow stress, upset test for, 23-24
hardening, 122
neck, vs bulk strain rate, 154
principal, in flow localization parameter, 53
sensitivity parameter, predicted grid distortions, 81
strain hardening rate, defined, 53-54
-stress-strain relationships, defined, 17-18

Strain-rate gradient(s)
attributable to chilling, 124
calculated, in nonisothermal upsetting, 129
dependence on strain in tensile testing, 63, 64
in process modeling of shear band development, 76-77
and temperature gradients, equiaxed alpha microstructure, 130

Strain-rate sensitivity
index, definitions, 179
influence on growth of geometric imperfections, 162
large, as stabilizing influence, 123
and thermal softening rate, ratio of, 129

Strength (metallurgical) defects
effects of flow softening, $65n$
flow localization in presence of, 68-69
and geometric defects, 69

Strengthening, precipitation, 97-98

Strengthening mechanisms, flow softening due to reversal of, 97-100

Stress
axial true, 24

axial and uniaxial, 19
defined, 14-15
effective, defined, 19-23
Mohr's circle for, 15
principal directions of, 15
-strain-strain rate relationships, defined, 17-18
tensor, 14-15
triaxiality, effect on necks and bulges, 251-256
uniaxial, stress-strain-strain rate relationships, 17-18. See also *Effective stress; Strain; Strain rate.*
Stretching, tensile testing, 13. See also *Sheet metal stretching.*
Subtransus compression, 98, 99
Superalloys
gamma-prime-strengthened, precipitation strengthened, precipitation strengthening in, 97
nickel-based, as upset test die material, 24
Superplastic flow
curves, at constant overall true strain rates, 174-176
flow localization under, 174-177
and flow softening, 174-175
Surface
cracks, failure loci, 25
failure during bulk forming, 275
fracture, 44-50
imperfections, 46-50
inhomogeneities, 44. See also *Inhomogeneities.*
shear strain, workability analysis, 30
strains, and Hill's criteria, 203
strains, principal, and Swift's criterion, 203
tractions, external (applied) loadings as, 14
Swift cup test, as workability test, 13
Swift's diffuse instability criterion, 200-203
and M-K localization strains, compared, 273

T

Taylor factor, mean, 103, 106
Teflon. See *PTFE (teflon) film.*

Temperature(s)
cold working, flow localization and workability at, 2-7
and deformation resistance, upset test for, 23-24
dependence of flow stress during flow localization, 121
during flow localization, 228
elevated, and work softening, 93-97
in flow localization parameter, 52
flow localization at warm working, 7-9
and flow stress, upset test for, 23-24
gradients. See *Temperature gradients.*
hot working, workability at, 2, 3
solidus, 2
specimen preheat, effect on shear banding, 133-134
twist and twist gradients, in torsion, 143-144
warm working, workability at, 2, 3
of workpiece, 2. See also *Heat treatment; Heat transfer; Homologous temperature.*
Temperature gradients
effect on flow localization, 122-123
effects in titanium alloy torsion testing, 146-147
expected in upsetting cylinders, 123-124
from heat transfer between tooling and workpiece, 147
minimizing effect on flow localization, 122-123
in nonisothermal upsetting, 122
and strain rate gradients, 130
Tempering completeness, and metallurgical defects, 68
Tensile deformation, area reduction during, 2
Tensile instability
Considère's analysis, 150-151
as determining amount of plastic deformation, 199
due to geometric softening, 199
and flow localization, 2. See also *Instability.*
Tensile loading
flow localization in, 149-198
and workability at cold working temperatures, 2

Tensile necking, flow softening in, 52
Tensile stresses, and bulging, 4
Tensile testing
 conventional, 13
 rate of strain-induced hardening for, 204
Tension testing
 of round bars, and flow localization, 154-177
 of round bars, instability, 149-154
 of sheet metals, 188-194
Tensor
 quantity, and strain, 16
 quantity, and stress, 14-15
 strain increment as, 17
 transformation law, 15, 16
Textural effects, due to flow softening, 100-103. See also *Texture; Texture softening.*
Texture
 development, in plane-strain compression and tension tests, 37
 development, in torsion testing, 30
 local variations as metallurgical defects, 68. See also *Textural effects; Texture softening.*
Texture softening, 100-103
 conditions for, 103
 method of full constraints as, 103-104
 practical examples of, 103-109
 R values, 108-109
Thermal contraction, upon cooling, nonuniform, 2
Thermal gradients
 calculated, in nonisothermal upsetting, 129
 effects on flow localization, 123
Thermal softening
 from deformation heating, 5
 rate, and strain-rate sensitivity, ratio of, 129
Thermodynamics, and maximum work, in effective strain, 21
Thinning, localized, and fracture, plasticity analysis, 47
Time of deformation, working speed as, 124
Titanium, pure mill annealed, flow localization under adiabatic shear band conditions, 111, 112

Titanium alloys
 bulging in, 58
 flow localization of, 249-250
 instability delay and useful deformation in, 184
 two-phase, microstructural softening, 98, 99
 values for upsetting, 57
Titanium alloys, specific types
 Ti-6242, flow localization parameters, alpha plus beta microstructure, 94
 Ti-6242, flow localization parameters, beta microstructure, 93
 Ti-6242, shear band initiation during sidepressing, 113-116
 Ti-6242, values for upsetting, 57
 Ti-6242Si, application of flow localization parameter to torsion in, 87-93
 Ti-6242Si, compression flow curves, 56, 58
 Ti-6242Si, flow localization between chill zone and deforming bulk, 8, 9
 Ti-6242Si, flow localization in nonisothermal hot working, 121-148
 Ti-6242Si, flow localization in nonisothermal sidepressing of, 131-140
 Ti-6242Si, flow localization during sidepressing, hydraulic press deformation rate, 135-138
 Ti-6242Si, flow localization in upsetting, 121, 124-128
 Ti-6242Si, flow softening, 56-58
 Ti-6242Si, lateral sidepressing of, 121
 Ti-6242Si, localized bulging, calculated, 56, 59
 Ti-6242Si, microstructures, effective strain-rate contours, 77-78
 Ti-6242Si, nonisothermal upsetting of lubricated, 124-128
 Ti-6242Si, physical properties, 129
 Ti-6242Si, process modeling of shear band development in, 76-79
 Ti-6242Si, range of flow behaviors, 71-74
 Ti-6242Si, shear band formation, 73, 74, 218
 Ti-6242Si, strain rates and temperatures for shear band formation, 73, 74

Ti-6242Si, tested in torsion, 145
Ti-6242Si, torque-twist curves, 87, 88, 89
Ti-6242Si, workability maps for, 74
Ti-6Al-4V, flow localization under adiabatic shear band formation, 111, 112
Ti-6Al-4V, flow stress as function of homologous temperature, 8
Ti-6Al-4V, metalcutting chip, 227
Ti-10-2-3, flow softening effects, 57, 58
Ti-10-2-3, localized bulging, 58, 59
Ti-10-2-3, shear band formation, 75
Tooling
heated to workpiece temperature, 8-9
hot workpiece deformed by, 7-8
thermal characteristics, 121
Tooling-workpiece
contact time, 121
effect on flow localization, 7
heated to same temperature, 8-9
heat transfer between, 7-8
interaction during flow localization, 121
and lubricant interface, effects on flow localization, 121
nonisothermal, 25, 26
temperature difference, 121
Tool steels, specific types
H11, in nonisothermal sidepressing, 131
H11, physical properties, 129
Torque equilibrium equation, 140-141
Torque softening, in stainless steels, 263
Torque-twist curve, for stainless steels, 263
Torsion
adiabatic shear band development in, 257-266
application of flow localization analysis, 142-147
degree of adiabaticity in, 258-259
flow localization in, 140-147
flow localization due to flow softening under, 85-93
of round bars, boundary-value problem for, 142-143
strain localization in, 259
of titanium alloys, flow localization parameter applied to, 87-93

See also *Torsion test(s)*.
Torsional deformation, flow localization parameter for, 85-87
Torsion test(s), 13, 26-30
analysis under adiabatic conditions, 258-259
by Costin, 257-258
development of strain localization in, 257-266
hot, application to titanium alloys, 90
with hot rolled steel (1020 HRS), 257-258
for localization of plastic flow from flow softening, 85-93
nomenclature, tubular specimen, 26
simulation results with 1020 HRS, 263-265
with steel alloys (1018 CRS), 257-258
stress field, 27. See also *Torsion*.
Total elongation, 154, 155
nominal (engineering) strain as measure of, 159
predicting, 155, 159-160
and strain-rate sensitivity, 160
as total useful deformation, 154. See also *Elongation*.
Tractions, surface, loadings as, 14
Transformed beta microstructure, influence of flow softening on flow localization in, 130
Transverse direction (T.D.), as axis in rolled sheet, 19
Transverse principal stresses, Bridgman analysis for sheet, 33
Triaxiality factor
with concave surface, 252, 253
with convex surface, 252, 253
influence on kinetics of plastic strain localization, 254-256
in tension or compression specimens, 252, 253
Triaxial stress state, analysis and development, 154
Triple point cracking, and workability, 7
True axial fracture strain, 33
True strain, axial, 24
True strain rates, superplastic flow curves at, 174-176
True stress, by uniaxial tension test, 33

Tungsten carbide, as upset test die material, 24
Turbine engine blades, sidepressing test for, 30
Twist rate gradient, in torsion, 143-144
Two-slice model(s)
 for adiabatic flow localization in simple shear, 234-238
 flow localization equations, $65n$
 for Staker's fragmenting shell experiments, 238-241
TZM molybdenum. See *Molybdenum alloys, specific types.*

U

Uniaxial compression
 extent of bulging during, 250
 flow softening under, 52
 kinetics of flow localization in, 64-68, 245-250
 test, 23-26. See also *Compression.*
Uniaxial stress
 and axial stress, 19
 -strain-strain rate relationships, 17-18. See also *Strain; Stress.*
Uniaxial tension
 flow localization and instability in, 149-198
 necking in, summary, 196-197
 test, 31-34
Upset tests, 23-26
 for barreling, 44. See also *Uniaxial compression.*
Upsetting
 bulging in, 128, 130-131
 flow localization modes, 55, 122-124
 nonisothermal, analysis of flow localization in, 122-124
 observations of flow localization in titanium alloy, 124-128
 shear band formation in, 131-140
 values for titanium and nickel alloys, 57
Uranium
 depleted, flow localization and softening, 57
 oxidized, bulging in isothermal upset, 55, 56

V

Viscous damping factor, 168
Voce relation, for strain dependence, 18
von Mises effective stress
 in Swift's diffuse instability criterion, 200
 -strain curves, 29
von Mises yield locus, defined, 19

W

Warm working temperatures
 flow localization at, 2-4, 7-9
 workability at, 2, 3
Wavelength, short and long necking, 154
Wave propagation, in impact loading of metals, 232
Weiner model
 for metalcutting, 231
 for shear zone temperature, 229
Widmanstätten microstructures
 break-up by spheroidization of lamellar structures, 98
 and texture softening, 101
Work
 maximum, and effective strain, 21
 maximum external, 22
Workability
 at cold working temperatures, 2, 3
 diagrams, 46, 71-76
 as function of homologous temperature, 2, 3
 at hot working temperatures, 2, 3
 as limited by grain-boundary cracking, 7
 maps, for shear band formation, 74, 75
 maps, for torsion simulations/testing, 147
 measured by in-plane and punch-stretching tests, 37-40
 measured by plane-strain compression and tension tests, 34-37
 measured by sidepressing test, 30-31
 measured by torsion test, 26-30
 measured by uniaxial compression test, 23-26

measured by uniaxial tension test, 31-34
tests, 13, 23-40
at warm and hot working temperatures, 2, 3, 7-9
at warm working temperatures, 2, 3
Work hardening
absolute, fixed, 95
negative, 51-69
rate, sensitivity rate of, 177-183
and texture softening, 102
and yield stress, effect on flow softening, 95
Working speed
analysis, of effects, 25-26
effect on chilling and thermal gradient development, 124
effect on shear banding, 133-134
effect on working load in nonisothermal sidepressing, 137
Workpiece
chilling, 121, 124, 138
compressive loading, cold working temperatures, 2
fracture on free surface, 44-46
homologous temperature, 2
and lubricant, 121
temperature, and flow localization, 2
thermal characteristics, 121, 124
Workpiece-die
effects of temperature differences, 123, 124
heat transfer between, 4. See also *Workpiece: Workpiece tooling*.
Workpiece-tooling
effect on flow localization, 7
heat transfer between, 7-8
interaction during flow localization, 121
and lubricant interface, effects on flow localization, 121
nonisothermal, 25, 26

Work softening
at elevated temperatures, by dynamic recovery process, 93-97
at elevated temperatures, from dynamic recrystallization, 96-97
from strain path changes, 95-96

Y

Yield drops
high temperature, 100
softening due to, 99-100
Yield function
and associated flow rule, defined, 18-23
of plasticity mechanics, 1
Yield locus, 19
Hill's, 19
plane-stress, in sheet metals, 19, 20
shape and R value under uniaxial tension, 22, 23
in Sowerby-Duncan interpretation of M-K analysis, 211
von Mises, defined, 19
Yield stress
in compression, von Mises locus as, 19
and work hardening, effect on flow softening, 95

Z

Zinc-titanium alloys, elongation as a function of strain-rate sensitivity, 156
Zirconium alloys, instability delay and useful deformation in, 184
Z model
for flow localization analysis, 47-50
locus of limit strains for, 51, 274
M-K analysis of failure locus, 275
M-K version of, 268-269